Accounting

for Cambridge IGCSE™ and O Level

COURSEBOOK

Catherine Coucom and Alistair McKenzie

Third edition with Digital access

Shaftesbury Road, Cambridge CB2 8EA, United Kingdom

One Liberty Plaza, 20th Floor, New York, NY 10006, USA

477 Williamstown Road, Port Melbourne, VIC 3207, Australia

314–321, 3rd Floor, Plot 3, Splendor Forum, Jasola District Centre, New Delhi – 110025, India

103 Penang Road, #05–06/07, Visioncrest Commercial, Singapore 238467

Cambridge University Press & Assessment is a department of the University of Cambridge.

We share the University's mission to contribute to society through the pursuit of education, learning and research at the highest international levels of excellence.

www.cambridge.org
Information on this title: www.cambridge.org/9781009814492

© Cambridge University Press & Assessment 2010, 2018, 2025

This publication is in copyright. Subject to statutory exception and to the provisions of relevant collective licensing agreements, no reproduction of any part may take place without the written permission of Cambridge University Press & Assessment.

First published 2010
Second edition 2018
Third edition 2025
20 19 18 17 16 15 14 13 12 11 10 9 8 7 6 5 4 3 2 1

Printed in Italy by L.E.G.O S.p.A

A catalogue record for this publication is available from the British Library

ISBN 978-1-009-81449-2 Student's book and ebook
ISBN 978-1-009-81450-8 Digital Student's book (2 years)
ISBN 978-1-009-81451-5 Digital Student's book (2 years)

Additional resources for this publication at www.cambridge.org/9781009814492

Cambridge University Press & Assessment has no responsibility for the persistence or accuracy of URLs for external or third-party internet websites referred to in this publication and does not guarantee that any content on such websites is, or will remain, accurate or appropriate.

For EU product safety concerns, contact us at Calle de José Abascal, 56, 1°, 28003 Madrid, Spain, or email eugpsr@cambridge.org.

Third-party websites and resources referred to in this publication are not endorsed.

Cambridge International Education material in this publication is reproduced under licence and remains the intellectual property of Cambridge University Press & Assessment.

Endorsement

Endorsement indicates that a resource has passed Cambridge International Education's rigorous quality-assurance process and is suitable to support the delivery of their syllabus. However, endorsed resources are not the only suitable materials available to support teaching and learning, and are not essential to achieve the qualification. For the full list of endorsed resources to support this syllabus, visit www.cambridgeinternational.org/endorsed-resources

Any example answers to questions taken from past question papers, practice questions, accompanying marks and mark schemes included in this resource have been written by the authors and are for guidance only. They do not replicate examination papers. In examinations the way marks are awarded may be different. Any references to assessment and/or assessment preparation are the publisher's interpretation of the syllabus requirements. Examiners will not use endorsed resources as a source of material for any assessment set by Cambridge International Education.

While the publishers have made every attempt to ensure that advice on the qualification and its assessment is accurate, the official syllabus, specimen assessment materials and any associated assessment guidance materials produced by the awarding body are the only authoritative source of information and should always be referred to for definitive guidance.

Our approach is to provide teachers with access to a wide range of high-quality resources that suit different styles and types of teaching and learning.

For more information about the endorsement process, please visit www.cambridgeinternational.org/endorsed-resources

Cambridge International Education material in this publication is reproduced under licence and remains the intellectual property of Cambridge University Press & Asessment.

Third-party websites and resources referred to in this publication are not endorsed.

2024 Cambridge Dedicated Teacher Awards

Our **Cambridge Dedicated Teacher Awards** are an opportunity to show appreciation for the incredible work teachers do every day.

Thank you to everyone who nominated this year; we have been inspired and moved by all of your stories. Well done to all of our nominees for your dedication to learning and for inspiring the next generation of thinkers, leaders and innovators.

Congratulations to our winners!

Global Winner
Southeast Asia & Pacific
Sydney Engelbert
Keningau Vocational College, Malaysia

East Asia
Pengfei Jiang
Zhuji Ronghuai Foreign Language School, China

Pakistan
Saeeda Salim
SISA – School of International Studies in Sciences & Arts, Pakistan

South Asia
Meena Mishra
Dr Sarvepalli Radhakrishnan International School, India

Middle East and North Africa
Gina Justus
Our Own English High school Sharjah-Girls, United Arab Emirates

Sub-Saharan Africa
Tajudeen Odufeso
Isara Secondary School, Nigeria

Europe
Aynur Bayazit
Menekşe Ahmet Yalçınkaya Kindergarten, Türkiye

Latin America & the Caribbean
Ramon Majé Floriano
Montessori sede San Francisco, Colombia

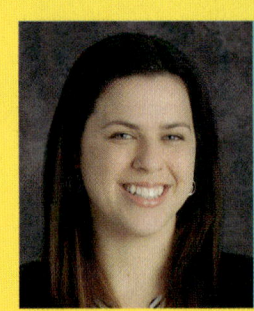

North America
Maria Medvetz Santos
Seminole Ridge Community High School, United States

For more information about our dedicated teachers and their stories, go to dedicatedteacher.cambridge.org

Contents

How to use this series — vi
How to use this book — vii
Introduction — ix

Section 1

1. Introduction to accounting — 2
2. Double entry book-keeping – Part A — 16
3. The trial balance — 42
4. Double entry book-keeping – Part B — 55
5. Petty cash books — 74

Section 1 practice questions — 87

Section 2

6. Business documents — 94
7. Books of prime entry — 112

Section 2 practice questions — 129

Section 3

8. Financial statements – Part A — 136
9. Financial statements – Part B — 158
10. Accounting rules — 173
11. Other payables and other receivables — 190
12. Accounting for depreciation and disposal of non-current assets — 217
13. Irrecoverable debts and allowance for irrecoverable debts — 241

Section 3 practice questions — 260

Section 4

14. Bank reconciliation statements — 270
15. Journal entries and correction of errors — 286
16. Control accounts — 313
17. Incomplete records — 331
18. Accounts of non-trading organisations (clubs and societies) — 356
19. Partnerships — 379
20. Manufacturing accounts — 396
21. Limited companies — 414
22. Analysis and interpretation — 431
23. Technology and sustainability — 456

Section 4 practice questions — 467

Glossary — 483
Appendix: commonly used accounting ratios — 488
Acknowledgements — 489
Index — 490

CAMBRIDGE IGCSE™ AND O LEVEL ACCOUNTING: COURSEBOOK

> How to use this series

All the components in the series are designed to work together.

The coursebook is designed for students to use in class with guidance from the teacher. It offers complete coverage of the *Cambridge IGCSE™, IGCSE (9-1)* and *O Level Accounting* syllabuses (0452/0985/7707). The coursebook is divided into four sections, and contains in-depth explanations of accounting concepts, a variety of independent and group activities, as well as engaging new features and images to help students make real-world connections.

A digital version of the coursebook is included with the print version and is also available separately. It includes simple tools for them to use in class or for self-study.

The workbook provides further practice of all the skills presented in the coursebook and is ideal for use in class or as homework. It provides engaging exercises, worked examples and opportunities for students to evaluate sample answers so they can put into practice what they have learnt.

A digital version of the workbook is included with the print version. It includes simple tools for students to use in class or for self-study, as well as downloadable templates to complete some of the activities.

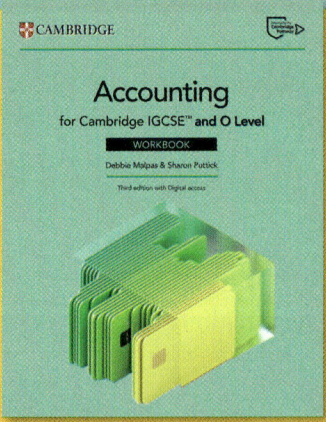

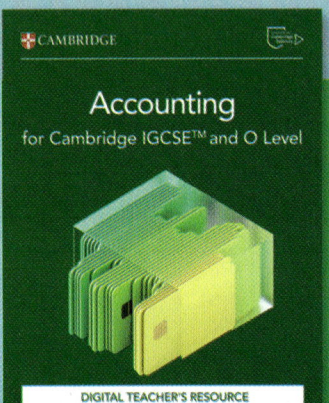

The digital teacher's resource provides everything teachers need to deliver the course. It is packed full of useful teaching notes and lesson ideas, with suggestions for differentiation to support and challenge students, ideas for formative assessment, overcoming common misconceptions and language support.

The digital teacher's resource contains downloadable resource sheets and worksheets.

All answers are available on Cambridge GO.

How to use this book

Throughout this coursebook, you will notice some features that are designed to help your learning. Here is a brief overview of what you will find.

LEARNING INTENTIONS

Learning intentions open each chapter. These help you navigate through the coursebook and indicate the important sections in each chapter.

ACTIVITY

There are various activities throughout this coursebook. These give you the opportunity to discuss sections or produce your own work either individually, in pairs or in groups.

ACCOUNTING IN CONTEXT

Accounting in context introduces you to the content in a chapter. It places some of the key ideas contained in each chapter within more of a real-world setting, and includes questions that allow you to discuss the section.

WORKED EXAMPLE

The Worked examples in the coursebook take you through the steps involved in completing an activity and will help you to understand what a successful answer looks like. These also provide support in developing the key skills that are needed for your course.

KEY TERMS

Key vocabulary is highlighted in the text when it is first introduced. An accompanying definition tells you the meaning of these words and phrases. You will also find definitions of these words and phrases in the Glossary at the back of this book.

ACCOUNTING IN ACTION

Accounting in action provides an insight into how the key concepts for this course might apply within a business or workplace setting. Designed to encourage group discussion, the short case studies and accompanying questions will help you to make connections between employment and studying accounting.

TIPS

Tips are provided throughout this coursebook to help with your learning. The tips might cover advice on answering questions, key skills for your course or how to avoid common errors or misconceptions.

DISCUSSION

Discussion questions are used throughout this coursebook to prompt thinking at key points within each chapter.

REFLECTION

Reflection activities enable you to look back on your work and encourage you to think about your learning. You will reflect on and assess the process that you used to arrive at your answers.

LINKS

These explain the links between sections in different sections of the coursebook.

> **SUMMARY**
>
> At the end of each chapter, you will find a list that brings together the key information you have learnt. This list can also be useful as a revision aid.

> **END-OF-SECTION PRACTICE QUESTIONS**
>
> These practice questions provide further examples of the sort of questions that you might find in your assessments. The questions focus on the assessment objectives that you will need for your course – knowledge and understanding, analysis and evaluation.

Practice questions

Each chapter contains a set of practice questions that are similar to questions you might find in your assessments. The questions focus on the syllabus assessment objectives – knowledge and understanding, analysis and evaluation.

> **CHECK YOUR PROGRESS**
>
> Each chapter ends with a grid showing the Learning intentions from the start of the chapter. When you are revising, you might find it helpful to rate how confident you are for each of these statements. You should also provide an example to support your score.

Introduction

This new and updated edition of the coursebook will help you while studying the Cambridge IGCSE™, IGCSE (9-1) or O Level Accounting syllabuses (0452 / 0985 / 7707) for examination from 2027.

You might be using this coursebook and studying accounting to enable you to take advantage of the wide range of opportunities which come from having a firm grounding in the purpose and role of accounting. You may wish to continue studying beyond Cambridge IGCSE or O Level. You may even be thinking about a career in accounting or a related profession, or hope to set up your own business in the future.

This coursebook covers all the sections included in the latest syllabuses and is divided into four sections. Each section is sub-divided into chapters based on sections from the syllabus. The sections are not necessarily included in the order in which they appear in the syllabus, but are arranged in a suitable order for an accounting student commencing a course at this level.

No prior knowledge is required, as this book provides an introduction to accounting and covers all the sections on the syllabus. Each chapter is complete in itself and contains detailed descriptions of the section supported by worked examples, activities, practice questions, tips and key terms. There are also discussion questions and sections on accounting in context and accounting in action, which allow you to develop your understanding of the role of accounting in the world of business.

The coursebook is designed to help you build your confidence and understanding of accounting. As you progress through your course and this coursebook, you will start to see links between the sections and chapters. For example, at the start of Section 3, you are introduced to elementary financial statements in Chapters 8 and 9, and then later chapters in the same section explain how these statements are affected by various year-end adjustments.

We hope that you enjoy using this coursebook and wish you every success in your accounting course.

Catherine Coucom and Alistair McKenzie

Section 1

This section introduces you to accounting and the ways in which financial information is recorded. You will study the difference between book-keeping and accounting. You will also learn about the assets, liabilities and capital of a business and how to prepare a simple statement of financial position.

The day-to-day transactions of a business are recorded using a system known as double entry book-keeping so this will be explained. You will cover the recording of transactions in the ledger, cash book, and petty cash book using the double entry system and the balancing of accounts.

You will study how to prepare a trial balance to check the accuracy of the double entry book-keeping and learn that some errors will not be revealed by a trial balance.

Chapter 1
Introduction to accounting

LEARNING INTENTIONS

By the end of this chapter, you will be able to:

- understand how book-keeping is different to accounting
- understand why businesses measure their profit and loss
- understand how accounting provides information which can be used to monitor progress and help with decision-making
- understand assets, liabilities and owner's equity, and use the accounting equation.

Introduction

All businesses, whatever their size, need to keep financial records. This is essential so that the owners of the business know whether the business is operating efficiently, whether it has made a profit or a loss, and to enable them to make suitable business decisions.

This chapter introduces you to accounting. Understanding the key terms and ideas in this chapter is the first step towards being able to keep records of financial transactions and being able to understand and interpret financial information.

Later chapters explain the double entry system of recording financial information, and the business documents which provide this information. You will also learn about the different types of businesses and how to prepare and interpret their financial statements.

ACCOUNTING IN CONTEXT

Keeping records

Figure 1.1: A new business owner might not have experience in keeping financial records

Every year many people set up their own business. Often these new business owners know a lot about the goods they are trading or the service they are offering, but they do not always know much about how to record and track the finances of the business.

Dhruv has always wanted to run his own mobile phone repair shop. He is very interested in technology and enjoys helping people.

Dhruv saved up some money and decided to rent a shop in a central location where many people pass by each day. Dhruv bought a selection of mobile phone accessories to sell in his shop as well as all the tools and equipment that he would need to carry out repairs.

Dhruv does not have any experience in keeping accounts, and during the first month of business, he does not keep any records of the money coming into his business or money he has spent. At the end of the first three months, a friend asks him how the business is going and how much profit he has made, but Dhruv has no idea.

Discuss in pairs or in a group:

1. What is the main reason most people go into business?
2. Why do you think it is important that Dhruv keeps a record of his business finances?

1.1 Book-keeping and accounting

It is very important for every business to record financial information. The owners of a business need this information in order to know how much profit has been earned, whether there is enough money in the business and whether the business is being run effectively. In order to have this information available, it is necessary to use book-keeping and accounting.

Book-keeping

Book-keeping is the process of recording the details of all the financial transactions of a business. Even the smallest business needs to make a record of every transaction which affects the business. If the records are not maintained, it is likely that something will be forgotten or overlooked. The system of double entry book-keeping is used to maintain these detailed records. The records maintained by one business may vary from those maintained by another business because each business is different. However, all businesses apply the same principles while maintaining double entry records.

Accounting

Accounting uses the book-keeping records to prepare financial statements at regular intervals. The owner of a business needs to know whether the business is making a profit or a loss. Periodically (often at yearly intervals), a statement of profit or loss is drawn up. This shows the calculation of the profit or loss earned by the business. If the business has earned a profit, then the owner is receiving a return on their investment and funds are available for expanding or improving the business. However, if the business has made a loss, then it may eventually close down as the owner is not receiving any return on their investment and funds are not available for running or maintaining the business.

The owner of the business also needs to know the financial position at regular intervals, so a statement of financial position is prepared. This shows:

- what the business owns and what is owing to it (its assets)
- what the business owes (its liabilities).

The term 'financial statements' is often used as a collective name for a statement of profit or loss and a statement of financial position.

The progress of a business can be measured by comparing the financial statements of one year with those of previous years, or with the financial statements of other similar businesses where these can be obtained. Various accounting ratios can be calculated to measure the relationship between figures within a set of financial statements. These are also useful for comparison purposes.

The information provided by the financial statements shows the owner of the business what has happened during a certain period of time and helps the owner to monitor the progress of the business. The plans for the future development of the business are also based on these financial statements.

> **KEY TERMS**
>
> **book-keeping:** the process of recording details of all the financial transactions of a business.
>
> **accounting:** the process of using book-keeping records to prepare financial statements and to assist in decision-making.

> **LINK**
>
> You will learn more about financial statements in Chapters 8–9.

1 Introduction to accounting

> **DISCUSSION**
>
> Thabo is about to open a business buying and selling handmade furniture. He does not know anything about book-keeping and has decided it will be too expensive to hire a book-keeper.
>
> Thabo says, 'I am not going to bother with writing anything down during the year. I am sure an accountant will be able to work out my profit at the end of the year.'
>
> Discuss what Thabo has said with a partner.
>
> List at least five reasons why Thabo's idea is not practical.

> **LINK**
>
> You will learn more about assets and liabilities in Chapter 9.

> **TIP**
>
> When you think about capital, remember that it is anything that is provided for a business by the owner. This is not necessarily in the form of money.

1.2 Assets, liabilities and capital

It is important to remember that the accounting records of a business relate only to the business and not to the owner. From an accounting viewpoint, the owner of the business is regarded as being completely separate from the business.

When a person decides to start a business, they will have to provide the necessary funds (resources). This is often in the form of money, but may include buildings, motor vehicles and goods. Any resources provided by the owner of the business is known as **capital**. Capital represents the amount owed by the business to the owner of that business.

Once the business is formed and capital has been provided, the business will own the money or other items provided by the owner. Things owned by the business (or owed to the business) are regarded as the resources of the business or the **assets** of the business.

In addition to the owner, other people may also provide assets to the business. Amounts which are owed to other people are known as **liabilities**.

> **KEY TERMS**
>
> **capital:** the total resources provided by the owner. It represents what the business owes the owner.
>
> **assets:** anything owned by or owing to the business.
>
> **liabilities:** anything owed by the business.

> **ACTIVITY 1.1**
>
>
>
> **Figure 1.2:** The sort of assets you might find in a young person's bedroom
>
> 1. Make a list of the assets you personally have. (Remember this is everything you own – clothes, books, bicycle, laptop and so on, as well as money that is yours and any money owing to you.) Try to put a value on each asset and then add them all up.
>
> 2. Make a list of any liabilities you have. (Remember this is anything you owe to someone else – family members, school friends and so on.) How much do you owe?

1.3 Sole trader businesses

Many businesses are set up and operated by one person. These are known as **sole traders**. The early chapters in this book cover accounts maintained by sole traders. Later chapters cover other types of business, such as partnerships and limited companies.

> **KEY TERM**
>
> **sole trader:** a person who owns and operates a business individually.

The advantages and disadvantages of a sole trader business

Before starting a business as a sole trader, a person must consider the advantages and disadvantages. These are summarised in Table 1.1.

Table 1.1: Advantages and disadvantages of a sole trader business

Advantages	Disadvantages
The business is easy to establish.	The owner has to provide all the capital that is required.
The owner is entitled to all the profit.	The owner is solely responsible for the debts of the business.
The owner has complete control.	
Decisions can be made quickly.	The owner has to make all the business decisions, take full responsibility and take all the risks.
It may offer greater flexibility than other types of business.	
	It may be difficult to obtain loans.

> **LINKS**
>
> You will learn about the accounting records of partnerships and limited companies in Chapters 19 and 21.

Buying and selling goods

Many businesses are formed with the aim of making a profit from buying items and selling them at a higher price. This is known as a trading business. The items which are bought and sold are often referred to as goods. The term 'purchases' is used to refer to goods bought, which are intended for resale. The term 'sales' is used to refer to the goods that are sold to customers.

Sometimes goods are bought and sold and payment is made or received immediately. The amount can be paid in cash or through a bank using a cheque. A cheque is a written order to pay a stated sum of money to the person or business named on the order. There are many other ways an amount can be paid using facilities provided by banks. (These are explained in Chapter 2.)

In business, it is quite common for goods to be bought and sold on credit. This means that instead of payment taking place immediately, payment is made sometime after the goods have been handed over. If a business has purchased goods on credit, the person from whom the goods have been purchased is known as a credit supplier or a **trade payable**. If a business sells goods on credit, the person to whom the goods have been sold is known as a credit customer or a **trade receivable**.

At any given point in time, the business may have some goods which have been bought but have not yet been sold. These goods, which are available for sale but have not yet been sold, are referred to as **inventory**.

> **LINK**
>
> You will learn more about buying and selling on credit in Chapter 2.

> **KEY TERMS**
>
> **trade payable:** a credit supplier of goods to whom the business owes money.
>
> **trade receivable:** a credit customer who owes money to the business.
>
> **inventory:** the goods a business has available for resale.

1.4 The accounting equation

The relationship between the assets, capital and liabilities of a business can be shown by the accounting equation:

Assets = Capital + Liabilities

Capital is sometimes referred to as owner's equity. So, the equation can also be written as:

Assets = Owner's equity + Liabilities

Like all mathematical equations, the two sides will always be equal, and the equation can be used to find any one of the three elements if the other two are known.

The accounting equation shows that the assets of a business (the resources used by a business) are always equal to the liabilities and capital of a business (the resources provided for the business by others). The assets represent how the resources are used by the business, and the liabilities and capital represent where these resources come from.

Any changes to the assets, liabilities and capital will affect the accounting equation but the two sides of the equation will still be equal.

ACTIVITY 1.2

1 Copy and complete the table by working out the missing values.

	Capital $	Assets $	Liabilities $
a	98 750	115 808	?
b	?	347 050	197 240
c	70 700	?	54 210

2 Write down how you would explain to a member of the class what capital is and why it is regarded as something the business owes.

TIP

Remember, purchasing on credit means that the business does not pay immediately. This means it does not affect the amount of money in the bank.

WORKED EXAMPLE 1.1

20–7

January 1   Usef set up a business to trade under the name of Usef's Spice Store
He opened a business bank account and paid in $80 000 as capital

2   The business purchased property for $50 000 and paid by cheque

3   The business purchased goods for $3 500 on credit

4   The business sold goods at the cost price of $500 on credit

Show the accounting equation after each of these transactions.

Date	Assets		=	Capital	+	Liabilities
January 1	Bank	$80 000		$80 000		Nil

- The assets of the business are equal to the capital of the business.

Date	Assets		=	Capital	+	Liabilities
January 2	Property	$50 000		$80 000		Nil
	Bank	$30 000				

- The money in the bank has decreased because a new asset has been bought.
- The total assets are equal to the capital.

Date	Assets		=	Capital	+	Liabilities
January 3	Property	$50 000		$80 000		Trade payable $3 500
	Inventory	$3 500				
	Bank	$30 000				

- The business has obtained inventory, which is an asset, but the business has also acquired a liability as it owes money to the supplier (who is known as a trade payable or a credit supplier).
- The total assets are equal to the capital plus the liabilities.

Date	Assets		=	Capital	+	Liabilities
January 4	Property	$50 000		$80 000		Trade payable $3 500
	Inventory	$3 000				
	Trade receivable	$500				
	Bank	$30 000				

- The inventory has decreased but a new asset has been acquired in the form of money owing to the business by a customer (who is known as a trade receivable or a credit customer).
- The total assets are equal to the capital plus the liabilities.
(For the sake of simplicity, the goods were sold to the customer at cost price. In practice, they need to be sold at a price above cost price to enable the business to make a profit.)

1 Introduction to accounting

> **REFLECTION**
>
> Worked example 1.1 used a lot of the new vocabulary that has been introduced in this chapter. Did you need to look back at the key term definitions to check what the words meant? There will be a lot of specialist terminology in this course that you will need to learn and be able to use.
>
> What strategies can you use to help you remember key terms?

1.5 The statement of financial position

The accounting equation may be shown in the form of a statement of financial position.

This shows the three elements of the accounting equation – the assets, the capital and the liabilities. The statement of financial position will be affected every time the business makes changes to the assets, liabilities or capital.

WORKED EXAMPLE 1.2

Prepare the statement of financial position of Usef's Spice Store after each of the transactions shown in **Worked example 1.1**.

Usef's Spice Store
Statement of financial position at 1 January 20–7

	$
Assets	
Bank	80 000
	80 000
Capital and liabilities	
Capital	80 000
	80 000

Usef's Spice Store
Statement of financial position at 2 January 20–7

	$
Assets	
Property	50 000
Bank	30 000
	80 000
Capital and liabilities	
Capital	80 000
	80 000

> **CONTINUED**

Usef's Spice Store	
Statement of financial position at 3 January 20–7	
	$
Assets	
Property	50 000
Inventory	3 500
Bank	30 000
	83 500
Capital and liabilities	
Capital	80 000
Trade payable	3 500
	83 500

Usef's Spice Store	
Statement of financial position at 4 January 20–7	
	$
Assets	
Property	50 000
Inventory	3 000
Trade receivable	500
Bank	30 000
	83 500
Capital and liabilities	
Capital	80 000
Trade payable	3 500
	83 500

> **TIP**
>
> When you complete a statement of financial position, the totals must always agree. If they do not, you know that you have made an error somewhere.

ACTIVITY 1.3

Figure 1.3: A bookshop owner in their store

Mpho owns a bookshop. She provided the following information about her business on 1 May 20–9.

On 2 May 20–9, the following transactions took place:

- Paid extra capital of $8 000 into the business bank account
- Repaid the loan in full from the business bank account
- Purchased goods for resale for $980 on credit
- Purchased additional shop fittings for $1 100 and paid by cheque

Copy the table and complete it by inserting the missing values.

Assets	1 May $	2 May $		Liabilities	1 May $	2 May $		Capital	1 May $	2 May $
Property	80 000	……..	Loan	5 000	……..		……..	……..
Shop fittings	7 600	……..	Trade payable	7 940	……..			
Inventory	9 010	……..						
Bank	2 760	……..						

Worked example 1.1 showed that every single transaction involves a change to the assets and/or the liabilities and/or the capital. This means that it is necessary to prepare a statement of financial position after every single transaction, as shown in Worked example 1.2. However, this is not possible in practice as many transactions can take place every hour of each working day. In practice, the day-to-day business transactions are recorded using double entry book-keeping and a statement of financial position is only prepared periodically. This is usually done at the close of a business on the last day of the financial year as part of the financial statements. As the business can be started on any day of the year, its financial year may not necessarily match the calendar year (i.e. from 1 January to 31 December). The financial statements are prepared for 12-month periods from the date the business started.

LINKS

You will learn more about double entry book-keeping in Chapters 2 and 4, and about statements of financial position in Chapter 9.

ACCOUNTING IN ACTION

Assets and liabilities

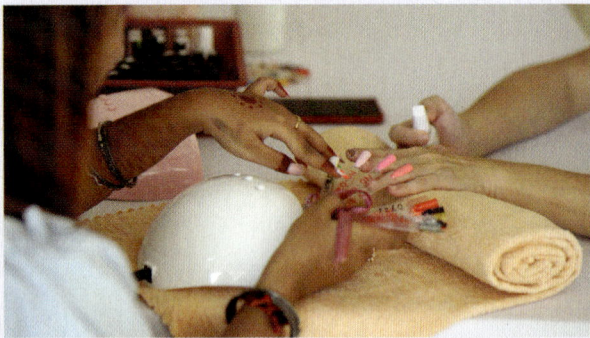

Figure 1.4: A client having their nails painted

Ambar is a beautician. She decided to set up her own business offering a range of beauty treatments and also selling beauty products.

Ambar invested a capital of $70 000. She used some of this to purchase the equipment that she needed and a quantity of beauty products to sell to her clients. The remainder of the money was placed in a business bank account. Ambar also provided the business with some furniture from her own home. She obtained a long-term bank loan to pay for business property.

Ambar intends to keep financial records for her business. At the end of the financial year, she plans to give all her financial records to an accountant to prepare her end-of-year financial statements.

Ambar knows that the statement of financial position is based on the accounting equation assets = capital + liabilities, but she does not really understand this equation and plans to ask her accountant what it means.

Discuss in pairs or in a group:

1. Which of the items mentioned are Ambar's assets and which are her liabilities?
2. How would you explain the accounting equation to Ambar?

SUMMARY

You should now know:

- Book-keeping is the detailed recording of all the financial transactions of a business. Accounting uses these book-keeping records to prepare financial statements.
- It is necessary to prepare financial statements to show the profit or loss of the business, the financial position of the business and to help with decision-making.
- The accounting equation shows that the assets are always equal to the capital plus the liabilities of the business.
- A statement of financial position shows the assets, liabilities and capital of a business on a certain date.

Chapter 1 practice questions

1 Which statements about book-keeping and accounting are correct?
   1 Accounting is dependent on the accuracy of the book-keeping records.
   2 Accounting takes place periodically rather than each day.
   3 Book-keeping includes recording financial transactions.
   4 Book-keeping includes the preparation of a statement of financial position.

   A 1, 2 and 3   B 1 and 3
   C 1, 3 and 4   D 2 and 4   [1]

2 Which one of the following best describes a statement of financial position?
   A a calculation of the total amount owed to the owner of the business
   B a list of assets, liabilities and capital of a business on a certain date
   C a list of everything owned by and owed to a business
   D a summary of money paid to and received by a business   [1]

3 A business had $6 250 in its bank account. The following transactions took place:

	$
Obtained a 3-year loan, which was paid directly into the bank account	5 000
Purchased office equipment and paid by cheque	2 000
Sold goods on credit	1 050

How much was there in the bank after these transactions?

   A $7 200   B $9 250
   C $9 300   D $11 250   [1]

4 A trader provided the following information:

	$
Property	88 000
Inventory	19 300
Trade payables	25 250
Trade receivables	27 420
Fixtures and fittings	31 300
Loan from bank	60 000
Cash at bank	3 170
Motor vehicle	18 360

   a Calculate the value of the assets.   [1]
   b Calculate the value of the liabilities.   [1]
   c Calculate the trader's capital using the accounting equation.   [1]

   [Total: 3]

5   Copy out the following table and complete it to show the effect of each of the following transactions.

The first one has been completed as an example.

A   Bought a motor vehicle and paid by cheque

B   Paid a credit supplier from the business bank account

C   Received a cheque from a credit customer

D   Sold goods (at cost price) and received a cheque

E   Paid off a loan by cheque [8]

	Effect on assets		Effect on liabilities
A	Motor vehicle Bank	Increase Decrease	No effect
B			
C			
D			
E			

6   Sam provided the following list of assets and liabilities on 31 October 20–4.

	$
Machinery	30 000
Furniture and fittings	8 500
Inventory	6 100
Trade receivables	4 950
Cash at bank	9 860
Trade payables	5 110
Capital	?

a   Calculate Sam's capital on 31 October 20–4. [2]

b   Prepare Sam's statement of financial position after the following transactions took place on 1 November 20–4:

   Paid $2 150 to a credit supplier from the business bank account

   Received a cheque for $450 from a credit customer

   A loan of $9 500 was paid directly into the bank account

   Paid $8 700 by cheque for an additional machine [8]

[Total: 10]

CHECK YOUR PROGRESS

How well do you think you have achieved the learning intentions for this chapter? Give yourself a score from 1 (still need a lot of practice) to 5 (feeling very confident) for each learning intention. Provide an example to support your score.

Now I can ...	Score	Example to support score
understand how book-keeping is different to accounting		
understand why businesses measure their profit or loss		
understand how accounting provides information which can be used to monitor progress and help with decision-making		
understand assets, liabilities and owner's equity, and use the accounting equation.		

Chapter 2
Double entry book-keeping – Part A

LEARNING INTENTIONS

By the end of this chapter, you will be able to:
- explain the double entry system of book-keeping and use it to process accounting data
- balance ledger accounts
- prepare and interpret ledger accounts and their balances
- record transactions using ledger accounts
- understand that ledger accounts can be maintained using a computer.

2 Double entry book-keeping – Part A

Introduction

A business would find it impossible to prepare a statement of financial position after every single transaction. The day-to-day transactions are recorded in the books of a business using the **double entry system of book-keeping**. The term 'double entry' is used because the two effects of a transaction (a giving and a receiving) are both recorded in the ledger.

A business maintains a separate ledger account for each type of asset, income, expense and liability, and also for each individual credit customer and credit supplier. Every transaction is recorded in the ledger account relating to that particular item or person.

A ledger is traditionally a bound book where each account appears on a separate page. Over the years, the ledger developed into a loose-leaf folder with separate sheets, each containing a ledger account. Many businesses now use accounting software, so a separate ledger account for each item or person can be maintained and accessed on a computer.

> **KEY TERM**
>
> **double entry book-keeping:** the process of making a debit entry and a credit entry for each transaction.

ACCOUNTING IN CONTEXT

Traditional or digital accounts?

Figure 2.1: A traditional accounting book

When a new business is formed, it is important that the owner sets up a system for recording all the transactions made by the business. These records can be kept using a traditional manual system or by using an accounting software package. Whether records are maintained manually or using a computer, the key principles of double entry book-keeping must always be maintained.

Haziz is starting a business as a wholesale furniture trader. He is very excited because he used to be a manager of the furniture department in a retail store, and thinks he will be able to make a large profit.

Haziz has a friend called Sarah, who is an accountant. Sarah has warned Haziz that to run a successful business he will need to keep careful records of all his business transactions. Sarah has explained that there are two methods Haziz could use for recording his transactions. He could use traditional accounting books, or he could use accounting software on his computer.

Haziz does not really know much about keeping accounts, but he thinks that buying accounting software sounds expensive, so to save money, he will record the financial transactions manually.

Discuss in a pair or a group:

1. Why do you think it is important for Haziz to keep accurate records of his business transactions?

2. What are the advantages and disadvantages of each of the two methods for keeping accounting records?

3. Do you think Haziz has made the correct decision? Why?

2.1 Recording transactions in the ledger

The layout of a ledger account which is maintained manually is as follows:

Debit			Account name			Credit
Date	Details	$	Date	Details		$

Ledger accounts are divided into two sections. The left-hand side is known as the debit side and the right-hand side is known as the credit side. The debit side of a ledger account is the side which is receiving or gaining value, and the credit side of a ledger account is the side which is giving value. The term debit is usually abbreviated to 'dr' and the term credit is usually abbreviated to 'cr'. On either side of the account, there are columns to record the date, details and amount of each transaction.

In order to record the two aspects of a transaction, each transaction is entered twice – on the debit side of one account and on the credit side of another account. The account which is receiving or gaining the value is debited and the account which is giving the value is credited.

The information entered in the accounting records is obtained from business documents. A business may maintain its ledger accounts either manually or on a computer. If the ledger is maintained manually, each ledger account will have its own page or sheet. If the ledger is maintained using computer software, each account will be located separately in the relevant ledger.

> **TIP**
>
> When you are entering transactions in a ledger, make sure that you enter every transaction twice: once on the debit side and once on the credit side.

WORKED EXAMPLE 2.1

20–7
January 1   Imran opened a business with a capital of $90 000 in the business bank account
         2   Equipment costing $20 000 was bought and paid for by cheque
Enter these transactions in Imran's ledger.

Debit			Imran Bank account			Credit
Date	Details		$	Date	Details	$
20–7				20–7		
Jan 1 **a**	Capital		90 000	Jan 2 **b**	Equipment	20 000

> **CONTINUED**
>
> | Debit | | | Capital account | | | Credit |
> |---|---|---|---|---|---|---|
> | Date | Details | $ | Date | Details | | $ |
> | | | | 20–7 | | | |
> | | | | Jan 1 **a** | Bank | | 90 000 |
>
> | Debit | | | Equipment account | | | Credit |
> |---|---|---|---|---|---|---|
> | Date | Details | $ | Date | Details | | $ |
> | 20–7 | | | | | | |
> | Jan 2 **b** | Bank | 20 000 | | | | |
>
> - The first transaction, **a**, is debited in the bank account, as this is the account which is receiving the money, and credited in the capital account, as this is where the money is coming from.
> - The second transaction, **b**, is debited in the equipment account, to show the value being received, and credited in the bank account, as this is where the money is coming from.
> - In each transaction, the details column shows the name of the account in which the other half of the double entry is made.
> - It is important that a double entry is made for every transaction.

Different methods of payment

In addition to paying by cheque, businesses can make payments electronically in various ways. Electronic payments are much quicker and safer, and funds can be transferred from one bank account to another instantly. Mobile and online banking are popular ways of operating bank accounts as transactions can be made immediately and do not require any paperwork.

Payments can be made by **bank transfer** (also called credit transfer) when a person instructs their bank to transfer an amount to the bank account of another person. Payments can also be made by standing order or direct debit:

- A standing order is when a person instructs the bank to pay a fixed sum at fixed intervals to another person. For example, a monthly payment of loan interest may be paid by standing order.
- A direct debit is when a person notifies the bank that permission has been given for a named person to collect an amount directly from their bank account. Direct debits are used for recurring payments where the amounts and dates vary. For example, a variable monthly payment for electricity may be paid by direct debit.

Other popular means of payment are debit cards and credit cards. When a person uses a debit card, the money comes directly from their bank account. When a person uses a credit card, the credit card company pays the person to whom money is owed and the cardholder pays the money back to the card company (usually at monthly intervals).

> **LINK**
>
> You will learn more about business documents, including cheques, in Chapter 6.

> **KEY TERM**
>
> **bank transfer:** a transaction where funds are moved directly from one bank account into another.

> CAMBRIDGE IGCSE™ AND O LEVEL ACCOUNTING: COURSEBOOK

> **DISCUSSION**
>
> Discuss with a partner the different ways payments can be made using the banking system. Try to think of an example of when each method of payment may be used.

2.2 Double entry records for assets and liabilities

A ledger account is opened for each type of asset and liability. Through applying the double entry principles, every transaction is entered twice. The account which is receiving the money is debited and the account which is giving the money is credited.

WORKED EXAMPLE 2.2

20–7

January	1	Imran opened a business with a capital of $90 000 in the business bank account
	2	Equipment costing $20 000 was bought and paid for by cheque
	3	A short-term loan of $10 000 from AB Loans was paid directly into the business bank account
	5	A motor vehicle costing $18 000 was bought and paid for by bank transfer
	6	A long-term loan of $4 000 from Imran's sister, Basma, was paid into the business bank account

Enter these transactions in Imran's ledger.

		Imran			
Debit		**Bank account**			**Credit**
Date	Details	$	Date	Details	$
20–7			20–7		
Jan 1	Capital	90 000	Jan 2	Equipment	20 000
3 *	AB Loans	10 000	5	Motor vehicles	18 000
6	Basma loan	4 000			

* It is not necessary to write the month against each transaction, only when it is the first entry for the month.

Debit		**Capital account**			**Credit**
Date	Details	$	Date	Details	$
			20–7		
			Jan 1	Bank	90 000

Debit		**Equipment account**			**Credit**
Date	Details	$	Date	Details	$
20–7					
Jan 2	Bank	20 000			

CONTINUED

Debit			AB Loans account			Credit
Date	Details	$	Date	Details		$
			20–7			
			Jan 3	Bank		10 000

Debit			Motor vehicles account			Credit
Date	Details	$	Date	Details		$
20–7						
Jan 5	Bank	18 000				

Debit			Basma loan account			Credit
Date	Details	$	Date	Details		$
			20–7			
			Jan 6	Bank		4 000

It may be decided that some cash is required by the business for use on a day-to-day basis. A cash account is opened in the ledger and the rules of double entry are applied. Any cash received is debited to the cash account and credited to the account giving the money. Any cash paid out is credited to the cash account and debited to the account receiving the money.

ACTIVITY 2.1

Figure 2.2: A business owner might need to discuss taking out a loan from a family member

Open the necessary ledger accounts and enter the following transactions in the books of Mandy.

20–4

May 1	Mandy opened a business with a capital of $60 000, of which $50 000 was paid into a business bank account and $10 000 was placed in a cash box for business use
2	Purchased business property for $40 000 and paid by bank transfer
4	Purchased fixtures and fittings for $5 400 and paid by cheque
5	A loan of $15 000 from Mandy's father, Clive, was paid into the business bank account
6	Purchased a motor vehicle for $9 400 and paid in cash

2.3 Double entry records for expenses and income

A ledger account is opened for each type of expense and income. The same double entry principles applied to assets and liabilities are applied to expenses and income.

The account which is receiving the money is debited and the account which is giving the money is credited.

WORKED EXAMPLE 2.3

20–7

January 1	Imran opened a business with a capital of $90 000, of which $88 000 was placed in a business bank account and the rest was kept in cash for business use
1	Rent of property, $400, was paid by bank transfer
1	Equipment costing $20 000 was bought and paid for by cheque
3	Insurance, $250, was paid by cheque
3	A short-term loan of $10 000 from AB Loans was paid directly into the business bank account
5	A motor vehicle costing $18 000 was bought and paid for by bank transfer
5	Motor expenses, $50, were paid in cash
6	A long-term loan of $4 000 from Imran's sister, Basma, was paid into the business bank account
7	Part of the premises was rented out to another business and $120 was received in cash

Enter these transactions in Imran's ledger.

Imran

Debit			Bank account	Credit		
Date	Details		$	Date	Details	$
20–7				20–7		
Jan 1	Capital		88 000	Jan 1	Rent expense	400
3	AB Loans		10 000	*	Equipment	20 000
6	Basma loan		4 000	3	Insurance	250
				5	Motor vehicles	18 000

* If there is more than one entry on the same side of an account on the same date, it is not necessary to write the day of the month each time.

Debit			Cash account	Credit		
Date	Details		$	Date	Details	$
20–7				20–7		
Jan 1	Capital		2 000	Jan 5	Motor expenses	50
7	Rent income		120			

Debit			Capital account	Credit		
Date	Details		$	Date	Details	$
				20–7		
				Jan 1	Bank	88 000
					Cash	2 000

CONTINUED

Debit			Rent expense account			Credit
Date	Details	$	Date	Details		$
20–7						
Jan 1	Bank	400				

Debit			Equipment account			Credit
Date	Details	$	Date	Details		$
20–7						
Jan 1	Bank	20 000				

Debit			Insurance account			Credit
Date	Details	$	Date	Details		$
20–7						
Jan 3	Bank	250				

Debit			AB Loans account			Credit
Date	Details	$	Date	Details		$
			20–7			
			Jan 3	Bank		10 000

Debit			Motor vehicles account			Credit
Date	Details	$	Date	Details		$
20–7						
Jan 5	Bank	18 000				

Debit			Motor expenses account			Credit
Date	Details	$	Date	Details		$
20–7						
Jan 5	Cash	50				

Debit			Basma loan account			Credit
Date	Details	$	Date	Details		$
			20–7			
			Jan 6	Bank		4 000

Debit			Rent income account			Credit
Date	Details	$	Date	Details		$
			20–7			
			Jan 7	Cash		120

> **CONTINUED**
>
> - The motor expenses, such as fuel and repairs, are shown in an expense account as they do not increase the value of the motor vehicle.
> - The rent received from a tenant is shown in an income account and is kept separate from the expense of rent.
> - No lines are left blank in the middle of ledger accounts as each entry is made on the next available line.
> - In practice, accounts of the same class (e.g. assets, expenses and so on) are kept in the same area of the ledger for ease of reference.

> **LINK**
>
> You will learn more about the different classes of accounts in Chapters 3–4.

> **TIP**
>
> Be careful with items, such as rent or interest, that a business may both pay and receive. When this happens, two separate accounts must be maintained, one for expense and one for income.

> **DISCUSSION**
>
> Discuss with a partner:
>
> 1. Why does each type of asset need its own account?
> 2. Why cannot the rent income and the rent expenses be entered in the same account?
> 3. Why cannot all the business expenses be put in the same account?

2.4 Balancing ledger accounts

At the end of each month, it is usual to **balance** any account of assets and liabilities which contain more than one entry. The balance is the difference between the two sides of the account and represents the amount left in that account.

The steps necessary to balance a ledger account are summarised in Figure 2.3.

> **KEY TERM**
>
> **balance:** the difference between the debit side and the credit side in a ledger account.

2 Double entry book-keeping – Part A

Add up each side of the account on a calculator or a separate sheet of paper, and find the difference between the two sides.

Enter this difference on the next available line on the side which is smaller in money. Enter the date (usually the last day of the month) in the date column and the word 'Balance' in the details column. The abbreviation 'c/d' for 'carried down' is inserted and shows where the double entry for this item will be made.

Total each side of the account. This is done by drawing total lines and inserting the figure between these lines. It is usual to show a single line above the total and either a single or a double line below the total. The totals of an account must be on the same level and must be the same figure.

Make the double entry for the balance carried down. On the line below the totals, write the amount of the balance on the opposite side to where the words 'Balance c/d' were written. Enter the date (the day after that shown for the balance carried down – usually the first day of the next month) in the date column and the word 'Balance' in the details column. The abbreviation 'b/d' for 'brought down' is inserted and shows where the double entry for this item was made.

> **TIP**
>
> When balancing an account, add up each side of the account and find the difference between them before drawing total lines and before writing the word 'balance'.

Figure 2.3: The steps for balancing a ledger account

WORKED EXAMPLE 2.4

The bank account prepared in **Worked example 2.3** shows the entries made by Imran during the first week of trading. Balance the bank account in Imran's books on 7 January 20–7.

Imran

Debit			Bank account				Credit
Date	Details		$	Date	Details		$
20–7				20–7			
Jan 1	Capital		88 000	Jan 1	Rent expense		400
3	AB Loans		10 000		Equipment		20 000
6	Basma loan		4 000	3	Insurance		250
				5	Motor vehicles		18 000
				7	Balance	c/d	63 350
			102 000				102 000
20–7							
Jan 8	Balance	b/d	63 350				

25

2.5 Double entry records for sales, purchases and returns

It is necessary to open an account to record goods which are purchased for resale and also an account to record goods which are sold by the business. While these are actually the same goods coming into the business and going out of the business, it is necessary to record them in separate accounts as the purchases will be at cost price and the sales at selling price. A purchases account and a sales account are used rather than a goods account. An inventory account is only used to record the goods left at the end of the financial year and not for day-to-day transactions.

The same double entry principles applied to assets and liabilities are applied to purchases, sales and returns.

Purchases

Goods purchased and paid for immediately

Whenever goods are purchased, the purchases account will be debited because the goods are coming into the business and the purchases account is receiving that value. As the payment is being made immediately, the credit entry will be made in the cash account if cash is being used, or in the bank account if payment is being processed through the business bank account.

Goods purchased on credit

It is common for businesses to buy on credit and pay for the goods at a later date rather than at the time of purchase. The purchases account will be debited in the usual way.

The credit entry will be made in the account of the supplier of the goods to show the value coming from that person. The supplier of goods is known as a trade payable.

When payment is made to the supplier, the bank or cash account will be credited (to show value going out of that account) and the account of the supplier will be debited (to show value going into that account).

Only goods bought for resale are entered in the purchases account. A business will also purchase things such as stationery, fuel for motor vehicles, tea and coffee for the office and so on. These are for use within the business and are not for resale, so will not be recorded in the purchases account.

2 Double entry book-keeping – Part A

> **WORKED EXAMPLE 2.5**
>
> 20–7
> January 9   Imran bought goods for $2 340 on credit from Ameerah
> 10   Imran bought goods for $975 and paid by cheque
> 13   Imran paid the amount owing to Ameerah by bank transfer
>
> Enter these transactions in Imran's ledger.
>
> **Imran**
>
> | Debit | | | Bank account | | | Credit |
> |---|---|---|---|---|---|---|
> | Date | Details | $ | Date | Details | | $ |
> | | | | 20–7 | | | |
> | | | | Jan 10 | Purchases | | 975 |
> | | | | 13 | Ameerah | | 2 340 |
>
> | Debit | | | Purchases account | | | Credit |
> |---|---|---|---|---|---|---|
> | Date | Details | $ | Date | Details | | $ |
> | 20–7 | | | | | | |
> | Jan 9 | Ameerah | 2 340 | | | | |
> | 10 | Bank | 975 | | | | |
>
> | Debit | | | Ameerah account | | | Credit |
> |---|---|---|---|---|---|---|
> | Date | Details | $ | Date | Details | | $ |
> | 20–7 | | | 20–7 | | | |
> | Jan 13 | Bank | 2 340 | Jan 9 | Purchases | | 2 340 |
> | | | 2 340 | | | | 2 340 |
>
> - The account of Ameerah is 'in balance' as both sides equal $2 340.
>   The account has been totalled to indicate that the account is now closed.

Sales

Goods sold and money received immediately

Whenever goods are sold, the sales account will be credited as the goods are going out of the business and the sales account is giving out that value. As the amount is being received immediately, the debit entry will be made in the cash account if cash is being used, or in the bank account if the amount is being processed through the business bank account.

Goods sold on credit

In addition to purchasing goods on credit and paying for them at a later date, a business may also sell goods on credit. The sales account will be credited in the usual way. The debit entry will be made in the account of the customer to whom the goods are sold, to show the value going to that person. The customer who bought the goods on credit is known as a trade receivable. When payment is received from the customer, the bank or cash account will be debited (to show value coming into that account) and the account of the customer will be credited (to show value going out of that account).

WORKED EXAMPLE 2.6

20–7

January 16   Imran sold goods, $149, for cash
         17   Imran sold goods, $1 050, on credit to Hamza
         20   Hamza gave Imran a cheque for $750 on account*

Enter these transactions in Imran's ledger.

* The term 'on account' indicates that only part of the amount outstanding is being paid. The remainder will be paid at a later date.

Imran

Debit			Bank account			Credit
Date	Details	$	Date	Details		$
20–7						
Jan 20	Hamza	750				

Debit			Cash account			Credit
Date	Details	$	Date	Details		$
20–7						
Jan 16	Sales	149				

Debit			Sales account			Credit
Date	Details	$	Date	Details		$
			20–7			
			Jan 16	Cash		149
			17	Hamza		1 050

Debit			Hamza account			Credit
Date	Details	$	Date	Details		$
20–7			20–7			
Jan 17	Sales	1 050	Jan 20	Bank		750
				Balance	c/d	300
		1 050				1 050
20–7						
Jan 21	Balance	b/d	300			

- Hamza's account has been balanced following the stages mentioned in Section 2.4 (although this is usually done at the end of the month).
- On 21 January, Hamza owes Imran $300 and from Imran's viewpoint is a trade receivable.

Returns

Sometimes goods which have been purchased have to be returned to the supplier. They may be faulty, damaged or not what was ordered. These goods are known as purchases returns or returns outward. A special account known as a purchases returns account (or returns outward account) is opened and any returns are credited to this account to show the value going out. The debit entry will be made in the account of the supplier to whom the goods are being returned (to show the value going to that person).

Similarly, a customer may return goods to the business. These goods are known as sales returns or returns inwards. An account known as the sales returns account (or returns inwards account) is opened and any returns are debited to this account to show the value coming in. The credit entry will be made in the account of the customer who returned the goods (to show the value coming from that person).

> **DISCUSSION**
>
> Discuss with a partner the reasons why sales returns are entered in a sales returns account rather than being debited in the sales account.

Figure 2.4: Goods being returned

WORKED EXAMPLE 2.7

20–7

January	21	Imran sold goods for $380 on credit to Robena
	22	Robena returned damaged goods for $60 to Imran
	23	Imran purchased goods for $980 on credit from Shaima
	25	Robena paid her account by bank transfer
	27	Imran returned faulty goods for $30 to Shaima
	30	Imran gave Shaima a cheque for $500 on account

Enter these transactions in Imran's ledger. Balance or total the accounts for Robena and Shaima as required.

		Imran				
Debit		**Bank account**				**Credit**
Date	Details		$	Date	Details	$
20–7				20–7		
Jan 25	Robena		320	Jan 30	Shaima	500

Debit		**Purchases account**				**Credit**
Date	Details		$	Date	Details	$
20–7						
Jan 23	Shaima		980			

CONTINUED

Debit		Sales account				Credit
Date	Details	$	Date	Details		$
			20–7			
			Jan 21	Robena		380

Debit		Robena account				Credit
Date	Details	$	Date	Details		$
20–7			20–7			
Jan 21	Sales	380	Jan 22	Sales returns		60
			25	Bank		320
		380				380

Debit		Sales returns account				Credit
Date	Details	$	Date	Details		$
20–7						
Jan 22	Robena	60				

Debit			Shaima account				Credit
Date	Details		$	Date	Details		$
20–7				20–7			
Jan 27	Purchases returns		30	Jan 23	Purchases		980
30	Bank		500				
31	Balance	c/d	450				
			980				980
				20–7			
				Feb 1	Balance	b/d	450

Debit		Purchases returns account				Credit
Date	Details	$	Date	Details		$
			20–7			
			Jan 27	Shaima		30

ACTIVITY 2.2

Kwame is a trader. Thabisa is one of his credit customers.

On 1 June 20–4, Thabisa owed Kwame $122.

During the month of June 20–4, the following transactions took place:

June 4 Kwame sold goods, $94, on credit to Thabisa

   8 Thabisa returned goods, $14, because they were damaged

   29 Thabisa paid the amount she owed on 1 June by bank transfer

a   Prepare the account of Thabisa as it would appear in the books of Kwame for the month of June 20–4. The account should start with an opening balance of $122 on the debit side to show the amount Thabisa owed Kwame on 1 June 20–4.
Balance the account and bring down the balance on 1 July 20–4.

b   Copy and complete the table to show the entries Thabisa would make in her ledger on each date.

Date	Account to be debited	Account to be credited
June 4		
June 8		
June 29		

2.6 Double entry records for carriage inwards and carriage outwards

The term **carriage** refers to the cost of carrying or transporting goods. **Carriage inwards** is part of the cost of purchasing goods as it occurs when a business has to pay for goods it has purchased to be delivered to its premises. **Carriage outwards** is a selling expense as it occurs when a business pays for goods to be delivered to a customer's premises. It is important that these two expenses are treated separately in the accounts.

When a payment is made for carriage inwards, the carriage inwards account is debited as this is the account receiving the money, and either the bank account or the cash account is credited as this is the account where the money is coming from.

> **KEY TERMS**
>
> **carriage:** the cost of transporting goods.
>
> **carriage inwards:** the cost of bringing the goods to the business.
>
> **carriage outwards:** the cost of delivering the goods to the customer.

When a payment is made for carriage outwards, the carriage outwards account is debited as this is the account receiving the money, and either the bank account or the cash account is credited as this is the account where the money is coming from.

If the carriage is not actually paid for at the time, the account of the supplier of the carriage service will be credited instead of the cash account or the bank account.

WORKED EXAMPLE 2.8

20–7

February	1	Imran sold goods for $450 on credit to Anwar
		Imran paid $15 in cash for the cost of carriage on goods sold to Anwar
	14	Imran purchased goods for $870 on credit from Sabena
		Imran paid $36 by bank transfer for carriage on goods purchased from Sabena
	21	Imran returned faulty goods for $20 to Sabena
	26	Imran received a cheque from Anwar to settle his account
	28	Imran paid $400 on account to Sabena by an online bank transfer

Enter these transactions in Imran's ledger. It is not necessary to balance or total any of the accounts.

Imran

Debit			Bank account			Credit
Date	Details	$	Date	Details		$
20–7			20–7			
Feb 26	Anwar	450	Feb 14	Carriage inwards		36
			28	Sabena		400

Debit			Cash account			Credit
Date	Details	$	Date	Details		$
			20–7			
			Feb 1	Carriage outwards		15

Debit			Purchases account			Credit
Date	Details	$	Date	Details		$
20–7						
Feb 14	Sabena	870				

Debit			Sales account			Credit
Date	Details	$	Date	Details		$
			20–7			
			Feb 1	Anwar		450

Debit			Purchases returns account			Credit
Date	Details	$	Date	Details		$
			20–7			
			Feb 21	Sabena		20

CONTINUED

Debit			Anwar account			Credit
Date	Details	$	Date	Details		$
20–7			20–7			
Feb 1	Sales	450	Feb 26	Bank		450

Debit			Carriage outwards account			Credit
Date	Details	$	Date	Details		$
20–7						
Feb 1	Cash	15				

Debit			Carriage inwards account			Credit
Date	Details	$	Date	Details		$
20–7						
Feb 14	Bank	36				

Debit			Sabena account			Credit
Date	Details	$	Date	Details		$
20–7			20–7			
Feb 21	Purchases returns	20	Feb 14	Purchases		870
28	Bank	400				

ACTIVITY 2.3

Figure 2.5: A wholesaler might be unsure about what accounting records to maintain

Joseph has just started trading as a wholesaler and is unsure about what accounting records he should maintain.

He has asked the following questions:

- Why can I not record sales and purchases in the same account as they are the same goods?
- Why can I not use one account for carriage?
- Why do I have to keep a separate account for each credit supplier?

Write an email or a short note to Joseph to answer his questions.

2.7 Double entry records for drawings

Whenever the owner of a business takes value from the business for their own use, this is known as **drawings**. This value may be in the form of money, non-current assets or goods from the inventory held by the business. It is usual to open a drawings account to record these values so that the capital account does not have a large number of entries.

> **KEY TERM**
>
> **drawings:** any value taken from the business by its owner.

The entries are as follows:

When money is taken from the business by the owner

- Debit the drawings account.
- Credit either the cash account or the bank account.

When goods are taken from the business by the owner

- Debit the drawings account.
- Credit the purchases account.

When any other asset is taken from the business by the owner

- Debit the drawings account.
- Credit the asset account.

At the end of the financial year

- Debit the capital account.
- Credit the drawings account.

When goods are taken from the business by the owner, the purchases account is credited because these goods were originally purchased for resale and the amount of goods now available for resale has been reduced.

> **LINK**
>
> You will learn more about double entry book-keeping in Chapter 4.

ACTIVITY 2.4

Copy the table and write the name of the account to be debited and the name of the account to be credited for each transaction.

Transaction	Account to be debited	Account to be credited
Bought machinery and paid by cheque		
Repaid money borrowed from QQ Loans by bank transfer		
Paid for stationery in cash		
Received commission in cash for work done for another business		
The owner of a business took money from the business bank account for their own use		
The owner of a business took unused office equipment from the business for personal use		

DISCUSSION

Justify to a partner why goods taken by the owner of a business for personal use are credited to the purchases account rather than the sales account.

ACTIVITY 2.5

Jia is a trader. He provided the following information.

20–8

Nov 3   Purchased goods, $1 350, on credit from Chao

Paid $10 in cash for carriage on the goods purchased from Chao

8   Returned goods, $125, to Chao

13   Sold goods for cash, $210

16   Sold goods, $2 160, on credit to Mei

17   Paid $70 by bank transfer for cost of carriage of goods sold to Mei

21   Goods, $340, were taken for personal use

27   Cash, $100, was taken for personal use

Enter the transactions in Jia's ledger. It is not necessary to total or balance any of the accounts.

REFLECTION

How confident are you that you can record business transactions in the ledger of a business?

How would you explain the rules of double entry to a member of the class who is finding it difficult to understand?

2.8 Three-column running balance accounts

The ledger accounts presented so far have been in the traditional form. This form is also known as the 'T' account format.

There is another method of presenting ledger accounts, which is commonly used on bank statements, known as the three-column running balance format. This form of presentation uses only one column each for the date and details, and has three money columns side by side: one for debit, one for credit and one for the balance after each transaction. The layout of a ledger account using this format is as follows:

Date	Details	Debit	Credit	Balance
		$	$	$

The advantage of this method is that it shows the balance of the account after every transaction. However, when the accounts are prepared manually, it involves extra calculations, which may lead to errors.

> **WORKED EXAMPLE 2.9**
>
> 20–7
>
> January 1 Imran opened a business with a capital of $90 000, of which $88 000 was placed in a business bank account and the rest was kept in cash for business use
>
> Rent of premises, $400, was paid by bank transfer
>
> 2 Equipment costing $20 000 was bought and paid for by cheque
>
> 3 Insurance, $250, was paid by cheque
>
> A short-term loan of $10 000 from AB Loans was paid directly into the business bank account
>
> 5 A motor vehicle costing $18 000 was bought and paid for by bank transfer
>
> Motor expenses, $50, were paid in cash
>
> 6 A long-term loan of $4 000 from Imran's sister, Basma, was paid into the business bank account
>
> 7 Part of the premises was rented out to another business and $120 was received in cash
>
> Enter these transactions in the bank account and the cash account in Imran's ledger using the three-column running balance format.
>
> **Imran**
> **Bank account**
>
> | Date | Details | Debit $ | Credit $ | Balance $ |
> |---|---|---|---|---|
> | 20–7 | | | | |
> | Jan 1 | Capital | 88 000 | | 88 000 |
> | | Rent expense | | 400 | 87 600 |
> | 2 | Equipment | | 20 000 | 67 600 |
> | 3 | Insurance | | 250 | 67 350 |
> | | AB Loans | 10 000 | | 77 350 |
> | 5 | Motor vehicles | | 18 000 | 59 350 |
> | 6 | Basma loan | 4 000 | | 63 350 |
>
> **Imran**
> **Cash account**
>
> | Date | Details | Debit $ | Credit $ | Balance $ |
> |---|---|---|---|---|
> | 20–7 | | | | |
> | Jan 1 | Capital | 2 000 | | 2 000 |
> | 5 | Motor expenses | | 50 | 1 950 |
> | 7 | Rent income | 120 | | 2 070 |

2.9 Interpreting ledger accounts and their balances

It is important that the owner of a business understands the entries made in the ledger accounts.

WORKED EXAMPLE 2.10

The following account appeared in the ledger of Imran.

Debit					Imran Robena account			Credit
Date	Details		$	Date	Details			$
20–7				20–7				
Mar 1	Balance	b/d	135	Mar 3	Cash			135
4	Sales		460	9	Sales returns			95
22	Sales		525	30	Bank			400
				31	Balance	c/d		490
			1 120					1 120

Explain each entry in the account of Robena and state where the double entry for each item will be found.

March 1 Robena owed Imran $135 for goods supplied on credit in previous months
 Double entry: Robena account for February 20–7 credit side

 3 Imran received cash, $135, from Robena
 Double entry: Cash account debit side

 4 Imran sold goods on credit to Robena, $460
 Double entry: Sales account credit side

 9 Robena returned goods, $95, to Imran
 Double entry: Sales returns account debit side

 22 Imran sold goods on credit to Robena, $525
 Double entry: Sales account credit side

 30 Robena paid Imran $400 by cheque (or by bank transfer)
 Double entry: Bank account debit side

 31 Robena owed Imran $490
 Double entry: Robena account for April 20–7 on the debit side

ACCOUNTING IN ACTION

Trading options

Figure 2.6: Different accounting records are needed for different ways of trading

Jacinda is starting a business as a wholesaler selling stationery and office supplies. She has bought premises and office equipment, and has also purchased inventory. Jacinda paid for the inventory by bank transfer, and the supplier is willing to consider offering credit terms after six months.

Jacinda is now preparing to visit local retail businesses, manufacturing businesses and hotels to introduce her business and to start taking orders. She is considering what terms of trade she should offer:

A Sales for cash only

B Sales for cash, debit or credit cards, or other electronic payments made at the time the goods are exchanged

C Sales on credit terms

Discuss the following questions with a partner and write down your ideas so you can share them with the class.

1 What accounting records will Jacinda need to maintain for each of the three options?

2 What other things should Jacinda think about when deciding on option A, B or C?

SUMMARY

You should now know:

- Every business transaction is entered in the accounting records using the double entry system.
- A ledger account is opened for each type of asset, liability, expense and income.
- Separate accounts are maintained for sales, sales returns, purchases and purchases returns.
- A drawings account records all value taken from the business by the owner of that business.
- Carriage is the cost of transporting goods; separate accounts for carriage inwards and carriage outwards are required.
- Ledger accounts can be balanced at the end of a trading period.

Chapter 2 practice questions

1. Mark is a trader. He took goods costing $100 for his own use.

   How would Mark record this in his ledger?

	Account to be debited	Account to be credited
A	drawings	inventory
B	drawings	purchases
C	inventory	drawings
D	purchases	drawings

   [1]

2. George sold goods to Cindy, who paid in cash.

   How would Cindy record this in her ledger?

	Account to be debited	Account to be credited
A	cash	purchases
B	George	purchases
C	purchases	cash
D	purchases	George

   [1]

3. Dinesh returned goods to his credit supplier, Thisara.

   How would Thisara record this in his ledger?

	Account to be debited	Account to be credited
A	Dinesh	purchases returns
B	Dinesh	sales returns
C	purchases returns	Dinesh
D	sales returns	Dinesh

   [1]

4. On 1 July 20–6, Malala started a business. The following are her transactions for the first two weeks of trading:

   July 1 Paid capital, $100 000, into the business bank account

   2 Bought property, $85 000, and paid by bank transfer

   4 Bought equipment, $6 000, and paid by cheque

   6 Bought goods, $1 900, on credit from Yousef

   7 Paid advertising expenses, $48, by cheque

   9 Sold goods, $395, and received a cheque

   12 Sold goods, $562, on credit to Tanya

   13 Tanya returned goods, $24

   14 Paid $900 by bank transfer on account to Yousef

   Enter these transactions in the ledger of Malala. Balance the bank account and the accounts of Yousef and Tanya on 14 July and bring down the balances on 15 July 20–6. [20]

5   Kanuki is a trader. On 1 October 20–4, the balances in her ledger included the following:

		$
Credit balances	Capital	120 000
	Trade payable Udani	1 845
	AB Finance loan	12 000
Debit balances	Bank	17 580
	Inventory	5 800
	Trade receivable Pinidu	960

a   Enter these balances in the appropriate accounts. [3]

b   The following transactions took place in October 20–4:

October 2   Bought goods on credit from Udani, $1 350

7   Returned goods to Udani, $65

10   Repaid the loan by bank transfer

14   Paid Udani for the amount owing on 1 October 20–4 by bank transfer

21   Cash received from the sale of goods, paid directly into the bank, $1 230

28   Kanuki took goods for her own use, $260

30   Pinidu paid the amount due by cheque

Enter these transactions in Kanuki's ledger. Balance the bank account and Udani's account and bring down the balances on 1 November 20–4. Total the accounts of Pinidu and AB Finance. [17]

[Total: 20]

6   The following account appeared in the ledger of Sadil:

Sadil							
Debit				**Abdul account**			**Credit**
Date	Details		$	Date	Details		$
20–6				20–6			
Oct 1	Balance	b/d	344	Oct 14	Sales returns		80
12	Sales		783	25	Bank		600
				31	Balance	c/d	447
			1 127				1 127

Explain each entry in this account and also state where the corresponding double entry for each item will be found. [10]

CHECK YOUR PROGRESS

How well do you think you have achieved the learning intentions for this chapter? Give yourself a score from 1 (still need a lot of practice) to 5 (feeling very confident) for each learning intention. Provide an example to support your score.

Now I can …	Score	Example to support score
explain the double entry system of book-keeping and use it to process accounting data		
balance ledger accounts		
prepare and interpret ledger accounts and their balances		
record transactions using ledger accounts		
understand that ledger accounts can be maintained using a computer.		

Chapter 3
The trial balance

LEARNING INTENTIONS

By the end of this chapter, you will be able to:

- explain why a trial balance is required and its limitations
- prepare a trial balance from ledger accounts and from a list of balances
- correct a trial balance which contains errors
- explain the errors which do not affect the balancing of a trial balance.

Introduction

A **trial balance** is a list of the balances on the accounts in the ledger at a certain date.

A trial balance is prepared to check the arithmetical accuracy of the double entry book-keeping. The name of each account is listed in the trial balance. The balance on each account is shown according to whether it is a debit balance or a credit balance. The trial balance will show if the total of the debit balances is equal to the total of the credit balances.

It is important to remember that the trial balance is **not** a part of the double entry system of book-keeping as it is simply a list of balances. If the ledger accounts are balanced monthly, then a trial balance may also be drawn up at the end of each month.

The trial balance should be headed with the term 'trial balance' along with the date on which it was prepared.

The layout of a trial balance is as follows.

Trial balance at		
Details	Debit $	Credit $

> **KEY TERM**
>
> **trial balance:** a list of the balances on the accounts in the ledger at a certain date.

ACCOUNTING IN CONTEXT

Is it really necessary to prepare a trial balance?

Figure 3.1: The owner of a bakery might not have any knowledge of book-keeping

It is important that the financial records of a business are accurate. One of the ways in which accuracy can be verified is to prepare a trial balance. This checks that the total of the debit balances is equal to the total of the credit balances.

Waseem has been working in a bakery for several years and has decided to start a business supplying bread, cakes and desserts to cafes and restaurants. Waseem is an experienced baker, but he has very little knowledge of book-keeping. He does understand that all business transactions should be recorded accurately and has heard about a trial balance, but he wonders if it is really necessary or whether it is just a waste of time.

Waseem's daughter, Zainab, has recently completed a book-keeping course, and he is considering employing Zainab to maintain his day-to-day accounting records. Alternatively, Waseem is considering employing someone who is able to maintain accounting records using accounting software.

Whoever he employs, Waseem is sure that a trial balance will not be necessary: Zainab did very well in her course and will not make any mistakes, or if accounting software is used, it will be 100% accurate.

Discuss in pairs or in a group:

1. Can Waseem be confident that:

   a. accounting software will have no errors?

   b. Zainab will maintain accurate records?

2. Why is it important to Waseem that his accounting records do not contain any errors?

3.1 The purpose of a trial balance

There are two main reasons for producing a trial balance:

1. A trial balance can help with locating arithmetical errors.
2. A trial balance is useful in preparing financial statements.

If the total of the credit balances and the total of the debit balances are not equal, then it means there is at least one error in the accounts. However, if the totals of the trial balance are equal, it does not guarantee that the entries in the ledger accounts are completely free of errors. Later in the chapter, you will learn about errors that will not be detected by a trial balance.

> **LINK**
>
> You will learn about financial statements in Chapters 8–9.

3.2 The preparation of a trial balance

All the ledger accounts which are 'open' (those which still have an amount of money showing in the account) are listed in the trial balance together with the balance on the account. If the debit side of an account is larger in money than the credit side, then that account has a debit balance and the amount of the balance (or difference) is entered in the debit column of the trial balance. If the credit side of an account has more money than the debit side, then that account has a credit balance and the amount of the balance (or difference) is entered in the credit column of the trial balance.

The debit column and the credit column are totalled. If the totals agree, it indicates that the double entry book-keeping is arithmetically correct.

> **WORKED EXAMPLE 3.1**
>
> Imran started his business on 1 January 20–7. His transactions for his first week of trading were shown in the solution to **Worked example 2.3** in Chapter 2.
>
> Prepare a trial balance for Imran at 7 January 20–7.
>
> **Imran**
> **Trial balance at 7 January 20–7**
>
> | Detail | Debit $ | Credit $ |
> |---|---|---|
> | Bank | 63 350 | |
> | Capital | | 90 000 |
> | Equipment | 20 000 | |
> | AB Loans | | 10 000 |
> | Motor vehicles | 18 000 | |
> | Basma loan | | 4 000 |
> | Cash | 2 070 | |
> | Rent expense | 400 | |
> | Insurance | 250 | |
> | Motor expenses | 50 | |
> | Rent income | | 120 |
> | | 104 120 | 104 120 |
>
> - It is common to abbreviate 'debit' to 'dr' and 'credit' to 'cr'.

3 The trial balance

In practice, a trial balance is drawn up using the actual ledger accounts. It is necessary to know the type of accounts which have a debit balance and those which have a credit balance. These are shown in Table 3.1.

Table 3.1: Types of accounts which have debit balances and those which have credit balances

Debit balances	Credit balances
Assets	Liabilities
Expenses	Incomes
Drawings	Capital
Purchases	Sales
Sales returns	Purchases returns

ACTIVITY 3.1

Copy and complete the following table by inserting a tick (✓) to indicate in which column of a trial balance each of the following accounts would be recorded.

Account	Debit	Credit
Property		
Cash		
Carol (a credit supplier)		
Wages		
Mark (a credit customer)		
Repairs to fixtures		
Bank loan		
Carriage outwards		
Carriage inwards		
Capital		

Compare your answers to Activity 3.1 with a partner. Discuss any differences and then check your answers.

DISCUSSION

Working in a small group, think about a local business and discuss the following:

1. What are some of the ledger accounts the business would need to keep?
2. Would the balance of each of these accounts be recorded in the debit column or the credit column of a trial balance?

WORKED EXAMPLE 3.2

The following trial balance was prepared by an inexperienced book-keeper and contains errors. Prepare a corrected trial balance at 31 December 20–9.

Farida
Trial balance for the year ended 31 December 20–9

	Debit $	Credit $
Bank (balance at bank)	2 950	
Cash		100
Capital		51 500
Drawings		820
Property	40 000	
Office equipment		2 520
Loan from AB Company	3 500	
Inventory	6 950	
Purchases		10 130
Sales	15 280	
Sales returns		810
Purchases returns	940	
Carriage inwards		220
Wages	6 900	
Rent income	1 200	
General expenses	880	
Trade receivables		1 270
Trade payables	1 130	
	79 730	67 370

CONTINUED

Farida
Corrected trial balance at 31 December 20–9

	Debit $	Credit $
Bank	2 950	
Cash	100	
Capital		51 500
Drawings	820	
Property	40 000	
Office equipment	2 520	
Loan from AB Company		3 500
Inventory	6 950	
Purchases	10 130	
Sales		15 280
Sales returns	810	
Purchases returns		940
Carriage inwards	220	
Wages	6 900	
Rent income		1 200
General expenses	880	
Trade receivables	1 270	
Trade payables		1 130
	73 550	73 550

- The heading of the trial balance was incorrect as a trial balance shows the balances in the books on a particular day. It does not cover a period of time.
- Each item had to be considered to decide whether it was in the correct column or if it needed to be amended.

3.3 The trial balance and errors

If the trial balance fails to balance

Figure 3.2: If a trial balance does not balance, it means an error has been made in the financial records

When a trial balance fails to balance, it is obvious that an error has been made somewhere. This may be from:

1. adding incorrectly within the trial balance
2. adding incorrectly within one of the ledger accounts
3. entering a different figure on the credit side to that entered on the debit side when making a double entry in the ledger
4. making a single entry for a transaction rather than a double entry
5. entering a transaction twice on the same side of the ledger.

> **TIP**
>
> If the totals of a trial balance do not agree, you know an error has been made in the ledger or in the preparation of the trial balance.

How to locate an error

The steps that need to be followed to locate an error are shown in Figure 3.3.

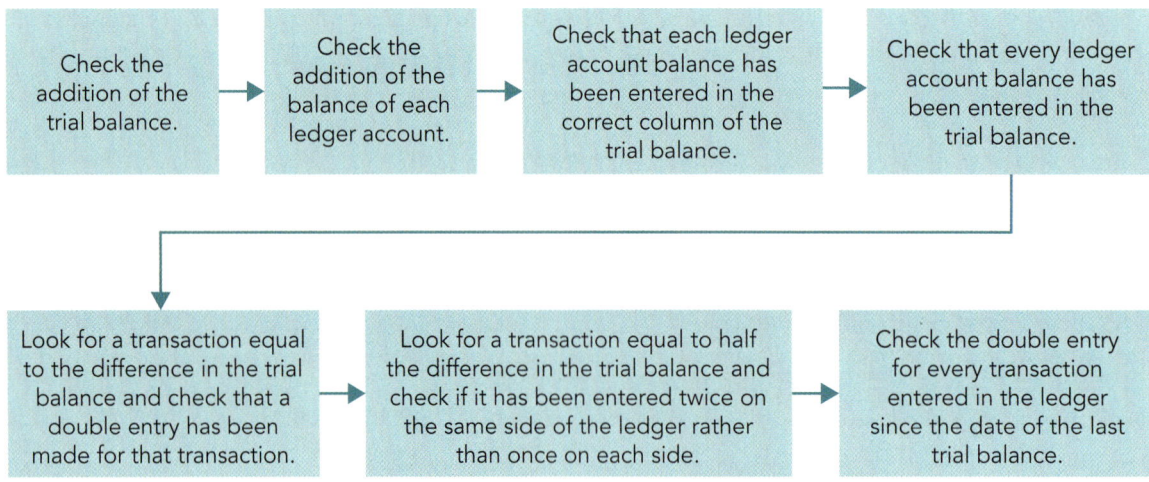

Figure 3.3: The steps to follow to locate an error in a trial balance

If the trial balance balances

When a trial balance balances, it simply means that the total of the debit balances is equal to the total of the credit balances. It does not imply that the double entry has no errors. The trial balance will still balance if any of the errors described in Table 3.2 are made.

Table 3.2: Errors which do not affect the trial balance

Name of error	Description of error	Example
Error of commission	This occurs when a transaction is entered using the correct amount and on the correct side, but in the wrong account of the same class.	Cash received from Malini credited to Mallika's account.
Error of complete reversal	This occurs when the correct amount is entered in the correct accounts, but the entry has been made on the wrong side of each account.	Cash drawings debited to the cash account and credited to the drawings account.
Error of omission	This occurs when a transaction has been completely omitted from the accounting records. Neither a debit entry nor a credit entry has been made.	Payment of wages not entered in the books.
Error of original entry	This occurs when an incorrect figure is used when a transaction is first entered in the accounting records. The double entry will therefore use the incorrect figure.	Purchase of goods on credit, $100, but recorded as $1 000.
Error of principle	This occurs when a transaction is entered using the correct amount and on the correct side, but in the wrong class of account.	Motor expenses debited to the motor vehicles account.
Compensating errors	These occur when two or more errors cancel each other out.	Purchases account understated by $100 and sales returns account overstated by $100.

> **REFLECTION**
>
> Look at the names for the different types of error in Table 3.2.
>
> Sometimes it is helpful to use (or invent) a word to help you remember a list of items. How might remembering 'COCROP' help you to remember the different types of error?
>
> Work with a partner to think of some other strategies that you could use to help you remember the names of the different types of error and when they occur.

ACTIVITY 3.2

For each for the following errors, state whether it would affect the balancing of a trial balance. Give a reason for each answer.

Error 1 No entry had been made for cash sales.

Error 2 Commission received had been correctly entered in the cash account but had been credited to the sales account.

Error 3 Goods returned to Violet had been correctly entered in her account but had been debited to the purchases returns account.

Error 4 Drawings had been correctly entered in the bank account but had been debited to the wages account.

Error 5 The sales account had been overstated by $100 and the purchases account had been understated by $100.

Error 6 Goods purchased on credit from Joseph were correctly entered in the purchases account and debited to the account of Jacob.

> **LINK**
>
> You will learn more about errors in the accounting records in Chapter 15.

ACTIVITY 3.3

Copy and complete the table by naming the type of error which has been made.

Error	Type of error
Repairs to fixtures debited to the fixtures account	
Sales to N Smith debited to the account of M Smith	
Balance on cash account overstated by $100 and balance on sales account understated by $100	
Cash purchases credited to the purchases account and debited to the cash account	
No entry made for cash sales	
Goods returned to Hassan, $30, debited to Hassan's account and credited to purchases returns account as $80	

3 The trial balance

ACCOUNTING IN ACTION

Finding the errors in financial records

Figure 3.4: If a trial balance does not balance, the financial records must be checked for errors

Tumelo opened a sportswear wholesale business a year ago. He attended a course on book-keeping for small businesses and was able to maintain a full set of double entry records during his first year of trading.

At the end of the financial year, Tumelo prepared a trial balance. He was very disappointed to find that the trial balance totals did not agree. The debit column of the trial balance totalled $61 330 and the credit column totalled $60 095.

Tumelo decided that the first thing to do was to check the double entry for every transaction.

Eventually, the following errors were found.

A   Wages, $1 650, had been recorded as $165 in the bank account. (The bank balance in the trial balance was a debit of $6 580.)

B   Cash sales, $460, had been omitted from the books

C   The sales returns account had been overstated by $10

D   Motor expenses, $95, had been debited to the general expenses account

E   The credit balance of Thabo's account had been overstated by $200

F   The credit column of the trial balance had been overstated by $60

Answer the following questions:

1   Explain, giving a reason, whether you agree with Tumelo that the first thing to do is to check the double entry for every transaction?

2   Which of the errors A–F would not have affected the total of the trial balance? Explain why.

3   Calculate the correct trial balance totals.

Compare your answers with a partner and discuss any differences.

SUMMARY

You should now know:

- A trial balance is a list of the balances on the accounts in the ledger at a certain date.
- A trial balance is prepared to check the arithmetical accuracy of the double entry book-keeping.
- If a trial balance fails to balance, it indicates that an error has been made.
- There are six types of error which are not revealed by a trial balance.

Chapter 3 practice questions

1. The balance of which account may appear on the debit side of a trial balance?

   A Carriage inwards

   B Purchases returns

   C Rent income

   D Sales [1]

2. The totals of a trial balance did not agree.

   Which error may have caused this?

   A General expenses paid in cash omitted from the accounting records

   B Goods purchased on credit from Muzhir credited to Muzdahir's account

   C Repairs to motor vehicle debited to motor vehicle account

   D Total of the sales returns account overstated [1]

3. A trader had $6 000 in his business bank account. Rent received from a tenant by bank transfer, $550, was entered in the accounts as $555. How will this affect the trial balance?

	Debit balances in trial balance	Credit balances in trial balance
A	bank overstated	no effect
B	bank overstated	rent income overstated
C	no effect	rent income overstated
D	rent income overstated	bank overstated

   [1]

4. William is a trader. The following balances appeared in his books on 31 March 20–8:

	$
Capital	53 600
Drawings	15 350
Bank	2 100
Cash	50
Sales	97 090
Purchases	57 600
Purchases returns	410
Inventory	11 100
Trade receivables	7 250
Trade payables	5 300
Wages	26 900
General expenses	2 750
Rent expense	4 800
Fixtures and equipment	28 500

   Prepare a trial balance at 31 March 20–8 to check the arithmetical accuracy of William's double entry book-keeping. [6]

5 Sayeeda provided the following list of balances on 30 April 20–4, but was not able to provide her capital account balance.

	$
Capital	?
Drawings	13 500
Property	190 000
Fixtures and fittings	51 500
Inventory	10 100
Trade receivables	12 990
Trade payables	10 950
Loan from FH	30 000
Bank	4 560
Cash	60
Sales	149 200
Purchases	136 750
Rates	3 100
General expenses	5 450
Wages	85 040

Prepare Sayeeda's trial balance at 30 April 20–4, inserting the missing capital account balance. [7]

6 A trial balance drawn up at the end of Jim's financial year balanced. However, a number of errors were later found that had not affected the balancing of the trial balance.

   a State the type of error made in **each** of the errors 1–4. [4]

      1 Goods returned by Jamil had been credited to Jamella's account.

      2 Repairs to property had been debited to the property account.

      3 An invoice, $1 000, for goods purchased on credit from Joseph had been recorded in the accounts as $100.

      4 Goods sold on credit to Martha had been credited to Martha's account and debited to the sales account.

   b Name two further types of error not revealed by a trial balance. [2]

[Total: 6]

CHECK YOUR PROGRESS

How well do you think you have achieved the learning intentions for this chapter? Give yourself a score from 1 (still need a lot of practice) to 5 (feeling very confident) for each learning intention. Provide an example to support your score.

Now I can ...	Score	Example to support score
explain why a trial balance is required and its limitations		
prepare a trial balance from ledger accounts and from a list of balances		
correct a trial balance which contains errors		
explain the errors which do not affect the balancing of a trial balance.		

Chapter 4
Double entry book-keeping – Part B

LEARNING INTENTIONS

By the end of this chapter, you will be able to:

- understand that the ledger is divided into sections – the sales ledger, the purchases ledger and the nominal (general) ledger
- enter transactions and process accounting data in the cash book
- understand and record cash discount
- understand that the cash book can be treated as both a book of prime entry and also as a ledger account for bank and cash
- record payments and receipts made using a range of payment methods.

Introduction

Chapter 2 explained how a business's transactions are recorded using the double entry system. It was explained that an account is maintained for each type of asset, liability, expense and income, as well as an account for each individual credit customer and credit supplier.

As the business grows, so does the number of transactions, and it becomes more convenient to divide the ledger into sections grouping the same types of account together.

The cash account and the bank account may contain a lot of entries as many transactions involve the transfer of money. These two accounts are often moved to a separate book known as the cash book where the cash account and the bank account are maintained side by side.

ACCOUNTING IN CONTEXT

Encouraging prompt payment

Figure 4.1: A wholesaler might sell home appliances to a retail store on credit

Businesses that sell goods on credit can sometimes find it difficult to get their customers to pay promptly. To encourage customers to make their payments more quickly, businesses may offer cash discount on the amount owed. This is a discount that credit customers can take advantage of if they pay the amount due within an agreed time (often 30 days). This will benefit them as they will pay a slightly smaller amount.

Milan is a wholesaler of home appliances. She sells on credit to retail stores. Selling on credit means Milan has to wait to receive payment on her sales. A lot of Milan's credit customers are taking a long time to make payment, which means that Milan is finding it difficult to pay her credit suppliers on time.

Milan is trying to think of ways to get her credit customers to pay more quickly. She is considering offering a cash discount to customers who pay within a certain time period and she hopes that this may encourage customers to pay sooner.

Discuss in pairs or in a group:

1. Do you think Milan's business would benefit from offering cash discount? Explain the reasons for your answer.
2. Can you think of anything else Milan could do to encourage her credit customers to pay their accounts early?

4.1 Division of the ledger into specialist areas

Dividing the ledger into sections makes it more convenient to use because the same types of account can be kept together and the task of maintaining the ledger can be divided between several people. It also enables checking procedures (in the form of control accounts) to be introduced and may reduce the possibility of fraud.

> **LINK**
>
> You will learn more about control accounts in Chapter 16.

4 Double entry book-keeping – Part B

The ledger is usually divided into the following specialised areas:

- **Sales ledger**: This is also referred to as the debtors ledger or trade receivables ledger. All the accounts of credit customers are kept in the sales ledger.
- **Purchases ledger**: This is also referred to as the creditors ledger or trade payables ledger. All the accounts of credit suppliers are kept in the purchases ledger.
- **Nominal ledger**: This is also referred to as the general ledger. Apart from the cash account, the bank account and the accounts of credit customers and credit suppliers, all the remaining accounts are kept in the nominal ledger. This ledger will contain accounts of assets, liabilities, expenses, income, sales, purchases and returns. Asset accounts are known as real accounts. Accounts for expenses, income and capital are known as nominal accounts.
- **Cash books**: These are the cash book (which contains the cash account and the bank account) and the petty cash book.

TIP

Remember that the accounts of individual credit suppliers go in the purchases ledger, but the purchases account goes in the nominal ledger. Similarly, the accounts of individual credit customers go in the sales ledger, but the sales account goes in the nominal ledger.

KEY TERMS

sales ledger: the ledger where the accounts of credit customers are maintained.

purchases ledger: the ledger where the accounts of credit suppliers are maintained.

nominal (general) ledger: the ledger where accounts for assets, liabilities, expenses, income, sales, purchases and returns are maintained.

LINK

You will learn about petty cash books in Chapter 5.

ACTIVITY 4.1

Figure 4.2: A ledger is often divided into specialist areas

Write down the name of the ledger in which each account would be maintained.

a Rent expense account
b AB Loan account
c XY Stores (credit supplier) account
d Capital account
e Sales returns account
f GT Traders (credit customer) account
g Purchases account

Compare your answers with a partner and discuss any differences.

4.2 The two-column cash book

Chapter 2 explained how two separate accounts – a cash account and a bank account – are maintained to record the movements of money. In practice, it is common for these accounts to be moved from the ledger and shown in a separate book known as the **cash book**. The cash account and the bank account appear side by side in the cash book.

The rules of double entry book-keeping are still applied. Any money received is debited in the cash book. If the money is placed in the cash, it will be entered in the cash column, and if it is paid into the bank, it will be entered in the bank column. Any money paid out is credited in the cash book. If the money is paid in cash, it will be entered in the cash column, and if it is paid out of the bank, it will be entered in the bank column.

While the cash account and the bank account appear side by side, they still keep their own identity and must be balanced separately as described in Chapter 2.

Since the cash book is part of the double entry system, it represents ledger accounts for both cash and bank. It is, however, also a book of prime entry because it is one of the books in which transactions should be recorded before being entered in the ledger.

> **KEY TERM**
>
> **cash book:** the book where the cash account and the bank account are maintained side by side.

> **LINK**
>
> You will learn more about books of prime entry in Chapter 7.

4.3 Contra entries

Sometimes surplus cash is paid into the bank, or money is withdrawn from the bank when more cash is needed. Such transactions are known as **contra entries** because they appear on both sides of the cash book, debited to one account and credited to the other. These transactions are recorded by applying the usual rules of double entry by debiting the account receiving the money and crediting the account giving the money. The name of the account where the double entry is made is written in the details column. The entries are as follows:

1 **To record cash paid into the bank**
   - Debit the bank account and write 'cash' in the details column.
   - Credit the cash account and write 'bank' in the details column.

2 **To record cash withdrawn from the bank for business use**
   - Debit the cash account and write 'bank' in the details column.
   - Credit the bank account and write 'cash' in the details column.

In each case, the letter 'c' may be entered to indicate that the double entry is on the opposite side of the same book.

> **KEY TERM**
>
> **contra entry:** an entry that appears on both sides of the cash book.

WORKED EXAMPLE 4.1

Enter these transactions in the books of Elina. The cash account and the bank account should be shown in a two-column cash book. The ledger should be divided into sales ledger, purchases ledger and nominal ledger. Balance the cash book on 31 December and bring down the balances on 1 January 20–7.

20–6

December	1	Elina started business with a capital of $20 000, which she paid into a business bank account
	2	Paid rent on property, $480, by standing order
	5	Purchased goods, $10 600, on credit from Aryan
	9	Withdrew $200 from the bank account for office use
	14	Paid advertising expenses, $55, in cash
	18	Sold goods, $3 900, on credit to Liyana
	23	Paid Aryan's account by cheque
	26	Bought fixtures and fittings, $6 100, and paid by credit transfer
	28	Elina took $2 500 from the business bank account for personal use

Elina

Sales ledger

Dr			Liyana account			Cr
			$			$
20–6						
Dec 18	Sales		3 900			

Purchases ledger

Dr			Aryan account			Cr
			$			$
20–6				20–6		
Dec 23	Bank		10 600	Dec 5	Purchases	10 600
			10 600			10 600

- The account of Aryan is 'in balance' as both sides equal $10 600. The account has been totalled to indicate that the account is now closed.

CONTINUED

Nominal Ledger

Dr	Capital account		Cr
	$		$
		20–6	
		Dec 1 Bank	20 000

Dr	Rent expense account		Cr
	$		$
20–6			
Dec 2 Bank	480		

Dr	Purchases account		Cr
	$		$
20–6			
Dec 5 Aryan	10 600		

Dr	Advertising expenses account		Cr
	$		$
20–6			
Dec 14 Cash	55		

Dr	Sales account		Cr
	$		$
		20–6	
		Dec 18 Liyana	3 900

Dr	Fixtures and fittings account		Cr
	$		$
20–6			
Dec 26 Bank	6 100		

Dr	Drawings account		Cr
	$		$
20–6			
Dec 28 Bank	2 500		

4 Double entry book-keeping – Part B

CONTINUED

Elina
Cash book

Dr			Cash $	Bank $				Cash $	Bank $	Cr
20–6					20–6					
Dec 1	Capital			20 000	Dec 2	Rent expense			480	
9	Bank	c	200		9	Cash	c		200	
					14	Advertising		55		
					23	Aryan			10 600	
					26	Fixtures and fittings			6 100	
					28	Drawings			2 500	
					31	Balance	c/d	145	120	
			200	20 000				200	20 000	
20–7										
Jan 1	Balance	b/d	145	120						

- The money paid out and received must be entered in the correct column depending on whether it was a cash transaction or a bank transaction.
- On 9 December, cash was withdrawn from the bank for office use. The money was credited in the bank column to show it going out and debited in the cash column to show it going in. A 'c' was inserted to indicate a contra item.
- At the end of the month, the cash columns and the bank columns were balanced separately as the cash and bank are two separate accounts.

> **TIP**
>
> When you record a contra entry, write the name of the account where the money has come from in the details column on the debit side, and the name of the account where the money is going to in the details column of the credit side.

ACTIVITY 4.2

Latif provided the following information for the month of April 20–9.

April 1 Cash balance $188

Bank balance (dr) $3 800

4 Received an online bank transfer of $3 106 from Reema

10 Paid insurance by standing order, $124

15 Bought office stationery, $68, and paid in cash

19 Wahid paid $966 by credit card

23 Farida paid her account, $486, by debit card

27 Cash sales, $3 620

29 Paid $3 500 cash into the business bank account

30 Latif withdrew $1 500 from the business bank account for his own use

Prepare Latif's cash book for the month of April 20–9. Balance the book and bring down the balances on 1 May 20–9.

REFLECTION

How confident were you at writing up Latif's cash book? Did you use Worked example 4.1 to help you? If so, how did using this example help you?

The worked examples and the activities are both designed to help you understand a section. Which of the features do you find is more helpful for your own learning style? Why do you think that is?

4.4 Bank overdraft

As explained earlier, the cash column and the bank column of a cash book are balanced separately as they represent two separate accounts.

The balance on the cash column will always be brought down as a debit balance at the start of the next trading period. The only exception to this is when there is no cash left in the cash account, in which case, the balance will be nil. It is not possible to have a credit balance on a cash account.

It is, however, possible to have a credit balance on a bank account. The bank may allow the business to have a **bank overdraft**. This means that the bank allows the business to pay out more from the bank than it has put into the bank (the bank will charge interest on the amount overdrawn). In the cash book, the bank account is balanced in the usual way and the balance will be brought down on the credit side. This represents the amount the business owes the bank, and is a liability.

KEY TERM

bank overdraft: when a business has taken more out of its bank account than has been paid in.

4 Double entry book-keeping – Part B

> **DISCUSSION**
>
> 'It is possible to have a credit balance on a bank account, but not on a cash account.'
>
> Discuss this statement with a partner and think of a way to explain it to another student. Try to think of an example to illustrate why it is not possible to have a credit balance on a cash account.

A bank overdraft is not the same as a bank loan – the features of each are shown in Table 4.1.

Table 4.1: Features of a bank overdraft and a bank loan

Bank overdraft	Bank loan
• A variable amount of borrowing agreed with the bank up to a set limit.	• A fixed amount of borrowing over a set term.
• The overdraft facility can be withdrawn or reduced at any time by the bank.	• The loan must be repaid by an agreed date or repayment by regular instalments may be required.
• Interest at a fixed rate is payable on the daily overdrawn balance.	• Interest at a fixed rate is payable on the total amount borrowed.
• The rate of interest is often higher than that of a bank loan, and may be even higher on an unauthorised overdraft.	• The rate of interest is often lower than that of a bank overdraft.
• The overdraft is often for smaller amounts than a bank loan.	• The loan is often for larger amounts than a bank overdraft, and may have a claim on some of the assets if the loan is not repaid.
• It is commonly used for short-term finance.	• It is commonly used for long-term finance.

WORKED EXAMPLE 4.2

Elina started business on 1 December 20–6. Her transactions for the first month of trading were the same as those shown in **Worked example 4.1**, except that the fixtures and fittings purchased on 26 December cost $6 300 rather than $6 100.

Enter Elina's transactions for December 20–6 in her two-column cash book. Balance the book on 31 December and bring down the balances on 1 January 20–7.

Elina

Dr					Cash book				Cr
				Cash $	Bank $			Cash $	Bank $
20–6						20–6			
Dec	1	Capital			20 000	Dec 2	Rent expense		480
	9	Bank	c	200		9	Cash	c	200
	31	Balance	c/d		80	14	Advertising	55	
						23	Ayran		10 600
						26	Fixtures and fittings		6 300
						28	Drawings		2 500
						31	Balance c/d	145	
				200	20 080			200	20 080
20–7						20–7			
Jan	1	Balance	b/d	145		Jan 1	Balance b/d		80

- The only difference in the cash book is that the credit entry for the fixtures and fittings is $200 larger than in **Worked example 4.1**. This means that by the end of the month the amount paid out of the bank is more than the amount that was paid into the bank, so there is a credit balance and the bank account is overdrawn by $80.

4.5 The three-column cash book

Many businesses maintain a three-column cash book rather than a two-column cash book. The difference is that a three-column cash book has an extra money column on each side to record cash discount.

Cash discount

Cash discount is an allowance given to a credit customer when an account is settled within a time limit set by the supplier. An account does not have to be paid in cash to qualify for cash discount. The time of payment is the deciding factor rather than how the account is paid. Cash discount is a way to encourage credit customers to pay their accounts promptly. The supplier will receive an amount slightly less than the due amount. However, the money is paid earlier and so it is available for use within the business.

> **KEY TERM**
>
> **cash discount:** an allowance given to a credit customer when an account is settled within a time limit set by the supplier.

4 Double entry book-keeping – Part B

Cash discount can be either allowed or received:

- Discount allowed is the discount a business allows its credit customers (trade receivables) when they pay their accounts within a set time. This is an expense of the business as it is the cost of having debts settled promptly.
- Discount received is the discount a business receives from its credit suppliers (trade payables) when it pays their accounts within a set time. This is an income of the business as it is the benefit received from settling debts promptly. It is important to realise that discount received does not involve the receipt of money: the supplier simply accepts less money in settlement of the account.

The amount of the cash discount is recorded at the same time as the transaction to settle a debt is recorded. The entries are as follows:

1 **When an account is paid by a credit customer and a discount is allowed**

   - Credit the discount in the credit customer's account to show that this amount is no longer owing.
   - Enter the amount of the discount in the discount allowed column of the cash book.

2 **When an account of a credit supplier is paid and a discount is received**

   - Debit the discount in the credit supplier's account to show that this amount is no longer owing.
   - Enter the amount of the discount in the discount received column of the cash book.

> **TIP**
>
> Do not attempt to balance the discount columns in the cash book. They represent different types of cash discount: the column on the debit side is discount allowed and the column on the credit side is discount received.

The discount columns in the cash book are not part of the double entry system. They are used for convenience to make a note of discount at the time an account is paid. At the end of the trading period, the totals must be transferred to the double entry system. The steps for this are shown in Figure 4.3.

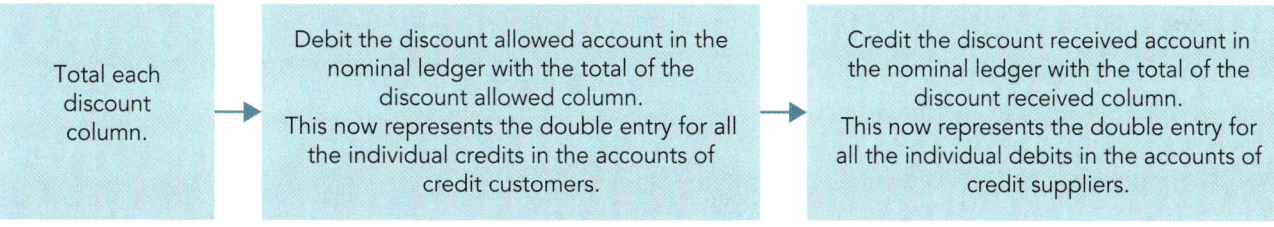

Figure 4.3: The steps for transferring discount allowed and discount received to the double entry system

> **DISCUSSION**
>
> Look at this statement:
>
> 'The total of the discount column on the debit side of the cash book is transferred to the debit of the discount allowed account in the nominal ledger.'
>
> Imagine a student in your class disagrees with this statement because they think it does not follow the rules of double entry.
>
> Discuss with a partner how you can convince this student that the statement is correct.

4.6 Dishonoured cheques

A **dishonoured cheque** is a cheque received by a business, but which the customer's bank refuses to pay. This may occur because there is not enough money in the customer's bank account, or it may be because there is an error on the cheque, for example: no signature, no date, or the amount in words and the amount in figures do not agree.

If a cheque is dishonoured, it is returned to the business that paid the cheque into the bank. The business must record the return of this cheque by crediting the bank account and debiting the credit customer's account (the reverse of the entries made when the cheque was received). The business will also inform the credit customer that this amount is unpaid.

A cheque issued to a credit supplier may be dishonoured if the business does not have enough money in the bank to meet the amount or if there is an error on the cheque. The business must record the return of this cheque by debiting the bank account and crediting the credit supplier's account (the reverse of the entries made when the cheque was issued).

> **KEY TERM**
>
> **dishonoured cheque:** a cheque which the bank will not accept when it is presented for payment.

ACTIVITY 4.3

Figure 4.4: A dishonoured cheque will be returned by the bank

On 14 May, Joseph gave his credit supplier Daniel a cheque to settle his account. The cheque was dishonoured and the bank returned the cheque to Daniel on 22 May.

Discuss these questions with a partner:

1. What entries should Daniel make in his accounting records on 22 May?

2. What steps should Daniel take to try to recover the money from Joseph?

3. What could Daniel do to prevent a similar situation occurring again with other credit customers?

4 Double entry book-keeping – Part B

WORKED EXAMPLE 4.3

Enter the following transactions in the books of Elina. She maintains a three-column cash book and divides the ledger into three sections – sales ledger, purchases ledger and nominal ledger.

20–7

January 1 Elina had a cash balance of $145 and a bank overdraft of $80
         4 Bought goods, $5 600, on credit from Ayran
         8 Returned goods, $200, to Ayran
       12 Sold goods, $660, on credit to Ahmad
       14 Cash sales, $790
       17 Paid $600 cash into the business bank account
       21 Received a cheque from Ahmad in settlement of his account
       24 Sold goods, $2 200, on credit to Shakir
       26 Ahmad's cheque was dishonoured and returned by the bank
       28 Paid Ayran the amount due, by online bank transfer, after deducting a cash discount of 2½%
       31 Shakir paid the amount due by debit card, less a cash discount of 3%

Balance the cash book on 31 January 20–7 and transfer the totals of the discount columns to the relevant accounts in the nominal ledger. Balance the accounts in the sales and purchases ledgers where necessary.

Elina
Sales ledger

Dr			Ahmad account				Cr
			$				$
20–7				20–7			
Jan 12	Sales		660	Jan 21	Bank		660
26	Bank			31	Balance	c/d	660
	(dishonoured cheque)		660				
			1 320				1 320
20–7							
Feb 1	Balance	b/d	660				

- The dishonoured cheque was debited to Ahmad's account to cancel the entry made on 21 January when the cheque was received. The account was then balanced to show that Ahmad still owes $660.

Dr		Shakir account				Cr
		$				$
20–7			20–7			
Jan 24	Sales	2 200	Jan 31	Bank		2 134
				Discount		66
		2 200				2 200

- The discount on 31 January was discount allowed and was entered in the discount allowed column in the cash book.
- The account of Shakir is 'in balance' as both sides equal $2 200. The account has been totalled to indicate that the account is now closed.

CONTINUED

Dr		Purchases ledger Ayran account				Cr
			$			$
20–7				20–7		
Jan 8	Purchases returns		200	Jan 4	Purchases	5 600
28	Bank		5 265			
	Discount		135			
			5 600			5 600

- The discount on 28 January was discount received and was entered in the discount received column in the cash book.
- The account of Ayran is 'in balance' as both sides equal $5 600. The account has been totalled to indicate that the account is now closed.

Dr		Nominal ledger Purchases account			Cr
			$		$
20–7					
Jan 4	Ayran		5 600		

Dr		Sales account			Cr
			$		$
				20–7	
				Jan 12 Ahmad	660
				14 Cash	790
				24 Shakir	2 200

Dr		Purchases returns account			Cr
			$		$
				20–7	
				Jan 8 Ayran	200

Dr		Discount allowed account			Cr
			$		$
20–7					
Jan 31	Total for month		66		

- The total of the discount allowed column in the cash book is transferred to this account at the end of the month.

4 Double entry book-keeping – Part B

CONTINUED

Dr	Discount received account		Cr
	$		$
		20–7	
		Jan 31 Total for month	135

- The total of the discount received column in the cash book is transferred to this account at the end of the month.

Elina
Cash book

Dr										Cr
			Discount allowed	Cash	Bank				Discount received	Cash	Bank
			$	$	$				$	$	$
20–7						20–7					
Jan 1	Balance	b/d		145		Jan 1	Balance	b/d			80
14	Sales			790		17	Bank	c		600	
17	Cash	c			600	26	Ahmad (dishonoured cheque)				660
21	Ahmad				660						
31	Shakir		66		2 134	28	Ayran		135		5 265
	Balance	c/d			2 611	31	Balance	c/d		335	
			66	935	6 005				135	935	6 005
20–7						20–7					
Feb 1	Balance	b/d		335		Feb 1	Balance	b/d			2 611

ACCOUNTING IN ACTION

Deciding who to sell to

Figure 4.5: Unsold goods being stored in a warehouse

Musa is a wholesaler. His terms of trade are 2% cash discount if the account is paid within 30 days. He has a large quantity of goods (cost price $36 000) which he has been unable to sell. Two customers have now offered to purchase these goods.

Nkosi has offered to purchase the goods at cost price of $36 000 on the usual terms. Nkosi has been a regular customer for many years. One cheque was dishonoured a few years ago, but since that time, Nkosi has paid his account monthly by bank transfer. If Musa sells the goods to Nkosi, Musa would have to pay carriage of $150.

Rabiah has offered to purchase the goods for $38 000. Her agent would collect the goods from Musa's warehouse and pay a deposit of $5 000 in cash. The balance would be paid in four equal monthly instalments by cheque. Musa has not traded with Rabiah previously.

Discuss in pairs or in a group:

Provide a short report advising Musa which customer he should sell the goods to. You should include both financial and non-financial factors.

> CAMBRIDGE IGCSE™ AND O LEVEL ACCOUNTING: COURSEBOOK

> **SUMMARY**
>
> You should now know:
>
> - The ledger is usually divided into three specialist areas – sales ledger, purchases ledger and nominal (general) ledger.
> - The cash account and the bank account are usually kept side by side in a cash book.
> - A contra entry appears on both sides of a cash book.
> - Payments can be made by online or mobile transfer, cheque, credit transfer, direct debit, standing order and credit and debit cards.
> - A credit balance brought down in the bank column of a cash book indicates a bank overdraft.
> - Cash discount encourages accounts to be paid within a set time limit.
> - The totals of the discount columns in the cash book are transferred to the discount accounts in the ledger.

Chapter 4 practice questions

1   Which account will appear in the sales ledger?

   A   Dan, a credit supplier

   B   Gill, a credit customer

   C   Sales

   D   Sales returns [1]

2   On 4 April 20–4, Raminder received a cheque, $975, from Kumar in full settlement of a debt of $1 000. How did Raminder record this transaction?

	Debit	$	Credit	$
A	Bank	975	Kumar	1 000
	Discount allowed	25		
B	Bank	975	Kumar	1 000
	Discount received	25		
C	Kumar	1 000	Bank	975
			Discount allowed	25
D	Kumar	1 000	Bank	975
			Discount received	25

[1]

3   Where is the total of the discount column on the debit side of a cash book posted?

   A   To the credit side of the discount allowed account

   B   To the credit side of the discount received account

   C   To the debit side of the discount allowed account

   D   To the debit side of the discount received account [1]

4 Double entry book-keeping – Part B

4 Dina is a trader. On 1 March 20–2, the balances in her cash book were:

Cash $150 debit

Bank $523 credit

The following transactions took place in March 20–2:

March	4	Purchased motor vehicle paying by credit transfer, $10 500
	7	Received a cheque from Jabari, $256
	11	Paid for repairs to property by credit card, $377
	13	Dina took $600 from the bank for personal use
	19	Paid general expenses in cash, $43
	21	Cash sales, $2 980
	27	Paid $318 to Layla by online bank transfer
	28	Paid wages in cash, $1 010
	31	Paid all cash into bank except $200

a Prepare Dina's cash book for March 20–2. Balance the cash book and bring down the balances on 1 April 20–2. [12]

b State the significance of the credit balance on the bank column on 1 March 20–2. [1]

c State why it is not possible to have a credit balance on the cash column. [1]

d Explain the term 'contra'. Illustrate your answer with reference to an appropriate entry in the cash book in **a**. [2]

[Total: 16]

5 Bayani maintains a full set of accounting records, including a three-column cash book. He provided the following information for October 20–5.

Oct	1	Cash balance $113, bank balance $8 260 (debit)
		Trade receivables – Dakila $125, Reyna $950
		Trade payables – Ligaya $280
	4	Paid a cheque to Ligaya in settlement of her account of $280, less 2½% discount
	9	Purchased a motor vehicle, $12 800, and paid by credit transfer
	12	Cash sales, $1 450, of which $1 300 was paid into the bank
	15	Received a cheque, $125, from Dakila
	19	Withdrew $900 by bank transfer for personal use
	24	Paid office expenses in cash, $33
	26	Received a credit card payment from Reyna for $931 in settlement of her account of $950

29 The cheque received from Dakila on 15 October was dishonoured by the bank

30 Paid all cash into the bank except $100

a   Enter the opening balances in the appropriate accounts on 1 October. **[2]**

b   Enter the transactions in the cash book and the ledgers. Balance the cash book on 31 October and bring down the balances on 1 November 20–5. **[20]**

c   Transfer the totals of the discount columns in the cash book to the ledger. **[2]**

d   Total or balance the accounts of the trade receivables and trade payables as required. **[2]**

[Total: 26]

6 Karl is a trader. On 1 February 20–8, he had the following balances on his books:

	$
Cash book – Cash	125
Bank overdraft	535
Sales ledger – Suzanne	300
Purchases ledger – Edward	440
Nominal ledger – Property	80 000
Fixtures	5 800
Capital	85 250

a   Enter these balances in the appropriate accounts on 1 February 20–8. **[3]**

The following transactions took place during the month of February 20–8:

February 3   Sold goods, $400, on credit to Suzanne

7   Suzanne returned faulty goods, $20

11 Purchased goods, $436, paying by cheque

Paid $12 by debit card for carriage on goods purchased

15 Cash sales, $610, of which $550 was paid into the bank

19 Suzanne paid the amount owing on 1 February by credit transfer, after deducting 3% cash discount

21 Paid general expenses, $75, in cash

23 Paid Edward by bank transfer the amount due, less a cash discount of 2½%

25 Let part of the premises to a tenant and received $360 rent in cash

27 Paid $35 with mobile bank transfer for repairs to fixtures

28 Paid all the cash into the bank except $120

4 Double entry book-keeping – Part B

b Enter these transactions in the books of Karl. [23]

c Balance the cash book and the personal accounts on 28 February. Transfer the totals of the discount columns to the nominal (general) ledger on 28 February. [5]

d Draw up a trial balance at 28 February 20–8. [9]

[Total: 40]

CHECK YOUR PROGRESS

How well do you think you have achieved the learning intentions for this chapter? Give yourself a score from 1 (still need a lot of practice) to 5 (feeling very confident) for each learning intention. Provide an example to support your score.

Now I can …	Score	Example to support score
understand that the ledger is divided into sections – the sales ledger, the purchases ledger and the nominal (general) ledger		
enter transactions and process accounting data in the cash book		
understand and record cash discount		
understand that the cash book can be treated as both a book of prime entry and also as a ledger account for bank and cash		
record payments and receipts made using a range of payment methods.		

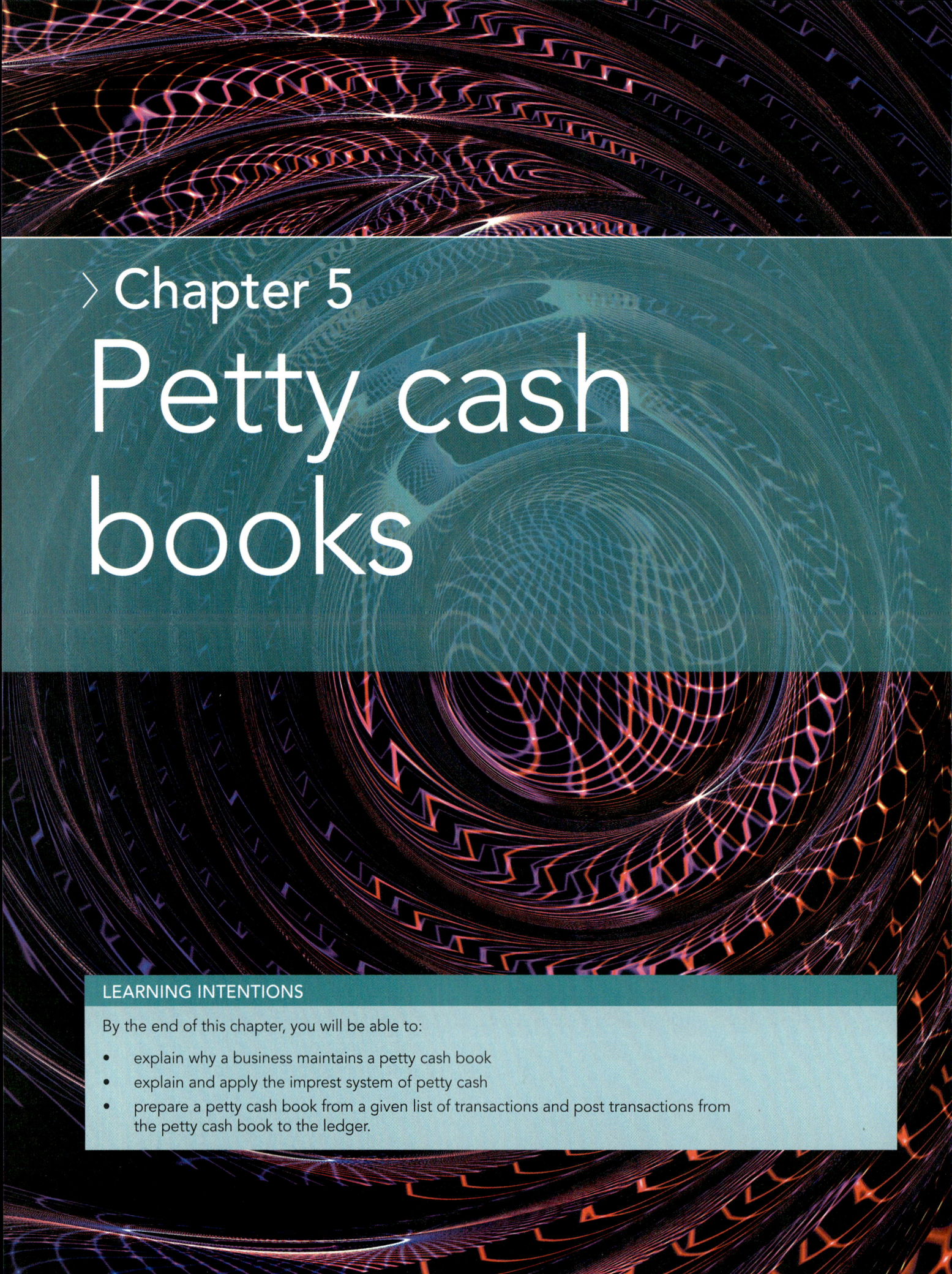

Chapter 5
Petty cash books

LEARNING INTENTIONS

By the end of this chapter, you will be able to:

- explain why a business maintains a petty cash book
- explain and apply the imprest system of petty cash
- prepare a petty cash book from a given list of transactions and post transactions from the petty cash book to the ledger.

5 Petty cash books

Introduction

Most businesses find it necessary to keep some cash on the premises. This can be used to make payments when using a cheque or bank transfer is not suitable. Occasionally, cash may also be received from a customer. Cash that is stored at the business property must be kept in a secure place because of the risk of theft and fraud. These threats can be reduced by monitoring and recording cash transactions. This can be done by maintaining a **petty cash book**.

A petty cash book is used to record low-value (petty) cash payments. These may include postage, stationery, cleaning, travelling expenses and even small cash payments to credit suppliers.

The petty cash book serves two purposes:

- it lists the transactions for transferring to ledger accounts
- it acts as a ledger account for petty cash transactions.

Like the cash book, the petty cash book is a book of prime entry and since it is part of the double entry system, it is also a ledger account.

> **KEY TERM**
>
> **petty cash book:** a book used to record low-value cash payments.

> **LINK**
>
> You will learn more about books of prime entry in Chapter 7.

ACCOUNTING IN CONTEXT

Small transactions

Figure 5.1: An office manager in their workplace

All businesses, large and small, make small cash payments for everyday items, such as items of stationery or postage stamps.

To avoid having to make entries in the main cash book every time a small transaction takes place, the business will have a petty cash book. The petty cash book is usually maintained by a junior member of the accounting staff, known as the petty cashier. The main cashier can then carry out the more important cash accounting tasks while overseeing the work of the petty cashier.

Lana is an office manager. A lot of the employees in the office have been coming to her to claim money for taxi fares, office refreshments and other small business expenses. This has been taking up a lot of time, so Lana has decided to appoint someone as a petty cashier who can be responsible for maintaining records of these expenses and making sure there is enough money in the petty cash box.

Discuss in pairs or in a group:

1. What are some of the small business expenses that the employees might be claiming?
2. What skills and experience will Lana be looking for when she appoints a petty cashier?

5.1 Maintaining a petty cash book

Maintaining a petty cash book means that it is not necessary to record small cash payments individually in either the cash book or the ledger. This reduces the number of entries in these books.

The task of maintaining a petty cash book is often given to a junior member of staff, who is given an amount of cash to act as a float from which small cash payments can be made. This allows the chief cashier to concentrate on more important tasks and it also provides valuable training for a junior member of staff. The chief cashier must check the work of the petty cashier at regular intervals.

When a member of staff wishes to obtain some petty cash, they should present the petty cashier with a completed petty cash voucher. This should show the purpose for which the money is required, the date and the signature of the person receiving the cash, and the voucher number. At regular intervals, the petty cashier should check these vouchers against the total cash spent.

It is possible to maintain a petty cash book using an accounting software package. The physical cash is paid and received in the usual way, but the records are maintained electronically and the monthly totalling and balancing is done automatically.

ACTIVITY 5.1

Figure 5.2: Clothes being packed in a small clothing warehouse

Jose owns a small clothing warehouse trading under the name of Jose's Fashion House. When a small amount of cash is required for business purposes, she usually takes it out of her own purse and then withdraws money from the business bank account to pay herself back.

Jose is considering introducing a petty cash system and appointing a junior member of staff to act as petty cashier. The only people who would be able to authorise petty cash payments would be Jose and the office manager, Ricardo.

Working in pairs or a small group, design a petty cash voucher for use in Jose's business.

5.2 The imprest system

Most petty cash books are maintained using the **imprest system**. Under this system, the petty cashier starts each period (week, fortnight, month and so on) with a fixed amount of money. This is known as the imprest amount or the float. During the period, payments are made out of this cash and are recorded in the petty cash book. At the end of the period, after the petty cash book is balanced, the chief cashier will provide the petty cashier with enough cash to restore the balance to the amount of the imprest (float). The petty cashier therefore starts each period with the same amount of cash.

Under this system, the chief cashier is aware of exactly how much petty cash has been spent in each period. This means that the petty cash expenditure can be controlled. The amount of the imprest can be adjusted as necessary if it is too much or not enough. The imprest system can also help to reduce fraud.

> **KEY TERM**
>
> **imprest system:** the amount spent each period is restored so the amount of petty cash at the start of each period is the same.

ACTIVITY 5.2

Jose introduced a petty cash system into her business, Jose's Fashion House. She decided that the imprest system should be used with a monthly imprest of $50.

After a few months, Cara, the petty cashier, found that at the end of each month she only had between $1 and $5 left.

- Discuss with a partner what action Cara should take.
- Write an email or a short note to Jose summarising your discussion, advising her what action she needs to take.

DISCUSSION

Figure 5.3: Small cash payments being recorded in a petty cash book

Imagine you have been asked to give a group of business owners some advice about introducing a petty cash system. Discuss with a partner the information it would be helpful for the business owner to know about, for example:

- What are the benefits of the imprest system of petty cash?
- What duties would a petty cashier need to carry out?
- What extra duties would the chief cashier have and would it save them time overall?

Be prepared to share your ideas with the rest of the class.

5.3 The layout of a petty cash book

A petty cash book resembles a ledger account with several money columns on the credit side. These are known as **analysis columns** and are used to divide the payments into different categories. A column is used for each of the main types of expenses paid out of petty cash. On the credit side, there is a column for recording the number of the voucher to which the payment relates.

The number of columns and the main types of expenses will be determined by each individual business.

A layout of a petty cash book is shown as follows:

Dr				Petty cash book					Cr
Total received	Date	Details	Vo. no.*	Total paid	←	Analysis columns			→
$				$	$	$	$		$

> **KEY TERM**
>
> **analysis columns:** columns in a petty cash book used to divide the payments into different categories.

* Vo. no. stands for voucher number.

5.4 Preparation of a petty cash book

The entries in a petty cash book are summarised as follows:

During the period

1 **Money received**

   a Debit the total received column with any money received from the chief cashier.

   Insert the word 'cash' or 'bank' in the details column.

   b Debit the total received column with any money received from any other source. Insert the name of the account to be credited in the details column, for example, the name of a credit customer (where a credit customer pays an account in cash), travel expenses (where an employee reimburses the petty cash for private travel expenses), telephone expenses (where an employee reimburses the petty cash for private telephone calls) and so on.

2 **Money paid**

   Credit the total paid column with any money paid out and also enter the amount in the analysis column for that particular expense. A brief description of the reason for the payment should be entered in the details column.

At the end of the period

1. Add the total paid column. Insert the total.
2. Add each of the analysis columns and insert the totals. If these totals are then added horizontally, they should agree with the total paid column. The analysis columns are now complete.
3. Balance the total received column and the total paid column in the same way as balancing any other ledger account. Carry down the balance from the credit side to the debit side to start the new period.
4. When the imprest is restored, enter as described earlier.
5. Complete the double entry for the totals of the analysis columns.
   a. The totals of the analysis columns for expenses should be debited to the appropriate expense account in the nominal ledger.
   b. Any entries in the analysis column headed 'ledger accounts' should be debited individually to the purchases ledger account of the credit supplier to whom the payment was made.

> **TIP**
> Remember to insert the total in the total paid column before balancing the petty cash book. This is important as it allows you to check that the totals of the analysis columns agree with the total paid.

WORKED EXAMPLE 5.1

Ming keeps an analysed petty cash book using the imprest system. The amount of the imprest is $250. He provided the following information:

20–1			$	Voucher number
March	1	Balance	250	
	5	Paid window cleaner	8	1
	8	Bought pens and pencils	6	2
	14	Paid Hoa, a credit supplier	50	3
	17	Paid train fare	12	4
	21	Bought computer paper	10	5
	25	Paid bus fares	8	6
	27	Paid Xuan, a credit supplier	42	7
	29	Paid office cleaner	25	8

a. Write up Ming's petty cash book for the month of March 20–1. The petty cash book should have four analysis columns – cleaning, stationery, travel expenses and ledger accounts.

b. Balance the petty cash book on 31 March 20–1 and carry down the balance. Show the restoration of the imprest on 1 April 20–1.

c. Make the necessary entries in Ming's nominal ledger and purchases ledger on 31 March 20–1.

CONTINUED

a & b

Ming
Petty cash book

Total received $	Date	Details		Vo. no.	Total paid $	Cleaning $	Stationery $	Travel expenses $	Ledger accounts $
	20–1								
250	Mar 1	Balance	b/d						
	5	Window cleaner		1	8	8			
	8	Pens and pencils		2	6		6		
	14	Hoa		3	50				50
	17	Train fare		4	12			12	
	21	Computer paper		5	10		10		
	25	Bus fares		6	8			8	
	27	Xuan		7	42				42
	29	Office cleaner		8	25	25			
					161	33	16	20	92
	31	Balance	c/d		89				
250					250				
	20–1								
89	Apr 1	Balance	b/d						
161		Cash							

- Every payment is entered in the appropriate analysis column and the total paid column. Total each of the analysis columns. They should be equal to the total amount paid.

CONTINUED

c

Dr	Ming Nominal ledger Cleaning account		Cr
	$		$
20–1			
Mar 31 Petty cash	33		

Dr	Stationery account		Cr
	$		$
20–1			
Mar 31 Petty cash	16		

Dr	Travel expenses account		Cr
	$		$
20–1			
Mar 31 Petty cash	20		

Dr	Purchases ledger Hoa account		Cr
	$		$
20–1			
Mar 14 Petty cash	50		

Dr	Xuan account		Cr
	$		$
20–1			
Mar 27 Petty cash	42		

- The total of each expense analysis column is transferred to the appropriate ledger account.
- The individual entries in the ledger account column are transferred to the personal accounts of the credit suppliers.
- Each of the accounts in the purchases ledger would have shown a credit balance representing the amount due. The payment from petty cash will cancel this amount.

ACTIVITY 5.3

Swati maintains a petty cash book using the imprest system. The imprest of $70 is restored at the beginning of each week.

Copy the petty cash book below and fill in the missing words and figures where appropriate.

Total received $	Date	Details		Vo. no.	Total paid $	Cleaning $	Refreshments $	Ledger accounts $
	20–6							
13	May 1	Balance	b/d					
....		Bank						
	2	Hari		1	10	....	....	....
18	3	Daksh						
	4	Tea and coffee		2	8	....	....	....
	5	Anika		3	11	....	....	....
		Cleaning		4	30	....	....	....
					....	....	....	....
		Balance	c/d		....			
_____					_____			
....					....			
....	6	Balance	b/d					
....	7	Bank						

REFLECTION

Completing a petty cash book like the one in Activity 5.3 is a task a book-keeper might do in the workplace. How does completing an activity based on a real workplace task help you to understand a section?

5 Petty cash books

ACCOUNTING IN ACTION

Different methods of recording

Figure 5.4: A petty cash book can be maintained digitally

Suyin is the office manager of a medium-sized company. Khalid is a junior member of staff who has recently taken over the role of petty cashier. The previous petty cashier used a paper-based system for recording all the petty cash transactions. Suyin was very happy with this system because it seemed to work smoothly and everyone understood how it worked. However, Khalid has recently learnt about an accounting software package that can be used to help with keeping a petty cash book and he hopes to persuade Suyin to let him try using this computerised system.

Discuss in pairs or in a group:

1. What might be the benefits of using a computerised system?
2. What might be the disadvantages of using a computerised system?
3. What other things might Suyin need to consider before she makes a decision?

SUMMARY

You should now know:

- A petty cash book is used to record small cash payments (and occasionally small cash receipts).
- The imprest system of petty cash means that the petty cashier starts each period with the same amount.
- A petty cash book is a book of prime entry and also a ledger account.
- The totals of the analysis columns are posted to the appropriate nominal ledger accounts at the end of each period.
- Any payments to credit suppliers are posted individually to the purchases ledger account of the supplier to whom the payment was made.

Chapter 5 practice questions

1. A trader maintains a petty cash book using the imprest system. The monthly imprest is $150. During the month of November, $104 was spent on petty cash transactions and $15 was received for the sale of postage stamps to an employee.

   How much was given to the petty cashier on 1 December to restore the imprest?

   A $89

   B $104

   C $119

   D $150 [1]

2. On 1 March, a trader's petty cash balance was $250 after the restoration of the imprest. During March, the petty cashier spent $145 and received a refund of $10 from a supplier.

   What entry will be made on 31 March to restore the imprest?

	Debit	$	Credit	$
A	bank	135	petty cash	135
B	bank	145	petty cash	145
C	petty cash	135	bank	135
D	petty cash	145	bank	145

   [1]

3. A trader maintains a petty cash book with analysis columns for cleaning, office expenses and ledger accounts.

   On 30 April, the petty cash book showed payments for each category with Karim being the only credit suppliers account being paid.

   What entries are made in the ledger on 30 April?

   A Credit cleaning account, office expenses account, ledger accounts

   B Credit cleaning account, office expenses account, Karim account

   C Debit cleaning account, office expenses account, ledger accounts

   D Debit cleaning account, office expenses account, Karim account [1]

4 Rahim is a sole trader. He operates a petty cash book using the imprest system with a float of $100.

On 1 August, the balance of the petty cash book had been restored to $100.

Details of petty cash vouchers presented during August are shown in the table below.

Date August	Details	Voucher number	Amount $
1	Tea and milk	91	6.80
4	Postage stamps	92	10.75
7	Window cleaner	93	20.00
12	Copy paper	94	12.25
18	Parcel postage	95	2.90
21	Coffee and sugar	96	3.10
24	Cleaner's wages	97	26.00
28	Printer ink	98	6.35

Prepare Rahim's petty cash book for the month of August. Balance the petty cash book on 31 August and bring the balance down on 1 September.

Use analysis columns for postage, cleaning, stationery and refreshments. **[10]**

5 Herman maintains a petty cash book with an imprest of $200, which is restored on the first day of each month.

On 31 October, he provided the following information:

	$
Total of refreshments column	13
Total of postage and stationery column	29
Total of cleaning column	35
Total of ledger accounts column	42

a Explain the imprest system of petty cash. **[2]**

b State the total amount spent by the petty cashier in October. **[1]**

c State the double entry which will be made for the total of the postage and stationery column on 31 October. **[1]**

d State the double entry which will be made in the ledger for the items in the ledger accounts column. **[1]**

e State what entry will appear for petty cash in the statement of financial position on 31 October. **[1]**

f State how much the petty cashier will receive on 1 November to restore the imprest. **[1]**

[Total: 7]

CHECK YOUR PROGRESS

How well do you think you have achieved the learning intentions for this chapter?
Give yourself a score from 1 (still need a lot of practice) to 5 (feeling very confident)
for each learning intention. Provide an example to support your score.

Now I can ...	Score	Example to support score
explain why a business maintains a petty cash book		
explain and apply the imprest system of petty cash		
prepare a petty cash book from a given list of transactions and post transactions from the petty cash book to the ledger.		

> Section 1 practice questions

1 Which task is performed by a book-keeper?

   A calculation of accounting ratios

   B monitoring the progress of a business

   C recording day-to-day transactions

   D preparation of financial statements [1]

2 Habeeb is a credit customer of Yasmin. Which entries would Yasmin make to record goods returned by Habeeb?

	Account debited	Account credited
A	Habeeb	purchases returns
B	Habeeb	sales returns
C	purchases returns	Habeeb
D	sales returns	Habeeb

[1]

3 What is a trial balance?

   A a list of assets and liabilities on a certain date

   B a list of the balances in the books on a certain date

   C a summary of the financial position on a certain date

   D a summary of the transactions for an accounting period [1]

4 On 1 February, Ann owed Becky $560. On 10 February, Ann purchased goods, $480, on credit from Becky. Ann returned ¼ of these goods on 14 February. On 27 February, Ann paid Becky the amount owed by bank transfer, less a cash discount of 2½%.

   How much did Ann pay Becky?

   A $546

   B $663

   C $897

   D $920 [1]

5 At the end of July, the totals of the discount columns in a trader's cash book were:

   Discount column on debit side total $44

   Discount column on credit side total $58

How would these be recorded in the ledger?

	Discount allowed account	Discount received account	
A	Credit $44	Debit $58	
B	Debit $44	Credit $58	
C	Credit $58	Debit $44	
D	Debit $58	Credit $44	[1]

6 a State the meaning of each of the following terms and give two examples of each:

   i Assets

   ii Liabilities [2]

b State what is meant by the term capital. [1]

c State the accounting equation. [1]

George started a business on 1 September 20–8 with a capital of $150 000, which was placed in a business bank account.

   The following transactions took place in the first week:

   Purchased property, $84 000, and equipment, $13 600

   Purchased goods on credit, $2 320

   Obtained a loan from LL Loans, $10 000, which was paid directly into the bank account

   Sold goods on credit at cost price, $500

d Prepare the statement of financial position at 7 September 20–8. [8]

[Total: 12]

7 Geetha is trader. She has very little knowledge of book-keeping but attempted to prepare a trial balance at the end of her first year of trading.

The following is the trial balance she prepared, which contains errors.

Geetha Trial balance at 31 July 20–6		
	Debit $	Credit $
Capital		125 000
Drawings		12 200
Bank overdraft	2 250	
Cash	200	
Sales	76 300	
Purchases		58 850
Purchases returns		410
Trade receivables		4 600
Trade payables	6 980	
Carriage outwards		1 000
Wages	40 000	
Office expenses	2 940	
Rates and insurance	8 650	
Fixtures and equipment	19 500	
Property	63 000	
	219 820	202 060

a Prepare a corrected trial balance for Geetha on 31 July 20–6. [8]

b Identify three types of error which would not be revealed by a trial balance. Give an example of each. [6]

c Identify three errors which would be revealed by a trial balance. [3]

[Total: 17]

8 Naledi maintains a petty cash book. The monthly imprest of $200 is restored on the first day of each month. Naledi provided the following information for May 20–4.

			$
May	1	Balance of petty cash	38
	4	Purchased refreshments for office	6
	11	Paid bus fares for members of staff	10
	16	Paid Kabelo, a credit supplier	66
	19	Paid for taxi for a member of staff	24
	24	Paid office cleaner	72
	28	Paid for refreshments for office	7

a Prepare Naledi's petty cash book for May 20–4, using analysis columns for travel expenses, refreshments, cleaning expenses and ledger accounts. Balance the petty cash book on 31 May and bring down the balance on 1 June 20–4. [10]

b Prepare the necessary entries in Naledi's ledgers on 31 May 20–4. [4]

c State the double entry for the restoration of the imprest on 1 June 20–4. [2]

d Suggest two benefits to Naledi of using an accounting software package rather than maintaining the petty cash book manually. [2]

[Total: 18]

9 Mushan started a business on 1 March 20–1. He provided the following information for his first month of trading:

March 1 Introduced capital of $150 000, of which $10 000 was placed in a cash box for use in the business, and the remainder was placed in a business bank account

2 Purchased property by bank transfer, $80 000

4 Purchased fixtures and equipment, $19 800, and paid by online bank transfer

6 Purchased goods for resale on credit from Sitha, $14 600

8 Returned goods, $280, to Sitha

12 Paid general expenses, $356, in cash

14 Paid rates by direct debit, $320

19 Sold goods, $9 200, on credit to Mauna

Paid carriage on goods sold to Mauna in cash, $94

21 Took goods for own use, $80

24 Rented out part of premises and received $1 400 by mobile bank transfer

28 Paid Sitha $10 000 on account by cheque

29 Cash sales, $15 500

30 Mauna paid her account by cheque, less a cash discount of 2½%

31 Paid all cash into bank except $9 000

a Record the above transactions in the books of Mushan for March 20–1. Balance the cash book and Sitha's account and bring down the balances on 1 April 20–1. [20]

b Prepare a trial balance at 31 March 20–1. [8]

[Total: 28]

10 Ben is a trader. His cash book for February 20–4 is shown below.

Dr				Ben Cash Book					Cr
			Cash $	Bank $				Cash $	Bank $
20–4					20–4				
Feb 1	Balance	b/d	100		Feb 1	Balance	b/d		2 087
4	Yasmin			120		Petty cash			173
13	Capital			6 000	11	Amit			2 450
26	Sales		2 320		14	Fixtures			1 200
28	Cash	c		2 200	21	Stationery		62	
	Balance	c/d		740	27	Wages			3 150
					28	Bank	c	2 200	
						Balance	c/d	158	
			2 420	9 060				2 420	9 060

Explain each entry in the cash book. State where the double entry for each transaction will be found. [26]

Section 2

This section focuses on how business documents are used to record day-to-day financial information. You will study the documents that are exchanged between the buyer and seller of goods. You will learn about the purpose and the content of each document. This section also explains how the information on these documents is entered in the accounting records of the buyer and the seller.

You will also be introduced to books of prime entry and learn how sales and purchases on credit and any subsequent returns are recorded in separate journals. You will also study how and why the ledger is divided into different sections.

Chapter 6
Business documents

LEARNING INTENTIONS

By the end of this chapter, you will be able to:

- recognise and understand the purpose of business documents: invoice, debit note, credit note, cheque, counterfoil, paying-in slip, receipt, statement of account
- understand how these business documents are sources of information for preparing accounting records
- account for trade discount and explain the difference between trade discount and cash discount.

6 Business documents

Introduction

As explained in Chapter 2, the entries in the accounting records of a business are made using business documents. Both documents received and documents issued by a business are used.

The main business documents and their uses are described in this chapter. The exchange of documents starts when a buyer places a purchase order with a seller for goods to be supplied on credit and ends when the payment is made for those goods. Not all the documents described in this chapter will necessarily be required in every transaction.

The main business documents are shown in Figure 6.1.

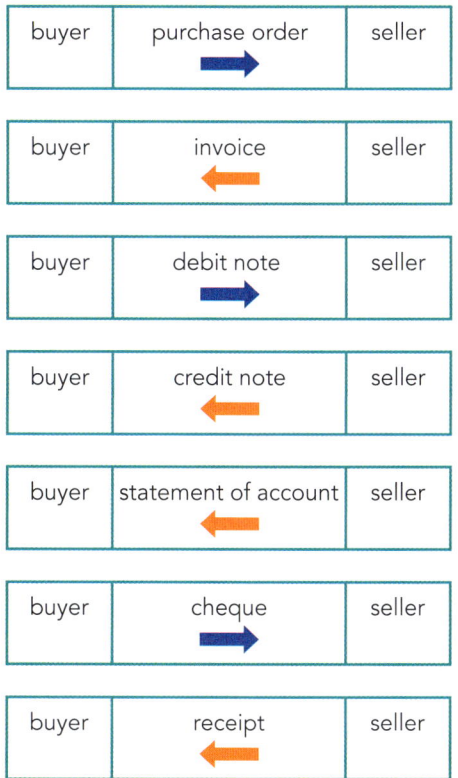

Figure 6.1: The exchange of business documents

ACCOUNTING IN CONTEXT

Are business documents really necessary?

Figure 6.2: Letting business documents build up can make things hard to manage

Business documents form the basis of the entries in the day-to-day accounting records of businesses. They help the owner or manager of a business to keep track of the movement of inventory and provide information about the amounts owed to credit suppliers and amounts owed by credit customers.

Jaleel is a business owner who does not really like paperwork. He would rather be out making new business contacts or dealing with customers than sitting at his desk maintaining the accounts.

Jaleel is considering whether all these business documents are really necessary or whether he can operate his business without them.

Jaleel has also heard that using accounting software could make his life easier. He would be able to record all the information electronically and the software would automatically generate some of the necessary documents, which could then be sent electronically. Jaleel quite likes this idea because, in addition to saving him time, it would mean he could use less paper, which he thinks would be good for the environment.

Discuss in pairs or in a group:

1. a Why does Jaleel need to use business documents?
   b What might happen if he decided not to use business documents?
2. Are there any disadvantages to using accounting software that Jaleel should consider?

6.1 Purchase order

When a business wishes to purchase goods, it will issue a **purchase order** to the supplier. Each business has its own style of purchase order, but they all contain the following information:

- the name and address of the supplier
- the name and address of the customer
- the date
- a full description of the goods, reference numbers, quantity required and unit price
- the name of the person authorised to place the order.

> **KEY TERM**
>
> **purchase order:** a document issued by a buyer to a credit supplier showing the goods or services they wish to purchase.

6.2 Invoice

When a business sells goods on credit, it will issue an **invoice** to the purchaser. Each business has its own style of invoice, but they all contain the following information:

- the name and address of the supplier
- the name and address of the customer
- the date
- full details, quantities and prices of the goods supplied.

Sometimes the supplier allows the customer **trade discount**, which is a reduction in the selling price of the goods. The rate of this discount often increases according to the quantity purchased, and so encourages customers to buy in bulk. It is also given to businesses in the same trade who would not be prepared to pay the full rate as they need to make a profit when they sell the goods.

It is important to distinguish between cash discount and trade discount. Trade discount is shown as a deduction on the invoice. Cash discount is not shown as a deduction on an invoice as it is only allowed if the invoice is paid within a set time limit.

KEY TERMS

invoice: a document issued by a credit supplier showing details, quantities and prices of goods supplied.

trade discount: a reduction in the selling price of goods.

LINK

You have already learnt about cash discount in Chapter 4.

TIP

You should show trade discount as a deduction on an invoice because it is a reduction in the price of the goods. You do not deduct cash discount on an invoice because it is only granted if the customer pays within a set period of time.

Figure 6.3: Trade discounts encourage customers to buy in bulk

Example of an invoice

J Dhoni owns JD's Gadget Shop. On 2 May 20–9, he purchased drones on credit from Drones4all, who issued the following invoice.

> ## *Invoice* Invoice number 484
>
> Drones4all
> Unit 6 Industrial Estate
> Lowtown
> Telephone: 0011223344
>
> JD's Gadget Shop
> 4 Main Street
> Hightown
>
> 2 May 20–9
>
> | Quantity | Description | Unit price $ | Amount $ |
> |---|---|---|---|
> | 10 | Model KD2 Drone for children | 75.00 | 750.00 |
> | 20 | Model AD4 Drone for adults | 125.00 | 2500.00 |
> | | | | 3250.00 |
> | | Less 20% trade discount | | 650.00 |
> | | | | 2600.00 |
>
> Terms: 2% cash discount if account paid by 30 June 20–9.

TIP

From the supplier's viewpoint, an invoice may be described as a sales invoice; from the customer's viewpoint, it may be described as a purchase invoice.

- The customer receives the original invoice and uses it to record the purchase of goods on credit.
- The supplier keeps a copy of the invoice and uses it to record the sale of goods on credit.

Figure 6.4: A customer inspecting a drone he has purchased on credit

ACTIVITY 6.1

Figure 6.5: A business owner preparing invoices for goods she is selling

Katie is a wholesaler trading in computers and related products. She allows her customers 20% trade discount on laptops and 15% trade discount on tablets and also a cash discount of 2% provided payment is made within 30 days.

On 1 March 20–5, Katie sold 10 KYT laptops, list price $540 each, and 24 XDW tablets, list price $400 each, to Amir.

Design a suitable heading for Katie to use on all her business documents.

Use this heading and prepare the invoice for the transaction on 1 March 20–5.

Include details such as Katie's address and telephone number, the invoice number, Amir's address and any other details you think are necessary.

DISCUSSION

Imagine that you own a business that supplies goods on credit.

You offer credit customers both trade discount and cash discount.

Discuss with a partner:
1. When would a customer be entitled to both discounts?
2. When would a customer only be entitled to trade discount?
3. When would a customer only be entitled to cash discount?

6.3 Debit note

The customer should check that goods received are in a satisfactory condition and that they are exactly what was ordered in respect of price, quantity and quality.

The supplier must be informed of any shortages, overcharges and faults. This is done by issuing a **debit note** to the supplier. Each business has its own style of debit note, but they all contain the following information:

- the name and address of the supplier
- the name and address of the customer
- the date
- full details and quantities (and sometimes the prices) of the goods returned or overcharged.

When a price is included on a debit note, it is the price which the customer was actually charged for those goods (the price after the deduction of trade discount).

> **KEY TERM**
>
> **debit note:** a document issued by a credit customer to request a reduction in the invoice received.

Example of a debit note

On 5 May 20–9, JD's Gadget Shop returned goods to Drones4all and issued the following debit note.

Debit Note

Debit note number 26

JD's Gadget Shop
4 Main Street
Hightown

Drones4all
Unit 6 Industrial Estate
Lowtown

5 May 20–9

The following goods have been returned:

	Unit price $	Amount $
2 Model AD4 Drone for adults	125.00	250.00
Less 20% trade discount		50.00
		200.00

Reason for return: Faulty goods

Please issue a credit note

- Neither the supplier nor the customer makes any entries in their accounting records in respect of a debit note.
- A debit note is merely a request to the supplier to reduce the total of the original invoice.

6.4 Credit note

When goods are returned, reported faulty or where there has been an overcharge on an invoice, the supplier may issue a **credit note**. As with all documents, each business has its own style of credit note, but they all contain the following information:

- the name and address of the supplier
- the name and address of the customer
- the date
- full details, quantities and prices of the goods returned or overcharged.

To distinguish them from invoices, credit notes are sometimes printed in red.

> **KEY TERM**
>
> **credit note:** a document issued by a credit supplier to notify of a reduction in a previous invoice.

Example of a credit note

On 5 May 20–9, JD's Gadget Shop returned goods to Drones4all and issued a debit note. Drones4all issued the following credit note to JD's Gadget Shop on 7 May 20–9:

Credit note

Credit note number 44

Drones4all
Unit 6 Industrial Estate
Lowtown
Telephone: 0011223344

JD's Gadget Shop
4 Main Street
Hightown

7 May 20–9

Quantity	Description	Unit price $	Amount $
2	Model AD4 Drone for adults	125.00	250.00
	Less 20% trade discount		50.00
			200.00
	Reason for issue of credit note: Faulty goods		

- The customer receives the original credit note and uses it to record the purchases returns.
- The supplier keeps a copy of the credit note and uses it to record the sales returns.

> **TIP**
>
> Trade discount is shown as a deduction on both the debit note and the credit note so that the amount is equal to that charged on the invoice.

6.5 Statement of account

At the end of each month, a supplier will usually issue each customer with a **statement of account**. This is a summary of the transactions for the month and reminds the customer of the amount owing. The styles of a statement of account may vary, but they all contain the following information:

- the name and address of the supplier
- the name and address of the customer
- the date
- the balance owing at the start of the period
- invoices and credit notes issued
- payments received
- any cash discounts allowed
- the balance owing at the end of the period.

> **KEY TERM**
>
> **statement of account:** a document issued by a credit supplier to summarise the transactions for the month.

Example of a statement of account

Drones4all issued the following statement of account to JD's Gadget Shop on 31 May 20–9.

Statement of account

Drones4all
Unit 6 Industrial Estate
Lowtown
Telephone: 0011223344

JD's Gadget Shop
4 Main Street
Hightown

31 May 20–9

Date	Reference	Debit $	Credit $	Balance $
20–9				
May 2	Invoice number 484	2600.00		2600.00
7	Credit note number 44		200.00	2400.00

The last amount shown in the balance column is the amount due.

Terms: 2% cash discount if account is paid by 30 June 20–9.

- A statement of account is a summary of the transactions which have already taken place, so it is not necessary for either the supplier or the customer to make any entries in their accounting records for this document.

- A statement of account is a reminder to the customer of the amount outstanding. This can be checked against the customer's own records to ensure that no errors have been made by either the supplier or the customer.

6.6 Cheque

Many accounts are paid by **cheque**, which is a written order to a bank to pay a stated sum of money to the person or business named on the order. A book of preprinted cheques is issued by the bank and the customer is only required to complete the necessary details of date, amount and payee (the person or business to whom the money is to be paid). The actual cheque is given to the payee.

Each cheque has a counterfoil attached, which is kept by the person paying the cheque. This allows a record to be made of the date, the payee and the amount of the cheque. The counterfoil is used to make entries in the cash book and the appropriate ledger account.

LINK

Other methods of payment are available through the bank.

Direct debits, online banking, bank transfers and so on were explained in Chapter 2.

KEY TERM

cheque: a written order to a bank to pay a stated sum of money to the person or business named on the order.

Example of a cheque

On 29 June 20–9, JD's Gadget Shop sent a cheque to Drones4all for the amount due on that date, less the cash discount.

The cheque and its counterfoil are shown:

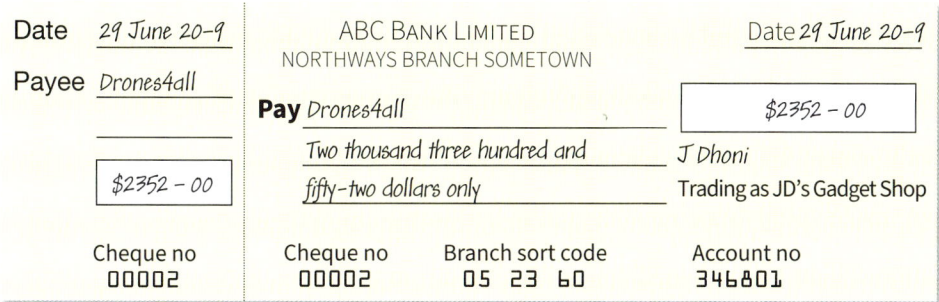

Cheque counterfoil   Actual cheque

- The customer keeps the cheque counterfoil and uses it to make the entry in the cash book to show the money paid out of the bank and to make a note of the discount in the discount received column.
- The supplier receives the cheque. A paying-in slip is completed when the cheque is paid into the bank. The counterfoil of this paying-in slip is used to make the entry in the cash book to show the money paid into the bank and to make a note of the discount in the discount allowed column.

6.7 Paying-in slip

When a customer deposits cash or cheques at the bank, they must present a completed **paying-in slip** at the same time. The paying-in slip gives details of exactly what is being paid into the bank.

A book of preprinted paying-in slips is issued by the bank, and the customer is only required to complete the necessary details of date, amount of notes, coins and cheques which are being paid into the bank, the total, and the name of the person who paid in the money. The actual paying-in slip is retained by the bank together with the cash and cheques paid in. The counterfoil is kept by the customer and is evidence of money paid into the bank.

Example of a paying-in slip

On 30 June 20–9, Drones4all paid the following into its bank account:

the cheque received from JD's Gadget Shop on 29 June 20–9

100 $10 notes

50 $5 notes

The paying-in slip and its counterfoil are shown.

> **KEY TERMS**
>
> **paying-in slip:** a document showing the amounts of coins, notes and cheques being paid into a bank account.
>
> **receipt:** a written acknowledgement of money received and acts as proof of payment.

Paying-in slip counterfoil

Date 30 June 20-9

Cash $1250
Cheques $2352

Total $3602

Paying-in slip number
000546
Account number
992927

Actual paying-in slip

XYZ Bank Limited, High Street, Lowtown

Paid in by K Singh

Date 30 June 20-9

Notes	$50		
	$10	1000	00
	$5	250	00
Coins	$2		
	$1		
	other		
Total cash		1250	00
Cheques		2352	00
		3602	00

Paying in slip No   Branch sort code   Account No
000546   08 05 34   992927

6.8 Receipt

A **receipt** is a written acknowledgement of money received and acts as proof of payment. Where goods are sold for cash, the customer is usually provided with a receipt. It is not necessary for a business to issue receipts for amounts paid through the banking system (by cheque or by bank transfer), as proof of payment will be shown on the statement issued by the bank.

> **LINK**
>
> You will learn about bank statements in Chapter 14.

6 Business documents

Example of a receipt
Drones4all issued the following receipt to JD's Gadget Shop on 29 June 20–9.

RECEIPT   Drones4all   **Number 57**
Unit 6 Industrial Estate
Lowtown

Received from _JD's Gadget Shop_
the sum of _$2352 (Two thousand three hundred and fifty-two dollars) by cheque_

Date _29 June 20–9_   _K Singh_ Chief cashier

- The customer receives the original receipt and uses it to record the payment.
- The supplier keeps a copy of the receipt and uses it to record the receipt of the money.

ACTIVITY 6.2

Copy the table and fill in the missing words to complete the summary of accounting entries for documents which are exchanged between a supplier and a credit customer.

Document	Books of credit customer	Books of credit supplier
Purchase order	No entry	No entry
Invoice	Debit Purchases account Credit	Debit .... Credit Sales account
Debit note	....	No entry
Credit note	Debit .... Credit	Debit Sales returns account Credit Customer's account
Statement of account	No entry	....
Cheque	Debit .... Credit	Debit Bank account Credit Customer's account
Receipt	Debit Supplier's account Credit Cash account	Debit .... Credit ....

Using digital records

If accounting software is used, the information about transactions is recorded electronically and all the necessary documents are generated automatically. The documents can then be forwarded electronically, which saves time and also reduces the amount of paperwork that businesses exchange. The accounting software will also automatically update the ledger accounts, which saves time and also reduces the likelihood of errors being made when the transactions are recorded.

> ### REFLECTION
>
> How confident do you feel about being able to recognise individual business documents and explain their purpose?
>
> Can you remember which business documents are not recorded in the accounting records? What can you do to help you remember this?

> ### ACCOUNTING IN ACTION
>
> **So many documents!**
>
>
>
> **Figure 6.6:** Large businesses can generate a lot of paperwork if the accounting records are maintained manually
>
> Robin is a wholesaler. He has 40 employees who work in his warehouse and five employees who work in the office. Robin's business exchanges a lot of documents with customers and suppliers, and all the accounting records are maintained manually.
>
> Robin is concerned that the office workers have a lot of documents to process.
>
> **Discuss in pairs or in a group:**
>
> 1. Do you think business documents are really necessary? Explain why you think they are or are not.
> 2. Do you think that businesses will still be using paper documents in 10 years' time? Explain why or why not?
> 3. Robin does not expect to have adequate funds to install a fully computerised system for his office records next year. Suggest some other ways Robin can reduce the workload of the office staff.

SUMMARY

You should now know:

- A supplier issues an invoice to a customer for goods sold on credit.
- A supplier may allow a customer trade discount if the businesses are in the same trade and also for buying in bulk.
- If goods are returned or there is an overcharge, a customer may issue a debit note to the supplier asking for a reduction in the invoice.
- A supplier issues a credit note to notify the customer of any reduction in the total of an invoice.
- A supplier issues a statement of account at the end of each month to notify the customer of the amount owing and provide a summary of the account.
- Many accounts are paid by cheque or bank transfer, in which case it is not necessary to issue a receipt as proof of payment.

Chapter 6 practice questions

1. Tilda returned goods, previously purchased on credit, to Lee.

    Which document did Lee issue when he received these goods?

    A credit note

    B debit note

    C invoice

    D statement [1]

2. Mahendra sells goods on credit. Her terms of trade are 20% trade discount for orders over $8 000 and 2% cash discount for payment within 30 days. On 4 June, Mahendra sold goods, list price $9 000, on credit to Arjun.

    How much did Mahendra debit to Arjun's account on 4 June?

    A $7 056

    B $7 200

    C $8 800

    D $8 820 [1]

3   Karen sells goods on credit to Kylie. Karen allows cash discount at 2% (rounded up to the next whole dollar where necessary) for payment by the end of the month following that in which the goods are supplied.

The following documents were exchanged in June:

		$
June 5	Invoice	420
11	Debit note	100
13	Credit note	100
24	Invoice	330

Kylie settled her account by bank transfer on 2 August. How much did she pay?

A $637

B $650

C $931

D $950   [1]

4   Mary is a credit customer of Paul. The following documents were exchanged in July.

Copy the following table. Complete the table by naming the person who issued each document and the entries (if any) made in the books of Mary and Paul.   [12]

Document	Person issuing document	Entries in Mary's books		Entries in Paul's books	
		Account debited	Account credited	Account debited	Account credited
Invoice					
Debit note					
Credit note					
Statement of account					

5 Study the following incomplete document and answer the questions below.

> **Debit Note**
>
> K Smith
> Unit 4 Industrial Estate
> Hightown
>
> L Jones
> 123 High Street
> Anytown   11 May 20–2
>
> | | Unit price $ | Amount $ |
> |---|---|---|
> | 6 Washing machines Model WM144 | 300.00 | i .... |
> | Less 20% ii .... discount | | iii .... |
> | | | iv .... |

a Calculate the missing words or figures in i–iv on the document. [2]

b Name the person who issued the debit note. [1]

c Suggest one reason why the document was issued. [1]

d State how L Jones would record this document in his accounting records. [1]

e Name the document which would be issued by the person receiving this document. [1]

[Total: 6]

6 Study the following incomplete document and answer the questions below.

```
..........................................
                    Trade Supplies
                    345 London Road
                        Littleton
Diana
14 High Street
Southmere                                        31 October 20-6
```

Date	Details	Debit $	Credit $	Balance $
20-6				
Oct 1	Balance	1 200.00		1 200.00
6	Sales	520.00		....
14	Sales returns		90.00	....
28	Online bank transfer		1 164.00	....
	Discount		36.00	....

a Name this document. [1]

b Suggest one reason for the issue of the document. [1]

c State the amount owing by Diana on 15 October and 31 October. [2]

d Name the documents sent by Trade Supplies to Diana on 6 October and 14 October. [1]

e Calculate the percentage rate of discount allowed on 28 October. [1]

f Suggest one reason why this discount was granted. [1]

[Total: 7]

6 Business documents

CHECK YOUR PROGRESS

How well do you think you have achieved the learning intentions for this chapter? Give yourself a score from 1 (still need a lot of practice) to 5 (feeling very confident) for each learning intention. Provide an example to support your score.

Now I can …	Score	Example to support score
recognise and understand the purpose of business documents: invoice, debit note, credit note, cheque, counterfoil, paying-in slip, receipt, statement of account		
understand how these business documents are sources of information for preparing accounting records		
account for trade discount and explain the difference between trade discount and cash discount.		

Chapter 7
Books of prime entry

LEARNING INTENTIONS

By the end of this chapter, you will be able to:

- enter transactions in the sales journal, purchases journal, sales returns journal and purchases returns journal
- post transactions from the books of prime entry to the ledger
- explain the advantages and disadvantages of using manual and digital methods to maintain books of prime entry.

7 Books of prime entry

Introduction

In Chapter 4, it was explained how the ledger is divided into specialist areas and how the cash and the bank account are usually maintained in a cash book rather than in the ledger. Businesses use **books of prime entry** to record goods sold on credit, goods purchased on credit, sales returns and purchases returns. These books are basically listing devices. They group together similar types of transactions, which is useful when posting to the ledger. Using these books means that a lot of detail is removed from the ledger and also that book-keeping can be divided between several people. Books of prime entry are helpful when certain accounting information needs to be collated and summarised. They are also used to obtain information when control accounts are being prepared.

Some businesses use an accounting software package to maintain books of prime entry instead of keeping records manually.

Books of prime entry are also known as books of original entry or subsidiary books. They have been given this name because all transactions should be recorded in one of these books before being entered in the ledger.

The books of prime entry are:

- Cash book
- Petty cash book
- Sales journal
- Purchases journal
- Sales returns journal
- Purchases returns journal
- General journal.

This chapter concentrates on the sales, purchases and returns journals.

> **KEY TERM**
>
> **book of prime entry:** a book where transactions are recorded before being entered in the ledger.

> **LINKS**
>
> You have already learnt about cash books and petty cash books in Chapters 4–5.
>
> You will learn about the general journal in Chapter 15 and control accounts in Chapter 16.

ACCOUNTING IN CONTEXT

Different types of transactions

Figure 7.1: Tools and construction materials being sold for cash and also on credit

As you saw in earlier chapters, the double entry system is used to record all business transactions. As a business expands and there are more transactions, more financial records will need to be maintained. This means that it is often necessary to divide the task of recording the transactions between several people.

Sandhya owns a business selling tools and construction materials to local builders, and home decorating supplies to customers who want to decorate or make repairs to their home. Builders who buy a lot of their supplies from Sandhya often like to buy on credit and pay their bills at the end of the month. However, other customers are required to pay for their purchases immediately.

> **CAMBRIDGE IGCSE™ AND O LEVEL ACCOUNTING: COURSEBOOK**

> **CONTINUED**
>
> Sandhya purchases all her goods from wholesalers and pays at the end of each month.
>
> Sandhya's business is doing well, and she has three employees who work in the office dealing with general enquiries, administration and book-keeping. At present, only one of the employees carries out book-keeping tasks and Sandhya is thinking of dividing the tasks so that the book-keeping work can be shared out between the employees.
>
> **Discuss in pairs or in a group:**
>
> 1 What sort of transactions take place each month in Sandhya's business?
>
> 2 How could the book-keeping tasks be divided between the three employees?
>
> 3 How might it help Sandhya's business if she uses different books of prime entry to record transactions?

7.1 Sales journal

When a business sells goods on credit, the **sales journal** is used to record the name of the customer, the total of the sales invoice and the date of that invoice. The sales journal is sometimes referred to as the sales book or the sales day book.

In a manual book-keeping system, this journal is written up using copies of the invoices sent to credit customers. The entries are as follows:

1 When goods are sold on credit

- Enter the date, customer name and the invoice total in the sales journal.
- Debit the customer's account in the sales ledger with the invoice total.

2 At the end of the month

- Credit the sales account in the nominal ledger with the sales journal total.
- This will now form the double entry for all the individual debit entries in the sales ledger.

> **KEY TERM**
>
> **sales journal:** a record of the names of credit customers, the value of the goods sold and the date of the sale.

7.2 Sales returns journal

When a credit customer returns goods, the business records the name of the customer, the total of the credit note issued and the date of that credit note in the **sales returns journal**. The sales returns journal is also known as the sales returns book or the returns inwards book (or returns inwards journal).

In a manual book-keeping system, this journal is written up using copies of the credit notes sent to credit customers. The entries are as follows:

1 When goods are returned by a credit customer

- Enter the date, customer name and credit note total in the sales returns journal.
- Credit the customer's account in the sales ledger with the credit note total.

> **KEY TERM**
>
> **sales returns journal:** a record of the names of credit customers who have returned goods, the value of the goods returned and the date of the return.

7 Books of prime entry

2 **At the end of the month**
- Debit the sales returns account in the nominal ledger with the sales returns journal total.
- This will now form the double entry for all the individual credit entries in the sales ledger.

Figure 7.2: A customer with a recently purchased drone

LINK
You learnt about trade discount in Chapter 6.

TIP
Remember that you should only post the totals of the journals to the sales and sales returns accounts at the end of the month, and not the individual transactions.

WORKED EXAMPLE 7.1

Drones4all provided the following information about invoices and credit notes issued in May 20–9.

May 2 Issued an invoice to JD's Gadget Shop for goods, $3 250, subject to a trade discount of 20%

7 Issued a credit note to JD's Gadget Shop for goods returned, list price $250

13 Sold goods on credit to Hassan, $4 400, subject to a trade discount of 25%, and issued an invoice on the same day

20 Sent Mira an invoice for $600 for goods supplied on credit

28 Issued a credit note to Mira for $90 because of an overcharge

Make the necessary entries in the books of Drones4all for May 20–9.

Drones4all		
Sales journal		
Date	Name	Amount $
20–9		
May 2	JD's Gadget Shop	2 600
13	Hassan	3 300
20	Mira	600
31	Transfer to sales account	6 500

CONTINUED

Sales returns journal		
Date	Name	Amount $
20–9		
May 7	JD's Gadget Shop	200
28	Mira	90
31	Transfer to sales returns account	290

- The amounts shown in the sales journal and the sales returns journal in this example are the values of the goods after trade discount has been deducted. Alternatively, the amount of trade discount may be shown in the journals for information. (This is shown after **Worked example 7.1**.)

Sales ledger

Dr	JD's Gadget Shop account			Cr
		$		$
20–9			20–9	
May 2	Sales	2 600	May 7 Sales returns	200

Dr	Hassan account			Cr
		$		$
20–9				
May 13	Sales	3 300		

Dr	Mira account			Cr
		$		$
20–9			20–9	
May 20	Sales	600	May 28 Sales returns	90

- The amount entered in the ledger accounts is the total invoice or credit note, which represents the value of the goods after trade discount has been deducted. The amount of trade discount may be shown in the journals for information, but it is never entered in the double entry records.

Nominal ledger

Dr	Sales account			Cr
		$		$
			20–9	
			May 31 Credit sales for month	6 500

- The entry in the sales account on 31 May is the double entry for the three individual debits in the credit customers' accounts in the sales ledger.

CONTINUED

Dr	Sales returns account		Cr
	$		$
20–9			
May 31 Returns for month	290		

- The entry in the sales returns account on 31 May is the double entry for the two individual credits in the credit customers' accounts in the sales ledger.

In order to show the trade discount, the journals in **Worked example 7.1** may be displayed as follows:

Drones4all			
Sales journal			
Date	Name	Amount $	Amount $
20–9			
May 2	JD's Gadget Shop		
	Goods	3 250	
	Less Trade discount	650	2 600
13	Hassan		
	Goods	4 400	
	Less Trade discount	1 100	3 300
20	Mira		
	Goods		600
31	Transfer to sales account		6 500

Sales returns journal			
Date	Name	Amount $	Amount $
20–9			
May 7	JD's Gadget Shop		
	Goods	250	
	Less Trade discount	50	200
28	Mira		
	Goods		90
31	Transfer to sales returns account		290

> **TIP**
>
> If trade discount was allowed when goods were sold (or purchased), then remember to deduct it when those goods are returned so that the actual price charged for those goods is recorded in the accounts.

ACTIVITY 7.1

Chamila supplies goods on credit to Inesh. Chamila's terms of trade are 20% trade discount on orders over $1000 and 2% cash discount for payment within 30 days.

a   Copy and complete the table to name the book of prime entry Chamila would use to record each of the following transactions which took place in June 20–8.

Date	Transaction	Book of prime entry
June 10	A bank transfer was received from Inesh to settle the amount he owed on 1 June	
June 14	Inesh purchased goods on credit, list price $600	
June 20	Inesh purchased goods on credit, list price $3 800	
June 22	Inesh returned goods, list price $400, purchased by him on 20 June	

b   On 1 June 20–8, Inesh owed $2 100 for goods purchased on 20 May 20–8.

Prepare the account of Inesh as it would appear in Chamila's ledger for June 20–8. Balance the account and bring down the balance on 1 July 20–8.

REFLECTION

In Activity 7.1, Chamila offered both trade discount and cash discount.

Write a short explanation of when each type of discount is given and how each is recorded in the accounting records.

Swap explanations with a partner and discuss:

- Which explanation was easier to understand?
- What was it that made that explanation easier to understand?

7.3 Purchases journal

When a business purchases goods on credit, the **purchases journal** is used to record the name of the credit supplier, the total of the purchases invoice and the date of the invoice. The purchases journal is also known as the purchases book or the purchases day book.

In a manual book-keeping system, this journal is written up using the invoices received from credit suppliers. The entries are as follows:

1 **When goods are bought on credit**

   - Enter the date, supplier name and the invoice total in the purchases journal.
   - Credit the supplier's account in the purchases ledger with the invoice total.

2 **At the end of the month**

   - Debit the purchases account in the nominal ledger with the purchases journal total.
   - This will now form the double entry for all the individual credit entries in the purchases ledger.

> **KEY TERM**
>
> **purchases journal:** a record of the names of credit suppliers, the value of the goods purchased and the date of the purchase.

7.4 Purchases returns journal

When a business returns goods they have purchased on credit, the **purchases returns journal** is used to record the name of the supplier, the total of the credit note received and the date of that credit. The purchases returns journal is also known as the purchases returns book or the returns outward book (or returns outward journal).

In a manual book-keeping system, this journal is written up using the credit notes received from suppliers. The entries are as follows:

1 **When goods are returned to a credit supplier**

   - Enter the date, supplier name and the credit note total in the purchases returns journal.
   - Debit the supplier's account in the purchases ledger with the credit note total.

> **KEY TERM**
>
> **purchases returns journal:** a record of the names of credit suppliers to whom goods have been returned, the value of the goods returned and the date of the return.

2   **At the end of the month**

- Credit the purchases returns account in the nominal ledger with the purchases returns journal total.
- This will now form the double entry for all the individual debit entries in the purchases ledger.

ACTIVITY 7.2

Figure 7.3: Business owners need to think about what accounting records they need to keep

Zain has just started a business as a wholesaler of men's clothing, and he is thinking about the accounting records he needs to keep.

Working in pairs, write a list of reasons why it would be useful for Zain to maintain sales, purchases and returns journals.

WORKED EXAMPLE 7.2

JD's Gadget Shop provided the following information about invoices and credit notes received in May 20–9.

May 2   Received an invoice for goods purchased from Drones4all for $3 250, less a trade discount of 20%

7   Received a credit note from Drones4all for goods returned, list price $250

19   Received an invoice for goods purchased on credit from Model Car Store for $600, less 15% trade discount

25   Discovered that half of the goods purchased on 19 May were faulty and these goods were returned to Model Car Store, who issued a credit note

7 Books of prime entry

> **CONTINUED**

Make the necessary entries in the books of JD's Gadget Shop for May 20–9.

JD's Gadget Shop		
Purchases journal		
Date	Name	Amount $
20–9		
May 2	Drones4all	2 600
19	Model Car Store	510
31	Transfer to purchases account	3 110

Purchases returns journal		
Date	Name	Amount $
20–9		
May 7	Drones4all	200
25	Model Car Store	255
31	Transfer to purchases returns account	455

Purchases ledger

Dr		Drones4all account			Cr
		$			$
20–9			20–9		
May 7	Purchases returns	200	May 2	Purchases	2 600

Dr		Model Car Store account			Cr
		$			$
20–9			20–9		
May 25	Purchases returns	255	May 19	Purchases	510

Nominal ledger

Dr		Purchases account			Cr
		$			$
20–9					
May 31	Credit purchases for month	3 110			

- The entry in the purchases account on 31 May is the double entry for the two individual credits in the credit suppliers' accounts in the purchases ledger.

> **CAMBRIDGE IGCSE™ AND O LEVEL ACCOUNTING: COURSEBOOK**

CONTINUED

Dr	Purchases returns account		Cr
	$		$
		20–9	
		May 31 Returns for month	455

- The entry in the purchases returns account on 31 May is the double entry for the two individual debits in the credit suppliers' accounts in the purchases ledger.

The transactions between Drones4all and JD's Gadget Shop are recorded by both businesses. In Worked example 7.1, the transactions are shown from the viewpoint of Drones4all (who sell the goods) and in Worked example 7.2, they are shown from the viewpoint of JD's Gadget Shop (who purchase the goods).

After Worked example 7.1, an alternative presentation for the journals was shown, which included the trade discount. In the same way, the format of the purchases journal and purchases returns journal can also be amended so that the trade discount is included.

> **TIP**
>
> Remember that you should only post the totals of the journals to the purchases and purchases returns accounts at the end of the month, and not the individual transactions.

ACTIVITY 7.3

Lakshani became a credit customer of Banduka on 1 June 20–3. They exchanged the following documents in June 20–3:

cheque, credit note, debit note, invoice, purchase order and statement of account.

a   Copy the table and extend as necessary. Complete the table by listing the documents in the order in which they would be issued and stating the name of the book of prime entry in which they would be recorded by each trader.

If any of the documents are not entered in a book of prime entry, write 'No entry'.

Document	Book of prime entry used by Lakshani	Book of prime entry used by Banduka

b   If you wrote 'No entry' for any of the documents, give a short explanation why that document is not recorded in the books of prime entry.

122

7.5 Using accounting software

A computerised accounting system can be used to record transactions in the books of prime entry instead of keeping records manually in actual books. The books of prime entry, which are often referred to as reports, can be produced more easily using a computerised accounting system than by using a manual system.

Different software packages may have slight differences, but a common feature is that an invoice is generated automatically when an item of stock is sold. This in turn causes the computer program to make the posting to the correct accounts in the ledgers. This is the same thing that a book-keeper would do using a manual system, but with the computerised system, there is less opportunity for errors to occur as the program is designed to ensure that the postings are correct.

Table 7.1 describes some of the benefits and limitations of changing from a manual system of book-keeping to an accounting software package.

Table 7.1: Benefits and limitations of using accounting software

Benefits of accounting software	Limitations of accounting software
Reduced costs as fewer book-keepers may be required.	Errors can still occur because of operator error or because incorrect original data is entered.
Improved credit control as invoices will be issued more promptly.	Risk that the computer system could crash resulting in a loss of data.
Reduced risk of fraud as the system uses secure passwords and may highlight any attempts at inappropriate entry.	Initial high cost of the software package and staff training.
More effective decision-making as data will be more readily available.	Loss of privacy as employees may be able to access financial information relating to the business.
	Possible risk of external threats, such as hacking.
	Staff could be resistant to change and become demotivated.

DISCUSSION

Mustapha has recently started a business. He purchases goods on credit from his suppliers and sells to customers who pay immediately using cash, debit or credit card, or bank transfer. Mustapha pays his suppliers and other large amounts either by cheque or bank transfer, and he makes small cash payments out of his own wallet.

Mustapha has little experience of maintaining accounting records, but he knows that it is a good idea to record his financial transactions as they occur.

Discuss these questions in pairs:

1 What records would you advise Mustapha to maintain on a daily basis?

2 What ledgers and books of prime entry should Mustapha use and what should he record in each?

3 Consider the list of benefits and limitations in Table 7.1. Would you advise Mustapha to keep records manually or use a software package? Why?

ACCOUNTING IN ACTION

Explaining the books of prime entry

Figure 7.4: As a business grows, more staff might be needed to help with the accounts

Sandhya's business of selling supplies for building and home decoration has continued to grow. She has continued to sell to local builders on credit terms and to require other customers to pay for their purchases immediately. Sandhya buys her supplies on credit terms.

The office staff have started to use different books of prime entry for recording the business's transactions. Each month more and more transactions are taking place, and it has become necessary to employ a new member of staff to help with the book-keeping activities.

Discuss in pairs or in a group:

1 What sort of training do you think would be helpful for the new member of staff so that they understand what the different books of prime entry are and how they are used?

2 One of the office staff has suggested that, instead of appointing a new member of staff, it might be better to use accounting software. What would you recommend to Sandhya and why?

SUMMARY

You should now know:

- All transactions should be entered in a book of prime entry before they are entered in the ledger.
- The sales journal is written up from copies of invoices sent to credit customers, and the sales returns journal is written up from copies of credit notes sent to credit customers.
- The purchases journal is written up from invoices received from credit suppliers, and the purchases returns journal is written up from credit notes received from credit suppliers.
- At the end of each month, the totals of the sales, purchases and returns journals are transferred to the sales, purchases and returns accounts, respectively.

Chapter 7 practice questions

1. Jennie sold goods, list price $2 800, to Dale on 13 April. Jennie offered Dale 20% trade discount and a 2½% cash discount for prompt payment.

    Which entry will Dale make in his books of prime entry on 13 April?

    A   purchases journal $2 184

    B   purchases journal $2 240

    C   sales journal $2 184

    D   sales journal $2 240   [1]

2. In which book of prime entry will Lee record credit notes he has received?

    A   purchases journal

    B   purchases returns journal

    C   sales journal

    D   sales returns journal   [1]

3. Which entries are posted from the sales returns journal?

	Account(s) to be debited	Account(s) to be credited
A	individual credit customer	sales
B	individual credit customer	sales returns
C	sales	individual credit customer
D	sales returns	individual credit customer

    [1]

4 Alice maintains a full set of books of prime entry.

   a State **one** advantage of maintaining purchases and sales journals. [1]

   b Copy and complete the following table to name the business documents which Alice will use to make entries in her books of prime entry.
      In each case, state whether Alice will receive or issue the document. [4]

Book of prime entry	Business document
Sales journal	
Purchases journal	
Sales returns journal	
Purchases returns journal	

   c Copy and complete the table by stating how Alice would enter the monthly totals of the following books of prime entry in her ledger.
      The first one has been completed as an example. [3]

Book of prime entry	Ledger entry
Sales journal	Sales account Credit
Purchases journal	
Sales returns journal	
Purchases returns journal	

   d Name two other books of prime entry which Alice may use. [2]

   e Name the ledger in which Alice will maintain the following accounts:

      i   sales account

      ii   purchases returns account

      iii Charles (a credit supplier) [3]

   f Alice provided the following information about Charles, one of her credit suppliers:

      20–1

      June 1   Alice owed Charles $750

            5   Purchased goods from Charles, list price $600, less 20% trade discount

            13 Returned goods to Charles, list price $100, purchased on 5 June

            23 Purchased goods from Charles, list price $60 (no trade discount was granted)

            28 Paid Charles the balance on his account on 1 June by bank transfer and deducted 2% cash discount

      Prepare the account of Charles in the ledger of Alice.
      Balance the account and bring down the balance on 1 July 20–1. [4]

   [Total: 17]

5   Ravi is a trader. His transactions in September 20–4 included the following:

   September 2   Bought goods on credit from Kumar, list price $8 800, less 20% trade discount

             4   Sold goods on credit to Mona, list price $1 200, less 25% trade discount

             10 Mona returned half of the goods purchased on 4 September

             14 Bought goods on credit from Dimuth, at list price, $770

             19 Sold goods on credit to Mona, list price $900, less 20% trade discount

             20 Returned to Dimuth goods purchased on 14 September, list price $130

             21 Mona returned goods bought on 19 September, list price $200

   a   Prepare Ravi's sales, purchases and returns journals for September 20–4. [11]

   b   Prepare the following accounts in Ravi's ledger for September 20–4: sales, purchases, sales returns, purchases returns, Kumar, Dimuth and Mona. It is not necessary to balance or total any of the accounts. [9]

   [Total: 20]

6   Thembi is a trader. She maintains a full set of accounting records and posts the totals of the sales, purchases and returns journals to the ledger each month.

   On 1 March 20–1, the balances in her accounts included the following:

	$
Sales	165 450
Purchases	89 690
Sales returns	960
Purchases returns	1 860
Karabo, a credit customer	900
Motle, a credit supplier	750

   The following transactions took place in March 20–1.

   March 4   Sold goods on credit to Karabo, list price $700, less 20% trade discount

          11 Karabo returned half of the goods purchased on 4 March

          17 Purchased goods on credit from Motle, list price $880, less 15% trade discount

          20 Returned goods to Motle, purchased on 17 March, list price $400

          27 Paid Motle a cheque for the amount owing on 1 March, less 2% cash discount

          30 Karabo paid $800 by bank transfer on account

a	Enter the balances on 1 March in the appropriate accounts.	[3]
b	Enter the transactions for March in the sales journal, purchases journal, sales returns journal and purchases returns journal.	[8]
c	Post the entries from the journals to the ledger accounts.	[8]
d	Enter the transaction on 27 March in the account of Motle and the transaction on 30 March in the account of Karabo.	[2]
e	Balance the accounts of Karabo and Motle and bring down the balances on 1 April 20–1.	[2]

[Total: 23]

CHECK YOUR PROGRESS

How well do you think you have achieved the learning intentions for this chapter? Give yourself a score from 1 (still need a lot of practice) to 5 (feeling very confident) for each learning intention. Provide an example to support your score.

Now I can …	Score	Example to support score
enter transactions in the sales journal, purchases journal, sales returns journal and purchases returns journal		
post transactions from the books of prime entry to the ledger		
explain the advantages and disadvantages of using manual and digital methods to maintain books of prime entry.		

Section 2 practice questions

1 Where is trade discount shown?

   1 invoice
   2 credit note
   3 sales ledger
   4 purchases ledger

   A 1 only
   B 1 and 2
   C 3 and 4
   D 1, 2, 3 and 4   [1]

2 Where is the total of the discount column on the debit side of a cash book posted?

   A credit discount allowed account
   B credit discount received account
   C debit discount allowed account
   D debit discount received account   [1]

3 Aziz sell 50 items, list price $20 each, to a trader with a trade discount of 10%. The trader returns eight of these items.

   What amount will be shown on the credit note issued?

   A $128
   B $144
   C $160
   D $178   [1]

4 Zhao sells goods on credit terms and allows his customers a trade discount of 25%. In July, the list price of goods returned by customers totalled $4 800.

   What entry will Zhao make in his nominal ledger on 31 July?

   A sales returns account $3 600 debit
   B sales returns account $4 800 debit
   C purchases returns account $3 600 credit
   D purchases returns account $4 800 credit   [1]

5   On 1 March, Sarah owed Rashid $675. On 18 March, Sarah purchased goods, list price $1 250, subject to a trade discount of 20% from Rashid. On 24 March, she returned one half of these goods.

How much did Sarah owe Rashid on 31 March?

A $1 175

B $1 300

C $1 540

D $1 675   [1]

6   On 2 September 20–4, Klara received the following document.

Lyons Limited 3 High Street Medtown				
Date 20–4	Details	Debit $	Credit $	Balance $
Aug 1	Balance			5 000
Aug 4	Sales	2 470		7 470
Aug 10	Returns		600	6 870
Aug 15	Payment received		4 800	
Aug 15	Discount		200	
Aug 31	Sales	3 600		

a   State the name of the document received by Klara on 2 September 20–4.   [1]

b   State two purposes of the document received by Klara on 2 September 20–4.   [2]

c   State the names of the documents issued on 4 August and 10 August 20–4.   [2]

d   Calculate the balance owing to Lyons Limited on 31 August 20–4.   [2]

e   Prepare the account of Lyons Limited in the books of Klara for the month of August 20–4.   [8]

[Total: 15]

7 Phanos is a trader. He maintains a full set of accounting records.

   a Copy and complete the table by stating the name of **one** source document from which Phanos will complete each book of prime entry. [5]

Book of prime entry	Source document
Petty cash book	
Purchases journal	
Purchases returns journal	
Sales journal	
Sales returns journal	

Phanos sells goods on a credit basis to Petra.

On 1 May 20–3, the balance owing to Phanos by Petra was $850.

During May 20–3, the following transactions took place between Phanos and Petra:

May	3	Petra purchases goods on credit, $1 350
	6	Petra pays the balance owing on 1 May 20–3 by credit transfer after deducting a 2% cash discount
	10	Petra returns goods, $200
	21	Petra purchases goods on credit, $3 600
	31	Petra pays the balance owing on this day by credit transfer after deducting a 2% cash discount

   b Prepare the account of Petra in Phanos's books for the month of May 20–3. [9]

   c State **one** reason why Phanos may offer Petra a trade discount. [1]

   d State **one** reason why Petra deducted cash discount when making his payments. [1]

   e Name the ledger in which Phanos maintains the account of Petra. [1]

   f State **one** advantage and **one** disadvantage to Phanos of purchasing a software package for producing his invoices. [2]

[Total: 19]

8 Daud sells goods on credit. He maintains a full set of accounting records.

The following information was extracted from his accounting records for December 20–5:

1 December 20–5		$
Debit balances in sales ledger:	Afsah	350
	Hazer	200

Daud

Sales journal

			$	$
20–5				
Dec 6	Afsah	Goods	620	
		Less Trade discount	62	558
15	Hazer	Goods		214
23	Afsah	Goods	500	
		Less Trade discount	50	450
31	Transfer to sales account			1 222

Daud

Sales returns journal

			$	$
20–5				
Dec 18	Hazer	Goods		84
26	Afsah	Goods	180	
		Less Trade discount	18	162
31	Transfer to sales returns account			246

Extract from debit side of cash book

		$ Discount allowed	$ Cash	$ Bank
20–5				
Dec 10	Afsah	14		336
17	Hazer		200	
24	Afsah			450

a Prepare the following accounts for the month of December 20–5: sales, sales returns, Afsah and Hazer. Balance the accounts of Afsah and Hazer on 31 December 20–5 and bring down the balances on 1 January 20–6. [8]

b State **two** differences between cash discount and trade discount. [2]

c Calculate the rate of trade discount that Daud allowed Afsah on 23 December. [1]

d Calculate the rate of cash discount that Daud allowed Afsah on 10 December. [1]

e Explain how the introduction of a computerised accounting package could benefit Daud when processing his credit transactions. [3]

[Total: 15]

9 On 1 January 20–6, Adelia opened a wholesale clothing business.

During the month of January 20–6, she received the following documents:

Invoices

January 6 From Nadia, for goods, list price $1 960, less 20% trade discount

17 From Johor, for goods, list price $700

22 From Nurin, for goods, list price $4 660, less 25% trade discount

Credit notes

January 12 From Nadia, for return of faulty goods, list price $320, purchased on 6 January

28 From Nurin, for return of all the goods purchased on 22 January, as was not what was ordered

During the month of January 20–6, she issued the following documents:

Invoices

January 9 To Eva, for goods, list price $3 210

16 To Siti, for goods, list price $4 250, less 20% trade discount

26 To Eva, for goods, list price $2 220

Credit note

January 30 To Eva, for half of the goods purchased on 26 January, returned as faulty

a Prepare the purchases journal, sales journal, purchases returns journal and sales returns journal. [10]

b Make the necessary posting to the appropriate accounts in the purchases ledger, sales ledger and nominal ledger. It is not necessary to balance or total any of the accounts. [10]

c Suggest two reasons why Adelia allowed Siti a trade discount. [2]

d Name the document which Adelia may have issued before she received a credit note from Nadia on 12 January. [1]

On 10 February 20–6, Adelia paid the amount owing to Nadia on 31 January, less a cash discount of 5%.

    e   Calculate the amount paid to Nadia on 10 February 20–6. [1]

    f   State how the discount offered to Adelia on 10 February would be recorded in the books of account of both businesses. [2]

    g   State one reason why Adelia should offer a cash discount to her credit customers. [1]

[Total: 27]

Section 3

This section focuses on financial statements, which are prepared at the end of a trading period. You will learn how to prepare a statement of profit or loss, which sets out the calculation of the gross profit or loss and the calculation of the profit or loss for the year. You will also study the preparation of a detailed statement of financial position separating the assets and liabilities into different types.

The section also introduces you to year-end adjustments. These include accrued and prepaid expenses and incomes, irrecoverable debts and allowances for irrecoverable debts, and depreciation and disposal of non-current assets. You will learn how to record these in the ledger and why it is necessary to make adjustments for them in the financial statements.

There is also a chapter which summarises all the accounting rules which are applied to the recording of financial information. These rules are also referred to in other sections so that you can see how they are applied to different accounting scenarios.

Chapter 8
Financial statements – Part A

LEARNING INTENTIONS

By the end of this chapter, you will be able to:
- explain the difference between a trading business and a service business and understand how a business can be a combination of these
- prepare statements of profit or loss for different types of business and understand why they are important
- adjust the statement of profit or loss for goods taken by the owner for own use
- transfer the balances of ledger accounts to financial statements.

8 Financial statements – Part A

Introduction

When a person starts a business, the aim is to make a profit. The profit (or loss) is calculated in the financial statements. These are usually prepared at the end of each financial year, but they can be prepared at any time to give the owner information about how their business is progressing.

Financial statements consist of:

- a **statement of profit or loss**, which shows the profit for the year
- statement of financial position, which shows the assets and liabilities of a business at a certain date.

In this chapter, you will learn about statements of profit or loss. You will learn about statements of financial position in Chapter 9.

> **KEY TERM**
>
> **statement of profit or loss:** a statement prepared for a trading period to show the gross profit and profit for the year.

ACCOUNTING IN CONTEXT

The health of a business

Figure 8.1: Items for sale in a furniture shop

Financial statements provide information about a business. They show the business's profit (or loss) for the year and also the assets and liabilities of a business at a certain date. It is important for all business owners to understand financial statements so that they have a clear understanding of the health of their business.

Anyone who is considering investing in or buying a business should also look at the financial statements of the business before they make a decision about their investment.

Avia has owned a successful furniture shop for many years, but has recently decided to sell the business. Maryam is considering buying the business from Avia, but before she makes a decision, she would like to look at the business's statements of profit or loss for the last few years.

Discuss in pairs or in a group:

1. Why do you think Maryam wants to see the statements of profit or loss?
2. What other things might Maryam consider when deciding whether or not to buy the business?

8.1 The statement of profit or loss

The statement of profit or loss was previously known as the income statement. The statement is in two sections:

- a trading section in which the business's gross profit is calculated
- a profit and loss section in which the business's profit for the year is calculated.

The trading section and the profit and loss section of the statement of profit or loss are part of the double entry system.

Using a trial balance

Financial statements are usually prepared from a trial balance. Every item in a trial balance appears **once** in a set of financial statements. As each item is used, it is useful to place a tick (✓) against the item. This ensures that no items are overlooked.

It is common to find notes accompanying a trial balance about various adjustments which are to be made. Any notes to a trial balance are used **twice** in a set of financial statements. To ensure that this is done, it is useful to place a tick (✓) against the notes each time they are used.

The items in the trial balance have already been entered twice in the books of account, unlike the adjustments in the notes which are entered twice to comply with the double entry principles of book-keeping.

The following trial balance was extracted from the books of Jagdeep at 31 May 20–8.
This trial balance will be used in this chapter for Worked examples 8.1–8.3.

8 Financial statements – Part A

Jagdeep Trial balance at 31 May 20–8	Dr $	Cr $
Bank	4 050	
Capital		102 000
Carriage inwards	1 900	
Cash	150	
Discount allowed	400	
Discount received		500
Drawings	8 000	
Fixtures and equipment	15 000	
General expenses	1 600	
Inventory 1 June 20–7	7 900	
Loan interest	600	
Long-term loan		12 000
Property	91 000	
Purchases returns		800
Purchases	68 300	
Rates and insurance	2 700	
Revenue		105 500
Sales returns	1 800	
Trade payables		6 300
Trade receivables	7 400	
Wages	16 300	
	227 100	227 100

Additional information

1 The inventory at 31 May 20–8 was valued at $8 100.

2 During the year ended 31 May 20–8, Jagdeep took goods costing $400 for his own use. No entries have been made in the accounting records.

8.2 Trading section of the statement of profit or loss

The trading section is concerned with buying and selling, and its purpose is to calculate the profit earned on the goods sold. This is known as the **gross profit**. The formula for calculating gross profit is:

Gross profit = Selling price of goods – Cost of sales

The selling price represents the total revenue less any sales returns.

> **TIP**
>
> The term 'revenue' is used instead of 'sales' in a trial balance and in a statement of profit or loss, so the figure for 'revenue' comes from the sales account.

> **KEY TERM**
>
> **gross profit:** the difference between the selling price and the cost price of the goods.

The cost of sales represents the total cost of the goods actually sold. This is not necessarily the cost of goods purchased during the year because some goods may have been in stock at the start of the year, and some of the goods purchased during the year may remain unsold at the end of the year. The formula for calculating cost of sales is:

Cost of sales = Opening inventory + Purchases − Closing inventory

The purchases figure represents the total cost of purchases less any purchases returns. If carriage inwards has been paid on goods purchased, this must be added to the purchases as it increases the cost of the goods. If the owner of the business has withdrawn goods for personal use, the cost of these goods is credited to the purchases account, so reducing the cost of goods available for sale. If goods taken by the owner have not already been recorded, they must be deducted from the purchases. This means that the formula for cost of sales becomes:

Cost of sales = Opening inventory + Purchases − Purchases returns − Goods for own use + Carriage inwards − Closing inventory

The calculation of gross profit is shown in the trading section of the statement of profit or loss. This must have a heading which includes the period of time covered by the statement. It is also usual to include the name under which the business trades.

WORKED EXAMPLE 8.1

Use the trial balance and accompanying notes shown in Section 8.1 to prepare the trading section of the statement of profit or loss of Jagdeep for the year ended 31 May 20–8.

Jagdeep
Statement of profit or loss (trading section) for the year ended 31 May 20–8

	$	$	$
Revenue		105 500	
Less Sales returns		1 800	103 700
Less Cost of sales			
Opening inventory		7 900	
Purchases	68 300		
Less Purchases returns	800		
	67 500		
Less Goods for own use	400		
	67 100		
Carriage inwards	1 900	69 000	
		76 900	
Less Closing inventory		8 100	68 800
Gross profit			34 900

8 Financial statements – Part A

> **CONTINUED**
>
> - The first two money columns have been used for adding and subtracting items and the final column for the total. For example, the first column has been used to adjust the purchases for returns, goods for own use and carriage, and the final cost of purchases has been entered in the second column.
> - As the items are entered in the trading section of the statement of profit or loss, they should be ticked off in the trial balance and accompanying notes.

ACTIVITY 8.1

George is a sole trader who runs a business buying and selling plants for houses and gardens. He provided the following information for the year ended 31 December 20–9.

	$
Carriage inwards	850
Closing inventory	9 870
Opening inventory	8 730
Purchases returns	3 000
Purchases	76 800
Revenue	120 000
Sales returns	8 000

Prepare the trading section of the statement of profit or loss for the year ended 31 December 20–9.

8.3 Profit and loss section of the statement of profit or loss

The profit and loss section of a statement of profit or loss is concerned with other income and expenses. Its purpose is to calculate the final profit after all running expenses and other items of income have been accounted for. This is known as the **profit for the year**. The formula for calculating profit for the year is:

Profit for the year = Gross profit + Other income − Expenses

The **profit from operations** is also shown on the statement of profit or loss. This is the profit after deducting all expenses from the gross profit except for any finance charges, such as interest paid on a loan. This may also be called profit for the year before interest.

The difference between cash and profit

All businesses are required to have a reasonable amount of cash to pay their day-to-day expenses and short-term debts. However, this value will not always be the same as the amount of profit that a business earns.

Profit is defined as the amount by which income exceeds the expenses for a specific period, but there are some expenses which do not require a movement of cash, for example, discount allowed, irrecoverable debts and depreciation of non-current assets. In these circumstances, the increase in expenses will not be matched by a decrease in cash.

A business which buys and sells goods on credit will see an immediate effect on their profit when goods are sold or purchased, but it may be some time before the cash is received or paid out and this means there will be a difference between the two figures of cash and profit.

There are several other transactions, such as the purchasing of non-current assets or the repayment of a loan, which will reduce the cash balance of a business but have no effect on its profit.

> **KEY TERMS**
>
> **profit for the year:** the final profit after any other income has been added to the gross profit and the running expenses have been deducted.
>
> **profit from operations:** the profit after deducting all expenses from the gross profit with the exception of finance charges such as interest paid.

> **LINKS**
>
> You will use gross profit, profit for the year and profit for the year before interest when working out profitability ratios in Chapter 22. You will learn more about irrecoverable debts in Chapter 13 and depreciation of non-current assets in Chapter 12.

Figure 8.2: Cash and profit are not the same thing

If a business owner takes cash drawings for their own use, this would reduce the cash balance but have no effect on the profit. If a business owner introduces additional capital, it will increase the cash balance but will not increase the profit of the business.

WORKED EXAMPLE 8.2

Use the trial balance and accompanying notes shown in Section 8.1 to prepare the profit and loss section of the statement of profit or loss of Jagdeep for the year ended 31 May 20–8.

Jagdeep Statement of profit or loss (profit and loss section) for the year ended 31 May 20–8			
	$	$	$
Gross profit			34 900
Add Discount received			500
			35 400
Less Discount allowed		400	
Wages		16 300	
General expenses		1 600	
Rates and insurance		2 700	21 000
Profit from operations			14 400
Less Loan interest			600
Profit for the year			13 800

- The items should be ticked off in the trial balance as they are entered in the profit and loss section of the statement of profit or loss.

ACTIVITY 8.2

The following balances remained in the books of Reena at 30 June 20–4 after calculating the gross profit for the year.

	$
Gross profit	67 800
Carriage outwards	1 800
Discount allowed	2 982
Discount received	3 907
Insurance	2 200
Motor expenses	3 200
Rent and rates	6 400
Wages	12 000

Prepare the profit and loss section of the statement of profit or loss for the year ended 30 June 20–4.

Combining the trading section and the profit and loss section

The two sections of the statement of profit or loss are usually presented in the form of one combined statement. The profit and loss section follows on immediately after the trading section, with the words 'gross profit' being written only once. The heading of the statement of profit or loss includes the period of time covered by the statement and the name under which the business trades.

> ### WORKED EXAMPLE 8.3
>
> Using either the trial balance and accompanying notes shown in Section 8.1, or the separate sections of the statement of profit or loss prepared in **Worked examples 8.1–8.2**, prepare the statement of profit or loss of Jagdeep for the year ended 31 May 20–8.
>
> | Jagdeep
Statement of profit or loss for the year ended 31 May 20–8 | | | |
> |---|---:|---:|---:|
> | | $ | $ | $ |
> | Revenue | | 105 500 | |
> | Less Sales returns | | 1 800 | 103 700 |
> | Less Cost of sales | | | |
> | Opening inventory | | 7 900 | |
> | Purchases | 68 300 | | |
> | Less Purchases returns | 800 | | |
> | | 67 500 | | |
> | Less Goods for own use | 400 | | |
> | | 67 100 | | |
> | Carriage inwards | 1 900 | 69 000 | |
> | | | 76 900 | |
> | Less Closing inventory | | 8 100 | 68 800 |
> | Gross profit | | | 34 900 |
> | Add Discount received | | | 500 |
> | | | | 35 400 |
> | Less Discount allowed | | 400 | |
> | Wages | | 16 300 | |
> | General expenses | | 1 600 | |
> | Rates and insurance | | 2 700 | 21 000 |
> | Profit from operations | | | 14 400 |
> | Less Loan interest | | | 600 |
> | Profit for the year | | | 13 800 |

> **LINKS**
>
> You will learn more about statements of profit or loss in Chapters 11–13.

8.4 Transferring ledger account totals to the statement of profit or loss

As the statement of profit or loss is part of the double entry system, each amount entered in the statement of profit or loss must have a double entry in another account.

Anything credited to the statement of profit or loss must be debited in the appropriate ledger account.

Anything debited to the statement of profit or loss must be credited in the appropriate ledger account.

WORKED EXAMPLE 8.4

Using the statement of profit or loss prepared for Jagdeep in **Worked example 8.3**, prepare the following ledger accounts to show how each is closed by transfer to the statement of profit or loss:

a   purchases account

b   purchases returns account

c   discount received account

d   wages account

a

Jagdeep
Nominal ledger

Dr			Purchases account			Cr
			$			$
20–8				20–8		
May 31	Total to date		68 300	May 31	Statement of profit or loss	68 300
			68 300			68 300

b

Dr			Purchases returns account			Cr
			$			$
20–8				20–8		
May 31	Statement of profit or loss		800	May 31	Total to date	800
			800			800

c

Dr			Discount received account			Cr
			$			$
20–8				20–8		
May 31	Statement of profit or loss		500	May 31	Total to date	500
			500			500

> CAMBRIDGE IGCSE™ AND O LEVEL ACCOUNTING: COURSEBOOK

CONTINUED

d

Dr		Wages account			Cr
		$			$
20–8			20–8		
May 31	Total to date	16 300	May 31	Statement of profit or loss	16 300
		16 300			16 300

- The entries shown as 'total to date' represent the total of the individual entries made in the account for the year ended 31 May 20–8.
- All the other items in the statement of profit or loss (excluding inventory, gross profit and profit for the year) have similar transfers from the appropriate ledger accounts.

There are two entries for inventory in the statement of profit or loss – the inventory at the start of the year and the inventory at the end of the year. The inventory account will have a debit balance representing the inventory at the start of the year – this is credited to the inventory account and transferred to the debit of the statement of profit or loss. The inventory at the end of the year is shown as a deduction from the debit entries in the statement of profit or loss (which is equal to a credit entry), so this must be debited in the inventory account.

WORKED EXAMPLE 8.5

Using the statement of profit or loss prepared for Jagdeep in **Worked example 8.3**, prepare the inventory account in Jagdeep's ledger on 31 May 20–8.

Jagdeep
Nominal ledger

Dr			Inventory account			Cr
			$			$
20–7				20–8		
Jun 1	Balance	b/d	7 900	May 31	Statement of profit or loss	7 900
			7 900			7 900
20–8						
May 31	Statement of profit or loss		8 100			

- The entry of $8 100 on the debit side, representing the inventory at the end of the financial year on 31 May 20–8, becomes the opening inventory for the year beginning 1 June 20–8.

8 Financial statements – Part A

A profit for the year represents the return on the owner's investment. This should be transferred to the credit of the capital account as it increases the amount the business owes the owner. A loss for the year should be transferred to the debit of the capital account as it reduces the amount the business owes the owner.

As explained in Chapter 2, the total of the drawings account is transferred to the capital account at the end of the year.

Sometimes, the owner of a business may take goods from the business for their own use. As the amount of purchases available for sale is now reduced, the purchases shown in the statement of profit or loss will also need to be reduced and charged to the owner as drawings.

The owner of a business may also use a business asset for their personal use or they may pay a private expense from the business bank account. This must be adjusted in the statement of profit or loss and charged to the owner as drawings.

WORKED EXAMPLE 8.6

On 1 June 20–7, the credit balance on Jagdeeps's capital account was $102 000. During the year ended 31 May 20–8, he had withdrawn $8 000 in cash and $400 in goods. His profit for the year ended 31 May 20–8 was $13 800.

Prepare the capital account and the drawings account in Jagdeeps's ledger on 31 May 20–8.

Jagdeep
Nominal ledger

Dr				Capital account				Cr
			$					$
20–8					20–7			
May 31	Drawings		8 400		Jun 1	Balance	b/d	102 000
	Balance	c/d	107 400		20–8			
					May 31	Statement of profit or loss		13 800
			115 800					115 800
					20–8			
					Jun 1	Balance	b/d	107 400

Dr			Drawings account			Cr
			$			$
20–8				20–8		
May 31	Total to date			May 31	Capital	8 400
	Cash		8 000			
	Purchases		400			
			8 400			8 400

> **TIP**
>
> Remember, if a business makes a profit, you credit the amount to the capital account as it increases the owner's capital. If a business makes a loss, you debit the amount to the capital account as it reduces the owner's capital.

> **DISCUSSION**
>
> Nadia runs a music shop. She has completed her statement of profit or loss for the year and has discovered that her business has made a loss.
>
> Discuss with a partner:
> 1. Why will making a loss reduce Nadia's capital?
> 2. What can Nadia do to try avoid making a loss in the future?

8.5 Statement of profit or loss of a service business

A **service business** is a business which does not buy or sell goods – for example, an accountant, insurance company, travel agent and hairdresser. At the end of the financial year, these businesses still need to prepare financial statements. However, they do not need to prepare the trading section of the statement of profit or loss as no goods are bought and sold. Only the profit and loss section of the statement of profit or loss and a statement of financial position are prepared.

In the statement of profit or loss, the starting point is all the income the business received for work done, which is added together, and then all the expenses are deducted to give the profit or loss for the year.

The statement of financial position for a service business is exactly the same as the statement of financial position of a **trading business**.

> **KEY TERMS**
>
> **service business:** a business which provides a service.
>
> **trading business:** a business which buys and sells goods.

WORKED EXAMPLE 8.7

Anita is a business consultant. She provided the following information at the end of her financial year on 30 September 20–5.

	$
Rates	3 200
General expenses	7 630
Insurance	3 800
Printing and stationery	4 560
Loan interest	1 500
Wages	43 500
Rent income	7 300
Commissions received	106 500

Prepare the statement of profit or loss for Anita for the year ended 30 September 20–5.

Anita
Statement of profit or loss for the year ended 30 September 20–5

	$	$	$
Commissions received			106 500
Add Rent income			7 300
			113 800
Less Rates		3 200	
General expenses		7 630	
Insurance		3 800	
Printing and stationery		4 560	
Wages		43 500	62 690
Profit from operations			51 110
Less Loan interest			1 500
Profit for the year			49 610

ACTIVITY 8.3

Figure 8.3: A travel consultant preparing his statement of profit or loss

Malik is in business as an online travel consultant. He provided the following information at the end of his financial year on 31 December 20–5.

	$
Commission received from tour operators	185 600
Marketing expenses	6 890
Rent expense	5 621
Travel expenses	17 643
Wages	45 000
Website hosting fees	2 321

Prepare the statement of profit or loss for Malik for the year ended 31 December 20–5.

> **TIP**
>
> A consultancy is a service business so you do not need to include a trading section in the statement of profit or loss.

8.6 Statement of profit or loss of a combined trading and service business

A trading business is one which buys and sells goods, and a service business is one which provides a service to its customers. However, some businesses are a combination of these – the main part of the business might be providing a service to their customers, but they also buy and sell products. For example, a hairdresser who sells haircare products.

At the end of the financial year, these businesses need to show the income from the different activities separately in the statement of profit or loss. The income from the service section of the business is added to the net revenue from the trading section of the business. The cost of sales will then be deducted in order to ascertain the gross profit. Any other income is added to the gross profit and the expenses of running the business are deducted in order to ascertain the profit for the year.

WORKED EXAMPLE 8.8

New Wave Hairdressing provided the following information at the end of their financial year on 31 March 20–7.

	$
Revenue – services	95 200
retail	4 800
Inventory 1 April 20–6	430
Heat and light	12 750
Wages and salaries	44 100
Maintenance	2 500
Purchases	2 145
Advertising	650

On 31 March 20–7, closing inventory was valued at $575.

Prepare the statement of profit or loss for New Wave Hairdressing for the year ended 31 March 20–7.

New Wave Hairdressing
Statement of profit or loss for the year ended 31 March 20–7

	$	$	$
Revenue – services		95 200	
retail		4 800	100 000
Less Cost of sales			
Opening inventory		430	
Purchases		2 145	
		2 575	
Less Closing inventory		575	2 000
Gross profit			98 000
Less Heat and light		12 750	
Wages and salaries		44 100	
Maintenance		2 500	
Advertising		650	
			60 000
Profit for the year			38 000

> CAMBRIDGE IGCSE™ AND O LEVEL ACCOUNTING: COURSEBOOK

DISCUSSION

Think about some of the different businesses you know. They may be local businesses that you use or larger businesses that you have heard about.

Discuss with a partner whether each business is a trading business, a service business or a combination of a trading and a service business.

Try to think of at least two businesses that are a combination of a trading and a service business.

REFLECTION

How confident were you at deciding whether each business was a trading business, a service business or a combination of a trading and a service business? What factors did you take into consideration when making your decision?

Were there any businesses you and your partner disagreed about? If so, how did you come to an agreement?

8 Financial statements – Part A

ACCOUNTING IN ACTION

Traditional or digital accounts?

Figure 8.4: Three business owners comparing their statements of profit or loss

Amar, Sai and Naya met on their first day at high school and have been friends ever since. All three had the ambition to run their own business one day, and after working hard for several years, they each managed to accumulate enough capital to start their own business.

- Amar opened a laundry business. He rented property on an industrial estate and borrowed money from the bank to purchase washing machines, drying machines and ironing equipment. He has ten employees.
- Sai opened a food store in rented property in the town centre. He was able to pay for the opening inventory and the shop fittings from his initial capital. He has six employees.
- Naya purchased property and equipment and opened a photographic studio. She buys and sells cameras and related equipment and also takes photos that appear in the online catalogue of a fashion retailer.

At the end of their first year of operating their businesses, the three friends compared their statements of profit or loss. They noticed that the presentation and content of the statements was slightly different.

Working in pairs

1 Explain why:

   a Amar's statement of profit or loss does not show a gross profit

   b the statement of profit or loss for both Sai and Naya show a gross profit, but the trading section of Naya's statement includes items not shown in Sai's statement.

2 Suggest:

   a one item of expense which will only appear in Amar's statement of profit or loss

   b two items of expense which will appear in both Amar's and Sai's statement of profit or loss, but not in Naya's statement of profit or loss

   c three items of expense which may appear in the statement of profit or loss of all three businesses.

CAMBRIDGE IGCSE™ AND O LEVEL ACCOUNTING: COURSEBOOK

> **SUMMARY**
>
> You should now know:
>
> - The difference between the selling price and the cost price is known as the gross profit. This is calculated in the trading section of the statement of profit or loss.
>
> - The difference between the gross profit, plus other income, less expenses is known as the profit for the year. This is calculated in the profit and loss section of the statement of profit or loss.
>
> - All the items appearing in the statement of profit or loss are transferred from the ledger accounts to complete the double entry.
>
> - A profit for the year is transferred to the credit of the capital account, and a loss for the year is transferred to the debit of the capital account.
>
> - A business which provides a service only prepares the profit and loss section of the statement of profit or loss.
>
> - A business which is a combination of a trading and a service business will need to calculate the cost of sales for the products that it sells.

Chapter 8 practice questions

1 How is the cost of sales calculated?

   A opening inventory + purchases − carriage inwards − purchases returns − closing inventory

   B opening inventory + purchases − carriage inwards + purchases returns − closing inventory

   C opening inventory + purchases + carriage inwards − purchases returns − closing inventory

   D opening inventory + purchases + carriage inwards + purchases returns + closing inventory [1]

2 At the end of his first year of trading, Nasheeb provided the following information:

	$
Revenue	89 500
Purchases	60 260
Closing inventory	5 120
Carriage inwards	920
Carriage outwards	2 140

   What was Nasheeb's gross profit?

   A $29 240

   B $32 220

   C $33 440

   D $34 360 [1]

8 Financial statements – Part A

3 Mai, a fashion retailer, did not record goods costing $500 taken for personal use. What was the effect of this error? [1]

	Gross profit		Profit for the year	
	Overstated	Understated	Overstated	Understated
A	✓		✓	
B		✓		✓
C	✓			✓
D		✓	✓	

4 Lydia is a wholesaler. She has little knowledge of accounting and prepared the following statement of profit or loss, which contains some errors.

Lydia
Statement of profit or loss for the year ended 30 April 20–1

	$	$
Revenue		114 800
Add Discount received		200
Opening inventory		5 180
		120 180
Less Purchases	63 370	
Returns from customers	2 940	
	66 310	
Less Closing inventory	6 450	59 860
Profit on goods		60 320
Add Discount allowed		100
		60 420
Less Rent expense	7 400	
Less Rent income	3 600	
	3 800	
Wages	22 660	
Carriage inwards	1 160	
General expenses	2 840	30 460
Final profit		29 960

Prepare a corrected statement of profit or loss for Lydia for the year ended 30 April 20–1. [9]

5 Lee has been in business as a retailer for one year. He is unsure about some of the terms used in business.

  a Explain the difference between the following terms and how they are recorded in a statement of profit or loss.

    i gross profit and profit for the year

    ii carriage inwards and carriage outwards

    iii discount allowed and discount received

    iv purchases returns and sales returns [8]

Lee provided the following totals for the year ended 31 December 20–5:

	$
Insurance	2 600
Motor vehicle expenses	1 950
Commission income	4 480
Sales returns	990

  b Enter these totals in the appropriate accounts. Close the accounts by making transfers to the statement of profit or loss. [8]

[Total: 16]

6 Xiang provided the following information at the end of his financial year on 30 September 20–3:

	$
Capital at 1 October 20–2	200 000
Fees received from clients	80 200
Wages	66 800
Rent and rates	8 200
Insurance	1 940
Commission income	880
Light and heat	2 740
Office expenses	3 350
Drawings	10 400

  a State whether Xiang's business is a trading business or a service business. Give a reason for your answer. [2]

  b Prepare Xiang's statement of profit or loss for the year ended 30 September 20–3. [5]

  c Prepare Xiang's capital account on 30 September 20–3. Balance the account and bring down the balance on 1 October 20–3. [4]

[Total: 11]

7   Selia operates a secretarial agency providing clerical services to small businesses. She also provides these businesses with their stationery needs such as copier paper, etc.

Selia provided the following information at the end of her financial year on 31 December 20–3:

	$
Income from clients	65 000
Stationery sales	6 480
Motor expenses	900
Stationery purchases	3 200
Wages and salaries	35 000
Sundry expenses	5 000
Telephone expenses	650
Inventory 1 January 20–3	1 200
Inventory 31 December 20–3	950

Prepare a statement of profit or loss for the year ended 31 December 20–3. [7]

CHECK YOUR PROGRESS

How well do you think you have achieved the learning intentions for this chapter? Give yourself a score from 1 (still need a lot of practice) to 5 (feeling very confident) for each learning intention. Provide an example to support your score.

Now I can …	Score	Example to support score
explain the difference between a trading business and a service business and understand how a business can be a combination of these		
prepare statements of profit or loss for different types of business and understand why they are important		
adjust the statement of profit or loss for goods taken by the owner for own use		
transfer the balance of ledger accounts to financial statements.		

Chapter 9
Financial statements – Part B

LEARNING INTENTIONS

By the end of this chapter, you will be able to:
- understand why it is important to prepare a statement of financial position and that it shows the assets, liabilities and capital on a particular date
- recognise and understand the contents of a statement of financial position: non-current assets, intangible assets, current assets, current liabilities, non-current liabilities and capital
- understand the interrelationship of items in a statement of financial position
- draw up statements of financial position for trading businesses, service businesses and businesses which are both trading and service businesses.

9 Financial statements – Part B

Introduction

As explained in Chapter 8, the financial statements are prepared at the end of each financial year. These consist of a statement of profit or loss and a **statement of financial position**.

A statement of the financial position shows the assets of a business (what the business owns and what is owing to the business) and the liabilities and capital of a business (what the business owes) on a certain date. The assets show how the resources are being used and the liabilities show where they come from.

> **KEY TERM**
>
> **statement of financial position:** a statement of the assets, liabilities and capital of a business on a certain date.

> **LINK**
>
> You learnt how to prepare some very simple statements of financial position in Chapter 1.

ACCOUNTING IN CONTEXT

Who needs a statement of financial position?

Figure 9.1: A statement of financial position gives important information about the photography business

The statement of financial position provides information about a business's financial position at a specific time. It lists the assets (what the business owns and what is owing to the business), the liabilities (what the business owes) and the capital of the business (the owner's investment in the business).

Mona has always been interested in photography. After leaving school, she attended a course on photography and then got a job as an assistant to a professional photographer. After a few years, she decided to open her own business taking commercial photos for businesses and taking photos for important family occasions. Mona enrolled on a short course for book-keeping for small businesses and was able to maintain a full set of double entry records during her first year. All her purchases were paid for at the time of purchase by bank transfer and her sales were made on credit terms.

At the end of her first year, Mona got some help to prepare a statement of profit or loss and was told that she should also prepare a statement of financial position. Mona could not understand why this was recommended. She said, 'I have kept a cash book, so I know exactly how much money came in and how much went out during the year and how much is left. Is that not enough to tell me my financial position?'

Discuss in small groups:

1. How is a cash book different from a statement of financial position?
2. Why is an annual statement of financial position useful to a business owner?

9.1 Assets

The assets section of a statement of financial position shows what the business owns, what is owing to the business and how these resources are being used by the business. Assets are divided into different groups according to their type, as shown in Figure 9.2.

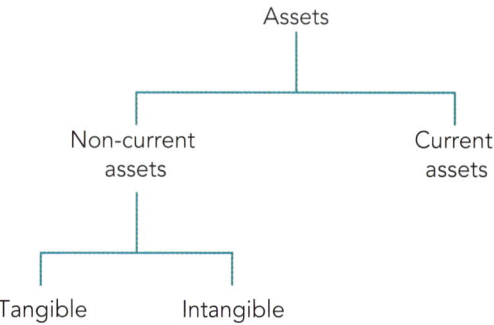

Figure 9.2: The different types of assets

There are two main types of assets: non-current assets and current assets.

1 **Non-current assets**

   There are two types of **non-current assets**:

   a **Tangible non-current assets**

      Tangible non-current assets are long-term assets which are obtained for business use rather than for resale. They help the business earn revenue.

      Examples of tangible non-current assets include: land and buildings, machinery, fixtures and motor vehicles.

      In a statement of financial position, it is usual for the non-current assets to be arranged in order of permanence. This means that the most permanent assets are shown first. The assets which have the longest useful life in the business are placed first, so property will come before assets such as motor vehicles, which lose value more quickly.

      A typical order for showing tangible non-current assets in a statement of financial position is:

      Property

      Machinery

      Fixtures and equipment

      Motor vehicles

> **KEY TERM**
>
> **non-current assets:** the assets which are obtained for use and not for resale, which help the business earn revenue.

Figure 9.3: Property and motor vehicles are non-current assets

b Intangible non-current assets

Intangible non-current assets are long-term assets which do not have material substance (they cannot be seen or touched). However, they belong to the business and do have a value.

Examples of intangible non-current assets include: **goodwill**, brand names and trademarks.

In a statement of financial position, the intangible non-current assets are shown before the tangible non-current assets.

2 Current assets

Current assets are short-term assets. Their amounts are constantly changing because of the normal trading activities of the business. These are assets which are either in the form of cash or which can be turned into cash relatively easily.

Examples of current assets include: inventory, trade receivables, bank and cash.

In a statement of financial position, it is usual for current assets to be arranged in increasing order of liquidity. This shows how quickly and easily the assets can be turned into actual money to settle liabilities when they fall due. This means that the assets furthest away from cash are shown first. Inventory is the least liquid as it needs to be sold and then the money collected. The trade receivables are closer to being liquid as the business only has to collect the money from them. Money in the bank can be withdrawn easily to become actual cash, which is the most liquid asset.

A typical order for showing current assets in a statement of financial position is:

Inventory

Trade receivables

Bank

Cash

> **KEY TERMS**
>
> **goodwill:** the amount by which the value of a business as a whole exceeds the value of the separate assets and liabilities.
>
> **current assets:** short-term assets whose amounts are constantly changing.

Figure 9.4: Inventory is a current asset

> **DISCUSSION**
>
> Working with a partner, think of a trading business and a service business which are known to you both.
>
> For each business, discuss the following questions:
>
> 1 What assets might that business possess?
>
> 2 How should the assets be ordered in a statement of financial position?

9.2 Capital and liabilities

The capital and liabilities section of a statement of financial position shows what the business owes and where the resources being used by the business have come from.

The amount owing to the owner(s) of a business is known as capital. The amounts owing to other people or businesses are known as liabilities, which are divided into different groups according to their type, as shown in Figure 9.5.

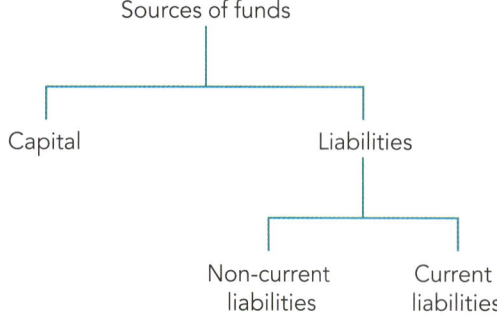

Figure 9.5: The providers of resources for a business

1   **Capital**

    Capital represents the owner's investment in the business and is the amount owed by the business to the owner.

2   **Non-current liabilities**

    Non-current liabilities are amounts owed by the business which are not due for repayment within the next 12 months. The amounts do not constantly change.

    Examples of non-current liabilities include: long-term loan and mortgage.

3   **Current liabilities**

    Current liabilities are short-term liabilities. Just like current assets, their amounts are constantly changing because of the normal trading activities of the business. They are amounts owed by the business which are due for repayment within the next 12 months.

    Examples of current liabilities include: trade payables and bank overdraft.

> **KEY TERMS**
>
> **non-current liabilities:** amounts owed which are not due for repayment within the next 12 months.
>
> **current liabilities:** amounts owed which are due for repayment within the next 12 months.

> **ACTIVITY 9.1**
>
> Working in a small group, write a short speech (to last no more than two minutes) in which you explain:
>
> - how to distinguish between a non-current liability and a current liability
> - why current liabilities are always changing
> - why capital is regarded as something the business owes.
>
> Provide examples to illustrate your answers.
>
> Choose one member of the group to present the speech to the rest of the class.

9.3 The statement of financial position

Both of the financial statements (the statement of profit or loss and the statement of financial position) are produced from a trial balance.

The following trial balance was extracted from the books of Jagdeep at 31 May 20–8.

This trial balance was used in Chapter 8 to prepare a statement of profit or loss for the year ended 31 May 20–8. It will be used in Worked example 9.1 to prepare a statement of financial position.

It was explained in Chapter 8 that each item in the trial balance is used once in the preparation of a set of financial statements, and any notes to a trial balance are used twice. The items already used in the preparation of the statement of profit or loss in Chapter 8 have been ticked.

Jagdeep		
Trial balance at 31 May 20–8		
	Dr $	Cr $
Bank	4 050	
Capital		102 000
✓ Carriage inwards	1 900	
Cash	150	
✓ Discount allowed	400	
✓ Discount received		500
Drawings	8 000	
Fixtures and equipment	15 000	
✓ General expenses	1 600	
✓ Inventory 1 June 20–7	7 900	
✓ Loan interest	600	
Long-term loan		12 000
Property	91 000	
✓ Purchases returns		800
✓ Purchases	68 300	
✓ Rates and insurance	2 700	
✓ Revenue		105 500
✓ Sales returns	1 800	
Trade payables		6 300
Trade receivables	7 400	
✓ Wages	16 300	
	227 100	227 100

Additional information:

1 ✓ The inventory at 31 May 20–8 was valued at $8 100.

2 ✓ During the year ended 31 May 20–8, Jagdeep took goods costing $400 for his own use. No entries have been made in the accounting records.

A statement of financial position must have a heading which includes the date to which it relates. It is also usual to include the name under which the business trades.

The assets and liabilities are arranged in their different categories. The assets are listed in the part first of the statement showing how the resources of the business are being used. The capital and liabilities are shown in the second part of the statement, which shows where the resources to run the business have come from.

The statement of financial position of a service business is prepared in exactly the same way as that of a trading business. The only difference is that the service business does not hold an inventory of goods for resale.

> **TIP**
>
> If the totals of your trial balance are equal, the totals of the statement of financial position should balance. If they do not balance, you know there is an error somewhere in the financial statements.

WORKED EXAMPLE 9.1

Using the trial balance and accompanying notes extracted from the books of Jagdeep, prepare a statement of financial position for Jagdeep at 31 May 20–8.

The profit for the year, calculated in the statement of profit or loss prepared in **Worked examples 8.2–8.3** in Chapter 8, was $13 800.

Jagdeep
Statement of financial position at 31 May 20–8

	$	$
Assets		
Non-current assets		
Property	91 000	
Fixtures and equipment	15 000	106 000
Current assets		
Inventory	8 100	
Trade receivables	7 400	
Bank	4 050	
Cash	150	19 700
Total assets		125 700
Capital and liabilities		
Capital		
Opening balance		102 000
Plus Profit for the year		13 800
		115 800
Less Drawings (8 000 + 400)		8 400
		107 400
Non-current liabilities		
Loan		12 000
Current liabilities		
Trade payables		6 300
Total capital and liabilities		125 700

- As these items are entered in the statement of financial position, they should be ticked off in the trial balance and in the accompanying notes.

- Once the statement of financial position is completed, all the items in the trial balance should have a tick and the notes to the trial balance should have two ticks.

- The balance on the capital account has changed. The amount owing to the owner went up because the business made a profit (which the business owes to the owner of the business). But the amount owing to the owner also went down because the owner made drawings (money and goods).

- The first money column has been used to list the assets in each category and the section totals are shown in the second money column.

In Chapter 1, you learnt that every transaction affects the items in a statement of financial position. Because the transaction will have two effects, the statement will still balance after every transaction. A new statement can be produced after each transaction, weekly or monthly, showing how the assets, liabilities and capital have been affected. As you learnt in Chapter 1, it is not practical to prepare a statement of financial position after each transaction, so the day-to-day transactions are recorded using double entry book-keeping.

ACTIVITY 9.2

Figure 9.6: Goods being paid for in cash

The statement of financial position of Jagdeep on 31 May 20–8 was prepared in Worked example 9.1.

After that statement was prepared, it was found that the following transactions which took place on 31 May 20–8 had not been recorded.

- Additional fixtures and equipment, $1 200, had been purchased and paid for by bank transfer
- $320 had been received in cash from Dilip, a credit customer
- Inventory, $1 840, was purchased on credit from Rajesh, a credit supplier
- Goods, cost price $1 500, were sold to Archana, a credit customer, for $1 800
- The organisation which provided the loan agreed to lending a further $10 000, and the money was used to purchase a motor vehicle

Prepare the statement of financial position for Jagdeep on 31 May 20–8 after the above transactions have been recorded.

REFLECTION

Imagine a student in your class is finding Activity 9.2 difficult. What advice could you give them? For example:

- What things do they need to think about?
- How do they decide where to include the motor vehicle?
- How do they decide if the capital is affected by any of these transactions?
- What can they check at the end to help them spot any errors?

Working capital and capital employed

A statement of financial position can be used to calculate two important figures. These are the **working capital** and the **capital employed**.

The formula used to calculate working capital is:

>   current assets – current liabilities

This shows whether the business can pay its immediate liabilities from its immediate assets. The working capital must be adequate to keep the business running efficiently on a day-to-day basis.

There are several formulae which can be used to calculate capital employed. These are:

>   non-current assets + (current assets – current liabilities)
>   non-current assets + working capital
>   owner's capital + non-current liabilities

The capital employed represents the total long-term finance which is being used by the business. These are the funds provided by the owners of the business and any long-term liabilities which will be available to the business for a considerable length of time. It does not include finance from current liabilities because these must be repaid relatively quickly from the current assets.

Whichever formula is applied, the answer will be the same. The first two versions of the formula calculate the net value of the assets being used in the business, and the last formula calculates the long-term finance which is being used.

KEY TERMS

working capital: the difference between the current assets and the current liabilities.

capital employed: the total long-term finance which is being used by a business.

LINKS

You will learn more about working capital and capital employed in Chapter 22.

WORKED EXAMPLE 9.2

Using the statement of financial position of Jagdeep on 31 May 20–8 prepared in **Worked Example 9.1**, calculate the:

a working capital
b capital employed

    a Working capital = current assets – current liabilities
                         = $19 700 – $6 300 = $13 400

    b Capital employed = non-current assets + (current assets – current liabilities)
                            = $106 000 + ($19 700 – $6 300) = $119 400

       (Alternative calculation = capital + non-current liabilities
                             = $107 400 + $12 000 = $119 400)

ACCOUNTING IN ACTION

Why bother with a statement of financial position?

Figure 9.7: A statement of financial position can provide the gardening business owner with useful information about their business

Jordan is the owner of a business which trades as Spring Blossom Plants. She has always been a keen gardener, and a year ago finally achieved her ambition of running a business that grows and sells a wide range of indoor and outdoor plants.

The number of customers visiting Spring Blossom Plants' premises during the year has increased and Jordan now employs three assistants to offer gardening advice and assist customers with their choice of plants.

At the end of her financial year, Jordan's accountant prepared a statement of profit or loss, which shows that the business has made a satisfactory profit. The accountant has said he will also prepare a statement of financial position. Jordan is not quite sure why the accountant is preparing a statement of financial position or why it is necessary.

Discuss in pairs or in a group:

1. How is the statement of financial position different from the statement of profit or loss, and what is the purpose of each statement?

2. What sort of items would you expect to see in Jordan's
   a. statement of profit or loss
   b. statement of financial position?

SUMMARY

You should now know:

- A statement of financial position shows the assets, liabilities and capital of a business on a certain date.
- Non-current assets are long-term assets. In a statement of financial position, the most permanent are shown first.
- Current assets are short-term assets and their values are constantly changing. In a statement of financial position, the furthest away from cash are shown first.
- Non-current liabilities are amounts which are not due for repayment within the next 12 months.
- Current liabilities are amounts which are due for repayment within the next 12 months and their values are constantly changing.

Chapter 9 practice questions

1. David's assets and liabilities on 29 April 20–1 were as follows:

	$
Fixtures and fittings	28 200
Motor vehicles	14 100
Inventory	6 650
Trade payables	5 870
Trade receivables	4 990
Cash at bank	3 240

   David invested $15 000 additional capital on 30 April 20–1.

   What was David's capital after this transaction?

   A $57 180

   B $66 310

   C $68 070

   D $72 180 [1]

2. A trader took cash from the business for personal use.

   What effect would this have on the financial statements?

	Current assets	Profit for the year
A	decrease	increase
B	decrease	no effect
C	increase	decrease
D	increase	increase	[1]

3. A trader repaid a long-term loan of $10 000. She used all the money in the business bank account, $7 000, and paid the balance from her personal bank account.

   How did this affect the statement of financial position?

	Assets	Liabilities	Capital
A	no effect	decrease $3 000	increase $3 000
B	decrease $7 000	decrease $10 000	increase $3 000
C	decrease $10 000	decrease $7 000	decrease $3 000
D	decrease $10 000	decrease $10 000	no effect	[1]

4   Halima is a wholesaler. She has very little knowledge about accounting, but attempted to prepare a statement of financial position. The statement she prepared contains errors.

Halima	
Statement of financial position at 31 July 20–5	
	$
Assets	
Property	88 000
Capital	115 000
Profit for the year	9 990
Inventory	5 640
Motor vehicle	14 360
Cash	100
Fixtures and fittings	10 870
Trade payables	4 570
	248 530
Liabilities	
Trade receivables	5 130
Loan (repayable August 20–7)	10 000
Drawings	8 500
Cash at bank	6 960
	30 590

Prepare a corrected statement of financial position at 31 July 20–5. [8]

5 Anika is a business adviser. Her financial year ends on 30 September.
She provided the following trial balance at 30 September 20–3:

	Dr $	Cr $
Capital		130 000
Drawings	16 000	
Property	90 000	
Office equipment	30 050	
Fees from clients		75 600
Rates and insurance	3 010	
Printing and stationery	1 960	
Wages	68 800	
Office expenses	2 000	
Rent income		7 500
Trade receivables	6 150	
Bank overdraft		5 070
Cash	200	
	218 170	218 170

Prepare Anika's statement of profit or loss for the year ended 30 September 20–3 and a statement of financial position at 30 September 20–3. **[11]**

6 Dilip is a trader.

Using the following information taken from Dilip's books on 30 June 20–8:

	$
Capital	83 300
Drawings	2 400
Property	60 000
Fixtures	5 000
Revenue	94 000
Purchases	81 100
Inventory 1 July 20–7	17 400
Carriage inwards	600
Carriage outwards	870
Trade receivables	15 100
Trade payables	6 900
Discount received	180
Rates and insurance	1 720
General expenses	300
Wages	13 000

(*Continued*)

	Loan interest	1 000
	Long-term loan from ABC Loans	10 000
	Bank overdraft	4 110

Inventory at 30 June 20–8 was valued at $18 100

a Prepare a trial balance at 30 June 20–8 [7]

b Prepare a statement for profit or loss for the year ended 30 June 20–8 [10]

c Prepare a statement of financial position at 30 June 20–8. [7]

[Total: 24]

CHECK YOUR PROGRESS

How well do you think you have achieved the learning intentions for this chapter? Give yourself a score from 1 (still need a lot of practice) to 5 (feeling very confident) for each learning intention. Provide an example to support your score.

Now I can …	Score	Example to support score
understand why it is important to prepare a statement of financial position and that it shows the assets and liabilities on a particular date		
recognise and understand the contents of a statement of financial position: non-current assets, intangible assets, current assets, current liabilities, non-current liabilities and capital		
understand the interrelationship of items in a statement of financial position		
draw up statements of financial position for trading businesses, service businesses and businesses which are both trading and service businesses.		

Chapter 10
Accounting rules

LEARNING INTENTIONS

By the end of this chapter, you will be able to:

- explain the application of the following accounting concepts: business entity, consistency, duality, going concern, historic cost, matching/accruals, materiality, money measurement, prudence and realisation
- calculate the value of inventory, and understand the effect on profits and asset values of an incorrect inventory valuation
- understand the differences between capital expenditure and revenue expenditure, and between capital receipts and revenue receipts
- understand how capital expenditure, revenue expenditure, capital receipts and revenue receipts are treated in the books of account
- explain the effect on the profit for the year and the asset valuations if the capital and revenue items are treated incorrectly
- understand why a business needs an ethical framework in accounting and understand the fundamental principles of integrity, objectivity, professional competence and due care, confidentiality and professional behaviour.

Introduction

Accounting has developed a number of rules which must be applied by everyone who is involved with recording financial information. This makes it possible to understand and compare the financial results of different businesses. The accounting principles which must be applied by every business are explained in this chapter.

There is a need for an ethical framework in accounting as it is important for accountants to be ethical in all aspects of their work. This chapter explains the fundamental principles of the framework.

This chapter also describes how capital and revenue expenditure and capital and revenue receipts should be recorded, and how a business should value its inventory. It is important that all businesses follow the same procedures for these items.

ACCOUNTING IN CONTEXT

Following the accounting rules

Figure 10.1: All businesses should follow the same accounting rules

A number of accounting rules have been developed over many years. It is important that these rules are recognised and applied by everyone who is involved in recording financial information. It does not matter how big or small the business is, what it trades in or whether the business is a sole trader business or a large international company – all businesses should follow the same rules.

Giuseppe runs a bakery selling bread, cakes and desserts. During the first year of operating the business, Giuseppe employed a book-keeper to maintain the day-to-day accounting records.

At the start of the second year, Guiseppe's daughter, Maria, took over the day-to-day accounting records. Maria saw what the book-keeper did the previous year, but she decided that she would do things differently to try save some time.

Giuseppe asked an accountant to prepare the year-end financial statements at the end of the first year and at the end of the second year. Giuseppe compared the two statements and noticed that the profit for the year in the second year was much higher than in the first year. He concluded that Maria must be better at maintaining the accounts.

Discuss in pairs or in a group:

1. What is wrong with Giuseppe's conclusion?
2. What advice would you give Giuseppe about whether to continue to employ Maria to maintain the accounts or to go back to employing a qualified book-keeper?

10.1 Accounting concepts

Accounting concepts are sometimes referred to as principles. A concept is a rule which sets down how the financial activities of a business are recorded. If all businesses follow the same rules, accounting users can have confidence that the financial statements are accurate. Some of the main accounting concepts have already been applied to the examples in the previous chapters.

Table 10.1 describes each concept and how it is applied.

Table 10.1: The application of accounting concepts

Accounting concept	Description	Application
Business entity	This means that the business is treated as being completely separate from the owner of the business.	The accounting records relate only to the business and record only the assets and liabilities of the business. The owner's personal expenditure is not recorded.
Consistency	Where a choice of accounting methods is available, the selected method must be used consistently from one accounting period to the next.	When a business chooses, for example, the straight line method of depreciation, this method must be applied every year. This allows the financial results of one year to be compared fairly with the results of another year.
Duality	This forms the basis of double entry book-keeping as explained in Chapter 2. Each business transaction must be recorded twice.	If you purchase a motor vehicle for cash, you would gain the asset of the motor vehicle but the asset of cash would reduce by the same amount.
Going concern	This assumes that the business will continue to operate for an indefinite period of time and that there is no intention to close down the business or reduce the size of the business by any significant amount.	Assets are valued at their net book values, which is the cost less the accumulated depreciation. This is known as their carrying value. They are not valued at their resale value.
Historic cost	This requires that all assets and expenses are initially recorded in the ledger accounts at their actual cost. No adjustments must be made if an asset's value has increased or decreased.	Any increases in non-current asset valuations, such as land, due to market conditions must be ignored when producing the statement of financial position.

(Continued)

> **LINKS**
>
> The practical application of the principle of business entity has already been explained in Chapters 2, 4 and 9.
>
> You will learn about depreciation in Chapter 12.

> **KEY TERMS**
>
> **business entity concept:** this means that the business is treated as being completely separate from the owner of the business.
>
> **consistency concept:** this means that accounting methods must be used consistently from one accounting period to the next.
>
> **duality concept:** this means that every transaction is recorded twice – once on the debit side and once on the credit side.
>
> **going concern concept:** this means that the accounting records are maintained on the basis that the business will continue to operate for an indefinite period of time.
>
> **historic cost concept:** this means that all assets and expenses are initially recorded at their actual cost.

Accounting concept	Description	Application
Matching/ accruals	This is often referred to as either the matching concept or the accruals concept. It means that the revenue of the accounting period is matched against the costs of the same period.	When preparing the statement of profit or loss at the end of the year, it is necessary to adjust for any payments owing or payments made in advance, to ensure that only the expenses for that period are included.
Materiality	Items which have either a low or immaterial value are not worth recording as separate items.	The purchase of a low value item, such as a calculator for office use, is strictly a non-current asset because part of its value is 'lost' each year through normal use. The cost of calculating and recording this each year would be more than the cost of the asset, so it is regarded as an office expense in the year of purchase.
Money measurement	This means that only information which can be expressed in terms of money can be recorded in the accounting records. It does not rely on personal opinions and it is factual.	The morale of the workforce and the effectiveness of a good manager both play an important part in the success of the business, but they will not appear in the accounting records as their value cannot be expressed in monetary terms.
Prudence	When preparing financial statements, it is important to ensure that profits and assets are not overstated and that liabilities are not understated.	Prudence would be applied when creating an allowance for irrecoverable debts. In anticipation of a future irrecoverable debt, an adjustment is made in this year's financial statements to provide a prudent view of the trade receivables.
Realisation	This means that revenue is only regarded as being earned when the legal title to goods or services passes from the seller to the buyer, who then has an obligation (liability) to pay for those goods.	When selling goods, the profit earned on that sale should only be included when the cash is received or the promise to pay is received, not when the order is placed.

LINKS

In Chapter 11, you will learn why it is sometimes necessary to adjust the items of income and expense in a statement of profit or loss for amounts prepaid or accrued.

You will learn how the matching/accruals principle is applied to capital and revenue expenditure later in this chapter.

KEY TERMS

matching/accruals concept: this means that the revenue of the accounting period is matched against the costs of the same period.

materiality concept: this means that individual items which will not significantly affect either the profit or the assets of a business do not need to be recorded separately.

money measurement concept: this means that only information which can be expressed in terms of money can be recorded in the accounting records.

LINKS

You will learn about providing for the loss in value of non-current assets in Chapter 12.

You will learn about providing for the loss when customers do not pay their accounts in Chapter 13.

TIP

To help you remember these concepts, try to think of an example that demonstrates each one.

DISCUSSION

1. Think about the accounting concepts in Table 10.1 and arrange them in order, starting with the one you think is the most important and finishing with the one you think is the least important.
2. Compare your list with a partner and discuss any differences.
3. Agree on a list together and be prepared to justify your decision to the rest of the class.

KEY TERMS

prudence concept: this means that profits and assets should not be overstated, and losses and liabilities should not be understated.

realisation concept: this means that revenue is only regarded as being earned when the legal title to goods passes from the seller to the buyer.

cost: the purchase price of the goods plus any additional costs to bring the goods to their present position and condition.

net realisable value: the estimated receipts from selling the goods less any costs of completing or selling those goods.

10.2 Inventory valuation

The rule when valuing inventory is:

Inventory is always valued at the lower of cost or net realisable value.

This is an application of the prudence concept, as overvaluing the inventory causes both the profit and the assets to be overvalued.

The **cost** of the inventory is the actual purchase price plus any additional costs (such as carriage inwards) incurred in bringing the inventory to its present position and condition.

If goods are damaged, it may be necessary to repair or repackage them before they can be sold. This is known as completing the goods, and the additional costs incurred need to be deducted from the selling price.

The **net realisable value** is the estimated receipts from the sale of the inventory, less any costs of completing the goods or costs of selling the goods.

Usually, the cost of the inventory will be lower than the net realisable value. However, if the goods are damaged, or if there is no demand for this type of goods because of changes in taste or fashion, then the net realisable value will be lower than cost.

TIP

When you are valuing an inventory, you should start by working out the cost price and the net realisable value after any adjustments have been taken into account.

WORKED EXAMPLE 10.1

Doan sells two different types of goods (Types X and Y). He provided the following information at 30 June 20–8.

Type	No of units	Cost price per unit	Net realisable value per unit	Adjustments
X	102	$18	$15	The cost price does not include carriage inwards of $2 per unit.
				It will cost $0.75 per unit to bring goods into a saleable condition.
Y	46	$22	$26	20 units were damaged and can only be sold for $10 per unit.

Calculate the value of the closing inventory at 30 June 20–8.

Type	No of units	Cost price per unit	Net realisable value per unit	Valuation
X	102	$18 + carriage: $18 + $2 = $20	$15 – costs to complete: $15 – $0.75 = $14.25	Net realisable value is lower than cost price, so item is valued at net realisable value: $14.25 × 102 = **$1 453.50**
Y	46	20 units @ $22	$10	Net realisable value is lower than cost price, so item is valued at net realisable value: $10 × 20 = **$200**
		26 units @ $22	$26	Cost price is lower than the net realisable value, so item is valued at cost price: $22 × 26 = **$572**

The total value of the inventory = $1 453.50 + $200 + $572 = **$2 225.50**

ACTIVITY 10.1

Figure 10.2: When goods are damaged their value is reduced

At the end of the year, Anika discovered that 40 items of inventory costing $70 each were damaged. They would need to be repackaged, which would cost an additional $5 for each item. They could then be sold for $73 each. Normally the items could be sold for $80 each.

1. Calculate the value of these 40 items for inclusion in the financial statements.
2. Which accounting concept did you apply when valuing these items?

The effects of incorrect inventory valuation

The inventory at the end of one year becomes the inventory at the start of the next year. This means that if an incorrect value is placed on the inventory, it will affect the gross profit and the profit for the year for both the current financial year and the following financial year. In Chapter 8, it was explained that:

gross profit = revenue – cost of sales

cost of sales = opening inventory + purchases – closing inventory

- If a business overvalues their closing inventory, this reduces the figure for the cost of sales (as a larger figure will be subtracted in the calculation). As a result, the gross profit will increase. The profit for the year will also increase as the total expenses are deducted from the gross profit.

- If a business undervalues their closing inventory, this increases the figure for their cost of sales (as a smaller figure will be subtracted in the calculation). As a result, the gross profit would decrease. The profit for the year will also decrease as the total expenses are deducted from the gross profit.

An incorrect inventory valuation will also mean that incorrect values will be shown for both current assets and capital in the statement of financial position.

- If the closing inventory is overvalued, then the figure used in the current assets will increase. The figure for the owner's capital will also increase as the profit for the year will have increased in the statement of profit or loss.

- If the closing inventory is undervalued, then the figure used in the current assets will decrease. The figure for the owner's capital will also decrease as the profit for the year would have decreased in the statement of profit or loss.

> **LINK**
>
> You will learn about correcting errors in Chapter 15.

WORKED EXAMPLE 10.2

After the preparation of his financial statements for the year ended 30 June 20–8, Doan discovered that he had overvalued his closing inventory by $250.

Complete the following table by placing a tick in the correct columns to show the effect of this.

	Overstated	Understated	No effect
Gross profit for the year ended 30 June 20–8	✓		
Gross profit for the year ending 30 June 20–9		✓	
Profit for the year ended 30 June 20–8	✓		
Profit for the year ending 30 June 20–9		✓	
Doan's capital at 30 June 20–8	✓		
Doan's capital at 30 June 20–9			✓
Current assets at 30 June 20–8	✓		
Current assets at 30 June 20–9			✓

> **CONTINUED**
>
> Overvaluing the inventory at 30 June 20–8 will affect the financial statements for that year because:
>
> - the cost of sales is understated so both the gross profit and the profit for the year will be overstated
> - overstating the profit for the year means that the balance of the capital account on 30 June 20–8 will also be overstated
> - the total of the current assets at 30 June 20–8 will be overstated if the inventory at that date is overvalued.
>
> Overvaluing the inventory at 30 June 20–8 will affect the financial statements for the year ending 30 June 20–9 because:
>
> - the cost of sales is overstated so both the gross profit and the profit for the year will be understated
> - understating the profit for the year means that the balance of the capital account on 30 June 20–8 will have been corrected at 30 June 20–9
> - the total of the current assets at 30 June 20–9 will not be affected as they include only the closing inventory at that date.

> **REFLECTION**
>
> In Section 10.1, you learnt about the prudence concept.
>
> How is correctly valuing inventory related to the prudence concept?
>
> To understand the effects of overvaluing or undervaluing an inventory, you might have had to look back to what you learnt about financial statements in Chapters 8 and 9.
>
> Why is it important to make sure that you really understand one section before you move on to the next one?
>
> How can making connections between different sections help your understanding?

10.3 Capital expenditure and revenue expenditure

Capital expenditure

Capital expenditure is money spent by a business on purchasing non-current assets and improving or extending non-current assets. This includes all the legal costs incurred in the purchase of non-current assets, costs of carriage for the delivery of non-current assets and costs of installing non-current assets.

These costs will appear as non-current assets in the statement of financial position of a business. They should **not** be charged as expenses in the year of purchase as they benefit the business for several years. The value of non-current assets often decreases because of depreciation (see Chapter 12). This cost will be matched against the annual revenue which the non-current asset has helped the business to earn.

Revenue expenditure

Revenue expenditure is money spent on running a business on a day-to-day basis. This includes the administration expenses, the selling expenses, the financial expenses and the cost of maintaining and running non-current assets. It also includes the cost of goods purchased for the purpose of resale.

These costs will appear in the statement of profit or loss. They are matched against the revenue of the period.

> **KEY TERMS**
>
> **capital expenditure:** money spent on purchasing, improving or extending non-current assets.
>
> **revenue expenditure:** money spent on running a business on a day-to-day basis.

ACTIVITY 10.2

Figure 10.3: New factory machinery being installed and tested

Joshi owns a small factory and recently used some of his workers to install some new machinery he had purchased. He believes that these wages should be shown in the statement of profit or loss as wages is a business expense.

1. Discuss with a partner why Joshi is not correct.

2. Write a note to Joshi to explain:

   a. how the wages cost of the installation should be treated

   b. how the wages cost should be treated if he uses the workers to repair the existing machinery.

If capital expenditure and revenue expenditure are treated incorrectly, the profit for the year will be inaccurate and the statement of financial position (while still balancing) will also be incorrect. For example, if repairs to an office machine (revenue expenditure) were treated as an improvement to that machine (capital expenditure), the expenses in the statement of profit or loss would be understated, so the profit for the year would be overstated. In the statement of financial position, the non-current assets would be overstated and the capital would also be overstated because of the incorrect profit for the year.

10.4 Capital receipts and revenue receipts

Capital receipts

A **capital receipt** occurs when money is received other than from normal trading activities. This includes the receipt of capital from the owner, the receipt of loans and the proceeds of the sale of a non-current asset.

A capital receipt should **not** be entered in the statement of profit or loss. If, however, a profit or loss is made on the sale of a non-current asset, then this will be included in the statement of profit or loss for the year in which the asset was sold.

Revenue receipts

A **revenue receipt** is money received by a business from normal trading activities. This includes revenue from the sale of goods, fees from clients and other income such as rent income, commission income, discount received and so on. Because these arise from the normal trading activities, they are entered in the statement of profit or loss.

A summary of the differences between capital expenditure, revenue expenditure, capital receipts and revenue receipts is shown in Table 10.2.

Table 10.2: The differences between capital and revenue expenditure and receipts

> **LINK**
>
> You will learn about the disposal of non-current assets in Chapter 12.

> **KEY TERMS**
>
> **capital receipt:** money received by a business that is not from normal trading activities.
>
> **revenue receipt:** money received by a business from normal trading activities.

Type of expenditure or receipt	Description	Example	Frequency	Financial statement
Capital expenditure	Purchase of non-current assets	Purchase of an office machine	Non-recurring	Statement of financial position
Revenue expenditure	Day-to-day running expenses	Repairs to office machinery	Recurring	Statement of profit or loss
Capital receipt	Money received that is not from normal trading activities	Money received from the sale of a non-current asset	Non-recurring	Statement of financial position
Revenue receipt	Money received from trading activities	Money received from the sale of goods	Recurring	Statement of profit or loss

ACTIVITY 10.3

Figure 10.4: An electric vehicle being charged

Rula has recently purchased a factory to manufacture electric vehicles (EV). She purchased new machinery using a bank loan on which annual interest was payable.

Decide whether each of the following items is a capital expenditure, a revenue expenditure, a capital receipt or a revenue receipt:

a   Bank loan

b   Government grant for using renewable energy

c   Factory insurance

d   Installation of EV charging points for staff vehicles

e   Installing a new roof

f   Repairs to the staff car park

g   Loan interest

h   Staff training costs to use existing machinery

i   Purchase of new machinery

j   Staff training costs to use new machinery

Compare your answers with a partner. Discuss any items where you have different answers and try to agree on a category before checking your answers.

10.5 Ethical framework in accounting

In recent years, there has been more recognition of the need for accountants to be ethical in all aspects of their work. As a result, a code of ethics for professional accountants has been published, which provides fundamental principles that all accountants must follow.

Table 10.3 summarises these principles.

Table 10.3: Ethical principles for accountants

Principle	Description	Application
Integrity	Accountants must be straightforward and honest when dealing with clients.	Accountants must always behave in an honest, fair and ethical way, and act in the best interests of their clients, ensuring that all information provided is accurate, transparent and reliable.
Objectivity	Accountants must be impartial and unbiased.	Accountants must always report information to their clients without bias and without being under pressure from others.
Professional competence and due care	Accountants must have the skills, knowledge and understanding to perform a task to the appropriate professional standard.	Accountants must possess the necessary skills and knowledge to perform their duties. They must constantly update their skills and knowledge so that their clients can have confidence in their ability to provide accurate and effective services.
Confidentiality	Accountants must not disclose confidential information to third parties without authority.	Accountants must protect their clients' privacy and information, and provide a secure system for retaining their clients' data.
Professional behaviour	Accountants must comply with relevant laws and regulations and not damage the reputation of the profession.	Accountants must act within the law and behave in an appropriate manner. For example, they should always be polite and courteous when meeting clients and always act in an ethical way.

When these principles are followed, everyone involved with the business, and even the wider public, can be confident that the accountant is providing reliable and accurate information. If an accountant does not follow any of these principles, they may be investigated by a professional body. This might mean that the person will be prevented from working further as a professional accountant and, in extreme cases, the accountant could be charged with fraud or embezzlement.

10 Accounting rules

ACTIVITY 10.4

Imagine that you have recently been employed as a trainee accountant.

Read through the three situations and work with a partner to answer these questions:

1 Which of the ethical principles might be broken in each situation? Explain why.

2 What action should be taken in order to follow the code of ethics?

Situation 1
Your sister runs a small business from home and has asked you to prepare her financial statements for the year to present to the tax office.

Situation 2
A senior colleague has asked you to increase the income figures for your team in order to improve the annual bonus that all staff receive.

Situation 3
Due to staff shortages, a senior partner has asked you to supervise the work of a new client but you do not feel like you have had enough training. You bring this to the attention of the senior partner, but they insist that you carry out the work.

DISCUSSION

Tareq and Malika are discussing the benefits of having an ethical framework in accounting.

Tareq says, 'Having an ethical framework means that all accountants will work in an ethical way and maintain the reputation of the profession.'

Malika says, 'I disagree. I think we need a system where there are more checks on accountants by independent organisations.'

Discuss in a small group who you agree with and why.

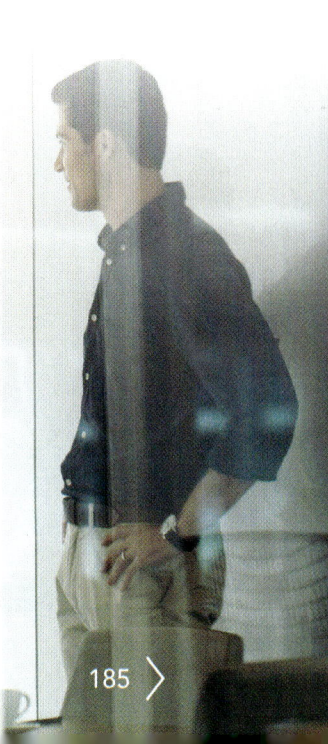

ACCOUNTING IN ACTION

Different types of expenditure

Figure 10.5: A herd of goats

Kgosi is a farmer. He has a large herd of goats and sells milk to the local dairy. He also uses some of the milk to make cheese, which he sells to local shops and cafes.

For several years, Kgosi employed Layla to run the farm office. Her duties were to maintain the day-to-day accounting records, pay the wages to the farm workers and deal with correspondence.

A month ago, Layla left Kgosi's farm and moved away from the area. Kgosi decided he would run the farm office himself until he managed to appoint a new office manager.

An invoice was received from a local business from whom Kgosi obtained many of his requirements to run the farm. The items listed on the invoice were:

- New tractor
- Delivery charge for new tractor
- Cost of extended guarantee and insurance of tractor
- Spare parts to repair milking machine
- Labour cost of repairing milking machine

Kgosi credited the account of the supplier and debited the machinery and equipment account with the total of the invoice.

Discuss in pairs or in a group:

1. Explain what is wrong with the double entry that Kgosi has made?
2. What would the effect be on the year-end financial statements of the entry made by Kgosi?

SUMMARY

You should now know:

- Accounting has developed a set of concepts which are applied in the preparation of accounting statements.
- The main accounting concepts are: business entity, consistency, duality, going concern, historic cost, matching/accruals, materiality, money measurement, prudence and realisation.
- Inventory must be valued at the end of every financial year. It is always valued at the lower of cost or net realisable value.
- It is important to distinguish between capital and revenue expenditure and also between capital and revenue receipts. If these items are treated incorrectly, the financial statements will also be inaccurate.
- Accountants must act ethically at all times and follow a set of principles.
- The fundamental principles of ethics are: integrity, objectivity, professional competence and due care, confidentiality and professional behaviour.

Chapter 10 practice questions

1. The cost of insuring the owner's personal motor vehicle was not included in the statement of profit or loss of the business. Which accounting concept was applied?

   A business entity

   B going concern

   C money measurement

   D prudence [1]

2. Dhalia provided the following information about her closing inventory.

	Number of units	Cost price per unit	Net realisable value per unit
Product A	500	$1.00	$1.80
Product B	2 000	$2.00	$1.90

   200 units of Product B were damaged and unsaleable.

   What was the total value of Dhalia's inventory?

   A $3 920

   B $4 100

   C $4 320

   D $4 700 [1]

3. Repairs to office machinery were entered as capital expenditure in the accounting records.

   How did this affect the financial statements?

	Profit for the year		Non-current assets	
	Overstated	Understated	Overstated	Understated
A	✓		✓	
B		✓		✓
C	✓			✓
D		✓	✓	

   [1]

4. Name the accounting concept applied in each of the following situations:

   a Rent for business premises relating to 20–7 was not included in the statement of profit or loss for 20–6. [1]

   b Credit sales were recorded when the goods were dispatched (sent), not when the customer placed the order. [1]

   c The value of the assets of a business was not reduced when the manager of the business retired. [1]

   d Cash purchases were debited to the purchases account and credited to the cash account. [1]

   [Total: 4]

5 a Explain the meaning of the terms 'cost' and 'net realisable value'. [2]

b State how a trader should value the inventory at the end of the financial year. [1]

c At the end of the financial year on 31 July 20–8, a trader discovered that he had undervalued his closing inventory by $2 100.

Copy and complete the following table by placing a tick in the correct column to show the effect, if any, of this undervaluation.

	Overstated	Understated	No effect
Profit for the year ended 31 July 20–8			
Gross profit for the year ended 31 July 20–9			
Current assets on 31 July 20–9			

[3]

[Total: 6]

6 a Explain the difference between each of the following pairs of terms. Give an example of each:

  i capital expenditure and capital receipts

  ii revenue expenditure and revenue receipts [8]

b Explain why it is important that capital receipts are not recorded as revenue receipts. [3]

[Total: 11]

7 State the ethical principle being described in each statement.

a You must always be straightforward and honest in all your dealings with clients. [1]

b You must have the necessary skills and knowledge to perform a task such as preparing financial statements. [1]

c You must be impartial and unbiased when dealing with clients. [1]

[Total: 3]

10   Accounting rules

CHECK YOUR PROGRESS

How well do you think you have achieved the learning intentions for this chapter? Give yourself a score from 1 (still need a lot of practice) to 5 (feeling very confident) for each learning intention. Provide an example to support your score.

Now I can …	Score	Example to support score
explain the application of the following accounting concepts: business entity, consistency, duality, going concern, historic cost, matching/accruals, materiality, money measurement, prudence and realisation		
calculate the value of inventory, and understand the effect on profits and asset values of an incorrect inventory valuation		
understand the differences between capital expenditure and revenue expenditure, and between capital receipts and revenue receipts		
understand how capital expenditure, revenue expenditure, capital receipts and revenue receipts are treated in the books of account		
explain the effect on the profit for the year and the asset valuations if the capital and revenue items are treated incorrectly		
understand why a business needs an ethical framework in accounting and understand the fundamental principles of integrity, objectivity, professional competence and due care, confidentiality and professional behaviour.		

Chapter 11
Other payables and other receivables

LEARNING INTENTIONS

By the end of this chapter, you will be able to:
- understand why it is important to apply the matching/accruals concept to incomes and expenses
- prepare ledger accounts to record accrued and prepaid expenses
- prepare ledger accounts to record accrued and prepaid incomes
- make adjustments in financial statements for accrued and prepaid expenses
- make adjustments in financial statements for accrued and prepaid incomes.

11 Other payables and other receivables

Introduction

It is often necessary to make adjustments to the accounting records in order to show the profit or loss of the business and the financial position of the business more accurately. These adjustments are referred to as year-end adjustments.

The Worked examples in previous chapters assumed that all the expenses in the profit and loss section of the statement of profit or loss were paid until the end of the financial year, with nothing paid beyond that date and nothing unpaid. Similarly, for revenue items within the profit and loss section of the statement of profit or loss, it was assumed that all the items were received up to the end of the financial year with nothing relating to a period beyond that date and nothing outstanding.

In practice, this is rarely the case. It is common to find expenses or income unpaid for a financial year, or to find expenses or income paid in one financial year but which relate to another financial year. This chapter explains what to do in these situations.

> **LINKS**
>
> You will learn more about year-end adjustments in Chapters 12–13.
>
> You learnt about statements of profit or loss in Chapter 8.

ACCOUNTING IN CONTEXT

Paying in advance or paying later

Figure 11.1: An artist's rented studio

Often a business will make and receive payments at the same time as goods or services are received or provided, but this is not always the case. Sometimes payments are made in advance before the goods or services are received, and other times the goods or services are received but not paid for until sometime later. It is quite common for businesses to have expenses or income unpaid at the end of the financial year, or to have expenses or income paid in one financial year but which relate to the following financial year.

Anastasia is an artist. She runs painting classes and workshops for both adults and children. Her financial year ends on 31 August.

Anastasia rents premises. She pays the rent quarterly in advance on 1 January, 1 April, 1 July and 1 October each year. Each week a cleaner comes to clean Anastasia's studio. On the first day of each month, Anastasia pays the cleaner for the work done in the previous month.

At the end of the financial year on 31 August 20–6, Anastasia had already paid the rent for the September 20–6 but she still owed the cleaner for the work done in August. As each of these items was for one month only, Anastasia decided to ignore them when preparing the year-end financial statements.

Discuss in a pair or a group:

1. Identify and explain the accounting concept which Anastasia is not applying. Why is Anastasia wrong to ignore the month's rent she has already paid and the month's cleaning that is unpaid?

2. Anastasia is considering asking her students to pay the fees for their art classes monthly in advance. What might be the advantages and disadvantages to Anastasia of doing this?

11.1 Accrued and prepaid expenses

A statement of profit or loss is prepared for a definite period of time (the period of time covered by the statement is included as part of the statement heading). Only items relating to that particular time period should be included in the statement: the timing of the actual receipts and payments is not relevant. This is a practical application of the matching/accruals concept.

It is necessary to adjust the items within the statement of profit or loss for amounts prepaid or accrued. This means that the profit or loss will be shown at a more accurate figure, and it allows for more meaningful comparisons of the financial statements from year to year.

It is often helpful to use a simple diagram when calculating the expense or income relating to a particular financial year. This is illustrated in the Worked examples in this chapter.

> **LINK**
>
> You learnt about the matching/accruals concept in Chapter 10.

Accrued expenses

An accrual is an amount due in an accounting period which remains unpaid at the end of that accounting period. Where there is an **accrued expense**, it means that some benefit or service has been received during the accounting period, but this benefit or service has not been paid for by the end of the period.

To apply the matching/accruals concept, the amount transferred to the statement of profit or loss should represent the expense for the accounting period covered by that statement. This means that any amount due but unpaid at the end of the financial year must be added to the amount paid and the total expense relating to the accounting period transferred to the statement of profit or loss.

The expense account will now show a balance equal to the amount unpaid. To complete the double entry, this balance is brought down on the credit side of the ledger account. As the balance represents an amount owing, due for payment in the near future, it will be included as a current liability in the statement of financial position.

The entries are as follows:

During the year

- Debit the expense account and credit the cash book with the amount paid.

At the year-end

- Debit the expense account with any amount due but unpaid and carry down as a credit balance.

- Credit the expense account with the difference on the account (this represents the expense for the year). Include this amount with the other expenses in the statement of profit or loss – this is equal to making a debit entry as the statement is part of the double entry system.

- Include the balance on the expense account as a current liability in the statement of financial position.

> **KEY TERM**
>
> **accrued expense:** an expense relating to a particular accounting period which is unpaid at the end of that period.

> **LINK**
>
> You learnt in Chapter 8 how the totals of the expense accounts and income accounts are transferred to the statement of profit or loss at the end of the financial year.

11 Other payables and other receivables

WORKED EXAMPLE 11.1

Zubair started a business on 1 April 20–7.

During the year ended 31 March 20–8, his payments for expenses included the following:

20–7	30 June	General expenses paid in cash, $56
	4 October	General expenses paid by bank transfer, $68
20–8	3 January	General expenses paid by cheque, $63

On 31 March 20–8, Zubair owed general expenses, $60, which was paid in cash on 5 April 20–8.

a Prepare the general expenses account in Zubair's nominal ledger for the year ended 31 March 20–8.

b Prepare a relevant extract from Zubair's statement of profit or loss for the year ended 31 March 20–8.

c Prepare a relevant extract from Zubair's statement of financial position at 31 March 20–8.

Before attempting to answer the question, it may be helpful to draw a diagram.

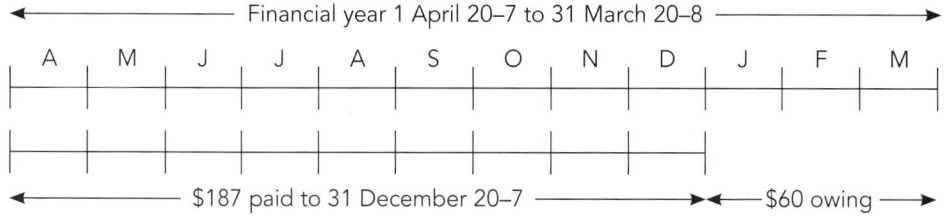

> **TIP**
>
> Only those expenses and incomes which relate to the current financial year are included in the statement of profit or loss, so you can use a diagram to help you see what adjustments are needed.

The diagram shows that the expenses paid do not match the period covered by the financial year. So, to calculate the value that is to be transferred to the statement of profit or loss, it is necessary to add the amount owing at the end of the year to the amount that has been paid during the year.

a

Zubair
Nominal ledger

Dr			General expenses account				Cr
			$				$
20–7				20–8			
Jun 30	Cash		56	Mar 31	Statement of profit or loss		247
Oct 4	Bank		68				
20–8							
Jan 3	Bank		63				
Mar 31	Balance	c/d	60				
			247				247
				20–8			
				Apr 1	Balance	b/d	60

> **CONTINUED**

- At the end of March 20–8, $60 is due but unpaid, so this is carried down as a credit balance to start the next financial year.
- At the end of the financial year, there were no entries on the credit side of the account, so the difference on the account was $247. This is credited to the general expenses account and included in the statement of profit or loss with the other expenses, which is equal to making a debit entry. (This represents the expense for the year and is the value calculated using the diagram.)

b

Zubair	
Extract from statement of profit or loss for the year ended 31 March 20–8	
	$
Expenses – General expenses	247

- General expenses relating to the financial year ended on 31 March 20–8 amount to $247, which is the total paid plus the amount unpaid.
- The general expenses would be listed with the other expenses in the statement of profit or loss and deducted from the gross profit.
- In a statement of profit or loss, adjustments to expenses or incomes are sometimes shown in brackets after the name of the expense for reference purposes. Here, this would be shown as:
Expenses – General expenses ($187 + $60)

c

Zubair	
Extract from statement of financial position at 31 March 20–8	
	$
Current liabilities	
Other payables	60

- Where there are several accrued expenses, it is usual to show one combined figure in the statement of financial position under 'Other payables' rather than showing the amount of each separate accrual.

11 Other payables and other receivables

> **ACTIVITY 11.1**
>
>
>
> **Figure 11.2:** A children's clothing store
>
> Adam has a store selling children's clothes and has just completed his first year of trading. He has maintained double entry records throughout the year with separate accounts for each type of expense. At the end of the year, Adam had an outstanding invoice for advertising expenses. He decided not to mention this to his accountant as he intends to pay the invoice in the next few weeks.
>
> Write a short email or note to Adam explaining why this invoice should be taken into consideration and how this should be recorded in the statement of profit or loss and the statement of financial position.

Prepaid expenses

A prepayment is an amount that is paid in advance. A **prepaid expense** means that a payment has been made during a particular accounting period for some benefit or service to be received in a future accounting period.

As with accrued expenses, the matching/accruals concept must be applied so that the amount transferred to the statement of profit or loss represents the expense for the accounting period covered by that statement. Any amount paid during the financial year relating to a future accounting period must be deducted from the amount paid so that only the expense relating to the accounting period is transferred to the statement of profit or loss.

The expense account will now show a balance equal to the amount paid in advance. To complete the double entry, this balance is brought down on the debit side of the ledger account. As the balance represents a short-term benefit which the business has paid for but not yet used up, it will be included as a current asset in the statement of financial position.

The entries are as follows:

During the year

- Debit the expense account and credit the cash book with the amount paid.

At the year-end

- Credit the expense account with any amount paid in advance and carry down as a debit balance.
- Credit the expense account with the difference on the account (this represents the expense for the year). Include this amount with the other expenses in the statement of profit or loss – this is equal to making a debit entry as the statement is part of the double entry system.
- Include the balance on the expense account as a current asset in the statement of financial position.

> **KEY TERM**
>
> **prepaid expense:** an expense paid during a particular accounting period which relates to a future accounting period.

195

WORKED EXAMPLE 11.2

Zubair started a business on 1 April 20–7.

Zubair rented premises until 1 July 20–7 when he purchased premises. He paid a cheque for $960 for one year's insurance on his premises on 1 July 20–7.

a Prepare the insurance account in Zubair's nominal ledger for the year ended 31 March 20–8.

b Prepare a relevant extract from Zubair's statement of profit or loss for the year ended 31 March 20–8.

c Prepare a relevant extract from Zubair's statement of financial position at 31 March 20–8.

Before attempting to answer the question, it may be helpful to draw a diagram.

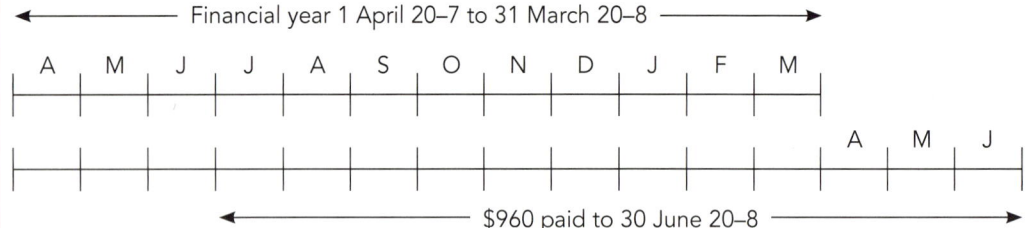

The diagram shows that the expenses paid do not match the period covered by the financial year, so it is necessary to deduct that part of the $960 which falls outside the financial year (3 months/12 months or ¼ of $960 relates to the following financial year).

a

Zubair							
Nominal ledger							
Dr			Insurance account				Cr
			$				$
20–7				20–8			
Jul 1	Bank		960	Mar 31	Statement of profit or loss		720
					Balance	c/d	240
			960				960
20–8							
Apr 1	Balance	b/d	240				

- At the end of March 20–8, $240 is paid in advance for the following year, so this is carried down as a debit balance to start the next financial year.

- At the end of the financial year, the difference on the account was $720. This is credited to the insurance account and included in the statement of profit or loss with the other expenses, which is equal to making a debit entry. (This represents the expense for the year and is the value calculated using the diagram.)

b

Zubair	
Extract from statement of profit or loss for the year ended 31 March 20–8	
	$
Expenses – Insurance	720

- The insurance relating to the financial year ended on 31 March 20–8 amounts to $720, which is the insurance from 1 July 20–7 to 31 March 20–8.

- The insurance expense would be listed with the other expenses in the statement of profit or loss and deducted from the gross profit.

11 Other payables and other receivables

> **CONTINUED**
>
> c
>
> | Zubair
Extract from statement of financial position at 31 March 20–8 | |
> |---|---:|
> | | $ |
> | **Current assets** | |
> | Other receivables | 240 |
>
> - Where there are several prepaid expenses, it is usual to show one combined figure in the statement of financial position under 'Other receivables' rather than showing the amount of each separate prepayment.

If a business has an inventory of stationery, postage stamps, wrapping paper and so on at the end of a financial year, this can be regarded as a prepaid expense. Money has been spent, but the benefit will not be received until the following accounting period when these are actually used. The entries are similar to those for a prepaid expense.

> **WORKED EXAMPLE 11.3**
>
> Zubair started a business on 1 April 20–7.
> During the year ended 31 March 20–8, he purchased stationery costing $230.
> On 31 March 20–8, the inventory of stationery was valued at $49.
> Prepare the stationery account in Zubair's nominal ledger for the year ended 31 March 20–8.
>
> | | | Zubair
Nominal ledger
Stationery account | | | | |
> |---|---|---:|---|---|---|---:|
> | **Dr** | | | | | | **Cr** |
> | | | $ | | | | $ |
> | 20–8 | | | 20–8 | | | |
> | Mar 31 | Bank/cash | 230 | Mar 31 | Statement of profit or loss | | 181 |
> | | | | | Balance | c/d | 49 |
> | | | 230 | | | | 230 |
> | 20–8 | | | | | | |
> | Apr 1 | Balance | b/d | 49 | | | |
>
> - The date of 31 March 20–8 has been used for the total paid as no individual dates and amounts were shown in the question.
> - The amount of $181 represents the cost of stationery used during the financial year and would be listed with the other expenses in the statement of profit or loss and deducted from the gross profit.
> - The balance representing the inventory at 31 March 20–8 would appear as a current asset in the statement of financial position.
> - The inventory of stationery must not be included in the inventory of goods for resale.

Figure 11.3: Businesses may maintain a stationery account

> **DISCUSSION**
>
> Cindy opened an advertising agency on 1 January 20–9. Her profit for the year ended 31 December 20–9 was $52 100. While inspecting her statement of profit or loss, she noticed that adjustments had not been made for commission income accrued of $2 910 and an inventory of stationery of $11.
>
> Discuss the following with a partner:
>
> 1. What would the profit for the year have been if adjustments had been made for these items?
>
> 2. Name and explain the accounting concept which was disregarded by the omission of these adjustments.
>
>   a. Explain, giving reasons, whether you can justify ignoring the adjustment for the stationery.
>
>   b. Explain whether your answer would have been different if the amount had been $110.
>
> Share your answers with the rest of the class.

11.2 Opening balances on expense accounts

In Worked examples 11.1–11.3, Zubair was in his first year of business, so none of the expense accounts prepared in these examples had an opening balance. However, there was a closing balance on each account, which becomes the opening balance for the second year of trading. This must be considered when calculating the expense relating to the next financial year.

11 Other payables and other receivables

WORKED EXAMPLE 11.4

Zubair's financial year ends on 31 March.

On 1 April 20–8, the general expenses account in Zubair's nominal ledger showed a credit balance of $60.

During the year ended 31 March 20–9, his payments for expenses included the following:

20–8	5 April	General expenses paid in cash, $60
	30 June	General expenses paid by cheque, $58
	2 October	General expenses paid by bank transfer, $67
	31 December	General expenses paid by online bank transfer, $49

An invoice for general expenses for $65 was received on 31 March 20–9. This was for general expenses up to the end of March but was not paid until 2 April 20–9.

Prepare the general expenses account in Zubair's nominal ledger for the year ended 31 March 20–9.

It may be helpful to draw a diagram before attempting to answer the question.

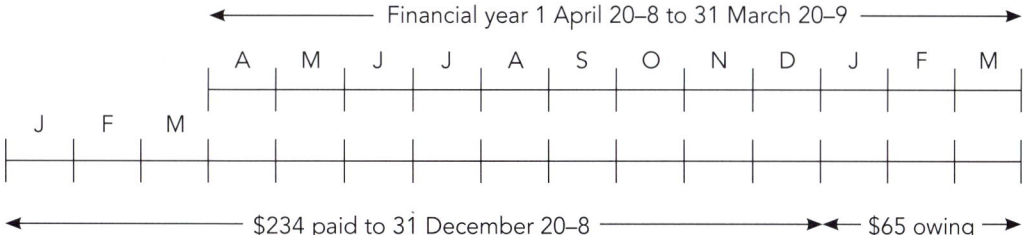

The diagram shows that the expenses paid do not match the period covered by the financial year, so it is necessary to:

- deduct the part of the $234 which falls outside the financial year ($60 was paid during this financial year but related to the previous accounting period)
- add the amount owing at the end of the present financial year to the amount that has been paid during the year.

Zubair
Nominal ledger

Dr				General expenses account				Cr
			$					$
20–8				20–8				
Apr 5	Cash		60	Apr 1	Balance		b/d	60
Jun 30	Bank		58	20–9				
Oct 2	Bank		67	Mar 31	Statement of profit or loss			239
Dec 31	Bank		49					
20–9								
Mar 31	Balance	c/d	65					
			299					299
				20–9				
				Apr 1	Balance		b/d	65

CONTINUED

- At the end of March 20–9, $65 is due but unpaid, so this is carried down as a credit balance to start the next financial year.
- At the end of the financial year, the difference on the account was $239. This is credited to the general expenses account and included in the statement of profit or loss with the other expenses, which is equal to making a debit entry. (This represents the expense for the year and is the value calculated using the diagram.)

WORKED EXAMPLE 11.5

Zubair's financial year ends on 31 March.

On 1 April 20–8, the insurance account in Zubair's nominal ledger showed a debit balance of $240.

He paid $1 080 for one year's insurance on his premises by direct debit on 1 July 20–8.

Prepare the insurance account in Zubair's nominal ledger for the year ended 31 March 20–9.

It may be helpful to draw a diagram before attempting to answer the question.

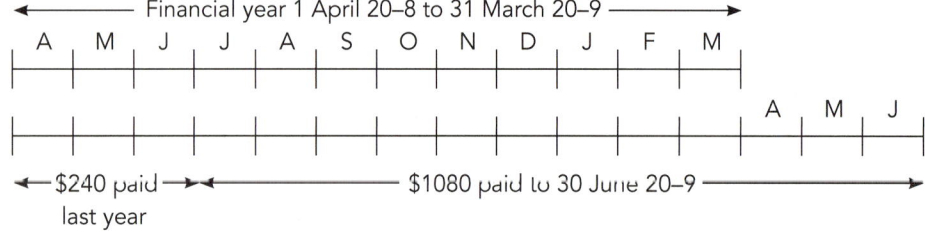

The diagram shows that the expenses paid do not match the period covered by the financial year, so it is necessary to:

- deduct the part of the $1 080 which falls outside the financial year (3 months/12 months or ¼ of $1 080 relates to the following financial year)
- add the amount of $240 paid in the previous financial year to the amount that has been paid during the year as it relates to the present financial year.

Zubair
Nominal ledger
Insurance account

Dr								Cr
				$				$
20–8					20–9			
Apr 1	Balance		b/d	240	Mar 31	Statement of profit or loss		1 050
Jul 1	Bank			1 080		Balance	c/d	270
				1 320				1 320
20–9								
Apr 1	Balance		b/d	270				

- At the end of March 20–9, $270 is paid in advance, so this is carried down as a debit balance to start the next financial year.
- At the end of the financial year, the difference on the account was $1 050. This is credited to the insurance account and included in the statement of profit or loss with the other expenses, which is equal to making a debit entry. (This represents the expense for the year and is the value calculated using the diagram.)

11 Other payables and other receivables

ACTIVITY 11.2

Kulsuma started a business on 1 April 20–1. She rented a shop and agreed to pay a total of $5 200 rent for the year ending 31 March 20–2 and a total of $5 720 for the year ending 31 March 20–3. Kulsuma paid rent totalling $5 000 during the year ended 31 March 20–2 and paid $6 360 during the year ended 31 March 20–3.

Calculate:

a   the balance brought down on the rent expense account on 1 April 20–2 and on 1 April 20–3, stating whether it was a debit or a credit balance

b   the amount of the rent expense in the statement of profit or loss for each of the years ended 31 March 20–2 and 31 March 20–3

c   the amount shown for rent in the statement of financial position on 31 March 20–2 and 31 March 20–3, indicating whether it was a current asset or a current liability.

11.3 Combined expense accounts

Sometimes a business may use one ledger account for two different, but related, expenses. The same principles are applied as those used for an account containing a single expense. The only difference is that there may be two opening and closing balances.

WORKED EXAMPLE 11.6

Martha's financial year ends on 31 March. She maintains a combined account for rent and rates. On 1 April 20–8, Martha had prepaid one month's rates, $240, and owed two months' rent, totalling $1 200. During the year ended 31 March 20–9, Martha made the following online payments:

20–8		$
1 May	Rent for 8 months to 30 September 20–8	4 800
1 June	Rates for 13 months to 31 May 20–9	3 120
1 December	Rent for 5 months to 28 February 20–9	3 000

Prepare the rent and rates account in Martha's nominal ledger for the year ended 31 March 20–9.

Before attempting to answer the question, it may be helpful to draw a diagram.

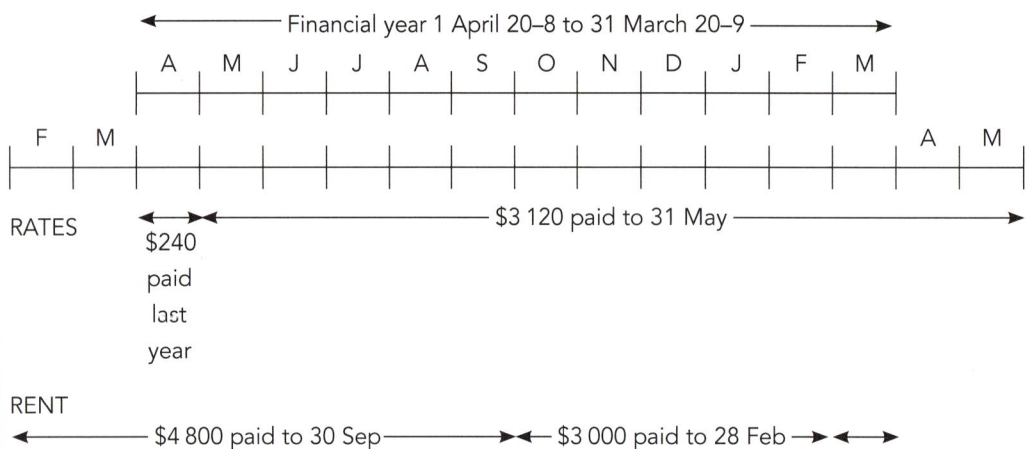

The diagram shows that the expenses paid for both the rent and the rates do not match the period covered by the financial year, so it is necessary to make some adjustments.

For the rates:

- deduct the part of the $3 120 which falls outside the financial year (2 months/13 months of $3 120 relates to the following financial year)

- add the amount of $240 paid in the previous financial year to the amount that has been paid during the year as it relates to the present financial year.

For the rent:

- add the $600 owing at the end of the present financial year to the amount that has been paid during the year

- deduct the part of the $4 800 paid in the current financial year which falls outside the financial year (2 months/8 months or ¼ of $4 800 relates to the previous financial year).

CONTINUED

Martha
Nominal ledger

Dr			Rent and rates account				Cr
			$				$
20–8				20–8			
Apr 1	Balance (rates)	b/d	240	Apr 1	Balance (rent)	b/d	1 200
May 1	Bank (rent)		4 800	20–9			
Jun 1	Bank (rates)		3 120	Mar 31	Statement of profit or loss		
Dec 1	Bank (rent)		3 000		Rent 7 200		
20–9					Rates 2 880		10 080
Mar 31	Balance (rent)	c/d	600		Balance (rates)	c/d	480
			11 760				11 760
20–9				20–9			
Apr 1	Balance (rates)	b/d	480	Apr 1	Balance (rent)	b/d	600

- There is an opening debit balance for rates because one month was prepaid and an opening credit balance for rent because two months was owing.

- At the end of March 20–9, rates of $480 is paid in advance, so this is carried down as a debit balance to start the next financial year. On the same date, rent of $600 is still owing, so this is carried down as a credit balance.

- At the end of the financial year, the difference on the account is $10 080. This is credited to the rent and rates account and included in the statement of profit or loss with the other expenses, which is equal to making a debit entry. (This represents the expense for the year of $7 200 for rent and $2 880 for rates, which are the values calculated using the diagram.)

11.4 Accrued and prepaid income

Accrued income

Accrued income (where an item of income is accrued) – it means that another person receiving a benefit or service from the business during the accounting period has not paid for that benefit or service by the end of the period.

The totals of income accounts in the nominal ledger are transferred to the statement of profit or loss at the end of the financial year. The matching/accruals concept is applied to income in the same way as it is to expenses so that the amount transferred to the statement of profit or loss represents the income for the accounting period covered by that statement. This means that any amount due but not yet received at the end of the financial year must be added to the amount received and the total income relating to the accounting period transferred to the statement of profit or loss.

> **KEY TERM**
>
> **accrued income:** income relating to a particular accounting period which has not been received at the end of that period.

The income account will now show a balance equal to the amount not yet received. To complete the double entry, this balance is brought down on the debit side of the ledger account. As the balance represents an amount owing to the business due to be received in the near future, it will be included as a current asset in the statement of financial position.

The entries are as follows:

During the year

- Credit the income account and debit the cash book with the amount received.

At the year-end

- Credit the income account with any amount due but not received and carry down as a debit balance.

- Debit the income account with the difference on the income account (this represents the income for the year). Include this amount with the other items of income in the statement of profit or loss which is equal to making a credit entry as the statement is part of the double entry system.

- Include the balance on the income account as a current asset in the statement of financial position.

WORKED EXAMPLE 11.7

Zubair started a business on 1 April 20–7.

On that date, he also agreed to act as an agent for Kohli & Company. Zubair was to be paid a commission at the end of every six months on all goods sold for Kohli & Company during that period.

Commission of $300 was received by direct debit on 1 October 20–7 and $280 was received by direct debit on 2 April 20–8.

a   Prepare the commission income account in Zubair's nominal ledger for the year ended 31 March 20–8.

b   Prepare a relevant extract from Zubair's statement of profit or loss for the year ended 31 March 20–8.

c   Prepare a relevant extract from Zubair's statement of financial position at 31 March 20–8.

Before attempting to answer the question, it may be helpful to draw a diagram.

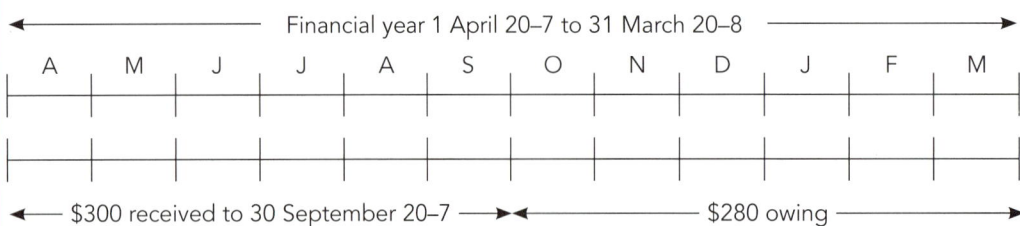

The diagram shows that the income received does not match the period covered by the financial year, so it is necessary to add the amount not yet received at the end of the year.

11 Other payables and other receivables

CONTINUED

a

Zubair
Nominal ledger

Dr			Commission income account					Cr
			$					$
20–8				20–7				
Mar 31	Statement of profit or loss		580	Oct 1	Bank			300
				20–8				
				Mar 31	Balance	c/d		280
			580					580
20–8								
Apr 1	Balance	b/d	280					

- At the end of March 20–8, commission of $280 has been earned but not received, so this is carried down as a debit balance to start the next financial year.

- At the end of the financial year, there were no entries on the debit side of the account, so the difference on the account was $580. This is debited to the commission income account and included in the statement of profit or loss with the other items of income, which is equal to making a credit entry. (This represents the income for the year and is the value calculated using the diagram.)

b

Zubair
Extract from statement of profit or loss for the year ended 31 March 20–8

	$
Gross profit	xxx
Add Commission income	580

- The commission income relating to the financial year ended on 31 March 20–8 amounts to $580, which is the total received plus the amount due but not yet received.

- The commission income would be listed with the other items of income in the statement of profit or loss and added to the gross profit.

c

Zubair
Extract from statement of financial position at 31 March 20–8

	$
Current assets	xxx
Income accrued	280

- The commission due but not yet received would appear in the statement of financial position as a current asset under the description of income accrued. Alternatively, it could be included in the other receivables (in this case, a note to the statement of financial position would show the breakdown of this figure).

> **DISCUSSION**
>
> Discuss these questions with a partner:
>
> 1 What is the difference between accruals and prepayments?
>
> 2 Imagine a member of the class is finding it difficult to understand why an accrued expense is a liability but an accrued income is an asset. How can you explain this to them?

Prepaid income

Prepaid income (where an item of income is prepaid) – it means that another person had paid for a benefit or service from the business, but this benefit or service has not been provided by the business at the end of the financial year.

Once again, the matching/accruals concept must be applied so that the amount transferred to the statement of profit or loss represents the income for the accounting period covered by that statement. Any amount received during the financial year relating to a future accounting period must be deducted from the amount received so that only the income relating to the accounting period is transferred to the statement of profit or loss.

The income account will now show a balance equal to the amount received in advance. To complete the double entry, this balance is brought down on the credit side of the ledger account. This balance will be included as a current liability in the statement of financial position as the business has a liability to provide some service or benefit for which the business has already been paid.

The entries are as follows:

During the year

- Credit the income account and debit the cash book with the amount received.

At the year-end

- Debit the income account with any amount received in advance and carry down as a credit balance.
- Debit the income account with the difference on the income account (this represents the income for the year). Include this amount with the other items of income in the statement of profit or loss, which is equal to making a credit entry as the statement is part of the double entry system.
- Include the balance on the income account as a current liability in the statement of financial position.

> **KEY TERM**
>
> **prepaid income:** income received during a particular accounting period which relates to a future accounting period.

11 Other payables and other receivables

WORKED EXAMPLE 11.8

Zubair started a business on 1 April 20–7.

Zubair rented premises until 1 July 20–7 when he purchased premises. On that date, he rented out part of his premises to another trader at an annual rent of $2 400, payable quarterly in advance.

The tenant paid rent of $600 by direct debit on 1 July 20–7, 1 October 20–7, 31 December 20–7 and 30 March 20–8.

a Prepare the rent income account in Zubair's nominal ledger for the year ended 31 March 20–8.

b Prepare a relevant extract from Zubair's statement of profit or loss for the year ended 31 March 20–8.

c Prepare a relevant extract from Zubair's statement of financial position at 31 March 20–8.

Before attempting to answer the question, it may be helpful to draw a diagram.

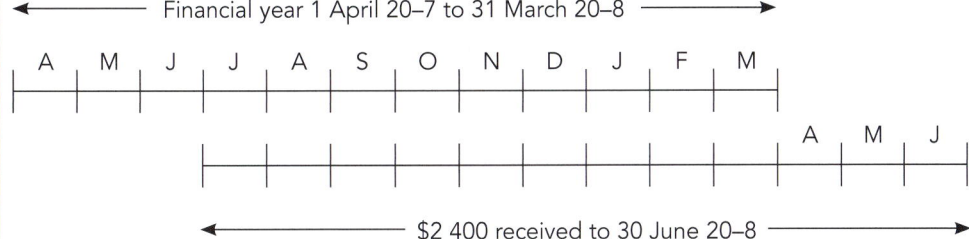

The diagram shows that the income received does not match the period covered by the financial year, so it is necessary to deduct that part of the $2 400, which falls outside the financial year ($600 relates to the following financial year).

a

Zubair
Nominal ledger

Dr		Rent income account					Cr
			$				$
20–8				20–7			
Mar 31	Statement of profit or loss		1 800	Jul 1	Bank		600
	Balance	c/d	600	Oct 1	Bank		600
				Dec 31	Bank		600
				20–8			
				Mar 30	Bank		600
			2 400				2 400
				20–8			
				Apr 1	Balance	b/d	600

- At the end of March 20–8, $600 is paid in advance for the following year, so this is carried down as a credit balance to start the next financial year.

- At the end of the financial year, the difference on the account is $1 800. This is debited to the rent income account and credited to the statement of profit or loss. (This represents the income for the year and is the value calculated using the diagram.)

CONTINUED

b

Zubair Extract from statement of profit or loss for the year ended 31 March 20–8	
	$
Gross profit	xxx
Add Rent income	1 800

- The rent income relating to the financial year ended on 31 March 20–8 amounts to $1 800, which is the rent received for the period 1 July 20–7 to 31 March 20–8.
- The rent income would be listed with the other items of income in the statement of profit or loss and added to the gross profit.

c

Zubair Extract from statement of financial position at 31 March 20–8	
	$
Current liabilities	xxx
Income prepaid	600

- The rent income in advance would appear in the statement of financial position as a current liability under the description of income prepaid. Alternatively, it could be included in the other payables (in this case, a note to the statement of financial position would show the breakdown of this figure).

11.5 Opening balances on income accounts

In the second and subsequent years of trading, a business may have opening balances on income accounts as well as opening balances on expense accounts. These must be considered when calculating the income relating to the particular financial year for which the accounts are prepared.

WORKED EXAMPLE 11.9

Zubair's financial year ends on 31 March.

He acts as an agent for Kohli & Company and is paid a commission at the end of every six months on all goods sold for Kohli & Company during that period.

On 1 April 20–8, the commission income account in Zubair's nominal ledger showed a debit balance of $280.

During the year ended 31 March 20–9, he received direct debits for commission as follows:

| 20–8 | 2 April | $280 |
| | 1 October | $295 |

At 31 March 20–9, commission due but not yet received amounted to $244.

Prepare the commission income account in Zubair's nominal ledger for the year ended 31 March 20–9.

Before attempting to answer the question, it may be helpful to draw a diagram.

CONTINUED

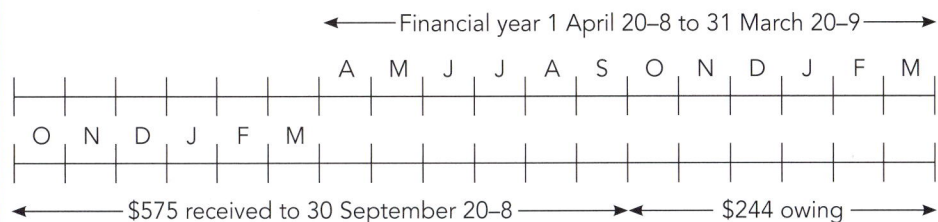

The diagram shows that the income received does not match the period covered by the financial year, so it is necessary to:

- deduct the part of the $575 which falls outside the financial year ($280 was received during this financial year but related to the previous accounting period)

- add the $244 owing at the end of present financial year to the amount that has been received during the year.

Zubair
Nominal ledger
Commission income account

Dr				$					Cr $
20–8					20–8				
Apr 1	Balance		b/d	280	Apr 2	Bank			280
20–9					Oct 1	Bank			295
Mar 31	Statement of profit or loss			539	20–9				
					Mar 31	Balance	c/d		244
				819					819
20–9									
Apr 1	Balance		b/d	244					

- At the end of March 20–9, $244 has been earned but not received, so this is carried down as a debit balance to start the next financial year.

- At the end of the financial year, the difference on the account is $539. This is debited to the commission income account and included in the statement of profit or loss with the other items of income. (This represents the income for the year and is the value calculated using the diagram.)

WORKED EXAMPLE 11.10

Zubair's financial year ends on 31 March.

He rents part of his premises to another trader at an annual rent of $2 400, payable quarterly in advance.

On 1 April 20–8, the rent income account in Zubair's nominal ledger showed a credit balance of $600.

The tenant paid rent of $600 by direct debit on 1 July 20–8 and 2 October 20–8. The rent due on 1 January 20–9 was not received until 2 April 20–9.

Prepare the rent income account in Zubair's nominal ledger for the year ended 31 March 20–9.

Before attempting to answer the question, it may be helpful to draw a diagram.

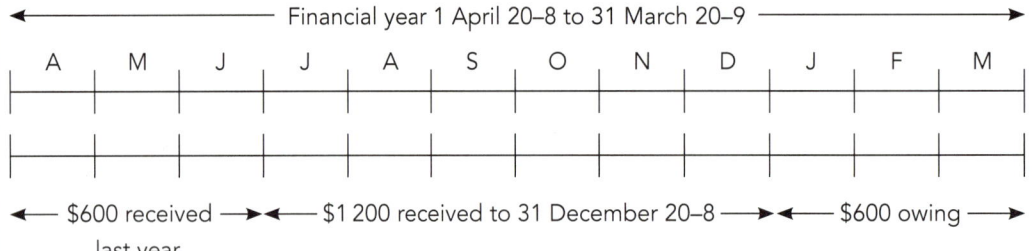

The diagram shows that the income received does not match the period covered by the financial year, so it is necessary to:

- add the $600 received in the previous financial year as it falls within the present financial year.

- add the $600 owing at the end of present financial year to the amount that has been paid during the year.

Zubair
Nominal ledger

Dr			Rent income account				Cr
			$				$
20–8				20–8			
Mar 31	Statement of profit or loss		2 400	Apr 1	Balance	b/d	600
				Jul 1	Bank		600
				Oct 2	Bank		600
				20–9			
				Mar 31	Balance	c/d	600
			2 400				2 400
20–9							
Apr 1	Balance	b/d	600				

- At the end of March 20–9, $600 is due but has not been received, so this is carried down as a debit balance to start the next financial year.

- At the end of the financial year, the difference on the account was $2 400. This is debited to the rent income account and included in the statement of profit or loss with the other items of income, which is equal to making a credit entry. (This represents the income for the year and is the value calculated using the diagram.)

11 Other payables and other receivables

ACTIVITY 11.3

Mukondi's financial year ends on 31 December. She acted as an agent for Barak and was paid a commission at the end of each calendar year on goods sold during that year. Barak cancelled the agreement on 31 December 20–7 and made full payment of all fees owed to Mukondi.

Mukondi provided the following information.

20–6

Jan	1	Commission, $219, was owing to Mukondi
Dec	30	Commission, $1 676, received by online bank transfer
	31	Commission, $199, was owing to Mukondi

20–7

| Dec | 31 | Commission, $1 816, received by cheque |

a Prepare the commission income account for the year ended 31 December 20–7.

b State the amount shown for commission income in the statement of profit or loss for each of the years ended 31 December 20–6 and 31 December 20–7.

c State the amount (if any) shown for commission income in the statement of financial position on 31 December 20–6 and 31 December 20–7, indicating whether it is a current asset or a current liability.

REFLECTION

This chapter has explained about accrued and prepaid expenses and accrued and prepaid incomes. There have been lots of examples showing how these are recorded in the ledger and in the year-end financial statements.

What can you do to help yourself remember? What methods can you use to summarise what you have learnt in this chapter to help you remember key bits of information? For example, you might find it helpful to draw diagrams, tables or mind maps, or to think of (or invent) a word to help you remember lists of information.

Share your ideas with others in your class and try using some different strategies to discover which ones you find the most helpful.

ACCOUNTING IN ACTION

Dealing with accrued and prepaid income

Figure 11.4: A fitness studio might benefit from prepaid income

Anya is the owner of Be Fit Stay Fit, a popular fitness studio. She offers various fitness classes, from yoga and Pilates to high-intensity training. She is determined to help people lead healthier lifestyles. Her financial year ends on 30 April.

For several years, Anya has operated a system where clients pay a monthly fee in advance, which entitles them to attend classes during that month.

In January 20–7, Anya decided to introduce a new scheme of prepaid class packages to try to attract new clients and to encourage them to commit to classes for several months. These packages require clients to pay for 30 classes in advance, which they can then book in for at their convenience over a period of six months. At the end of April 20–7, several clients had not attended all the classes for which they had already paid. This was recorded as prepaid income in Be Fit Stay Fit's financial statements for the year ended 30 April 20–7.

A few members attended classes in April 20–7 but had not paid their monthly fee. This was recorded as accrued income in Be Fit Stay Fit's financial statements for the year ended 30 April 20–7.

Discuss in pairs or in a group:

1. How should accrued income be recorded in the financial statements of Be Fit Stay Fit?
2. How does prepaid income benefit Be Fit Stay Fit?
3. What would be the effect on the profit of Be Fit Stay Fit for the year ended 30 April 20–7 if no adjustment was made for prepaid and accrued expenses?

SUMMARY

You should now know:

- The expenses for an accounting period must be matched against the income of that particular period.
- An accrual is an amount due in an accounting period which remains unpaid at the end of that period.
- A prepayment is an amount that has been paid or received in one accounting period which relates to a future period.
- In the statement of profit or loss, an accrued expense is added to the amount which has already been paid for that particular expense. The accrued amount is a current liability in the statement of financial position.
- In the statement of profit or loss, a prepaid expense is deducted from the amount which has been paid for that particular expense. The prepaid amount is a current asset in the statement of financial position.

> **CONTINUED**
>
> - In the statement of profit or loss, accrued income is added to the amount which has already been received for that particular item of income. The accrued amount is a current asset in the statement of financial position.
>
> - In the statement of profit or loss, prepaid income is deducted from the amount received for that particular item of income. The amount received in advance is a current liability in the statement of financial position.

Chapter 11 practice questions

1 Zaid's financial year ends on 31 October. On 1 November 20–6, he owed advertising costs of $40. During the year ended 31 October 20–7, he paid advertising costs of $530. This included $270 for an advertising campaign for six months to 29 February 20–8.

   How much was entered for advertising expenses in Zaid's statement of profit or loss for the year ended 31 October 20–7?

   A $220

   B $260

   C $310

   D $350   [1]

2 Aryani started a fashion boutique on 1 March 20–6. On that date, she purchased stationery, $395. During the year, she took stationery, $15, for her own use. On 28 February 20–7, the stationery was valued at $174. How much was entered for stationery in Aryani's statement of profit or loss for the year ended 28 February 20–7?

   A $206

   B $221

   C $236

   D $380   [1]

3 Nasir's financial year ends on 31 December. On 1 April 20–9, she moved into new premises and paid $3 000 for one year's rent of new premises.

   What entry would be made for rent in the statement of financial position on 31 December 20–9?

   A $750 asset

   B $750 liability

   C $2 250 asset

   D $2 250 liability   [1]

4 Wasim is a trader. His financial year ends on 31 December.
   He started to rent premises on 1 January 20–1. It was agreed that the rent would be $950 a month for the first 12 months and then increase to $1 050. Wasim paid six months' rent in advance by bank transfer on 1 January, 1 July and 31 December 20–1.

   a i   Prepare the rent expense account in Wasim's ledger for the year ended 31 December 20–1.

      ii Balance the account and bring down the balance on 1 January 20–2.

      iii Prepare a relevant extract from Wasim's statement of financial position at 31 December 20–1. [6]

Wasim sublet part of his business premises to a tenant named Sadil. The monthly rent was $240. The rent income account in Wasim's ledger for the year ended 31 December 20–2 was as follows:

Dr					Wasim Rent income account				Cr
				$					$
20–2					20–2				
Jan 1	Balance		b/d	480	Jan 10	Bank			1 920
Dec 31	Statement of profit or loss			2 880	Jun 1	Bank			2 160
	Balance		c/d	720					
				4 080					4 080
					20–3				
					Jan 1	Balance		b/d	720

   b i   Name the ledger in which this account would appear.

      ii Explain each entry in the account.

      iii State where the balance on the account on 31 December 20–3 would appear in the statement of financial position. [7]

On 1 January 20–2, Wasim had stationery valued at $50.

During the year ended 31 December 20–2, the following transactions took place:

February 1 Purchased stationery, $46, and paid in cash

August 31 Purchased stationery, $12, using petty cash

Wasim's inventory of stationery on 31 December 20–2 was valued at $33.

   c Prepare the stationery account in Wasim's ledger for the year ended 31 December 20–2. Balance the account and bring down the balance on 1 January 20–3. [4]

[Total: 17]

5 Reheeq owns a wholesale furniture store. His financial year ends on 30 June. He provided the following trial balance on 30 June 20–1:

	Dr $	Cr $
Revenue		125 600
Purchases	92 350	
Purchases returns		610
Inventory 1 July 20–0	8 150	
Property	100 000	
Fixtures and fittings	20 100	
Trade payables		8 070
Trade receivables	10 060	
Bank	6 710	
Rent income		1 020
Discount received		200
Insurance	1 120	
Rates	600	
Wages	28 300	
Office expenses	310	
Capital		124 000
Drawings	1 800	
4% 10-year loan from AB Finance		10 000
	269 500	269 500

Additional information:

1. At 30 June 20–1:
   Inventory was valued at $9 110
   Rent income prepaid amounted to $50
   Insurance prepaid amounted to $160
   Rates accrued amounted to $120
   A whole year's interest on the loan was outstanding.

2. During the year ended 30 June 20–1, Reheeq took goods, $620, for his own use. This was not entered in the accounting records.

Prepare a statement of profit or loss for the year ended 30 June 20–1 and a statement of financial position on 30 June 20–1. [20]

6 Magda is a business consultant. She provided the following information at the end of her first year on 30 September 20–4.

	$
Office expenses	5 970
Wages	33 600
Insurance	1 800
Rates	1 860
Motor vehicle expenses	1 180
Fees received from clients	52 150
Commission income	4 700

The following information is also available:

1. On 30 September 20–4:
   Rates due amounted to $540
   Office expenses due amounted to $110
   Commission income outstanding amounted to $180

2. The office expenses include stationery. On 30 September 20–4, the inventory of stationery was valued at $190.

3. The insurance covers a period of 15 months to 31 December 20–4.

4. Wages paid in cash, $210, have not been entered in the accounting records.

5. It is estimated that half of the motor vehicle expenses relate to Magda's personal use.

Prepare Magda's statement of profit or loss for the year ended 30 September 20–4. [8]

CHECK YOUR PROGRESS

How well do you think you have achieved the learning intentions for this chapter? Give yourself a score from 1 (still need a lot of practice) to 5 (feeling very confident) for each learning intention. Provide an example to support your score.

Now I can …	Score	Example to support score
understand why it is important to apply the matching/accruals concept to incomes and expenses		
prepare ledger accounts to record accrued and prepaid expenses		
prepare ledger accounts to record accrued and prepaid incomes		
make adjustments in financial statements for accrued and prepaid expenses		
make adjustments in financial statements for accrued and prepaid incomes.		

Chapter 12

Accounting for depreciation and disposal of non-current assets

LEARNING INTENTIONS

By the end of this chapter, you will be able to:
- explain the meaning of depreciation and the reasons for accounting for depreciation
- use the straight line, reducing balance and revaluation methods to calculate depreciation
- prepare ledger accounts for the provision for depreciation and to record the sale of non-current assets, including the use of asset disposal accounts.

Introduction

As explained in Chapter 11, it is often necessary to include year-end adjustments in a set of financial statements. This ensures that the accounts provide a more accurate view of the profit or loss of the business and the financial position of the business. This chapter focuses on the year-end adjustments made for depreciation of non-current assets.

Depreciation is an estimate of the loss in value of a non-current asset over its expected working life. Most of the non-current assets of a business lose value over the period of time that they are used by the business. If the accounting records continue to show these assets at their cost prices, then the accounts will provide misleading information. It is therefore necessary to record an estimate of the loss in value. The records can only show an estimate of the loss in value of a non-current asset through depreciation. The exact amount will only be known when the asset is disposed of or sold. Buildings depreciate over time, but land does not usually lose value (unless it is something like a well or a mine, where value is removed from the land).

> **KEY TERM**
>
> **depreciation:** an estimate of the loss in value of a non-current asset over its expected working life.

ACCOUNTING IN CONTEXT

Himari's bicycle repairs

Figure 12.1: Equipment for repairing bicycles is a non-current asset

Most businesses need non-current assets for use within the business to help the business earn revenue. These assets may be machinery, equipment, fixtures and fittings, motor vehicles and so on. Some of these assets may be purchased when the business is set up and others may be purchased later when they are needed.

Himari operates a bicycle repair business. He has a workshop where people can bring their bicycles for him to repair.

Himari has a built up a good reputation for high-quality work and fair prices, and his business has been doing very well. He hopes to expand the business by replacing some of his old tools and buying new equipment so that he can start to repair electric bikes. The bank balance of the business is quite healthy, and Himari is considering using some of this money to purchase the new equipment. He has also considered the possibility of obtaining a bank loan, which would provide more funds for expansion.

Discuss in pairs or in a group:

1. What factors should Himari consider when deciding whether to purchase new equipment?
2. What effect will purchasing new equipment have on his financial statements?

12 Accounting for depreciation and disposal of non-current assets

12.1 How depreciation affects the financial statements

The purchase of a non-current asset is capital expenditure.

The cost of a non-current asset is not charged as an expense in the year of purchase as it benefits the business for several years. Matching the capital expenditure against the sales it has helped the business to earn is done by an annual charge for depreciation. This means that the cost of the non-current asset is spread over the years in which the business benefits from the use of that asset. This is an application of the matching/accruals concept.

The depreciation for the year is included in the expenses in the statement of profit or loss, so the profit for the year is not overstated. This is an application of the prudence concept. If the profit is overstated, the owner of a business may think that the business is more profitable than it actually is. In these circumstances, they may be tempted to draw too much out of the business.

The prudence concept is also applied in the statement of financial position, as the non-current assets are recorded at a figure less than the cost price (which is known as the net book value or the written down value). This overrides the historic cost concept as it ensures that the non-current assets are shown at more realistic values.

Depreciation is a non-monetary expense as it does not involve an outflow of money, nor does it provide a cash fund to use for the replacement of a non-current asset.

> **LINKS**
>
> You learnt about capital expenditure and the accounting concepts of matching/accruals, prudence and historic cost in Chapter 10, and about year-end adjustments for other payables and other receivables in Chapter 11. You will learn about other year-end adjustments in Chapter 13.

12.2 Causes of depreciation

The four main causes of depreciation are: physical deterioration, economic reasons, passage of time and depletion.

Physical deterioration

This is the result of 'wear and tear' owing to the normal usage of the non-current asset. It can also be because the asset falls into a poor physical state from rust, rot, decay and so on.

Economic reasons

The non-current asset may become inadequate when it can no longer meet the needs of the business. It can also be because the non-current asset has become out of date as newer and more efficient assets become available.

Passage of time

This arises where a non-current asset, such as a lease, has a fixed life of a set number of years.

Depletion

This arises with non-current assets such as wells and mines. The worth of the asset reduces as value is taken from the asset.

ACTIVITY 12.1

Figure 12.2: Fishing boats will lose value over time

Copy out the following table and complete it by stating the most likely cause of depreciation for each of the non-current assets.

Non-current asset	Likely cause of depreciation
Office computer system	
Gold mine	
Property on a 99-year lease	
Wooden fishing boat	
Delivery van	
20-year-old printing machine	

DISCUSSION

With a partner, discuss a business you both know about.

1. What non-current assets might they have?
2. What would be the most likely cause of depreciation for each of these non-current assets?

12.3 Methods of calculating depreciation

There are several methods used to calculate the estimated loss in value of a non-current asset. Different types of non-current assets are often depreciated using different methods. The method selected should be the one which spreads the cost of the asset as fairly as possible over the periods which benefit from its use.

Once a method has been selected for a particular non-current asset, it should be applied each year. This is an application of the consistency concept.

In practice, many factors are considered before a depreciation method is selected. For example:

- How long is the asset expected to last?
- How much will the asset be sold for when it is put out of use?
- How can the benefits from the use of the asset be measured?

There are three main methods of depreciation:

- Straight line method
- Reducing balance method
- Revaluation method

LINK

You learnt about the consistency concept in Chapter 10.

12 Accounting for depreciation and disposal of non-current assets

Straight line method of depreciation

The **straight line method of depreciation** is also known as the fixed instalment method.

The formula used for calculating the annual depreciation using this method is:

$$\frac{\text{Cost of asset}}{\text{Number of expected years of use}}$$

This expresses the annual depreciation as an amount of money.

This method applies the same amount of depreciation (or the same percentage rate of the cost price) each year.

This method is used where each year is expected to benefit equally from the use of the asset.

> **KEY TERM**
>
> **straight line method of depreciation:** the method where the same amount of depreciation is charged each year.

WORKED EXAMPLE 12.1

Vijay's financial year ends on 30 June.

On 1 July 20–3, he purchased office equipment costing $30 000 and paid by credit transfer. Vijay estimated that he would be able to use the office equipment for four years.

Calculate the annual depreciation charge:

a as an amount of money
b as a percentage.

a Annual depreciation = $\dfrac{\text{Cost of asset}}{\text{Number of expected years of use}} = \dfrac{\$30\,000}{4 \text{ years}} = \$7\,500$

b $\dfrac{\$7\,500}{\$30\,000} \times \dfrac{100\%}{1} = 25\%$

When using the formula to calculate the annual depreciation charge in Worked example 12.1, it is assumed that the value of the asset has fallen to nil by the end of its working life. However, where it is estimated that the asset will have some value at the end of its working life, this must be included in the calculation. This value is known as a **residual value**. The formula then becomes:

$$\frac{\text{Cost of asset} - \text{Residual value}}{\text{Number of expected years of use}}$$

> **KEY TERM**
>
> **residual value:** the value of a non-current asset at the end of its useful life.

WORKED EXAMPLE 12.2

Vijay's financial year ends on 30 June.

On 1 July 20–3, he purchased office equipment costing $30 000 and paid by credit transfer. Vijay estimated that he would be able to use the office equipment for four years and then be able to sell it for $3 600.

Calculate the annual depreciation charge:

a as an amount of money

b as a percentage (based on the original cost).

a Annual depreciation = $\dfrac{\text{Cost of asset} - \text{Residual value}}{\text{Number of expected years of use}} = \dfrac{\$30\,000 - \$3\,600}{4 \text{ years}} = \$6\,600$

b $\dfrac{\$6\,600}{\$30\,000} \times \dfrac{100\%}{1} = 22\%$

Table 12.1: Advantages and disadvantages of the straight line method of depreciation

Advantages	Disadvantages
It is relatively easy to calculate.	It is necessary to estimate the useful life and the residual value of the non-current asset.
It is useful when a non-current asset provides equal benefit for each year of its working life.	It ignores the actual rate at which the non-current asset will lose value.

Reducing balance method of depreciation

With the **reducing balance method of depreciation**, the amount of depreciation reduces each year. The same percentage rate is applied, but it is calculated on a different value each year. At the end of the first year, the depreciation for that year is calculated on the cost of the asset. The depreciation for the following year is calculated (using the same percentage) on the cost of the asset less the depreciation previously written off. The figure of cost less depreciation is known as the **net book value** (or written down value) of the asset.

The value of the asset can never fall to nil as the depreciation is always calculated as a percentage of the net book value.

> **KEY TERMS**
>
> **reducing balance method of depreciation:** the method where the depreciation charged each year decreases as it is calculated on the net book value rather than the cost.
>
> **net book value:** the cost price of a non-current asset minus the accumulated depreciation to date.

12 Accounting for depreciation and disposal of non-current assets

This method is used when the greater benefits will be gained from the use of the asset in the early years of its life. Assets depreciated by this method often have lower maintenance costs in the early years. This method is often used for those assets which become out of date quickly because of advancing technological progress.

Any residual value is taken into consideration when the percentage rate is selected.

WORKED EXAMPLE 12.3

Vijay's financial year ends on 30 June.

On 1 July 20–3, he purchased office equipment costing $30 000 and paid by credit transfer. Vijay estimated that he would be able to use the office equipment for four years, and then be able to sell it for $3 500.

Calculate the depreciation for each of the four years of the working life of the office equipment using the reducing balance method at the rate of 40% per annum.

	$
Cost	30 000
Depreciation for year ended 30 June 20–4 at 40%	12 000
Book value at 1 July 20–4	18 000
Depreciation for year ended 30 June 20–5 at 40%	7 200
Book value at 1 July 20–5	10 800
Depreciation for year ended 30 June 20–6 at 40%	4 320
Book value at 1 July 20–6	6 480
Depreciation for year ended 30 June 20–7 at 40%	2 592
Book value at 1 July 20–7	3 888

> **TIP**
>
> Depreciation is always expressed in whole dollars so you may need to adjust a figure to eliminate any cents. Where this occurs, you should round the figure up to the next whole dollar.

Table 12.2: Advantages and disadvantages of the reducing balance method of depreciation

Advantages	Disadvantages
It follows the matching/accruals concept.	The depreciation has to be recalculated each year.
It is useful for those non-current assets where greater benefits are gained in the early years of usage.	The depreciation charge against profit is greater in the early years of the non-current asset's life.

ACTIVITY 12.2

Hashir makes and sells clothes. He purchased a new sewing machine costing $400. He thinks it will have a working life of four years and hopes to receive $40 when he trades it in against a new machine after four years.

a   Calculate the depreciation for each year using:

   i   the straight line method of depreciation

   ii   the reducing balance method of depreciation at 45% per annum (where necessary you should round up the amounts to the next whole number).

b   Discuss with a partner which method of depreciation is the most appropriate. Write a note to Hashir to advise him which method to use and why.

Revaluation method of depreciation

The **revaluation method of depreciation** is used where it is not practical (or where it is difficult) to keep detailed records of certain types of non-current assets. If detailed records are not available, then the straight line and the reducing balance methods of depreciation cannot be calculated. Small items of equipment used in offices and laboratories, packing cases, hand tools and so on are usually depreciated using the revaluation method as no detailed records are kept for these assets.

The assets are valued at the end of each financial year. This value is compared with the value at the end of the previous financial year, or with the cost if it is the first year of ownership. The amount by which the value of the asset has fallen is the depreciation for the year.

> **KEY TERM**
>
> **revaluation method of depreciation:** the method where the opening and closing values of a non-current asset are compared (after adjusting for any additions during the year) to determine the depreciation for the year.

WORKED EXAMPLE 12.4

Vijay's financial year ends on 30 June.

On 1 July 20–3, he purchased office equipment costing $30 000 and paid by credit transfer. Vijay decided to revalue the office equipment at the end of each year.

On 30 June 20–4, the office equipment was valued at $24 000.

Calculate the depreciation for the year ended 30 June 20–4.

	$
Cost of office equipment on 1 July 20–3	30 000
Value of office equipment on 30 June 20–4	24 000
Depreciation for the year ended 30 June 20–4	6 000

Table 12.3: Advantages and disadvantages of the revaluation method of depreciation

Advantages	Disadvantages
It is not necessary to estimate the useful life and the residual value of the non-current asset.	The non-current asset has to be revalued at the end of each year.
No complex calculations are required.	The valuation may be based on personal opinion.

> **REFLECTION**
>
> You have now learnt about the three main methods of depreciation.
>
> What will you do to help yourself remember the differences between the three methods, and the advantages and disadvantages of each? Discuss your strategies with a partner.

12.4 Recording depreciation in the ledger

Recording depreciation using the straight line method and the reducing balance method

The procedure for entering depreciation calculated using the straight line method and the reducing balance method is exactly the same.

Each type of non-current asset has two ledger accounts:

- an account for recording the cost of the asset (the asset account)
- an account for recording the depreciation (the provision for depreciation on asset account).

The asset account always has a debit balance and the provision for depreciation account always has a credit balance. These two accounts must always be considered together. The difference between the balances of these accounts represents the net book value of the asset.

The entries are as follows:

During the year (when the asset is purchased)

- Debit the non-current asset account.
- Credit either the bank account or the supplier's account (if purchased on credit).

At the end of the financial year

- Include the depreciation for the year with the other expenses in the statement of profit or loss – this is equal to making a debit entry as the statement is part of the double entry system.
- Credit the provision for depreciation on the asset account with the depreciation for the year.
- Balance the provision for depreciation on the asset account and carry down as a credit balance.
- Balance the non-current asset account if there have been any transactions during the year and carry down as a debit balance.

WORKED EXAMPLE 12.5

Vijay's financial year ends on 30 June.

On 1 July 20–3, he purchased office equipment costing $30 000 and paid by credit transfer. Vijay estimated that he would be able to use the office equipment for four years and then be able to sell it for $3 600.

Vijay decided to use the reducing balance method of depreciation at 40% per annum.

Prepare the office equipment account and the provision for depreciation on office equipment account in Vijay's nominal ledger for each of the years ended 30 June 20–4, 20–5, 20–6 and 20–7.

	Vijay		
	Nominal ledger		
Dr	**Office equipment account**		**Cr**
	$		$
20–3			
Jul 1 Bank	30 000		

- The non-current asset account is not balanced at the end of the year as there is only one entry in the account

CONTINUED

Dr				Provision for depreciation on office equipment account			Cr
			$				$
20–4				20–4			
Jun 30	Balance	c/d	12 000	Jun 30	Statement of profit or loss		12 000
			12 000				12 000
20–5				20–4			
Jun 30	Balance	c/d	19 200	Jul 1	Balance	b/d	12 000
				20–5			
				Jun 30	Statement of profit or loss		7 200
			19 200				19 200
20–6				20–5			
Jun 30	Balance	c/d	23 520	Jul 1	Balance	b/d	19 200
				20–6			
				Jun 30	Statement of profit or loss		4 320
			23 520				23 520
20–7				20–6			
Jun 30	Balance	c/d	26 112	Jul 1	Balance	b/d	23 520
				20–7			
				Jun 30	Statement of profit or loss		2 592
			26 112				26 112
				20–7			
				Jul 1	Balance	b/d	26 112

- Before the transfer to the statement of profit or loss can be made each year, it is necessary to calculate the depreciation for the year. These calculations are shown in **Worked example 12.3**.
- The difference between the balance on the non-current asset account and the balance on the provision for depreciation account on a particular date represents the net book value of the non-current asset on that date. So, on 1 July 20–7, the net book value of the office equipment is $30 000 – $26 112 = $3 888.

If the straight line method of depreciation had been used in **Worked example 12.5**, then:

- the entry in the office equipment account would be exactly the same
- the entries in the provision for depreciation on office equipment account would be very similar. The transfer to the statement of profit or loss would be $6 600 each year, so the totals and balances on the account would be different to those shown for the reducing balance method.

Where a non-current asset is purchased during the financial year, a business may decide to charge depreciation from the date of purchase. This means that in the first year of ownership, only a proportion of the annual depreciation will be charged to the statement of profit or loss.

WORKED EXAMPLE 12.6

Vijay's financial year ends on 30 June.

On 1 July 20–4, he purchased a motor vehicle costing $24 000 and paid by credit transfer. On 1 January 20–5, an additional motor vehicle costing $20 000 was purchased and paid for by bank transfer.

Vijay decided to use the straight line method of depreciation at 25% per annum, depreciation to be calculated from the date of purchase.

Prepare the motor vehicles account and the provision for depreciation on motor vehicles account in Vijay's nominal ledger for the year ended 30 June 20–5.

Vijay
Nominal ledger

Dr		Motor vehicles account					Cr
			$				$
20–4				20–5			
Jul 1	Bank (MV1)		24 000	Jun 30	Balance	c/d	44 000
20–5							
Jan 1	Bank (MV2)		20 000				
			44 000				44 000
20–5							
Jul 1	Balance	b/d	44 000				

Dr		Provision for depreciation on motor vehicles account					Cr
			$				$
20–5				20–5			
Jun 30	Balance	c/d	8 500	Jun 30	Statement of profit or loss		
					(MV1) 6 000		
					(MV2) 2 500		8 500
			8 500				8 500
				20–5			
				Jul 1	Balance	b/d	8 500

- The second motor vehicle (MV2) was bought on 1 January, so only half the annual depreciation has been charged.

Sometimes a business may decide to ignore the date of purchase when calculating depreciation. This means that a whole year's depreciation will be charged on all the assets held at the end of the financial year.

12 Accounting for depreciation and disposal of non-current assets

ACTIVITY 12.3

Sophia is a retail trader. Her first year of trading ended on 30 June 20–5.

She decided to depreciate her shop fixtures using the straight line method at a fixed annual percentage from the date of purchase.

Sophia's books include the following incomplete accounts for the year ended 30 June 20–5.

Sophia

Dr		Shop fixtures account			Cr
		$			$
20–4			20–5		
Jul 1	Bank (A)	2 500	Jun 30	Balance c/d	....
20–5					
Jan 1	YY Suppliers (B)	1 500			
		....			....
20–5					
....	Balance b/d	....			

Dr		Provision for depreciation on shop fixtures account			Cr
		$			$
20–5			20–5		
Jun 30	Balance c/d	....	Jun 30	Statement of profit or loss	
				(A) 500	
				(B)	....
		....			....
			20–5		
			Jul 1	.... b/d	....

a What annual percentage rate of depreciation did Sophia charge on her shop fixtures?

b Copy out the two accounts and insert the missing words and figures.

c Assuming no additional fixtures were purchased in the financial year ending 30 June 20–6, calculate the total depreciation charge for the year.

Recording depreciation using the revaluation method

The cost of the asset and the depreciation are recorded in the same account.

The entries are as follows:

During the year (when the asset is purchased)

- Debit the non-current asset account.
- Credit either the bank account or the supplier's account (if purchased on credit).

At the end of the financial year

- Credit the non-current asset account with the value of the asset at that date and carry down as a debit balance.
- Credit the non-current asset account with the difference on the account (which represents the depreciation for the year).
- Include the depreciation for the year with the other expenses in the statement of profit or loss – this is equal to making a debit entry as the statement is part of the double entry system.

12 Accounting for depreciation and disposal of non-current assets

WORKED EXAMPLE 12.7

Vijay's financial year ends on 30 June.

On 1 July 20–3, he purchased office equipment costing $30 000 and paid by credit transfer. Vijay decided to revalue the office equipment at the end of each year.

On 30 June 20–4, the office equipment was valued at $24 000.

Prepare the office equipment account and the provision for depreciation on office equipment account in the nominal ledger for the year ended 30 June 20–4.

Vijay
Nominal ledger

Dr			Office equipment account				Cr
			$				$
20–3				20–4			
Jul 1	Bank		30 000	Jun 30	Balance	c/d	24 000
					Statement of profit or loss		6 000
			30 000				30 000
20–4							
Jul 1	Balance	b/d	24 000				

12.5 Recording depreciation in the financial statements

Recording depreciation in the statement of profit or loss

The depreciation for the year for each type of non-current asset is credited to the provision for depreciation account in the nominal ledger and debited to the statement of profit or loss. This reduces the business's profit for the year. As depreciation is a non-monetary expense, it is usually shown after the monetary expenses in the statement of profit or loss.

If the business is a manufacturing business, depreciation of non-current assets used in the manufacturing process will be debited to the manufacturing account rather than the statement of profit or loss. This increases the cost of manufacturing, which in turn reduces the profit for the year.

Recording depreciation in the statement of financial position

It is usual to show the total cost of each type of non-current asset less the total depreciation written off up to the date of the statement of financial position (referred to as **accumulated depreciation**). The difference between these figures is the net book value.

> **LINK**
>
> You will learn about preparing manufacturing accounts in Chapter 20.

> **KEY TERM**
>
> **accumulated depreciation:** the total of all the depreciation which has been charged on a non-current asset.

> **WORKED EXAMPLE 12.8**

Vijay's financial year ends on 30 June.

On 1 July 20–3, he purchased office equipment costing $30 000 and paid by credit transfer. Vijay estimated that he would use the office equipment for four years and then be able to sell it for $3 600.

Vijay decided to use the reducing balance method of depreciation at 40% per annum.

a Prepare a relevant extract from Vijay's statement of profit or loss for **each** of the years ended 30 June 20–4 and 30 June 20–5.

b Prepare a relevant extract from Vijay's statement of financial position at 30 June 20–4 and at 30 June 20–5.

a

Vijay
Extract from statement of profit or loss for the year ended 30 June 20–4

	$
Expenses – Depreciation on office equipment	12 000

Vijay
Extract from statement of profit or loss for the year ended 30 June 20–5

	$
Expenses – Depreciation on office equipment	7 200

b

Vijay
Extract from statement of financial position at 30 June 20–4

Non-current assets	Cost $	Accumulated depreciation $	Net book value $
Office equipment	30 000	12 000	18 000

Vijay
Extract from statement of financial position at 30 June 20–5

Non-current assets	Cost $	Accumulated depreciation $	Net book value $
Office equipment	30 000	19 200	10 800

The financial statements are prepared from a trial balance and its accompanying notes. In the trial balance, the balances on the asset accounts are shown in the debit column and the balances on provision for depreciation accounts are shown in the credit column. One of the notes will indicate the depreciation to be charged for the current financial year.

> **LINKS**
>
> You learnt how to prepare financial statements in Chapters 8–9.

12 Accounting for depreciation and disposal of non-current assets

The depreciation for the year will appear twice in the financial statements: it is an expense in the statement of profit or loss, and it is included in the statement of financial position as part of the accumulated depreciation (the depreciation for the year is added to the balance of the provision for depreciation account shown in the trial balance).

WORKED EXAMPLE 12.9

Vijay's financial year ends on 30 June.

He depreciates his office equipment using the reducing balance method of depreciation at 40% per annum.

Vijay's trial balance on 30 June 20–6 included the following:

	Dr	Cr
	$	$
Office equipment	30 000	
Provision for depreciation on office equipment		19 200

a Prepare a relevant extract from Vijay's statement of profit or loss for the year ended 30 June 20–6.

b Prepare a relevant extract from Vijay's statement of financial position at 30 June 20–6.

a

Vijay
Extract from statement of profit or loss for the year ended 30 June 20–6

	$
Expenses – Depreciation on office equipment	4 320

- The depreciation relating to the current financial year is included as an expense in the statement of profit or loss.

b

Vijay
Extract from statement of financial position at 30 June 20–6

	$	$	$
Non-current assets	Cost	Accumulated depreciation	Net book value
Office equipment	30 000	23 520	6 480

- In the statement of financial position, the total depreciation up to that date ($19 200 shown in the trial balance plus the depreciation for the year of $4 320) is deducted from the cost price of the asset to give the net book value of the asset.

> **TIP**
> Remember: a statement of profit or loss shows the depreciation of a non-current asset for that particular year, whereas a statement of financial position shows the cost and the accumulated depreciation of the asset.

12.6 Disposal of non-current assets

Figure 12.3: When a motor vehicle is sold it is a capital receipt

The purchase of a non-current asset is capital expenditure, so it is recorded in an account for the non-current asset rather than in the purchases account. When a non-current asset is sold, it is a capital receipt and is recorded in a special account known as an asset disposal account rather than in the sales account.

When a non-current asset is sold or disposed of, it must be removed from the ledger records. The cost of the asset and the depreciation on the asset are removed from the asset account and the provision for depreciation account and transferred to a disposal account. The proceeds of sale are also entered in the disposal account. It is quite likely that this account will not balance. This is because the depreciation was only an estimate of the loss in value. Only when the asset is sold can the actual loss in value be calculated. The difference on the disposal account represents either a loss on disposal (when the actual depreciation proved to be more than the estimate) or a profit on disposal (when the actual depreciation proved to be less than the estimate).

The entries are as follows:

On the day of sale

- Debit the asset disposal account and credit the non-current asset account with the original cost price of the asset.
- Debit the provision for depreciation on asset account and credit the asset disposal account with the total depreciation charged on the asset being sold.
- Debit either the bank account or the customer's account (if sold on credit) and credit the asset disposal account with the proceeds of sale.

At the end of the financial year

- If there is a loss on disposal:
  - credit the asset disposal account with the loss
  - include the loss in the expenses in the statement of profit or loss, which is equal to making a debit entry as the statement is part of the double entry system.

12 Accounting for depreciation and disposal of non-current assets

- If there is a profit on disposal:
  - debit the asset disposal account with the profit
  - include the profit with the other items of income in the statement of profit or loss, which is equal to making a credit entry as the statement is part of the double entry system.

WORKED EXAMPLE 12.10

Vijay's financial year ends on 30 June.

On 1 July 20–3, he purchased office equipment costing $30 000 and paid by credit transfer. Vijay decided to depreciate the office equipment using the reducing balance method.

On 1 July 20–7, the provision for depreciation on office equipment account showed a credit balance of $26 112.

Vijay sold all the office equipment on credit to Raminder for $2 900 on 1 July 20–7.

Prepare the office equipment account, the provision for depreciation on office equipment account and the disposal of office equipment account for the year ended 30 June 20–8.

Vijay
Nominal ledger

Dr		Office equipment account				Cr
			$			$
20–3				20–7		
Jul 1	Bank		30 000	Jul 1	Disposal	30 000
			30 000			30 000

Dr		Provision for depreciation on office equipment account					Cr
			$				$
20–7				20–7			
Jul 1	Disposal		26 112	Jul 1	Balance	b/d	26 112
			26 112				26 112

Dr		Office equipment disposal account				Cr
			$			$
20–7				20–7		
Jul 1	Office equipment		30 000	Jul 1	Provision for depreciation	26 112
					Raminder	2 900
				20–8		
				Jun 30	Statement of profit or loss	988
			30 000			30 000

> **CONTINUED**
>
> - The difference on the disposal account remains in that account until the end of the financial year when it is transferred to the statement of profit or loss.
> - In this case, the depreciation had been under-provided, so there was a loss of $988 to transfer to the statement of profit or loss.
> - If the total of the credit side of the account had exceeded the debit side, there would have been an over-provision of depreciation. The transfer to the statement of profit or loss would have been shown on the debit side of this account and added to the gross profit in the statement of profit or loss.

If only some of the assets of a particular type are being sold, it is important that only the entries relating to the assets being sold are removed from the ledger records.

Businesses may operate different policies in relation to depreciation when an asset is sold or disposed of partway through the year. Some ignore depreciation in the year of sale; others charge depreciation up to the date of disposal of the asset. Once a method has been selected, it should be employed consistently.

ACTIVITY 12.4

Figure 12.4: Providing cleaning services for offices

Chris started a business on 1 October 20–6 to provide cleaning services for offices and private houses. He decided to charge depreciation on his cleaning equipment using the straight line method at 20% per annum from the date of purchase, but not to charge depreciation in the year of disposal.

He provided the following information.

20–6 October 1	Purchased cleaning equipment, $3 000, by bank transfer
20–7 January 1	Purchased cleaning equipment, $1 000, on credit from K Y Cleaning
20–8 March 31	All the equipment purchased on 1 October 20–6 was sold as it was no longer suitable. The buyer paid $2 000 in cash.

Prepare the following accounts in Chris's nominal ledger for the two years ended 30 September 20–8:

- Cleaning equipment account
- Provision for depreciation on cleaning equipment account
- Cleaning equipment disposal account.

12 Accounting for depreciation and disposal of non-current assets

ACCOUNTING IN ACTION

Falling profits

Figure 12.5: The fleet of delivery vehicles may lose value over time

Salina operates a fleet of delivery vehicles and is concerned that her profits have been falling over the years. She believes that one of the main causes of this is the amount of depreciation, which is being charged each year.

Salina has asked you for advice and has suggested either changing her method of depreciation or not charging depreciation on all non-current assets.

1. Make a list of the effects each suggestion would have on Salina's business.

2. Can you suggest any other actions she can take?

SUMMARY

You should now know:

- Depreciation is an estimate of the loss in value of a non-current asset over its expected working life.

- The main causes of depreciation are physical deterioration, economic reasons, passage of time and depletion.

- The three main methods of calculating depreciation are straight line, reducing balance and revaluation.

- Depreciation is shown as an expense in the statement of profit or loss.

- In the statement of financial position, the total depreciation to date (the accumulated depreciation) is deducted from the cost of the asset to show the net book value.

- When a non-current asset is sold, it is removed from the ledger records and transferred to an asset disposal account.

Chapter 12 practice questions

1. Lydia's financial year ends on 30 June. She depreciates her non-current assets using the reducing balance method at 20% per annum. On 1 July 20–3, Lydia bought a motor vehicle costing $22 000. What was the depreciation charge for the year ended 30 June 20–5?

   A $3 520

   B $4 400

   C $7 920

   D $8 800 [1]

2 Hitash's financial year ends on 31 March. On 1 April 20–7, he purchased office machinery costing $2 000. He decided to depreciate it using the reducing balance method at 15% per annum. On 31 March 20–9, Hitash incorrectly charged depreciation using the straight line method at 15% per annum.

What was the effect on the profit for the year ended 31 March 20–9?

A   overstated by $45

B   understated by $45

C   overstated by $300

D   understated by $300 [1]

3 Maryam opened a hairdressing salon on 1 August 20–2. On that date, she purchased hairdressing equipment costing $1 200, which she expected to have a working life of five years. Maryam purchased additional equipment on 1 July 20–3 costing $400. She decided to depreciate her hairdressing equipment using the revaluation method and valued her hairdressing equipment at $1 100 on 31 July 20–3.

What was the depreciation charge for the year ended 31 July 20–3?

A $100

B $240

C $320

D $500 [1]

4 Khumo's financial year ends on 30 April. He depreciates his fixtures and fittings at 15% per annum on cost. Depreciation is calculated from the date of purchase.

On 1 May 20–3, the balances in Khumo's books included the following:

	$
Fixtures and fittings	1 600
Provision for depreciation on fixtures and fittings	360

He purchased additional fixtures and fittings by bank transfer on the following dates:

	$
31 October 20–3	1 400
1 February 20–4	800

a   Prepare the fixtures and fittings account and the provision for depreciation on fixtures and fittings account for the year ended 30 April 20–4. Balance the accounts and bring down the balances on 1 May 20–4. [8]

b   Prepare a relevant extract from Khumo's statement of profit or loss for the year ended 30 April 20–4. [1]

c   Prepare a relevant extract from Khumo's statement of financial position at 30 April 20–4. [2]

[Total: 11]

12 Accounting for depreciation and disposal of non-current assets

5 Beketele started a business on 1 July 20–6. On that date, she made the following payments:

	$
Property	215 000
Legal costs relating to purchase of premises	2 150
Motor vehicle	9 800
Delivery costs of motor vehicle	200
Fuel for motor vehicle	50
Insurance of motor vehicle	495

a State whether each of these payments is capital expenditure or revenue expenditure. **[6]**

Beketele decided to depreciate the motor vehicle by 20% per annum using straight line method.

b Calculate the provision for depreciation on the motor vehicle on 1 July 20–8. **[2]**

On 1 July 20–8, Beketele decided that the motor vehicle was no longer suitable and sold it for $6 700, which was received in cash.

c Prepare the motor vehicle disposal account as it would appear in Beketele's ledger. **[4]**

[Total: 12]

6 Tebogo owns a secretarial agency. His financial year ends on 31 May. He provided the following information for the year ended 31 May 20–1:

	$
Fees received from clients	33 950
Office expenses	11 760
Insurance	1 800
Wages	24 000
Rent received from tenant	7 500
Drawings	5 200

Tebogo also provided the following additional information:

1 On 31 May 20–1, fees due from clients amounted to $2 620.

2 The rent received included $500 which was owing on 1 June 20–0 and $1 000 which was paid in advance for the year ending 31 May 20–2.

3 The wages paid included $360 which was owing on 1 June 20–0. On 31 May 20–1, wages owing amounted to $200.

4 All the office equipment was sold on 1 September 20–0 for $2 500. This had cost $4 200 and had been depreciated by $1 575 at the date of sale.

5   New office equipment, $4 400, was purchased on 1 September 20–0. This is to be depreciated at the rate of 25% per annum from the date of purchase.

6   On 1 June 20–0 Tebogo's capital was $81 400.

a   Prepare Tebogo's statement of profit or loss for the year ended 31 May 20–1. [9]

b   Prepare Tebogo's capital account for the year ended 31 May 20–1. Balance the account and bring down the balance on 1 June 20–1. [3]

[Total: 12]

CHECK YOUR PROGRESS

How well do you think you have achieved the learning intentions for this chapter? Give yourself a score from 1 (still need a lot of practice) to 5 (feeling very confident) for each learning intention. Provide an example to support your score.

Now I can …	Score	Example to support score
explain the meaning of depreciation and the reasons for accounting for depreciation		
use the straight line, reducing balance and revaluation methods to calculate depreciation		
prepare ledger accounts for the provision for depreciation and to record the sale of non-current assets, including the use of asset disposal accounts.		

Chapter 13
Irrecoverable debts and allowance for irrecoverable debts

LEARNING INTENTIONS

By the end of this chapter, you will be able to:

- explain the meaning of irrecoverable debts and irrecoverable debts recovered
- make ledger entries to record irrecoverable debts and irrecoverable debts recovered
- explain the reasons for maintaining an allowance for irrecoverable debts
- make ledger entries to record, create and adjust an allowance for irrecoverable debts
- prepare financial statements that include irrecoverable debts, irrecoverable debts recovered and allowance for irrecoverable debts.

Introduction

When goods are sold on credit, the customer is allowed to pay for the goods at a later date.

There is always a risk that the customer may not pay for those goods. An **irrecoverable debt** is an amount owing to a business which will not be paid by the credit customer. This may be because the customer has disappeared, has gone out of business or is unable to pay.

> **KEY TERM**
>
> **irrecoverable debt:** an amount owing to a business which will not be paid by the credit customer.

ACCOUNTING IN CONTEXT

How to avoid irrecoverable debts

Figure 13.1: A sports equipment business might sell goods for cash and also sell on credit terms

When a business operates on a cash basis and does not sell on credit, there is no risk of any irrecoverable debts because everything is paid for straight away. However, if a business does not sell on credit, it might be limiting its number of customers, and therefore limiting the growth of the business. When a business owner is deciding whether to offer credit terms, they should consider the risk of irrecoverable debts in addition to the possibility of increasing profits by attracting more customers.

Jamil had been successfully running a sports clothing and equipment business for some years with trading on a cash basis. In order to expand his business, Jamil decided to offer his customers credit sales. He hoped that by offering credit sales, he would gain the business of sports teams and clubs.

One of his credit customers, Ravat, initially paid all his invoices on time. Over a period of six months, his payments were getting later and later and then he stopped paying altogether. At that point, he owed Jamil $1 500. Jamil then found out that Ravat had gone bankrupt.

Discuss in pairs or a group:

1. What things could Jamil have done to avoid this irrecoverable debt of $1 500?

2. What can Jamil do to try to avoid a situation like this with any new credit customers?

13 Irrecoverable debts and allowance for irrecoverable debts

13.1 Writing off irrecoverable debts

After a trader has tried unsuccessfully to obtain the amount owed by a credit customer, the trader may decide that the money is never going to be paid. When this happens, the debt is written off.

The customer's account is closed by transferring the amount written off to the irrecoverable debts account. At the end of the year, the total of the irrecoverable debts account is transferred to the statement of profit or loss, where it is regarded as an expense for the year.

The entries are as follows:

When a debt is written off

- Debit the irrecoverable debts account.
- Credit the trade receivable account.

At the end of the financial year

- Include the irrecoverable debts with the other expenses in the statement of profit or loss – this is equal to making a debit entry as the statement is part of the double entry system.
- Credit the irrecoverable debts account.

Writing off irrecoverable debts is an example of the application of the prudence concept.

If a debt cannot be paid, it is written off so that the assets are not overstated. The amount of the irrecoverable debt is regarded as an expense for the year, so it must be included in the statement of profit or loss otherwise the profit for the year will be overstated.

> **LINK**
>
> You learnt about the prudence concept in Chapter 10.

CAMBRIDGE IGCSE™ AND O LEVEL ACCOUNTING: COURSEBOOK

ACTIVITY 13.1

Kabelo is a trader. His financial year ends on 31 May. On 29 May 20–7, Kabelo decided to write off as irrecoverable $350 owed by Amara, a credit customer.

Copy out the following irrecoverable debts account and complete it by inserting the missing words and figures.

Kabelo
Nominal ledger
Irrecoverable debts account

Dr			$			Cr $
20–6				20–7		
Nov 1	Thato		128	May 31	....	......
20–7						
May 5	Bontle		66			
29	....		......			......
			......			......

13.2 Irrecoverable debts recovered

A debt written off may be recovered if a credit customer pays some or all of the amount owed, after the amount was written off. There are two possible methods for recording this.

Method 1

An **irrecoverable debt recovered** is debited to the bank account and credited to an irrecoverable debts recovered account. This is because the account of the customer has already been closed.

The entries are as follows:

When the amount is received

- Debit the bank account.
- Credit the irrecoverable debts recovered account.

> **KEY TERM**
>
> **irrecoverable debt recovered:** when a credit customer pays some or all of the debt after it was written off as irrecoverable.

13 Irrecoverable debts and allowance for irrecoverable debts

At the end of the financial year

- Debit the irrecoverable debts recovered account.
- Either include the irrecoverable debts recovered in the statement of profit or loss with the other items of income, which is equal to making a credit entry, or credit the irrecoverable debts account.*

Method 2

An alternative method is to reinstate the debt by crediting the irrecoverable debts recovered account and debiting the customer with the amount previously written off. The amount received would then be debited in the bank account and credited to the customer's account. The advantage of this method is that all the transactions relating to that customer appear in their account.

The entries are as follows:

When the amount is received

- Debit the trade receivable account.
- Credit the irrecoverable debts recovered account.
- Debit the bank account.
- Credit the trade receivable account.

At the end of the financial year

- Debit the irrecoverable debts recovered account.
- Either include the irrecoverable debts recovered in the statement of profit or loss with the other items of income, which is equal to making a credit entry, or credit the irrecoverable debts account.*

* Usually the total of the irrecoverable debts recovered account is added to the gross profit in the statement of profit or loss. However, some traders prefer to transfer it to the irrecoverable debts account and then transfer the difference on that account to the statement of profit or loss. The overall effect is the same.

Figure 13.2: Goods being traded

WORKED EXAMPLE 13.1

Latif is a trader. His financial year ends on 30 June. Latif sells goods on credit and offers 2% cash discount if invoices are paid within 30 days.

On 1 August 20–4, Shaheen purchased goods, $700, on credit from Latif. On 29 August 20–4, Shaheen settled her account by bank transfer after deducting the cash discount.

On 1 October 20–4, Latif sold further goods, $400, on credit to Shaheen. On 27 June 20–5, Latif wrote off the amount due from Shaheen as irrecoverable.

On 6 May 20–6, Shaheen paid Latif $400 in cash.

During the year ended 30 June 20–6, Latif wrote off irrecoverable debts totalling $830.

Prepare the following accounts in Latif's ledger for each of the years ended 30 June 20–5 and 30 June 20–6.

a Shaheen account

b Irrecoverable debts account

c Irrecoverable debts recovered account

a

Latif
Sales ledger

Dr			Shaheen account			Cr
			$			$
20–4				20–4		
Aug 1	Sales		700	Aug 29	Bank	686
Oct 1	Sales		400		Discount	14
				20–5		
				Jun 27	Irrecoverable debts	400
			1100			1100

b

Nominal ledger

Dr			Irrecoverable debts account			Cr
			$			$
20–5				20–5		
Jun 27	Shaheen		400	Jun 30	Statement of profit or loss	400
			400			400
20–6				20–6		
Jun 30	Trade receivables		830	Jun 30	Statement of profit or loss	830
			830			830

- The words 'Trade receivables' have been used as no individual names, dates and amounts have been provided.

13 Irrecoverable debts and allowance for irrecoverable debts

CONTINUED

c

Dr	Irrecoverable debts recovered account			Cr
		$		$
20–6			20–6	
Jun 30	Statement of profit or loss**	400	May 6 Cash*	400
		400		400

* Alternatively, the debt could have been reinstated by debiting Shaheen's account and crediting irrecoverable debts recovered account. The cash would then be debited to the cash account and credited to Shaheen's account.

** Alternatively, the irrecoverable debts recovered account could have been transferred to the credit of the irrecoverable debts account. This would result in $430 being transferred from irrecoverable debts to the statement of profit or loss on 30 June 20–6.

13.3 Reducing the possibility of irrecoverable debts

The only certain way of avoiding irrecoverable debts is not to sell goods on credit. In practice, this is not always an option. All possible steps must be taken to avoid irrecoverable debts.

- Before allowing credit to a new customer, credit references should be obtained – one from the customer's bank and one from a present or previous supplier.

- A credit limit is usually fixed for each customer, which places an upper limit on the amount the customer can owe at any one time (this credit limit can be reviewed periodically). Establishing a credit limit and then monitoring the customer's account is known as credit control.

- Invoices and month-end statements of account should be issued promptly.

- The accounts of trade receivables should be carefully monitored. Any overdue accounts should be investigated and the customers should be contacted by letters, emails and telephone calls if necessary.

- No further goods should be supplied until the amount due is paid.

- A more extreme measure involves taking legal action against the customer, but sometimes the amount of the debt is too small to justify costly legal proceedings.

ACTIVITY 13.2

Ronnie has worked for a home furnishings wholesaler for many years, and he has now decided to start his own wholesale business supplying retail stores with home furnishings. Ronnie is worried about the possibility of irrecoverable debts.

Discuss with a partner the ways Ronnie can try to avoid irrecoverable debts.

Use your ideas to design a poster to show what Ronnie can do. You should design and decorate your poster to try make the recommended actions easy to remember.

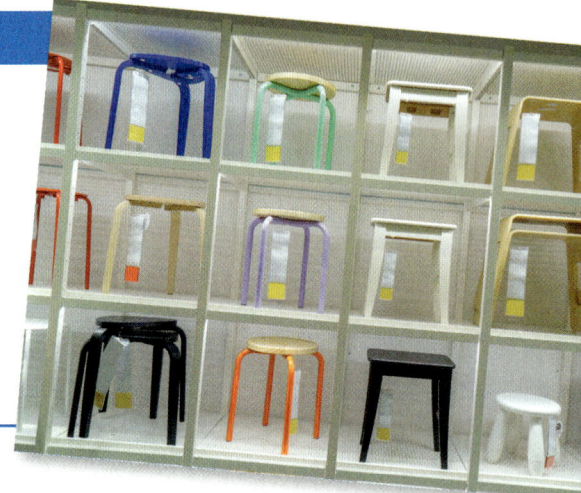

13.4 Allowance for irrecoverable debts

An allowance for irrecoverable debts is an estimate of the amount which a business will lose in a financial year because of irrecoverable debts.

At the end of their financial year, many businesses try to anticipate the amount which will be lost because of irrecoverable debts. This ensures that the profit for the year in the statement of profit or loss and the trade receivables in the statement of financial position are not overstated. This is an application of the prudence concept.

By maintaining an **allowance for irrecoverable debts**, a business also observes the matching/accruals concept. The amount of sales for which the business is unlikely to be paid is regarded as an expense of the year in which those sales are made.

In order to make an allowance for irrecoverable debts, it is necessary to estimate the amount of irrecoverable debts. The amount of the allowance may be established by:

- looking at each individual credit customer's account and estimating which ones will not be paid
- estimating, on the basis of past experience, the percentage of the total amount owing by credit customers that will not be paid
- considering the length of time debts have been outstanding using an ageing schedule. For older debts, a higher percentage may be used to calculate the allowance (the longer a debt is outstanding, the greater the risk it may become irrecoverable).

> **LINKS**
>
> You learnt about the concepts of prudence and matching/accruals in Chapter 10.

> **KEY TERM**
>
> **allowance for irrecoverable debts:** an estimate of the amount a business will lose in a financial year due to irrecoverable debts.

13 Irrecoverable debts and allowance for irrecoverable debts

> **DISCUSSION**
>
> Ting supplies components to several small engineering businesses through his website on a credit basis. He is concerned that several of his customers may not be able to pay their outstanding debts when they are due.
>
> Discuss with a partner:
>
> 1 What steps should Ting take to decide on an accurate allowance for irrecoverable debts?
>
> 2 How might the general economy of a region affect the size of a suitable allowance for irrecoverable debts?

> **ACTIVITY 13.3**
>
> Annie had a few irrecoverable debts during her first year of trading. She was advised to establish an allowance for irrecoverable debts.
>
> Imagine you are advising Annie. Write an email or a short note to explain the meaning of the matching/accruals concept and how maintaining an allowance for irrecoverable debts is an example of how the matching/accruals concept is applied.

13.5 Creating an allowance for irrecoverable debts

Once a business has decided to create an allowance for irrecoverable debts and the amount or percentage has been decided, this can be recorded in the books. These entries are made at the end of the financial year.

The entries are as follows:

- Include the allowance for irrecoverable debts with the other expenses in the statement of profit or loss – this is equal to making a debit entry as the statement is part of the double entry system.
- Credit the allowance for irrecoverable debts account.
- In the statement of financial position, deduct the balance on the allowance for irrecoverable debts account from the trade receivables in the current assets section.

CAMBRIDGE IGCSE™ AND O LEVEL ACCOUNTING: COURSEBOOK

WORKED EXAMPLE 13.2

Latif's financial year ends on 30 June.

During the year ended 30 June 20–7, he wrote off irrecoverable debts totalling $500.

On 30 June 20–7, Latif's trade receivables amounted to $13 500. He decided to create an allowance for irrecoverable debts of 4% of the trade receivables.

a   Prepare the irrecoverable debts account and the allowance for irrecoverable debts account in Latif's nominal ledger for the year ended 30 June 20–7.

b   Prepare a relevant extract from Latif's statement of profit or loss for the year ended 30 June 20–7.

c   Prepare a relevant extract from Latif's statement of financial position at 30 June 20–7.

a

Latif
Nominal ledger

Dr			Irrecoverable debts account			Cr
			$			$
20–7				20–7		
Jun 30	Trade receivables		500	Jun 30	Statement of profit or loss	500
			500			500

- The words 'Trade receivables' have been used as no individual names, dates and amounts have been provided.

Dr	Allowance for irrecoverable debts account		Cr
	$		$
		20–7	
		Jun 30 Statement of profit or loss	540

- The allowance has been calculated at 4% of $13 500.

b

Latif
Extract from statement of profit or loss for the year ended 30 June 20–7

	$
Expenses – Irrecoverable debts	500
Allowance for irrecoverable debts	540

c

Latif
Extract from statement of financial position at 30 June 20–7

	$	$
Current assets		
Trade receivables	13 500	
Less Allowance for irrecoverable debts	540	12 960

- Only the amount which is actually expected to be received from the trade receivables is added to the other current assets in the statement of financial position.

13.6 Adjusting an allowance for irrecoverable debts

In future years, a business may decide to maintain the allowance for irrecoverable debts using the same percentage of the trade receivables. If the amount owing has increased, the allowance needs to be increased and vice versa. If the original allowance for irrecoverable debts was based on an amount of money rather than a percentage, it may be decided that this amount needs to be changed. This adjustment to the allowance for irrecoverable debts is made at the end of the financial year.

The entries are as follows:

- Debit the allowance for irrecoverable debts account with the new provision and carry down.
- Credit the allowance for irrecoverable debts account with the new provision brought down.
- If the allowance has increased:
  - include the amount by which the allowance has increased in the statement of profit or loss with the other expenses – this is equal to making a debit entry as the statement is part of the double entry system
  - credit the allowance for irrecoverable debts account with the amount by which the allowance increased.
- If the allowance has decreased:
  - debit the allowance for irrecoverable debts account with the amount by which the allowance decreased
  - include the amount by which the allowance has decreased in the statement of profit or loss with the other items of income – this is equal to making a credit entry as the statement is part of the double entry system.
- In the statement of financial position, deduct the balance on the allowance for irrecoverable debts account (the new allowance) from the trade receivables in the current assets section.

> **TIP**
>
> When you first create an allowance for irrecoverable debts, the total amount is entered in the statement of profit or loss. In later years, you only need to enter the amount by which the allowance increases or decreases.

Increasing an allowance for irrecoverable debts

WORKED EXAMPLE 13.3

Latif's financial year ends on 30 June.

On 30 June 20–7, Latif created an allowance for irrecoverable debts of $540.

During the year ended 30 June 20–8, Latif wrote off debts totalling $490.

On 30 June 20–8, Latif's trade receivables amounted to $14 800. Latif decided to maintain the allowance for irrecoverable debts at the rate of 4% of the trade receivables.

a Prepare the irrecoverable debts account and the allowance for irrecoverable debts account in Latif's nominal ledger for the year ended 30 June 20–8.

b Prepare a relevant extract from Latif's statement of profit or loss for the year ended 30 June 20–8.

c Prepare a relevant extract from Latif's statement of financial position at 30 June 20–8.

> **CONTINUED**

a

Latif					
Nominal ledger					
Dr		Irrecoverable debts account			Cr
		$			$
20–8			20–8		
Jun 30	Trade receivables	490	Jun 30	Statement of profit or loss	490
		490			490

The words 'Trade receivables' have been used as no individual names, dates and amounts have been provided.

Dr		Allowance for irrecoverable debts account					Cr
			$				$
20–8				20–7			
Jun 30	Balance	c/d	592	Jun 30	Statement of profit or loss		540*
				20–8			
				Jun 30	Statement of profit or loss		52
			592				592
				20–8			
				Jul 1	Balance	b/d	592

- The item indicated with * was entered in the account on 30 June 20–7 at the end of the previous financial year.
- The balance (the new allowance) has been calculated at 4% of $14 800.

b

Latif	
Extract from statement of profit or loss for the year ended 30 June 20–8	
	$
Expenses – Irrecoverable debts	490
Increase in allowance for irrecoverable debts	52

- Only the amount by which the allowance needs to be increased is included in the expenses in the statement of profit or loss.

c

Latif		
Extract from statement of financial position at 30 June 20–8		
	$	$
Current assets		
Trade receivables	14 800	
Less Allowance for irrecoverable debts	592	14 208

- The amount of the allowance for irrecoverable debts at 30 June 20–8 (the balance on the allowance for irrecoverable debts account) is deducted from the trade receivables to show the amount expected to be received.

Reducing an allowance for irrecoverable debts

WORKED EXAMPLE 13.4

Latif's financial year ends on 30 June.

On 30 June 20–8, Latif's allowance for irrecoverable debts amounted to $592.

On 30 June 20–9, his trade receivables amounted to $13 300. He decided to maintain the allowance for irrecoverable debts at the rate of 4% of the trade receivables.

a Prepare the allowance for irrecoverable debts account in Latif's nominal ledger for the year ended 30 June 20–9.

b Prepare a relevant extract from Latif's statement of profit or loss for the year ended 30 June 20–9.

c Prepare a relevant extract from Latif's statement of financial position at 30 June 20–9.

a

Latif
Nominal ledger

Dr				Allowance for irrecoverable debts account				Cr
			$					$
20–9					20–8			
Jun 30	Statement of profit or loss		60		Jul 1	Balance	b/d	592
	Balance	c/d	532					
			592					592
					20–9			
					Jul 1	Balance	b/d	532

- The balance (the new allowance) has been calculated at 4% of $13 300.

b

Latif	
Extract from statement of profit or loss for the year ended 30 June 20–9	
	$
Gross profit	xxx
Add Decrease in allowance for irrecoverable debts	60

- The surplus allowance is added to the gross profit in the statement of profit or loss.
- Any irrecoverable debts would be included in the expenses in the statement of profit or loss in the usual way.

c

Latif		
Extract from statement of financial position at 30 June 20–9		
	$	$
Current assets		
Trade receivables		13 300
Less Allowance for irrecoverable debts		532	12 768

- The amount of the allowance for irrecoverable debts at 30 June 20–9 (the balance on the provision account) is deducted from the trade receivables to show the amount expected to be received.

> **TIP**
>
> When you prepare a statement of financial position on a particular date, remember to deduct the total amount of the allowance for irrecoverable debts at that date from the trade receivables.

ACTIVITY 13.4

At the end of her financial year on 31 March 20–1, Mariam decided to create an allowance for irrecoverable debts of $864 and to maintain it at the same percentage in future years. She provided the following information:

Trade receivables at 31 March 20–1 $43 200

31 March 20–2 $45 500

31 March 20–3 $42 800 (including $300, which is irrecoverable and should be written off)

1 Calculate the percentage rate of Mariam's provision for irrecoverable debts.

2 Calculate the amount which would appear for allowance for irrecoverable debts in the statement of profit or loss for the year ended 31 March 20–2. State the section of the statement of profit or loss in which that amount would appear.

3 Calculate the amount which would appear for allowance for irrecoverable debts in the statement of profit or loss for the year ended 31 March 20–3. State the section of the statement of profit or loss in which that amount would appear.

4 Explain the entry for trade receivables which would be made in the statement of financial position on 31 March 20–3.

ACCOUNTING IN ACTION

Going out of business

Figure 13.3: If a business cannot pay its debts, it may have to close down

Hyan is the owner of Zeta Systems. He has recently been informed that one of his major customers, Beta Products, has gone out of business, owing him $5 000.

Hyan has been advised that there is a possibility the customer may be able to pay 10% of the outstanding amount but this may take some time.

Working in pairs, answer these questions:

1 How should Hyan record the following in his accounting system:

   a Beta Products going out of business?

   b receiving 10% of the outstanding debt from Beta Products if this occurs?

2 How will each of the actions in **1a** and **1b** affect the financial statements for the current year and the following year?

REFLECTION

In the Accounting in action activity, you had to apply what you have learnt in this chapter to a real-life business situation. How does applying what you have learnt to a situation faced by a real accountant help you to understand a section?

> **SUMMARY**
>
> You should now know:
>
> - An irrecoverable debt is an amount owing to a business which will not be paid by a credit customer. Irrecoverable debts are shown as an expense in the statement of profit or loss.
>
> - A debt written off may later be recovered when a credit customer pays some or all of the debt. Debts recovered are added to the gross profit in the statement of profit or loss.
>
> - An allowance for irrecoverable debts is an estimate of the amount which a business will lose in a financial year because of irrecoverable debts.
>
> - The amount required to create or increase an allowance for irrecoverable debts is shown as an expense in the statement of profit or loss. Any surplus allowance is added to the gross profit in the statement of profit or loss.
>
> - The allowance for irrecoverable debts is deducted from the trade receivables in the statement of financial position.

Chapter 13 practice questions

1. At the end of his financial year, William wrote off a debt owed by a credit customer. What was the effect of this?

	Trade receivables	Profit for the year	Capital	Balance at bank
A	decreased	decreased	decreased	no effect
B	decreased	no effect	no effect	no effect
C	no effect	no effect	decreased	decreased
D	no effect	decreased	no effect	decreased

[1]

2. Rex maintains an allowance for irrecoverable debts. Which statements are correct?

    1. It is an application of the matching/accruals concept.
    2. It is an application of the prudence concept.
    3. It is an estimate of what may be lost because of irrecoverable debts.
    4. It is money set aside to cover losses because of irrecoverable debts.

    A 1, 2 and 3
    B 1 and 4
    C 2 and 3
    D 2, 3 and 4   [1]

3   Abi maintains an allowance for irrecoverable debts at 2% of trade receivables. On 1 January 20–5, the allowance for irrecoverable debts was $400. The trade receivables on 31 December 20–4 amounted to $20 550.

What entries did Abi make on 31 December 20–4 to adjust the allowance for irrecoverable debts?

	Debit	$	Credit	$
A	allowance for irrecoverable debts	11	statement of profit or loss	11
B	allowance for irrecoverable debts	411	statement of profit or loss	411
C	statement of profit or loss	11	allowance for irrecoverable debts	11
D	statement of profit or loss	411	allowance for irrecoverable debts	411

[1]

4   Raminder prepared the following trial balance after the preparation of the trading section of his statement of profit or loss for the year ended 31 January 20–8.

	Dr $	Cr $
Gross profit		55 000
Capital		103 500
Drawings	5 000	
Property at cost	86 000	
Fixtures and equipment at cost	32 000	
Provision for depreciation on fixtures and equipment		4 800
Inventory 31 January 20–8	7 500	
Trade receivables	9 400	
Allowance for irrecoverable debts		176
Irrecoverable debts	80	
Trade payables		6 800
5% Loan (repayable 1 July 20–8)		5 000
Rent income		1 200
Discount allowed	116	
Discount received		150
Wages	26 400	
Office expenses	11 100	
Insurance	1 300	
Cash	92	
Bank		2 362
	178 988	178 988

13 Irrecoverable debts and allowance for irrecoverable debts

Additional information at 31 January 20–8:

1 Insurance paid in advance amounted to $100.

2 The rent income was received from a tenant. The contract began on 1 November 20–7 for a monthly rent of $300.

3 Trade receivables include a debt of $200, which is regarded as irrecoverable.

4 The allowance for irrecoverable debts is to be maintained at 2½% of the trade receivables.

5 One year's interest on the loan is outstanding.

6 Fixtures and equipment are being depreciated at 15% per annum using the reducing balance method.

Prepare Raminder's statement of profit or loss to calculate the profit for the year ended 31 January 20–8 and a statement of financial position at that date. [19]

5 Chun is a trader. Her financial year ends on 30 September. She sells on credit and allows customers a trade discount of 20%. A cash discount of 2% is allowed if accounts are paid within 30 days. On 1 October 20–3, Chun's allowance for irrecoverable debts amounted to $340.

Chun provided the following information:

20–3

Oct 1   Hua, a credit customer, owed $650

2   Hua settled her account by an online payment after deducting cash discount

20–4

Jan 2   Hua purchased goods on credit from Chun, list price $900

31   Hua paid Chun $300 in cash

May 1   Hua was declared bankrupt. Her creditors received a bank transfer of 10 cents in the dollar in final settlement of the amount owed. Chun wrote off the remaining amount as an irrecoverable debt

Sep 30   Chun decided to increase her allowance for irrecoverable debts by $150

Prepare the following accounts in Chun's ledger for the year ended 30 September 20–4:

a   Hua account [5]

b   irrecoverable debts account [2]

c   allowance for irrecoverable debts account. [3]

The accounts should be closed by balancing, totalling or making an appropriate year-end transfer as necessary.

[Total: 10]

6 Musa owns an advertising agency. His financial year ends on 31 October. He provided the following information on 31 October 20–2.

	$
Capital	140 000
Drawings	10 120
Office equipment at cost	25 500
Provision for depreciation on equipment	3 825
Property at cost	142 000
Fees from clients	100 600
Commission income	4 000
Salaries	59 200
Office expenses	5 100
Insurance	1 326
Irrecoverable debts	300
Allowance for irrecoverable debts	200
Trade receivables	6 000
Loan (repayable 1 January 20–4)	20 000
Bank	18 820 debit
Cash	259

Additional information on 31 October 20–2:

1. Commission income outstanding amounted to $200.
2. Insurance covers a period of 13 months to 30 November 20–2.
3. One year's loan interest at 5% is accrued.
4. The allowance for irrecoverable debts is to be maintained at 3% of the trade receivables.
5. The office equipment is being depreciated at 15% per annum using the straight line method.

a. Prepare the statement of profit or loss of Musa for the year ended 31 October 20–2. [8]

b. Prepare the statement of financial position of Musa at 31 October 20–2. [8]

[Total: 16]

13 Irrecoverable debts and allowance for irrecoverable debts

CHECK YOUR PROGRESS

How well do you think you have achieved the learning intentions for this chapter? Give yourself a score from 1 (still need a lot of practice) to 5 (feeling very confident) for each learning intention. Provide an example to support your score.

Now I can …	Score	Example to support score
explain the meaning of irrecoverable debts and irrecoverable debts recovered		
make ledger entries to record irrecoverable debts and irrecoverable debts recovered		
explain the reasons for maintaining an allowance for irrecoverable debts		
make ledger entries to record, create and adjust an allowance for irrecoverable debts		
prepare financial statements that include irrecoverable debts, irrecoverable debts recovered and allowance for irrecoverable debts.		

Section 3 practice questions

1. Abdullah is a retailer. He took goods from his shop for his personal use and did not record this in his accounting records. An adjustment was made in the year-end financial statements.

   How did this adjustment affect the gross profit and the closing capital? [1]

	Effect on gross profit		Effect on closing capital		
	Increase	Decrease	Increase	Decrease	No effect
A	✓		✓		
B		✓		✓	
C	✓				✓
D		✓			✓

2. After the preparation of the year-end financial statements, two errors were discovered:

   1. 200 items of inventory were valued at the cost price of $14 each. This amount did not include carriage inwards of $1 per unit.

   2. An item of inventory costing $290 had been included at cost price, but damage to the item meant that it could only be sold for $210.

   How was the gross profit affected by these errors?

   A overstated by $120

   B overstated by $280

   C understated by $120

   D understated by $280 [1]

3. On 31 March 20–5, Basma wrote off $58 owed by Sabena as irrecoverable. Sabena sent a cheque for $58 to Basma on 1 January 20–6.

   What entries would Basma make on 1 January 20–6? [1]

	Account to be debited	Account to be credited
A	Allowance for irrecoverable debts	Sabena
B	Bank	Irrecoverable debts
C	Irrecoverable debts recovered	Irrecoverable debts recovered
D	Sabena	Bank

4 Joshua started a business on 1 May 20–8. He rented premises for the first six months. On 1 November 20–8, he purchased property and paid for 12 months' insurance on the property.

When the year-end financial statements were prepared an adjustment was made for the insurance prepaid.

Which accounting concept was applied?

A going concern

B matching/accruals

C money measurement

D prudence [1]

5 Usef is a manufacturer. At the end of every financial year, he depreciates his machinery using the reducing balance method.

Which accounting concepts is he applying?

A consistency, duality, historic cost

B consistency, matching/accruals, prudence

C duality, matching/accruals, realisation

D historic cost, prudence, realisation [1]

6 Maan is a retailer. He buys and sells computers and computer accessories. In addition, he also services and updates computer systems. Maan provided the following information at the end of the financial year on 31 May 20–9.

	$
Revenue – Retail	296 000
– Servicing	74 000
Inventory 1 June 20–8	22 000
Commission income	1 600
Repairs and maintenance	3 970
General expenses	1 810
Purchases	294 000
Carriage inwards	820
Purchases returns	12 000
Wages	52 400
Discount received	2 150
Rates and insurance	6 120

During the year ended 31 May 20–9, Maan took computers for his own use, $1 450.

On 31 May 20–9, the inventory was valued at $23 900.

a Prepare the statement of profit or loss for the year ended 31 May 20–9. [12]

Maan is hoping that he will have made a high profit. He said, 'I can use the profit to pay for the family holiday next month.'

b Explain why Maan's statement is incorrect. [3]

[Total: 15]

7 Aisyah has just completed her first year of trading. She has tried to maintain accounting records but is worried that she may have entered some transactions incorrectly.

a Explain the meaning of each of the following terms and give two examples of each.

   i Capital expenditure

   ii Revenue expenditure

   iii Capital receipts

   iv Revenue receipts [12]

b Explain why it is important to distinguish between capital and revenue items. [2]

Aisyah asked an accountant to check her books and to prepare financial statements. The accountant discovered the following errors.

Error 1 The purchase of fixtures and fittings, $740 on credit, had been debited to the purchases account but no other entry had been made.

Error 2 Loan interest paid, $150, had been recorded as part-repayment of the loan.

Error 3 The payment of an invoice from a local garage, $18 100, was credited to the cash book and debited to the motor vehicles account. This invoice was for the purchase of a new vehicle, $17 400, and repairs to an existing vehicle, $700.

Error 4 Rent income, $480, received from a tenant had been correctly recorded in the cash book and debited to the rent expense account.

c Copy out the following table. Where the error has an effect on the assets, liabilities or profit, write the amount for **each** error in the appropriate column. Where there is no effect, place a tick in the column headed no effect. [8]

Error	Effect on assets			Effect on liabilities			Effect on profit		
	Over-stated $	Under-stated $	No effect	Over-stated $	Under-stated $	No effect	Over-stated $	Under-stated $	No effect
1									
2									
3									
4									

[Total: 22]

8 a Suggest why it is important for an accountant to adhere to each of following ethical principles:

    i objectivity

    ii confidentiality [2]

b Name three other ethical principles which accountants should follow. [3]

c Suggest the consequences an accountant may face if they do not apply the ethical principles which all accountants are expected to follow. [2]

Joe, a sole trader, asked his friend, Paul, to prepare the year-end financial statements. Joe asked Paul to place an inflated value on the closing inventory so that the statement would show the business in a good light.

d   **i** Identify the accounting concept which has not been applied.

    ii Identify the ethical principle which has not been applied.

    iii State how the following items in the statement of financial position would be affected:

        closing balance of capital account

        total current assets

    iv Suggest how the following items in the financial statements for the following year may be affected:

        gross profit

        total current assets [6]

[Total: 13]

9 Kazin is a trader. His financial year ends on 31 May. He provided the following information about some of the accounts in his ledger:

Balances on 1 June 20–7	$
Capital	85 600
Inventory	14 340
Packing materials	270

Totals for the year ended 31 May 20–8	
Purchases returns	1 090
Carriage outwards	860
Drawings	9 330
Purchases of packing materials	1 830

On 31 May 20–8, the inventory of goods was valued at $15 280 and there was an inventory of packing materials valued at $190.

The loss for the year ended 31 May 20–8 was $2 710.

a Prepare a ledger account for each of the items listed. Record the year-end transfers or balances as appropriate. [12]

b Explain each entry in the following account which appeared in Kazin's ledger.

State where the double entry for each item would be made. [10]

Dr		Kazin Rent income account				Cr
		$				$
20–8			20–7			
May 31	Statement of profit or loss	9 600	Jun 1	Balance	b/d	800
	Balance c/d	1 600	Jul 3	Cash		4 800
			20–8			
			Jan 4	Bank		5 600
		11 200				11 200

[Total: 22]

10 Mia's accountant became ill before he was able to complete the financial statements at the end of the financial year. Mia decided that she would prepare the statement of financial position herself even though she has only a little knowledge of accounting. The statement of financial position prepared by Mia, which contains errors, is shown below.

Mia Statement of financial position at 31 January 20–1	
	$
Assets	
Property at cost	99 000
Loan (repayable 30 June 20–1)	9 000
Drawings	8 500
Fixtures and equipment at cost	19 750
Cash	1 060
Bank overdraft	4 280
Trade payables	9 850
	151 440
Liabilities	
Capital	150 000
Loss for the year	9 020
Trade receivables	7 500
Motor vehicle at cost	17 800
Inventory	10 500
	194 820

Section 3 practice questions

  a Prepare a corrected statement of financial position at 31 January 20–1. [8]

  b Suggest three ways in which Mia may be able to reduce the loss for the year. [3]

                                                                            [Total: 11]

11 Rohan is a wholesaler trading in home furnishings. His financial year ends on 31 December.

He maintains a combined account for rates and insurance. He provided the following information.

| 20–4 Jan 1 | Four months' rates accrued | $1 600 |
| | Five months' insurance prepaid | $1 200 |

During the year ended 31 December 20–4, the following payments were made by direct debit.

| | Rates – 18 months to 28 February 20–5 | $7 200 |
| | Insurance – 12 months to 31 May 20–5 | $2 880 |

  a Prepare the rates and insurance account for the year ended 31 December 20–4.

     Balance the account and bring down the balance on 1 January 20–5. [8]

  b Identify the section of the statement of financial position at 31 December 20–4 in which the balance of the rates and insurance account will appear. Give a reason for your answer. [2]

Rohan's customers often ask if he can recommend someone who can make curtains and covers for chairs and settees. Rohan always recommends Anika. Whenever Anika gets an order from these customers, she gives Rohan a commission.

Rohan provided the following information for the year ended 31 December 20–4.

		$
Jan 1	Commission accrued	250
Jun 30	Commission received by bank transfer	534
Dec 31	Commission accrued	310

  c Prepare the commission income account for the year ended 31 December 20–4.

     Balance the account and bring down the balance on 1 January 20–5. [4]

  d State where the commission income would be entered in the statement of profit or loss for the year ended 31 December 20–4. [1]

                                                                           [Total: 15]

12 Chen started a business on 1 January 20–6. He considered using the straight line method to depreciate all his non-current assets.

    a Name two other methods of depreciation Chen could use to depreciate his non-current assets. [2]

Chen decided to depreciate his office equipment at 15% per annum using the straight line method calculated on a month-by-month basis from the date of purchase to the date of disposal. He provided the following information:

			$
20–6 Jan	1	Cost of office equipment (A)	5 000
20–7 Jul	1	Cost of office equipment (B)	3 000
20–8 May	1	Cost of office equipment (C)	4 000
20–8 May	1	Proceeds of sale of office equipment (A) received by bank transfer	3 520

    b Calculate the deprecation on office equipment for each of the years ended 31 December 20–6, 20–7 and 20–8. [6]

    c Prepare the provision for depreciation on office equipment account for each of the three years ended 31 December 20–6, 20–7 and 20–8. Balance the account at the end of each year. [6]

    d Prepare the office equipment disposal account. [5]

[Total: 19]

13 a State the difference between irrecoverable debts and allowance for irrecoverable debts. [2]

    b Suggest two ways in which irrecoverable debts may be reduced. [2]

    c Identify two accounting concepts which are observed by maintaining an allowance for irrecoverable debts. [2]

Li's financial year ends on 31 July. She maintains an allowance for irrecoverable debts of 5% of the trade receivables at the end of each financial year.

On 31 July 20–4, the trade receivables owed $17 840. On 31 July 20–5, they owed $17 760 (including $200, which should be written off as irrecoverable).

    d Prepare the allowance for irrecoverable debts account. Balance the account and bring down the balance on 1 August 20–5. [3]

All Li's credit customers pay their accounts by bank transfer. She allows them a cash discount of 2½% if accounts are paid within 30 days. Li is considering increasing the discount to 3% if accounts are paid within 21 days.

    e Suggest how this may affect

        i Li's bank balance

        ii Li's profit for the year. [4]

[Total: 13]

14 Suella is a trader. Her financial year ends on 31 May. Her trial balance on 31 May 20–4 was as follows:

Suella Trial balance at 31 May 20–4	Dr $	Cr $
Capital		380 000
Drawings	51 000	
Trade receivables	49 270	
Trade payables		43 300
Bank	16 235	
Property at cost	290 000	
Fixtures and fittings at cost	40 000	
Motor vehicles at cost	24 000	
Provision for depreciation on fixtures and fittings		16 000
Provision for depreciation on motor vehicles		10 500
Allowance for irrecoverable debts		2 360
Revenue		609 500
Inventory 1 June 20–3	38 000	
Purchases	498 850	
Sales returns	1 110	
Carriage inwards	750	
Commission income		930
Rates and insurance	8 400	
Wages	39 700	
Administration expenses	5 275	
	1 062 590	1 062 590

Additional information:

1 At 31 May 20–4:

Inventory was valued at $40 650

Commission income outstanding amounted to $105

Insurance prepaid amounted to $180

Rates accrued amounted to $260

Wages accrued amounted to $1 600

2 A debt of $150 should be written off as irrecoverable and the allowance for irrecoverable debts should be maintained at 5% of the remaining trade receivables.

3 Fixtures and fittings are being depreciated at 20% per annum using the straight line method.

4 Motor vehicles are being depreciated at 25% per annum using the reducing balance method.

a Prepare the statement of profit or loss for the year ended 31 May 20–4. [13]

b Prepare the statement of financial position at 31 May 20–4. [11]

[Total: 24]

Section 4

This is a large section and covers several topics. First, you will study the ways in which the accounting records can be checked using bank reconciliation statements and control accounts and also how to correct errors using journal entries.

You will then focus on how to prepare financial statements for a trader who has not maintained a full set of accounting records. This section also introduces you to the preparation of financial statements for businesses such as partnerships and limited companies, where there is more than one owner. You will cover the preparation of the financial statements of a manufacturing business, including the preparation of an account to calculate the cost of production. The treasurer of a club or society is expected to prepare year-end financial statements, so you will learn how to prepare these.

The financial statements of a business are used to assess the performance and progress of that business and you will focus on how to do this by calculating and interpreting accounting ratios. In the final chapter of this section you will consider some of the ways that technology can be used to make accounting processes and the storage of data more sustainable.

> Chapter 14
Bank reconciliation statements

LEARNING INTENTIONS

By the end of this chapter, you will be able to:

- understand the purpose of a bank statement
- explain the purpose of a bank reconciliation statement and how it is used by a business
- prepare an updated cash book
- draw up a bank reconciliation statement
- explain how bank reconciliation statements are maintained in a computerised accounting system.

14 Bank reconciliation statements

Introduction

A business maintains a bank account in the cash book to record transactions involving money paid in and withdrawn from the bank. By using this account, the business owner can calculate how much money there is in the bank at any given time.

At regular intervals (usually monthly), the bank will send a bank statement to the customer detailing the transactions which have taken place during the period and showing the bank balance after each transaction. This gives the business owner the opportunity to compare the bank statement with their own records. Any differences between the balance shown on the bank statement and that shown in the bank column of the cash book will need to be investigated. This chapter shows how to compare the two records, explains why the differences occur and what actions might need to be taken.

ACCOUNTING IN CONTEXT

Figure 14.1: A customer having a haircut in a salon

At regular intervals (often at the end of each month), a business owner should balance the cash book and compare the balance on the bank column with the statement received from the bank. In an ideal world, the balance on the bank column in the cash book and the bank statement balance should be the same, but this is often not the case.

Sally is a hair stylist and owns her own hair salon. She employs a book-keeper to maintain her day-to-day accounts and to record the money which the business receives and spends. When Sally received her bank statement for April, she asked the book-keeper for the cash book so that she could check that everything was correct.

When Sally compared the balance on the bank column in the cash book with that on the bank statement, she found that the two balances did not agree.

The book-keeper assured Sally that there was no mistake in the cash book and suggested that the bank statement was wrong.

Discuss in pairs or in a group:

1. Can you suggest what Sally could use to check that the book-keeper had correctly recorded the money paid into the bank and the amounts paid by cheque?

2. Can you think of any reasons why the bank statement balance and the balance on the bank column in the cash book did not agree?

14.1 What is a bank statement?

A **bank statement** is a copy of the customer's account in the books of the bank. This is a record of transactions as they affect the bank. When money is paid into the bank, the customer's account will be credited as this is the amount owed by the bank to the customer. When money is taken out of the bank, the customer's account will be

> **KEY TERM**
>
> **bank statement:** a copy of a customer's account in the books of the bank which is sent to the customer at regular intervals.

debited, as this reduces the amount owed by the bank to the customer. A positive bank balance will appear as a credit balance and an overdrawn balance as a debit balance. The entries on a bank statement are recorded on the opposite sides of the account when compared to the entries in the bank account in the cash book.

The bank account is a record of transactions as they affect the business. Money paid into the bank is debited (the bank is a debtor for this amount) and money withdrawn from the bank is credited (the bank is a creditor for this amount).

It is important to compare the bank statement and the bank account in the cash book. If the two balances disagree, it is necessary to reconcile them to explain why the differences have arisen.

As mentioned in the introduction, banks issue bank statements to customers at regular intervals, often monthly. However, if customers use online banking, they can easily access their bank statements whenever they choose, which allows them to maintain better control of their finances.

> **LINK**
>
> You learnt about cash books in Chapter 4.

ACTIVITY 14.1

Figure 14.2: Understanding how to check a cash book against a bank statement is an important skill for trainee accountants

Joshi, a trainee accountant, is being shown how to check the bank columns of the cash book for May against the monthly statement received from the bank.

Prepare answers to the following questions Joshi has asked:

1. Why do the items we have debited in the cash book appear on the credit column on the bank statement?
2. Why have we made a credit entry for a direct debit payment?
3. Why does the cheque that we paid into the bank on 31 May not appear on the bank statement for that month?

14.2 Reasons why the bank account and the bank statement may differ

Differences between the bank account and the bank statement usually occur because:

- the same item is recorded at different times
- the business might not record certain items in the cash book.

Timing differences

There are two main reasons for timing differences: unpresented cheques and uncredited deposits.

1. **Unpresented cheques**

    These are cheques that have been issued by the business and entered on the credit side of the cash book, but do not appear on the bank statement. This may be because the payee has not paid the cheque into their bank or because the cheque is still in the banking system and has not yet been deducted from the business's account.

2. **Uncredited deposits**

    These are cash and cheques that have been paid into the bank and entered on the debit side of the cash book, but do not appear on the bank statement. This may happen if a payment is made into the bank late in the day and will not then be processed until the following day; or if the payment is made into a different branch of the bank from the one where the account is maintained.

Items not recorded in the cash book

Sometimes amounts paid and received may not be entered in the cash book until the bank statement is received. For items such as bank charges, bank interest and direct debit payments, the amounts will not be known until the statement is received. For items such as standing orders and credit transfer payments, the business owner may have overlooked them (especially if they are paid infrequently) or may deliberately wait for the bank statement as proof of payment.

Table 14.1 shows some of the items which a business may not record in a cash book until the bank statement is received.

> **LINK**
>
> You learnt about dishonoured cheques in Chapter 4.

Table 14.1: Items not recorded in a cash book until the bank statement is received

Item	Explanation
Amounts paid directly by the bank to others	These include standing orders and direct debits which the business has instructed the bank to pay directly from the account of the business.
Amounts paid directly into the bank	These occur when another business has instructed their bank to pay money directly into the bank account of the business. These can include payments made by customers using an online banking system and are often referred to as credit transfers.
Bank charges and bank interest paid	These are charges made by a bank to a business to cover the cost of running the account and for any interest charged on overdrafts and loans.
Bank interest received	This is money the business has earned on any deposit account or savings account that the business has with the bank.
Dishonoured cheques	These are cheques paid into the bank that the bank has refused to pay, possibly due to insufficient funds in that account.

Any other differences between the two records must be investigated. Errors made by the business should be corrected and the bank should be notified of any errors that they have made.

> **DISCUSSION**
>
> Discuss with a partner the reasons why any errors in a bank statement need to be investigated.

14.3 Stages of bank reconciliation

Businesses prepare a bank reconciliation statement in order to reconcile the balance in a business's bank account with the balance on the bank statement. A bank reconciliation statement is prepared at regular intervals in order to update the cash book and check for any errors in either the cash book or the bank statement. It will also act as a deterrent to fraud as any fraudulent entries would be identified.

Figure 14.3 shows the stages of bank reconciliation and the process for preparing a bank reconciliation statement.

> **TIP**
>
> When you compare the bank account in the cash book with the bank statement, remember that the entries appear on opposite sides, so you should compare the debit side of one with the credit side of the other.

When the bank statement is received, compare it with the entries in the bank account in the cash book. Put a tick (✓) against those items which appear in both records.

Update the cash book with items which appear on the bank statement but not in the cash book.

- Items debited on the bank statement (e.g. bank charges, standing orders) should be credited to the bank account in the cash book.
- Items credited on the bank statement (e.g. credit transfers) should be debited to the bank account in the cash book.

Make adjustments for any errors in the cash book.

Balance the cash book and carry down the balance.
The updated bank balance in the cash book appears in the statement of financial position.

Prepare a **bank reconciliation statement.**
Start with the balance shown on the bank statement and then:

- add any items which appear on the debit side of the cash book but do not appear on the bank statement (e.g. uncredited deposits)
- deduct any items which appear on the credit side of the cash book but do not appear on the bank statement (e.g. unpresented cheques)
- make any adjustments for bank errors.

The total should equal the updated bank balance in the cash book.

Figure 14.3: The stages of bank reconciliation

14 Bank reconciliation statements

It is possible to prepare the bank reconciliation statement by starting with the updated bank account balance. In this case, it is necessary to deduct uncredited deposits and add unpresented cheques.

A **bank reconciliation statement** does not form part of the double entry records of the business. It is a statement which shows the bank account and the bank statement balances were reconciled on a certain date.

> **KEY TERM**
>
> **bank reconciliation statement:** a document prepared by a business to explain why the updated bank balance in the cash book does not agree with the balance on the bank statement.

WORKED EXAMPLE 14.1

Ahana's cash book (bank columns) for the month of March 20–9 is shown below.

Dr				Ahana Cash book (bank columns only)				Cr
			$					$
20–9				20–9				
Mar	1	Balance b/d	6 800	Mar	8	Purchases		1 200
	19	J Dhalia	420		13	B Miurdhi		620
	22	Rio Stores	517		19	Terdi Ltd		1 582
	25	Sales	2 860		20	Dobinn		717
					31	Balance	c/d	6 478
			10 597					10 597
20–9								
Apr	1	Balance	b/d 6 478					

- It is important to remember that the bank columns are actually part of the main three-column cash book – not a separate ledger account.

On 1 April 20–9, Ahana received her bank statement for the month of March 20–9.

CONTINUED

REGIONAL BANK LTD
High Street Branch

Account: Ahana Bakshi
Account no: 987654
Date: 31 March 20–9

Date	Details	Debit $	Credit $	Balance $
20–9				
Mar 1	Balance			6 800 Cr
12	Cheque no 2388	2 100		4 700 Cr
13	Card payment – B Miurdhi	620		4 080 Cr
19	Bank transfer – J Dhalia		420	4 500 Cr
20	Bank interest received		600	5 100 Cr
31	Bank charges	100		5 000 Cr

It was discovered that Ahana had made an error in the cash book on 8 March and recorded purchases as $1 200, when the correct figure was $2 100.

a Make any additional entries which are required in the bank columns of Ahana's cash book and bring down an updated balance on 1 April 20–9.

b Prepare a bank reconciliation statement at 31 March 20–9.

Step 1

Compare the entries in the cash book with those on the bank statement.
Place a tick (✓) against the items appearing in both the records.

The cash book and the bank statement should now look like this:

Ahana
Cash book (bank columns only)

Dr				$					Cr $
20–9					20–9				
Mar 1	Balance b/d	✓		6 800	Mar 8	Purchases			1 200
19	J Dhalia	✓		420	13	B Miurdhi	✓		620
22	Rio Stores			517	19	Terdi Ltd			1 582
25	Sales			2 860	20	Dobinn			717
					31	Balance	c/d		6 478
				10 597					10 597
20–9									
Apr 1	Balance	b/d		6 478					

CONTINUED

	REGIONAL BANK LTD			
	High Street Branch			
Account: Ahana Bakshi			**Account no:** 987654	
			Date: 31 March 20–9	
Date	Details	Debit $	Credit $	Balance $
20–9				
Mar 1	Balance			6 800 Cr ✓
12	Cheque no 2388	2 100		4 700 Cr
13	Card payment – B Miurdhi	620 ✓		4 080 Cr
19	Bank transfer – J Dhalia		420 ✓	4 500 Cr
20	Bank interest received		600	5 100 Cr
31	Bank charges	100		5 000 Cr

Step 2

Update the bank account in the cash book with items which appear on the bank statement but not in the cash book and correct any errors in the cash book.

Items appearing in the debit column of the bank statement which have not been ticked off must be credited in the bank account (excluding 8 March as this card payment had previously been entered in the cash book but with an incorrect amount). Items appearing in the credit column of the bank statement which have not been ticked off must be debited in the bank account.

The bank account must then be adjusted for the error on 8 March.

The updated cash book is shown below.

a

Dr			Ahana Cash book (bank columns only)					Cr
			$					$
20–9				20–9				
Apr 1	Balance	b/d	6 478	Apr 1	Bank charges			100
	Bank interest received		600		Correction of error	c/d		900
					Balance			6 078
			7 078					7 078
20–9								
Apr 1	Balance	b/d	6 078					

- Ahana recorded purchases of $1 200 instead of $2 100, so to correct the error an additional $900 must be credited to the bank account.
- The balance on the bank columns of the cash book is now an accurate up-to-date balance and will appear in the statement of financial position.

CONTINUED

STEP 3

Starting with the balance shown in the bank statement, the bank reconciliation statement can now be prepared.

b

Ahana
Bank reconciliation statement at 31 March 20–9

	$	$
Balance shown on bank statement		5 000
Add Uncredited deposits – Rio Stores	517	
Sales	2 860	3 377
		8 377
Less Unpresented cheques – Terdi Ltd	1 582	
Dobinn	717	2 299
Balance shown in cash book		6 078

ACTIVITY 14.2

Rekha has been in business for several years and has never seen the point of preparing a bank reconciliation statement.

Write an email to Rekha explaining why she should prepare a bank reconciliation statement.

14.4 Bank reconciliation when there is a bank overdraft

A bank overdraft occurs when there is not enough money in the bank account to cover a transaction, but the bank still makes the payment. This will result in a credit balance in the bank account in the cash book and a debit balance in the bank statement. In this situation, the principles of bank reconciliation are the same as in Worked example 14.1, but care must be taken when dealing with negative bank balances.

WORKED EXAMPLE 14.2

On 31 August 20–9, the bank account in Ahana's cash book showed an overdrawn balance of $2 653. On the same date, her bank statement showed a debit balance of $3 189.

When comparing the cash book and the bank statement it was found that the following items appeared only in the cash book:
- a cheque paid on 30 August to RM Engineering, $2 384
- cash sales paid into the bank on 31 August, $2 900.

CONTINUED

The following items appeared only on the bank statement and not in the cash book:
- rent income paid directly into the bank, $75
- bank charges of $95.

a Make any additional entries which are required in the bank columns of Ahana's cash book and bring down an updated balance on 1 September 20–9.

b Prepare a bank reconciliation statement at 31 August 20–9.

a

Ahana
Cash book (bank columns only)

Dr								Cr
			$					$
20–9				20–9				
Sep 1	Rent income		75	Sep 1	Balance	b/d		2 653
	Balance	c/d	2 673		Bank charges			95
			2 748					2 748
				20–9				
				Sep 1	Balance	b/d		2 673

b

Ahana
Bank reconciliation statement at 31 August 20–9

	$
Balance shown on bank statement	(3 189)
Add Uncredited deposits - Sales	2 900
	(289)
Less Unpresented cheques – RM Engineering	2 384
Balance shown in cash book	(2 673)

- The overdrawn balance on the bank statement (a debit balance) is shown in brackets to indicate a negative balance. The overdrawn balance in the bank account in the cash book (a credit balance) is also shown in brackets to indicate that it is a negative value.

ACTIVITY 14.3

On 1 May 20–7, the cash book of Tarik's business showed a debit balance of $238.

Tarik received a bank statement for April 20–7 which showed a closing balance of $1 325 (Dr).

On investigation, he identified the following reasons for the difference:

- Bank interest for April 20–7 of $125 had been debited directly by the bank but had not yet been recorded in the cash book.

- The book-keeper had made an error when adding up the credit side of the cash book. The total had been overstated by $100.

- The bank statement included a direct debit for equipment rental, $1 200, which had not been recorded in the cash book.

- Cash takings, $2 199, banked by Tarik on 30 April 20–7 had not yet appeared on the bank statement.

- Two cheques sent to suppliers during the month of April 20–7 had not yet been presented for payment:

  - Cheque no: 2396   Arran $420
  - Cheque no: 2399   Skye $850

- A cheque received earlier in the month from Raul, a credit customer, $389, had been returned by the bank.

- An electronic payment, $980, received from a credit customer, Marta, had not been entered in the cash book.

1 Make any additional entries which are required in the bank columns of Tarik's cash book and bring down an updated balance on 1 May 20–7.

2 Prepare a bank reconciliation statement at 30 April 20–7.

REFLECTION

After completing Activity 14.3, how confident are you that you understand how to prepare a bank reconciliation statement?

What actions would you suggest to help someone who is still feeling unsure about this work?

14.5 Bank reconciliation in a computerised accounting system

The process for producing a bank reconciliation statement using a software package is the same as for a manual book-keeping system. When comparing the bank statement against the bank account, first check for missing items and adjust for any errors, which may have occurred in the cash book. Then check for any items which have not yet been processed by the bank, such as unpresented cheques. Once the updated balance in the cash book has been calculated, prepare the bank reconciliation statement. In the unlikely event that the two balances do not match, it may possibly be due to an error in either the cash book or the bank statement, which has not yet been detected.

If the business is operating an online bank account, it is possible to link the bank account in the nominal ledger to the bank's accounting system. This would automatically update both records and make bank reconciliation easier. This could also save the business owner time, which they could spend on other aspects of managing their business. The software can check the totals of different bank accounts in real time and ensure that the balances match with those in all the parts of the system.

Using a software package to prepare a bank reconciliation statement may eliminate some of the errors which might occur when using a manual system. The software package is programmed to match up figures from different documents and if there are places where the figures do not match, the software will alert the user to investigate.

> **DISCUSSION**
>
> Discuss with a partner whether the use of an online bank account would increase or reduce the instances of fraudulent transactions and errors in the books of the business or in the bank records.

14.6 Advantages of bank reconciliation

The advantages of reconciling the balance on the bank statement with that shown on the bank account in the cash book are:

1. After updating the bank account, an accurate bank balance is available.
2. Errors in the bank account or on the bank statement can be identified.
3. It helps business owners to uncover any fraud or embezzlement.
4. Uncredited deposits can be identified.
5. Unpresented cheques can be identified.
6. Any 'stale' cheques (these are usually cheques over six months old which will not be processed by the bank) can be identified and written back into the bank account.

> **ACCOUNTING IN ACTION**
>
> **Understanding bank reconciliation statements**
>
> Ha-eun, the head of the accounts department, decided that the new trainee, Ji-yoo, should learn about bank reconciliation statements. Ha-eun showed Ji-yoo the cash book for April and also the bank statement covering the same period. She told Ji-yoo that the first task was to compare the two records and note which transactions appeared in only one or the other. Ji-yoo made the following list:
>
> Things which are only in the cash book
>
> April 11   Cash paid into bank $1101
>
>   28   Cheque paid to Zu-min $420
>
>   30   Cash paid into bank $2578
>
>
>
> **Figure 14.4:** A new trainee learning about bank reconciliation statements

> **CONTINUED**
>
> Things which are only on the bank statement
>
> | April | 11 | Counter credit $1110 |
> |---|---|---|
> | | 19 | Direct debit to XY Insurance $3500 |
> | | 29 | Bank charges $126 |
> | | 30 | Credit transfer from Mi-Cha $494 |
>
> I think the items on 11 April may be the same transaction, but the figures are different.
>
> After completing this task, Ji-yoo asked Ha-eun the following questions:
>
> a Why does the bank statement seem to be the opposite way round to the cash book?
>
> b Why did the bank not record the transactions shown in the cash book on 28 and 30 April?
>
> c Why were the direct debit and the bank charges not recorded in the cash book?
>
> d Why can we not just assume the bank statement balance is the correct bank balance? Why do we need to compare the records?
>
> Discuss in pairs or in a group:
>
> 1 Imagine you are Ha-eun. What answers would you give to Ji-yoo's questions?
>
> 2 What steps could Ha-eun take to check the cash book entry for the transaction on 11 April?

> **SUMMARY**
>
> You should now know:
>
> - The purpose of the bank reconciliation is to explain the differences between the bank balance shown in the cash book and the balance on the bank statement.
> - Most of the differences between the balances are caused by differences in the time at which items are recorded and because some items cannot be recorded in the cash book until the bank statement is received.
> - The cash book should be updated by entering those items which appear on the bank statement but not in the cash book.
> - The bank reconciliation statement shows the balance on the bank statement adjusted for uncredited deposits, unpresented cheques and any bank errors. The final figure should agree with the balance shown in the bank account in the cash book.

Chapter 14 practice questions

1 Which statement is correct about a bank reconciliation statement?

    A It contains bank charges and standing orders.

    B It is part of the double entry book-keeping records.

    C It is prepared by the bank.

    D It is prepared by the trader. [1]

2 A bank reconciliation statement was prepared starting with the balance shown on the bank statement. Which item would be deducted?

  A bank error resulting in the account being incorrectly debited

  B cash book error resulting in the balance being overstated

  C uncredited cheque

  D unpresented cheque [1]

3 The bank column of a trader's cash book showed a debit balance of $952. This did not agree with the balance on the bank statement on the same date. The following differences were found:

	$
Unpresented cheque	134
Bank charges	11
Rent paid by credit transfer	310

What was the balance on the bank statement?

  A $765 credit

  B $765 debit

  C $1 139 credit

  D $1 139 debit [1]

4 Sota is a trader. He maintains a three-column cash book and compares this with his bank statement at the end of every month and prepares a bank reconciliation statement.

  a State two reasons why it is advisable for Sota to reconcile his cash book with the bank statement every month. [2]

  b Explain the difference between uncredited deposits and unpresented cheques. [2]

  c Copy and complete the following table by placing a tick in the correct column to indicate whether each item would be used to update the cash book or would appear in the bank reconciliation statement. [7]

	Updating cash book	Bank reconciliation statement
Bank charges		
Bank error		
Cash sales not yet credited		
Cheque from Adil dishonoured		
Credit transfer from Wahid		
Electricity paid by direct debit		
Unpresented cheque		

[Total: 11]

5 Esther provided her cash book for the month of December 20–8.

Esther

Dr				Cash book (bank columns only)				Cr
				$				$
20–8					20–8			
Dec 1	Balance	b/d	832		Dec 12	Lewis		280
10	George		146		21	Jonah		195
29	Sales		964		31	Balance	c/d	1 467
			1 942					1 942
20–9								
Jan 1	Balance	b/d	1 467					

On 1 January 20–9, Esther received her bank statement for the month of December 20–8.

SOUTHERN BANK LTD
Central Branch

Account: Esther Williams   Account no: 959477

Date: 31 December 20–8

Date	Details	Debit $	Credit $	Balance $
20–8				
Dec 1	Balance			732 Cr
12	Bank transfer – Lewis	280		452 Cr
18	Cheque 7890		146	598 Cr
24	Dishonoured cheque	146		452 Cr
29	DD RAK Finance	120		332 Cr
31	Bank charges	53		279 Cr

Esther checked the bank statement against her cash book and discovered the following errors:

- Esther had made an error when bringing down the balance in the cash book on 1 December 20–8. The correct figure was $732 (Dr).
- The direct debit payment on 29 December 20–8 related to a payment which should have been charged to Esther's personal bank account and not the business bank account.

a Identify items not recorded in the cash book. Update the bank columns the cash book and bring down an updated balance on 1 January 20–9. **[4]**

b Prepare a bank reconciliation statement at 31 December 20–8. **[5]**

c Prepare an extract from the statement of financial position at 31 December 20–8 showing the bank balance. **[2]**

[Total: 11]

14 Bank reconciliation statements

6 On 31 May 20–5, Temu's cash book showed a bank overdraft of $3 213.

He discovered the following differences between his cash book and the bank statement:

1. Unpresented cheques:

	$
Bilan	695
Astur	1 212

2. Cash sales, $2 872, had not been recorded in the bank statement.

3. The bank had debited $500 to the business bank account which should have been debited to Temu's personal bank account.

a Prepare a bank reconciliation statement at 1 June 20–5 to show the balance on the bank statement. [6]

b Explain the difference between a bank statement and a bank reconciliation statement. [4]

c Explain why the entries on a bank statement are on the opposite side to where they appear in the cash book. [4]

[Total: 14]

CHECK YOUR PROGRESS

How well do you think you have achieved the learning intentions for this chapter? Give yourself a score from 1 (still need a lot of practice) to 5 (feeling very confident) for each learning intention. Provide an example to support your score.

Now I can …	Score	Example to support score
understand the purpose of a bank statement		
explain the purpose of a bank reconciliation statement and how it is used by a business		
prepare an updated cash book		
draw up a bank reconciliation statement		
explain how bank reconciliation statements are maintained in a computerised accounting system.		

Chapter 15

Journal entries and correction of errors

LEARNING INTENTIONS

By the end of this chapter, you will be able to:

- record accounting data in the general journal and post entries to the ledger
- record the purchase and sale of non-current assets and depreciation of non-current assets in the journal
- record accrued and prepaid expenses and accrued and prepaid incomes in the journal
- record irrecoverable debts and irrecoverable debts recovered (where appropriate) in the journal
- record the creation of, and adjustments to, an allowance for irrecoverable debts in the journal
- prepare journal entries to correct errors
- understand the purpose of a suspense account and how to make entries in a suspense account
- calculate the profit or loss after errors have been corrected and understand the effect that correcting errors has on a statement of financial position.

15 Journal entries and correction of errors

Introduction

The **journal** or general journal is a book of prime entry. Chapter 7 explained how all transactions are recorded in a book of prime entry **before** they are entered in the ledger.

The journal is not a part of the double entry book-keeping system. It is regarded as a diary in which transactions are noted before they are entered in the ledger. Anything which is not entered in one of the other books of prime entry must be entered in the journal before being recorded in the ledger.

> **KEY TERM**
>
> **journal:** a book of prime entry used to record transactions which cannot be recorded in any other book of prime entry.

> **LINKS**
>
> You learnt about the other books of prime entry in earlier chapters. In Chapters 4–5, you learnt about cash books and petty cash books, and in Chapter 7, you learnt about sales, purchases and returns journals.

ACCOUNTING IN CONTEXT

Where are different transactions recorded?

Figure 15.1: A wholesaler trading in soft furnishings

Businesses use books of prime entry, which means that a lot of detail is removed from the ledger. Books of prime entry are also useful for collating and summarising accounting information. Every transaction should be recorded in one of these books before being posted to the ledger.

Mani is a wholesaler trading in soft furnishings for homes. He buys and sells cushions, curtains, rugs and all sorts of other items that people might want for their home. Goods are purchased on credit from various manufacturers and are then sold on credit to retail stores. Mani employs office staff, warehouse assistants and lorry drivers.

In addition to their other duties, the office staff maintain a full set of double entry records, including seven books of prime entry.

Discuss in pairs or in a group:

1. Suggest one type of transaction which will be recorded in each of the following books of prime entry:

    a cash book

    b petty cash book

    c sales journal

    d sales returns journal

    e purchases journal

    f purchases returns journal

2. If a transaction is not recorded in any of the books of prime entry listed in question 1, then it is recorded in the journal. Suggest two transactions which may be recorded in the journal. In each case, give a reason why the transaction you have named would appear in the journal and not in one of the other books of prime entry.

15.1 Layout of journal entries

An entry in the journal should show:

- the date of the transaction
- the name of the account to be debited and the amount
- the name of the account to be credited and the amount
- a narrative.

The narrative consists of a brief explanation of what is being recorded and why the entry is being made. This is useful because it is impossible to remember the reason for every entry, and the entries in the journal sometimes involve unusual transactions.

The layout of the journal is as follows:

	Journal		
Date	Details	Debit $	Credit $

The items usually recorded in the journal are:

- opening entries
- purchase and sale of non-current assets on credit
- non-regular transactions such as year end transfers, writing off irrecoverable debts, interest charged on overdue accounts
- correction of errors.

15.2 Opening journal entries

Opening journal entries are made when the business starts or when the business first keeps accounting records. An opening journal entry lists the assets owned by the business (shown in the debit column), the liabilities owed by the business (shown in the credit column) and the capital of the business (also shown in the credit column).

After the journal entry has been prepared, the items are posted to the appropriate ledger accounts.

Figure 15.2: A business's assets can include motor vehicles and inventory

15 Journal entries and correction of errors

> ### WORKED EXAMPLE 15.1
>
> Bhavin started business on 1 November 20–1. He did not maintain any accounting records during his first year of trading.
>
> On 1 November 20–2, Bhavin was able to provide the following information about his business:
>
> | | |
> |---|---|
> | Assets | Property $130 000, fixtures $28 700, motor vehicle $14 500, inventory $4 800, trade receivables $5 200, cash $300 |
> | Liabilities | Trade payables $6 100, bank overdraft $3 800 |
>
> Prepare an opening journal entry for Bhavin at 1 November 20–2.
>
> Record the appropriate entries in Bhavin's ledger and cash book.
>
> **Bhavin**
> **Journal**
>
> | Date | Details | Debit $ | Credit $ |
> |---|---|---|---|
> | 20–2 | | | |
> | Nov 1 | Property | 130 000 | |
> | | Fixtures | 28 700 | |
> | | Motor vehicle | 14 500 | |
> | | Inventory | 4 800 | |
> | | Trade receivables | 5 200 | |
> | | Cash | 300 | |
> | | Trade payables | | 6 100 |
> | | Bank | | 3 800 |
> | | Capital | | 173 600 |
> | | Assets, liabilities and capital on 1 November 20–2 | 183 500 | 183 500 |
>
> - It is usual to show the debit entries first.
> - It is usual to slightly indent the credit entries.
> - It is usual to draw a line after each separate journal entry.
> - The capital was calculated as the difference between the assets and the liabilities.
> - If the names of individual credit suppliers and customers are known, these could be listed separately with the amounts owing, instead of giving a combined total for trade receivables and trade payables.

> **CONTINUED**

Bhavin
Nominal ledger

Dr	Property account		Cr
	$		$
20–2			
Nov 1 Balance	130 000		

Dr	Fixtures account		Cr
	$		$
20–2			
Nov 1 Balance	28 700		

Dr	Motor vehicles account		Cr
	$		$
20–2			
Nov 1 Balance	14 500		

Dr	Inventory account		Cr
	$		$
20–2			
Nov 1 Balance	4 800		

Dr	Capital account		Cr
	$		$
		20–2	
		Nov 1 Balance	173 600

Cash Book

	Cash $	Bank $		Cash $	Bank $
20–2			20–2		
Nov 1 Balance	300		Nov 1 Balance		3 800

- If the names of the individual credit customers and credit suppliers were provided, an account would be opened in the:
    - sales ledger for each credit customer and the account debited with the balance owed by that customer
    - purchases ledger for each credit supplier and the account credited with the balance owed to that supplier.

15.3 Purchase and sale of non-current assets

As the purchase and sale of non-current assets on credit are not recorded in one of the other books of prime entry, they should be entered in the journal before being posted to the ledger.

After the journal entry has been completed, the transaction is posted to the appropriate ledger accounts.

> **LINK**
>
> You learnt about disposal of non-current assets in Chapter 12.

WORKED EXAMPLE 15.2

Bhavin's financial year ends on 31 October.

Prepare the journal entries to record the following transactions on 1 September 20–3:
- Purchased additional fixtures, $1 500, on credit from Office Supplies.
- Sold the motor vehicle (cost $14 500) for $8 600 on credit to AB Vehicles.

Bhavin
Journal

Date	Details	Debit $	Credit $
20–3			
Sep 1	Fixtures	1 500	
	Office Supplies		1 500
	Purchase of fixtures on credit		
	Disposal of motor vehicle	14 500	
	Motor vehicles		14 500
	Transfer of motor vehicle to disposal account		
	AB Vehicles	8 600	
	Disposal of motor vehicle		8 600
	Sale of motor vehicle on credit		
Oct 31	Statement of profit or loss	5 900	
	Disposal of motor vehicle		5 900
	Loss on disposal of motor vehicle transferred to the statement of profit or loss		

- The narrative is added after the debit and credit entries and a line is drawn after each separate journal entry.

> **TIP**
>
> When you write the narrative in a journal, you should briefly explain the reason for the entry and not simply state which account is debited and which account is credited.

ACTIVITY 15.1

Nyoni is an electrical goods wholesaler. She maintains a full set of accounting records.

State the book of prime entry in which Nyoni would record each of the following transactions:

1. Purchase of goods for resale on credit
2. Purchase of stationery on credit
3. Goods returned by a credit customer
4. Transfer of personal motor vehicle to the business
5. Personal travel expenses paid by cheque
6. Purchase of office equipment by cheque
7. Transfer of drawings to capital account at year end.

15.4 Non-regular transactions

As explained earlier, any transactions which cannot be recorded in another book of prime entry are recorded in the journal. These often consist of transactions which do not occur regularly, and year-end transfers to the statement of profit or loss. The transaction is posted to the appropriate ledger accounts after the journal entry is completed.

Worked example 15.3 shows how to prepare journal entries and make ledger postings for irrecoverable debts, irrecoverable debts recovered, and the creation of, and adjustment to, an allowance for irrecoverable debts. All of these are regarded as non-regular transactions.

The example also includes some journal and ledger entries for year-end transfers to the statement of profit or loss.

WORKED EXAMPLE 15.3

Bhavin's financial year ends on 31 October. He provided the following information for the year ended 31 October 20–3:

- Irrecoverable debts written off up to 30 October 20–3 amounted to $320.
- On 31 October 20–6, it was decided to:

  Write off as irrecoverable a debt of $90 owing by Annie

  Create an allowance for irrecoverable debts of $620.

a Prepare journal entries to record the decisions made on 31 October 20–3 and any necessary year-end transfers.

b Prepare the appropriate ledger accounts after posting these entries.

15 Journal entries and correction of errors

CONTINUED

a

Bhavin
Journal

Date	Details	Debit $	Credit $
20–3			
Oct 31	Irrecoverable debts	90	
	Annie		90
	Writing off Annie's account as an irrecoverable debt		
	Statement of profit or loss	410	
	Irrecoverable debts		410
	Transfer of irrecoverable debts to the statement of profit or loss		
	Statement of profit or loss	620	
	Allowance for irrecoverable debts		620
	Creation of allowance for irrecoverable debts		

b

Bhavin
Sales ledger

Dr			Annie account				Cr
			$				$
20–3				20–3			
Oct 1	Balance	b/d	90	Oct 31	Irrecoverable debts		90
			90				90

Nominal ledger

Dr			Irrecoverable debts account				Cr
			$				$
20–3				20–3			
Oct 30	Trade receivables		320	Oct 31	Statement of profit or loss		410
31	Annie		90				
			410				410

Dr		Allowance for irrecoverable debts account					Cr
			$				$
20–3				20–3			
Oct 31	Balance	c/d	620	Oct 31	Statement of profit or loss		620
			620				620
				20–3			
				Nov 1	Balance	b/d	620

> **CONTINUED**

On 31 October 20–4, Bhavin:

- agreed to accept equipment valued at $180 from Rita in settlement of a debt written off during the year ended 31 October 20–3.
- decided to increase the allowance for irrecoverable debts to $650.

c Prepare journal entries to record the above information, including year-end transfers.

d Prepare the appropriate ledger accounts after posting these entries.

c

Bhavin
Journal

Date	Details	Debit $	Credit $
20–4			
Oct 31	Equipment	180	
	Irrecoverable debts recovered		180
	Equipment accepted in settlement of debt previously written off		
	Irrecoverable debts recovered	180	
	Statement of profit or loss		180
	Transfer of irrecoverable debts recovered to the statement of profit or loss		
	Statement of profit or loss	30	
	Allowance for irrecoverable debts		30
	Increase in allowance for irrecoverable debts		

d

Bhavin
Nominal ledger

Dr		Irrecoverable debts recovered account				Cr
			$			$
20–4				20–4		
Oct 31	Statement of profit or loss		180	Oct 31	Equipment	180
			180			180

Dr		Equipment account		Cr
			$	$
20–4				
Oct 31	Irrecoverable debts recovered		180	

CONTINUED

Dr			Allowance for irrecoverable debts account			Cr
			$			$
20–3				20–3		
Oct 31	Balance	c/d	620	Oct 31	Statement of profit or loss	620
			620			620
20–4				20–3		
Oct 31	Balance	c/d	650	Nov 1	Balance b/d	620
				20–4		
				Oct 31	Statement of profit or loss	30
			650			650
				20–4		
				Nov 1	Balance b/d	650

- The alternative ways of recording irrecoverable debts recovered are explained in Section 13.2 of Chapter 13.

Worked example 15.4 shows how to prepare journal entries and make ledger postings for year-end transfers for items appearing in the trading section of the statement of profit or loss. It also shows the transfer of items which require an adjustment for an accrual or a prepayment to the profit and loss section of the statement of profit or loss.

> **LINKS**
>
> You learnt about irrecoverable debts and allowances for irrecoverable debts in Chapter 13.

WORKED EXAMPLE 15.4

Bhavin's financial year ends on 31 October. He provided the following information:

- At 31 October 20–5, Bhavin's ledger accounts included the following:

  Sales returns for the year $3 150

  Inventory at 1 November 20–4 $4 360

  Purchases for the year $51 000

  Rent income $1 500 (part of the property had been let to a tenant on 1 July 20–5 at an annual rent of $3 600)

  General expenses $3 990

  Insurance $2 040, which included a prepayment of $240

  Motor vehicle $18 000 (purchased 1 November 20–4)

- On 31 October 20–5:

  Inventory was valued at $4 880

  General expenses accrued amounted to $210

  The motor vehicle should be depreciated by $2 700

a Prepare journal entries to record the year-end transfers.

b Prepare the ledger accounts after posting these entries.

CONTINUED

a

	Bhavin Journal		
Date	Details	Debit $	Credit $
20–5			
Oct 31	Statement of profit or loss	3 150	
	Sales returns		3 150
	Transfer of sales returns for the year to the statement of profit or loss		
	Statement of profit or loss	4 360	
	Inventory		4 360
	Transfer of opening inventory to the statement of profit or loss		
	Statement of profit or loss	51 000	
	Purchases		51 000
	Transfer of purchases for the year to the statement of profit or loss		
	Inventory	4 880	
	Statement of profit or loss		4 880
	Transfer of closing inventory to the statement of profit or loss		
	Rent income	1 200	
	Statement of profit or loss		1 200
	Transfer of rent income for the year to the statement of profit or loss		
	Statement of profit or loss	4 200	
	General expenses		4 200
	Transfer of general expenses for the year to the statement of profit or loss		
	Statement of profit or loss	1 800	
	Insurance		1 800
	Transfer of insurance for the year to the statement of profit or loss		
	Statement of profit or loss	2 700	
	Provision for depreciation on motor vehicle		2 700
	Annual depreciation charge of motor vehicle transferred to the statement of profit or loss		

- The amounts transferred to the statement of profit of loss for rent income, general expenses and insurance are the amounts which relate to the year ended 31 October 20–5 (the amount received or paid was adjusted for the closing prepayment or accrual).

CONTINUED

b

Bhavin
Nominal ledger

Dr	Sales returns account			Cr
	$			$
20–5		20–5		
Oct 31 Total to date	3 150	Oct 31 Statement of profit or loss		3 150
	3 150			3 150

Dr	Purchases account			Cr
	$			$
20–5		20–5		
Oct 31 Total to date	51 000	Oct 31 Statement of profit or loss		51 000
	51 000			51 000

Dr	Inventory account			Cr
	$			$
20–4		20–5		
Nov 1 Balance b/d	4 360	Oct 31 Statement of profit or loss		4 360
	4 360			4 360
20–5		20–5		
Oct 31 Statement of profit or loss	4 880	Oct 31 Balance c/d		4 880
	4 880			4 880
20–5				
Nov 1 Balance b/d	4 880			

Dr	Rent income account			Cr
	$			$
20–5		20–5		
Oct 31 Statement of profit or loss	1 200	Oct 31 Total received		1 500
Balance c/d	300			
	1 500			1 500
		20–5		
		Nov 1 Balance b/d		300

CONTINUED

Dr		General expenses account				Cr
20–5			$	20–5		$
Oct 31	Total paid		3 990	Oct 31	Statement of profit or loss	4 200
	Balance	c/d	210			
			4 200			4 200
				20–5		
				Nov 1	Balance b/d	210

Dr		Insurance account				Cr
20–5			$	20–5		$
Oct 31	Total paid		2 040	Oct 31	Statement of profit or loss	1 800
					Balance c/d	240
			2 040			2 040
20–5						
Nov 1	Balance	b/d	240			

Dr		Provision for depreciation on motor vehicles account				Cr
20–5			$	20–5		$
Oct 31	Balance	c/d	2 700	Oct 31	Statement of profit or loss	2 700
			2 700			2 700
				20–5		
				Nov 1	Balance b/d	2 700

LINKS

You learnt about other payables and other receivables in Chapter 11 and about depreciation of non-current assets in Chapter 12.

15 Journal entries and correction of errors

> **ACTIVITY 15.2**
>
> Olivia is a trader. At the end of her financial year on 31 October 20–3, the balances in her books included:
>
> Carriage outwards $594
>
> Discount received $1 820
>
> Prepare journal entries to show the year-end transfers to the statement of profit or loss. Narratives should be shown.

15.5 Correction of errors

Errors made when recording day-to-day transactions can be divided into those which are not shown by the trial balance, and those which affect the totals of the trial balance so they do not agree.

Errors which are not shown by a trial balance

There are six types of errors that can be made which will not be revealed by the trial balance.

These are:

- Error of commission
- Error of complete reversal
- Error of omission
- Error of original entry
- Error of principle
- Compensating errors

When such errors are discovered, they should be corrected by first making a journal entry and then making entries in the appropriate ledger accounts.

> **LINK**
>
> You learnt about the errors which will not affect the balancing of a trial balance in Chapter 3.

WORKED EXAMPLE 15.5

Bhavin's financial year ends on 31 October.

The totals of the trial balance prepared on 31 October 20–6 agreed, but the following errors were later discovered:

- The purchase of stationery, $95, had been debited to the purchases account.
- A bank transfer, $750, received from K Singh had been credited to the account of H Singh.
- The wages account had been overstated by $1 000 and the purchases account had been understated by $1 000.

Prepare the necessary journal entries to correct these errors.

Bhavin
Journal

Date	Details	Debit $	Credit $
20–6			
Oct 31	Stationery	95	
	Purchases		95
	Error in posting stationery to purchases, now corrected		
	H Singh	750	
	K Singh		750
	Error in posting a bank transfer to wrong personal account, now corrected		
	Purchases	1 000	
	Wages		1 000
	Purchases understated and wages overstated, now corrected		

To help you decide where to debit and where to credit, you could prepare working notes in the form of ledger accounts. For example, in Worked example 15.5:

When considering Error 1

Entry made

Dr	Stationery account	Cr

Dr	Purchases account	Cr
95		

Entry which should have been made

Dr	Stationery account	Cr
95		

Dr	Purchases account	Cr

How to correct the error

Dr	Stationery account	Cr
95		

Dr	Purchases account	Cr
95		95

When considering Error 2

Entry made

Dr K Singh account Cr	Dr H Singh account Cr
	750

Entry which should have been made

Dr K Singh account Cr	Dr H Singh account Cr
750	

How to correct the error

Dr K Singh account Cr	Dr H Singh account Cr
750	**750** 750

Errors which affect a trial balance

Some errors may occur, which means the totals of the trial balance will not balance.

If the errors are not found immediately, the trial balance is balanced by inserting the difference between the two sides in a **suspense account**. This is a temporary account which is used to record the difference on the trial balance until the errors are discovered.

The flow chart in Figure 15.3 shows the steps that are taken when a trial balance does not balance and the errors are discovered later.

KEY TERM

suspense account: a temporary account opened in order to make the totals of a trial balance agree.

Totals of a trial balance do not balance. → Enter the difference in a suspense account. → When an error is found, correct it by making a journal entry. → Make appropriate entries in the ledger accounts.

Figure 15.3: Steps which are taken when a trial balance does not balance

When all the errors have been found and corrected, the suspense account will close automatically. So, if there is a balance remaining on a suspense account, it means that there are still some errors in the accounting records.

LINK

You learnt about the types of errors which result in the totals of a trial balance not balancing in Chapter 3.

TIP

If you prepare a trial balance and it does not balance, then you should use a suspense account so that you can balance the trial balance and prepare financial statements. Errors can then be corrected using double entry.

WORKED EXAMPLE 15.6

Bhavin's financial year ends on 31 October.

The totals of the trial balance prepared on 31 October 20–7 failed to agree. The difference of $590 was a shortage on the credit side. This was entered in a suspense account.

The following errors were later discovered:

a The sales account had been understated by $1 000.

b No entry had been made for office expenses, $29, paid in cash.

c Credit purchases, $650, from Anil had been correctly entered in the purchases journal but credited to Anil's account as $560.

d Capital introduced by Bhavin, $10 000 (paid into the bank), had been debited to the capital account and credited to the bank account.

e $310 paid to Yuvraj by bank transfer had been correctly entered in the bank account, but no other entry was made.

f The sales returns for October 20–7, totalling $95, had been correctly entered in the individual customers' accounts but had been credited to the purchases returns account.

Prepare the necessary journal entries to correct these errors.

Prepare the suspense account in Bhavin's ledger.

Bhavin
Journal

				Debit $	Credit $
	20–7				
a	Oct 31	Suspense		1 000	
			Sales		1 000
			Sales understated, now corrected		
b		Office expenses		29	
			Cash		29
			Omission of cash paid for office expenses, now corrected		
c		Suspense		90	
			Anil		90
			Purchases, $650, incorrectly entered in Anil's account as $560, now corrected		

15 Journal entries and correction of errors

CONTINUED

Bhavin
Journal

		Debit $	Credit $
d	Bank	20 000	
	Capital		20 000
	Capital introduced debited to capital and credited to bank, now corrected		
e	Yuvraj	310	
	Suspense		310
	Bank transfer from Yuvraj entered only in the bank, now corrected		
f	Sales returns	95	
	Purchases returns	95	
	Suspense		190
	Sales returns incorrectly credited to purchases returns, now corrected		

- Where an entry has been reversed (as in error **d**), it is necessary to double the amount of the error in order to correct it and to restore the accounts to the correct amount.
- Error **f** required two accounts to be debited (the sales returns and the purchases returns) with the corresponding credits in the suspense account in order to correct the error.

Bhavin
Nominal ledger
Suspense account

Dr			$			Cr $
20–7				20–7		
Oct 31	Sales		1 000	Oct 31	Difference on trial balance	590
	Anil		90		Yuvraj	310
					Sales returns	95
					Purchases returns	95
			1 090			1 090

- An entry was required in the suspense account to correct errors **a**, **c**, **e** and **f** as all these affected the balancing of the trial balance.
- No entry was required in the suspense account to correct errors **b** and **d** as these did not affect the balancing of the trial balance.

ACTIVITY 15.3

Figure 15.4: Repairs being made to factory machinery

a   Write down one reason why it may be necessary to open a suspense account.

b   A factory owner needed to make some repairs to one of the machines. When the accounts were completed, the machinery repairs, $500, was debited to the machinery account.

   i   State the type of error which was made.

   ii Prepare a correcting journal entry (a narrative is required) and explain why your correcting journal entry included or did not include an entry into a suspense account.

c   A business owner prepared a trial balance which did not balance, so a suspense account was opened. The owner discovered later that a bank overdraft, $200, had not been included in the trial balance. The following correcting journal entry was made:

Journal		
Details	Debit $	Credit $
Suspense (no credit entry required)	220	
Correction of error, bank overdraft omitted from trial balance		

Explain why no credit entry was required and only one entry was made.

REFLECTION

How confident were you in answering the questions in Activity 15.3?

Which of the questions did you find the simplest and which did you find the most difficult?

Why do you think that was?

What can you do to help yourself answer similar questions in future?

15.6 Effect on profit of correcting errors

If errors are discovered after the draft statement of profit or loss has been prepared, it may be necessary to amend the profit figure. Any corrections made to items appearing in the trading section of the statement of profit or loss will affect both the gross profit and the profit for the year. Any corrections made to items appearing in the profit and loss section of the statement of profit or loss will only affect the profit for the year.

15 Journal entries and correction of errors

WORKED EXAMPLE 15.7

Bhavin's financial year ends on 31 October.

The totals of the trial balance prepared on 31 October 20–7 failed to agree. The difference was entered in a suspense account and draft financial statements were prepared. The profit for the year was $15 000.

The following errors were later discovered:

a The sales account had been understated by $1 000.

b No entry had been made for office expenses, $29, paid in cash.

c Credit purchases, $650, from Anil had been correctly entered in the purchases journal but credited to Anil's account as $560.

d Capital introduced by Bhavin, $10 000 (paid into the bank), had been debited to the capital account and credited to the bank account.

e $310 paid to Yuvraj by bank transfer had been correctly entered in the bank account, but no other entry was made.

f The sales returns for October 20–7, totalling $95, had been correctly entered in the individual customers' accounts but had been credited to the purchases returns account.

Prepare a statement to show the corrected profit for the year ended 31 October 20–7.

Bhavin
Statement of corrected profit for the year ended 31 October 20–7

		$	$
Profit for the year from statement of profit or loss			15 000
Add	Sales understated		1 000
			16 000
Less	Office expenses omitted	29	
	Sales returns understated	95	
	Purchases returns overstated	95	219
Corrected profit for the year			15 781

- Errors **c**, **d** and **e** do not affect the calculation of the profit, as they affect items which appear in the statement of financial position and not items which appear in the statement of profit or loss.

- If the sales are understated, the profit will be understated and so $1 000 must be added.

- If expenses have been omitted, the profit will be overstated and so $29 must be deducted.

- If the sales returns have been understated, the profit will be overstated and so $95 must be deducted.

- If the purchases returns have been overstated, the profit will be overstated and so $95 must be deducted.

15.7 Effect on statement of financial position of correcting errors

If errors are discovered and corrected after the preparation of draft financial statements, the statement of financial position may have to be amended. If the profit for the year has been corrected, this will affect the capital section of the statement of financial position, but other items may also need to be amended.

> ### WORKED EXAMPLE 15.8
>
> Bhavin's financial year ends on 31 October.
>
> The totals of the trial balance prepared on 31 October 20–7 failed to agree. The difference was entered in a suspense account and draft financial statements were prepared.
>
> The following errors were later discovered:
>
> a   The sales account had been understated by $1 000.
>
> b   No entry had been made for office expenses of $29 paid in cash.
>
> c   Credit purchases of $650 from Anil had been correctly entered in the purchases journal but credited to Anil's account as $560.
>
> d   Capital introduced by Bhavin of $10 000 (paid into the bank) had been debited to the capital account and credited to the bank account.
>
> e $310 paid to Yuvraj by bank transfer had been correctly entered in the bank account, but no other entry was made.
>
> f   The sales returns for October 20–7, totalling $95, had been correctly entered in the individual customers' accounts but had been credited to the purchases returns account.
>
> The corrected profit for the year ended 31 October 20–7 was $15 781.
>
> Explain how correcting each of these errors will affect the statement of financial position at 31 October 20–7.
>
> **Errors a and f**
> These errors do not affect any of the assets and liabilities but do affect the profit. This means that the draft profit, which was added to the capital, will be increased by $810 (plus $1 000 and minus $190).
>
> **Error b**
> To correct this error, the figure for cash in the current assets section of the statement will have to be reduced by $29. The draft profit, which was added to the capital, will be reduced by $29.
>
> **Error c**
> To correct this error, Anil's account needed to be credited with $90, so the figure for trade payables in the current liabilities section will need to be increased by $90.
>
> **Error d**
> To correct this error, the capital account needed to be credited with $20 000, so the balance of the capital account will need to be increased by $20 000.
>
> This also affected the bank account. The bank account needed to be debited with $20 000, so the figure for bank in the current assets section will need to be increased by $20 000. If the bank was an overdrawn balance, then the current liabilities would be reduced by $20 000.
>
> **Error e**
> To correct this error, Yuvraj's account needed to be debited, so the figure for trade payables in the current liabilities section will need to be decreased by $310.

DISCUSSION

Belinda owns a small sewing business. Her financial year ends on 31 December.

Belinda purchased a machine on 1 January 20–5 for $1 200. On 30 December 20–7, she decided the machine was no longer suitable for her requirements and she sold it for $540. At the date of sale, the machine had been depreciated by $583.

In January 20–8, it was discovered that no entries had made in the books to record the sale of the machine.

Discuss with a partner:

1. What journal entries should have been made on 30 December 20–7?

2. How does correcting this error affect the profit for the year ended 31 December 20–7?

3. How does correcting this error affect the statement of financial position on 31 December 20–7?

ACCOUNTING IN ACTION

Correcting errors

Figure 15.5: A caterer preparing food for a special event

Amy owns a catering business which caters for family events such as weddings and birthday parties. She also provides a catering service for local businesses when they have special events such as staff parties and open days.

Amy purchases all her ingredients on credit from local food wholesalers. She sends her customers an account a few days after the event has taken place and allows 14 days credit.

Amy employs a part-time book-keeper to maintain the day-to-day accounting records, and her accountant prepares her statement of profit or loss and statement of financial position at the end of each financial year.

The totals of the trial balance prepared on 30 April 20–6 did not agree and the difference was entered in a suspense account. The following errors were later discovered:

i   An invoice issued for catering for a garden party had not been recorded.

ii The total of the general expenses account had been overstated.

iii Purchases returns had been debited to the account of Super Bakers Supplies instead of to the account of Super Chefs Supplies.

iv Repairs to catering equipment had been debited to the catering equipment account.

Discuss in pairs or in a group:

1. How would you explain to Amy whether each error did or did not:

   a   affect the balancing of the trial balance, giving a reason

   b   affect the calculation of the profit for the year, giving a reason?

2. What would you say to Amy when she asks if it is really necessary to open a suspense account?

> SUMMARY

You should now know:

- A journal can be regarded as a diary in which transactions are noted before they are entered in the ledger.

- Journal entries are made to open the accounting records, to record the purchase and sale of non-current assets, to record non-regular transactions and to correct errors.

- A narrative is a brief explanation of what is being recorded in the journal entry and why the entry is being made.

- A suspense account is opened if a trial balance fails to balance. This means that the draft financial statements can be prepared.

- Errors affecting the balancing of the trial balance are corrected by making entries in the suspense account.

Chapter 15 practice questions

1   Sara maintains an allowance for irrecoverable debts at 3% of the trade receivables at the end of each financial year. On 1 June 20–2, Sara's allowance for irrecoverable debts was $414. On 31 May 20–3, her trade receivables amounted to $12 600.

Which journal entry would Sara make on 31 May 20–3?

		Debit $	Credit $
A	Allowance for irrecoverable debts	36	
	Statement of profit or loss		36
B	Allowance for irrecoverable debts	378	
	Statement of profit or loss		378
C	Statement of profit or loss	36	
	Allowance for irrecoverable debts		36
D	Statement of profit or loss	378	
	Allowance for irrecoverable debts		378

[1]

2 Jabari's financial year ends on 31 March. On 1 April 20–7, he purchased furniture costing $4 400 for use in the office. He decided to depreciate the furniture using the reducing balance method at 15% per annum.

Which journal entry did Jabari make on 31 March 20–9?

		Debit $	Credit $
A	Provision for depreciation on furniture	99	
	Furniture		99
B	Provision for depreciation on furniture	1 221	
	Depreciation of furniture		1 221
C	Statement of profit or loss	561	
	Provision for depreciation on furniture		561
D	Statement of profit or loss	660	
	Provision for depreciation on furniture		660

[1]

3 Aaron discovered that goods bought on credit from Damon, $440, had been incorrectly debited to Damian's account.

Which journal entry corrects this error?

		Debit $	Credit $
A	Damian	440	
	Damon		440
B	Damian	440	
	Damon	440	
	Suspense		880
C	Damon	440	
	Damian		440
D	Suspense	880	
	Damian		440
	Damon		440

[1]

4 John owns a retail store. His financial year ends on 31 July.
On 31 July 20–1, John made the following transactions:

    Purchased stationery, $94, on credit from AB Supplies

    Took goods, costing $210, for his own use

    Depreciated shop fittings by $900

  a Prepare journal entries to record these items. Narratives are required.   **[6]**

On 31 July 20–1, the balances in John's ledger included the following:

	$
Rent	3 600
Sales	84 700
Purchases returns	1 940

One-third of the rent relates to John's apartment above the shop.

  b Prepare journal entries to adjust the rent and to record the year-end transfers to the statement of profit or loss for the three accounts. Narratives are required.   **[12]**

[Total: 18]

5 At the end of his financial year on 31 July 20–4, Sanjay opened a suspense account with a debit balance of $435.

  a Suggest one reason why the suspense account was required.   **[1]**

After preparing draft financial statements, Sanjay discovered the following errors:

  1 The sales returns journal was understated by $100.

  2 Carriage outwards, $194, had been debited to the carriage inwards account.

  3 The total of the analysis column for office expenses in the petty cash book, $23, had not been transferred to the ledger.

  4 $565 paid by Kimaya, a credit customer, had been credited to the account of Kinana, another credit customer.

  5 The balance of the petty cash book, $120, had not been entered in the trial balance.

  6 The July total of the discount allowed column in the cash book, $96, had been credited to the discount received account in the ledger.

  b Prepare journal entries to correct the errors. Narratives are not required. **[13]**

  c Prepare the suspense account. Balance or total the account as necessary.   **[6]**

[Total: 20]

6 Ezra is a wholesaler of men's clothing. His draft profit for the year ended 30 September 20–3 was $17 980. He then discovered the following errors:

1   One page of the sales returns journal had been overstated by $100.
2   Capital invested into the business bank account by Ezra, $10 000, had been recorded as drawings.
3   No entry had been made for cleaning expenses paid in cash, $50.
4   No entry had been made for the sale of fixtures. These had originally cost $5 000 and had been depreciated by $4 200. A bank transfer for $760 was received.
5   No entry had been made for cash discount, $23, received from Caleb, a credit supplier.
6   The amount of $630 received from Elisha, a credit customer, had been debited to the account of Elijah, another credit customer.

Copy out the following the statement of corrected profit for the year ended 30 September 20–3. Complete the statement by inserting the amount by which the profit will increase or decrease when each error is corrected. Where an error does not affect the profit, write 'no effect'. Insert the amount of the corrected profit for the year. [8]

Ezra
Statement of corrected profit for the year ended 30 September 20–3

	Effect on profit		$
	Increase $	Decrease $	
Draft profit for the year			....
Error 1	....	....	
Error 2	....	....	
Error 3	....	....	
Error 4	....	....	
Error 5	....	....	
Error 6	....	....	
	....	....	....
Corrected profit for the year			....

CHECK YOUR PROGRESS

How well do you think you have achieved the learning intentions for this chapter? Give yourself a score from 1 (still need a lot of practice) to 5 (feeling very confident) for each learning intention. Provide an example to support your score.

Now I can …	Score	Example to support score
record accounting data in the general journal and post entries to the ledger		
record the purchase and sale of non-current assets and depreciation of non-current assets in the journal		
record accrued and prepaid expenses and accrued and prepaid incomes in the journal		
record irrecoverable debts and irrecoverable debts recovered (where appropriate) in the journal		
record the creation of, and adjustments to, an allowance for irrecoverable debts in the journal		
prepare journal entries to correct errors		
understand the purpose of a suspense account and how to make entries in a suspense account		
calculate the profit or loss after errors have been corrected and understand the effect that correcting errors has on a statement of financial position.		

Chapter 16
Control accounts

LEARNING INTENTIONS

By the end of this chapter, you will be able to:
- understand how books of prime entry are used to prepare the purchases ledger control account and the sales ledger control account
- draw up purchases ledger control accounts and sales ledger control accounts
- explain the role of the purchases ledger control account and the sales ledger control account in identifying errors
- explain how control accounts are maintained in a computerised accounting system.

Introduction

Control accounts are also known as total accounts. If the totals of a trial balance do not agree and the error cannot be readily located, it is necessary to check all the accounting records. This can take a considerable amount of time. The checking process can be speeded up if a control account for the sales ledger (which contains the accounts of the trade receivables) and a control account for the purchases ledger (which contains the accounts of the trade payables) have been prepared.

These accounts act as a check on the individual accounts within these ledgers. The balance on the sales ledger control account on a certain date should be equal to the total of all the balances in the sales ledger on that date. Similarly, the balance on the purchases ledger control account on a certain date should be equal to the total of all the balances in the purchases ledger on that date. If these figures agree, it indicates that the accounts in the sales ledger and the purchases ledger are arithmetically accurate, so there must be an error elsewhere in the accounting records.

Like the trial balance, however, these accounts can only check the arithmetical accuracy – errors such as omission and commission will not be revealed by a control account.

> **LINKS**
>
> You learnt about the division of the ledger in Chapter 4 and about the errors not revealed by a trial balance in Chapter 3.

ACCOUNTING IN CONTEXT

Dividing up the ledger and using control accounts

Figure 16.1: Control accounts can save time when checking for errors

Before the year-end financial statements are prepared, a trial balance is drawn up. If the trial balance fails to balance and the error cannot be found easily, it is necessary to check all the accounting records. The amount of time needed for checking can be reduced if a control account is prepared for the sales ledger and the purchases ledger, as these control accounts act as a check on the individual accounts within these ledgers.

Marcus buys and sells supplies for the building trade. He purchases goods, such as building materials and supplies for plumbers and joiners, on credit from manufacturers. Most of the goods are sold on credit to local tradesmen, but a few sales are made for cash.

Marcus maintains sales, purchases and returns journals, and a cash book. Marcus has been recording all the ledger accounts in a single ledger, but he has recently been advised to divide the ledger into three sections: a sales ledger, a purchases ledger and a nominal ledger. Marcus has also been told that he should prepare control accounts for the sales ledger and the purchases ledger.

Discuss in pairs or in a group:

1. a Suggest two reasons why Marcus should divide the ledger into sections.

   b What sort of accounts should Marcus put in the sales ledger?

   c Which ledger is likely to contain more accounts: the sales ledger or the purchases ledger? Give a reason for your answer.

2. The sales ledger control account acts as a check on the individual accounts in the sales ledger. Similarly, the purchases ledger control account acts as a check on the individual accounts in the purchases ledger. How may this be useful if the trial balance totals do not agree?

16 Control accounts

16.1 Advantages of control accounts

Where a full set of accounting records is maintained, it is usual to prepare a **sales ledger control account** and a **purchases ledger control account**. The advantages of preparing these accounts are shown in Figure 16.2.

> **KEY TERMS**
>
> **sales ledger control account:** an account summarising the balances of all the accounts of the trade receivables.
>
> **purchases ledger control account:** an account summarising the balances of all the accounts of the trade payables.

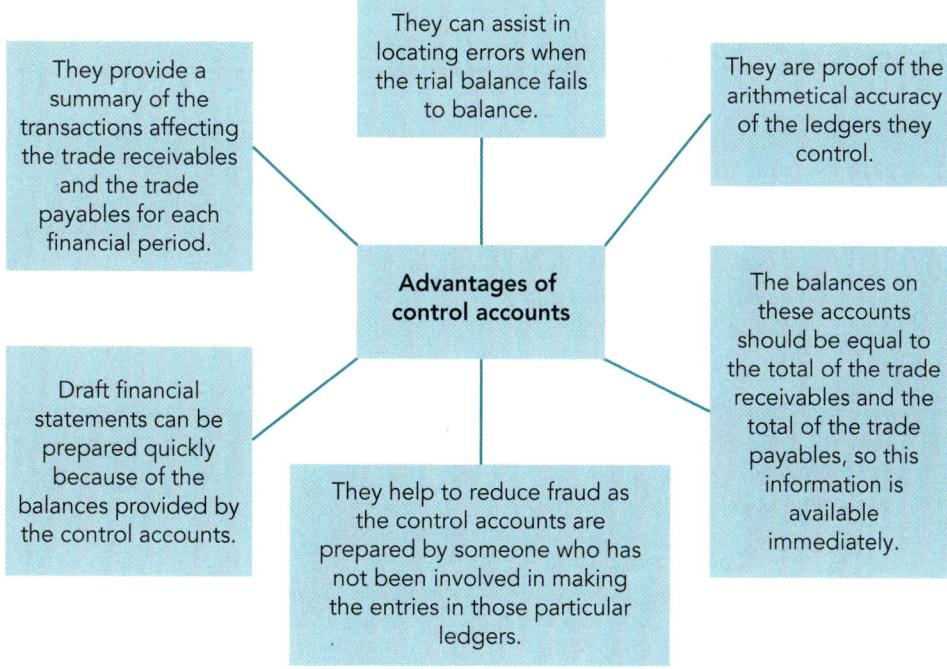

Figure 16.2: Advantages of control accounts

16.2 Sales ledger control account

The sales ledger control account is also referred to as a total trade receivables account. As this account acts as a check on the individual credit customers' accounts, it should be prepared independently and information in the individual accounts of the credit customers must **not** be used. (An error in the sales ledger would not be revealed if the control account is prepared from the accounts in that ledger.)

The information to prepare a sales ledger control account is obtained from the books of prime entry. The sources of information are summarised in Table 16.1.

Table 16.1: Sources of information for a sales ledger control account

Total	Source
Credit sales	Sales journal
Sales returns	Sales returns journal
Receipts from credit customers	Cash book
Discounts allowed to credit customers	Cash book
Dishonoured cheques	Cash book
Refunds to credit customers	Cash book
Irrecoverable debts	General journal
Interest charged	General journal

The sales ledger control account is similar to the account of a credit customer, but instead of containing individual transactions concerned with just one credit customer, it contains transactions relating to **all** the trade receivables.

The layout of a sales ledger control account is shown here.

Dr	Nominal ledger Sales ledger control account		Cr
	$		$
Balance b/d		Sales returns	
Sales		Cash	
Bank (dishonoured cheque)		Bank	
Bank/Cash (refunds)		Discount allowed	
Interest charged		Irrecoverable debts	
		Balance c/d	
Balance b/d			

The sales ledger control account is drawn up at the end of a financial period (often monthly) and balanced. The total of the balances on all the individual credit customers' accounts should agree with the balance on the control account. If they are different, it indicates that there is an error in one of the customers' accounts or an error in the control account, so further checks are required.

> **TIP**
>
> A sales ledger control account is a summary of the accounts of credit customers (trade receivables), so you should not include any items in the control account which do not appear in the account of a credit customer, such as cash sales or allowance for irrecoverable debts.

16 Control accounts

ACTIVITY 16.1

Martin is a trader. He maintains a full set of books of prime entry, which he uses to prepare monthly control accounts. On 31 May 20–4, he balanced his sales ledger control account and brought down a debit balance of $11 670 on 1 June 20–4.

The following errors were later discovered.

1 The sales journal had been understated by $1 000.

2 The total of the sales returns journal, $460, had not been recorded in the sales ledger control account.

3 An irrecoverable debt of $122 had not been entered in the sales ledger.

4 The discount allowed column in the cash book had been overstated by $100.

State how each of these errors would affect the balance of the sales ledger control account. Give a reason for your answers.

WORKED EXAMPLE 16.1

Sirima maintains a full set of accounting records and prepares control accounts at the end of each month. She provided the following information for the month of May 20–7:

		$
20–7 May 1	Sales ledger control account balance	1 500 debit
May 31	Totals for the month:	
	Sales journal	6 250
	Sales returns journal	250
	Cash received from credit customers	120
	Cheques and bank transfers received from credit customers	3 892
	Discount allowed	46
	Dishonoured cheque	70
	Cash refunds to credit customers	19
	Irrecoverable debts	94

> **CONTINUED**
>
> Prepare Sirima's sales ledger control account for the month of May 20–7.
>
> **Sirima**
> **Nominal ledger**
>
> | Dr | | | | Sales ledger control account | | | | Cr |
> |---|---|---|---|---|---|---|---|---|
> | | | | | $ | | | | $ |
> | 20–7 | | | | | 20–7 | | | |
> | May 1 | Balance | b/d | 1 500 | | May 31 | Sales returns | | 250 |
> | 31 | Sales | | 6 250 | | | Cash | | 120 |
> | | Bank (dishonoured cheque) | | 70 | | | Bank | | 3 892 |
> | | Cash (refunds) | | 19 | | | Discount allowed | | 46 |
> | | | | | | | Irrecoverable debts | | 94 |
> | | | | | | | Balance | c/d | 3 437 |
> | | | | 7 839 | | | | | 7 839 |
> | 20–7 | | | | | | | | |
> | Jun 1 | Balance | b/d | 3 437 | | | | | |
>
> - The balance brought down on 1 June should be equal to the total of the balances of the accounts of individual credit customers.

16.3 Purchases ledger control account

The purchases ledger control account is also known as a total trade payables account. This account serves a similar purpose to the sales ledger control account. It acts as a check on the individual credit suppliers' accounts, and must be prepared independently and not from information in the individual accounts of the credit suppliers.

The information to prepare a purchases ledger control account is obtained from the books of prime entry. The sources of information are summarised in Table 16.2.

16 Control accounts

Table 16.2: Sources of information for a purchases ledger control account

Total	Source
Credit purchases	Purchases journal
Purchases returns	Purchases returns journal
Payments to credit suppliers	Cash book
Discounts received from credit suppliers	Cash book
Refunds from credit suppliers	Cash book
Interest charged	General journal

> **TIP**
>
> You must not use information from the accounts in the sales and purchases ledgers to prepare a control account because doing this will not reveal any errors in the ledgers.

The purchases ledger control account is similar to the account of a credit supplier, but instead of containing individual transactions concerned with just one credit supplier, it contains transactions relating to **all** the trade payables.

The layout of a purchases ledger control account is shown here.

Nominal ledger

Dr	Purchases ledger control account			Cr
	$			$
Purchases returns		Balance	b/d	
Cash		Purchases		
Bank		Interest charged		
Discount received		Bank/Cash (refunds)		
Balance	c/d			
		Balance	b/d	

Like the sales ledger control account, a purchases ledger control account is drawn up at the end of the financial period (often monthly) and balanced. The total of the balances on all the individual credit suppliers' accounts should agree with the balance on the control account. If they are different, it indicates that there is an error in one of the suppliers' accounts or the control account, so further checks are required.

> **TIP**
>
> A purchases ledger control account is a summary of the accounts of credit suppliers (trade payables) so you should not include any items which do not appear in the account of a credit supplier, such as cash purchases.

WORKED EXAMPLE 16.2

Sirima maintains a full set of accounting records and prepares control accounts at the end of each month. She provided the following information for the month of May 20–7.

			$
20–7 May 1	Purchases ledger control account balance		3 189 credit
May 31	Totals for the month:		
	Purchases journal		5 853
	Purchases returns journal		180
	Cheques and bank transfers paid to credit suppliers		4 800
	Discount received from credit suppliers		185
	Interest charged on overdue account		21
	Cheque refunds from credit suppliers		100

Prepare Sirima's purchases ledger control account for the month of May 20–7.

Sirima
Nominal ledger

Dr			Purchases ledger control account					Cr
			$					$
20–7				20–7				
May 31	Purchases returns		180	May 1	Balance		b/d	3 189
	Bank		4 800	31	Purchases			5 853
	Discount received		185		Interest charged			21
	Balance	c/d	3 998		Bank (refunds)			100
			9 163					9 163
				20–7				
				Jun 1	Balance		b/d	3 998

- The balance brought down on 1 June should be equal to the total of the balances of the accounts of individual credit suppliers.

ACTIVITY 16.2

Charlotte has recently started a business. She intends to record the business transactions using a full double entry system of book-keeping.

Charlotte has been advised that it would be sensible to introduce the following measures to check on the accounting records:

- trial balance
- bank reconciliation
- control accounts.

Prepare a set of notes you can give to Charlotte explaining the purpose of each of these measures.

REFLECTION

In Activity 16.2, you thought about three different methods for checking accounting records.

What would you say to a business owner who thinks that carrying out these checks takes too much time and effort?

How regularly do you check your own work? Do you think checking your work is a good use of your time? Explain why or why not.

16.4 Balances on both sides of a control account

Occasionally a credit customer's account may show a credit balance. This may be due to:

- an overpayment by the customer
- the customer returning goods after paying the account
- the customer paying in advance for the goods
- cash discount not being deducted before payment was made.

In the sales ledger control account, it is usual to keep any credit balance separate from the debit balance. The control account will therefore have two balances – the usual debit balance representing money owing by credit customers, and the more unusual credit balance representing money owing to credit customers. Any credit balance is entered on the debit side of the control account and carried down as a credit balance. The account can then be balanced in the usual way.

WORKED EXAMPLE 16.3

Sirima maintains a full set of accounting records and prepares control accounts at the end of each month. She provided the following information for the month of July 20–7.

			$
20–7 July 1	Sales ledger control account balance		3 200 debit
July 31	Totals for the month:		
	Sales journal		6 510
	Sales returns journal		410
	Cheques and bank transfers received from credit customers		5 468
	Discount allowed		62
	Interest charged on overdue account		10

On 31 July 20–7, the total of the credit balances in the individual sales ledger accounts was $225.

Prepare Sirima's sales ledger control account for the month of July 20–7.

Sirima
Nominal ledger

Dr				Sales ledger control account				Cr
			$					$
20–7				20–7				
July 1	Balance	b/d	3 200	July 31	Sales returns			410
31	Sales		6 510		Bank			5 468
	Interest charged		10		Discount allowed			62
	Balance	c/d	225		Balance	c/d		4 005
			9 945					9 945
20–7				20–7				
Aug 1	Balance	b/d	4 005	Aug 1	Balance	b/d		225

In a similar way, a credit supplier's account can show a debit balance. This may occur due to:

- an overpayment to the supplier
- returning goods to the supplier after paying the account
- paying the supplier in advance for the goods
- cash discount not being deducted before payment was made.

As in the sales ledger control account, the debit balance and the credit balance are shown separately in the purchases ledger control account. The purchases ledger control account will therefore have two balances – the usual credit balance representing money owing to credit suppliers, and the more unusual debit balance representing money owing by credit suppliers. Any debit balance is entered on the credit side of the control account and carried down as a debit balance. The account can then be balanced in the usual way.

16.5 Contra entries in control accounts

Contra entries are also known as inter-ledger transfers or set-offs.

Sometimes a business may sell goods to another business and also buy different goods from that business. This means that there will be two ledger accounts for that business – one in the sales ledger and the other in the purchases ledger.

Instead of each business sending the other a payment to cover the amount due, they may agree to set one account balance off against the other. Any remaining amount will be settled by one business making another payment.

WORKED EXAMPLE 16.4

Sirima provided the following information for the month of August 20–7:

20–7

August 6	Sold goods, $300, on credit to Bhatia Road Stores
18	Bought goods, $480, on credit from Bhatia Road Stores
30	The balances of the two accounts for Bhatia Road Stores were set-off and Sirima sent a cheque for the remaining balance.

Record these transactions in the account of Bhatia Road Stores in the sales ledger and in the account of Bhatia Road Stores in the purchases ledger.

Sirima
Sales ledger

Dr		Bhatia Road Stores account			Cr
		$			$
20–7			20–7		
Aug 6	Sales	300	Aug 30	Purchases ledger	300
		300			300

Purchases ledger

Dr		Bhatia Road Stores account			Cr
		$			$
20–7			20–7		
Aug 30	Sales ledger	300	Aug 18	Purchases	480
	Bank	180			
		480			480

- A journal entry would be made for the transfer of $300 on 30 August as it is a non-regular transaction.
- As the transfer of $300 on 30 August affected both accounts in the sales ledger and the purchases ledger, it would affect both the sales ledger control account and the purchases ledger control account. (See **Worked example 16.5**.)

> **TIP**
>
> Remember that you must record a contra entry in both the sales ledger control account and the purchases ledger control account.

WORKED EXAMPLE 16.5

Sirima provided the following information for the month of September 20–7:

		$
20–7		
Sept 1	Sales ledger control account debit balance	2 750
	Sales ledger control account credit balance	234
	Purchases ledger control account credit balance	2 118
Sept 30	Totals for the month:	
	Sales journal	6 564
	Purchases journal	5 230
	Sales returns journal	125
	Purchases returns journal	116
	Cheques and bank transfers received from credit customers	4 895
	Cheques and bank transfers paid to credit suppliers	4 328
	Discount received	192
	Irrecoverable debt	225
	Interest charged by credit supplier	35
	Contra entry	325

On 30 September 20–7, the total of the debit balances in the individual purchases ledger accounts was $210.

Prepare Sirima's sales ledger control account and purchases ledger control account for the month of September 20–7. Balance the accounts and bring down the balances on 1 October 20–7.

Sirima
Nominal ledger

Dr			Sales ledger control account			Cr
			$			$
20–7				20–7		
Sep 1	Balance	b/d	2 750	Sep 1	Balance b/d	234
30	Sales		6 564	30	Sales returns	125
					Bank	4 895
					Irrecoverable debt	225
					Contra entry	325
					Balance c/d	3 510
			9 314			9 314
20–7						
Oct 1	Balance	b/d	3 510			

CONTINUED

Sirima
Nominal ledger

Dr				Purchases ledger control account				Cr
				$				$
20–7					20–7			
Sept 30	Purchases returns			116	Sept 1	Balance	b/d	2 118
	Bank			4 328	30	Purchases		5 230
	Discount received			192		Interest charged		35
	Contra entry			325		Balance	c/d	210
	Balance	c/d		2 632				
				7 593				7 593
20–7					20–7			
Oct 1	Balance	b/d		210	Oct 1	Balance	b/d	2 632

DISCUSSION

Discuss with another student the effect the omission of a contra entry would have on both the sales ledger control account and the purchases ledger control account.

ACTIVITY 16.3

Imagine you are responsible for completing the monthly sales ledger control account for your employer. You will be on holiday at the end of the next month, so a colleague who prepares the purchases ledger control account will be taking on your duties.

Prepare guidance notes to assist her in this task. These notes should highlight the main differences she will find between preparing the purchases ledger control account and preparing the sales ledger control account.

16.6 The role of control accounts in a computerised accounting system

When a business is using a software package to process their transactions, the control account is used to make the automatic double entry postings. When a sales invoice is entered onto the system, the total amount of the invoice will automatically be posted to the sales ledger control account. Therefore, you will only have to enter the invoice once and all the other postings will be completed automatically, saving time for the book-keeper. The balance of the control account will also be automatically posted to the statement of financial position at the end of the financial year, representing the total amount due from trade receivables.

Similarly, when a purchase invoice is entered into the system, the total amount of the invoice will be automatically posted to the purchases ledger control account. Therefore, you will only have to enter the invoice once, and all other postings will be completed automatically, saving time for the book-keeper. The balance of the control account will also be automatically posted to the statement of financial position at the end of the financial year, representing the total amount owing to trade payables.

> ### DISCUSSION
>
> Discuss these questions with a partner:
>
> 1 Your manager has asked you to train a new employee on how to complete the sales ledger control account. What are the main points you would want to include in your training of this new employee?
>
> 2 With the automatic posting of entries when using a computerised accounting system, is there any point in learning the double entry principles?

ACCOUNTING IN ACTION

Understanding control accounts

Figure 16.3: A business selling a selection of tyres

Miguel trades in tyres for cars, vans and heavy goods vehicles. He purchases the tyres on credit from manufacturers and sells them on credit to retail businesses that sell and fit tyres, local garages and large transport businesses that have their own vehicle repair departments.

Occasionally, Miguel is asked to supply tractor tyres. Miguel does not usually trade in tractor tyres, so when he is asked for them, he purchases them from one of his customers who owns a retail tyre business.

At the end of each month, Miguel's office manager prepares control accounts. Here is the sales ledger control account for the end of May 20–4:

CONTINUED

Miguel

Dr			Sales ledger control account					Cr
				$				$
20–4					20–4			
May 1	Balance	b/d		13 600	May 31	Sales returns		1 860
31	Sales			15 240		Bank		13 610
	Balance	c/d		200		Discount allowed		370
						Irrecoverable debts		140
						Contra entry		820
						Balance	c/d	12 240
				29 040				29 040
20–4					20–4			
Jun 1	Balance	b/d		12 240	Jun 1	Balance	b/d	200

Miguel does not really understand the purpose of a control account and he asks the office manager the following questions:

a Why it is useful to prepare monthly control accounts?

b Where does the information come from to prepare these accounts?

c What does the item 'contra entry' mean and how has it arisen?

d How it is possible to have two balances on the account on 1 June 20–4?

Discuss in pairs or in a group:

1 Imagine you are the office manager. How would you answer Miguel's questions?

2 Why is it important that the information for preparing the sales ledger control account is not taken from the individual sales ledger accounts?

SUMMARY

You should now know:

- The main purpose of control accounts is to assist in locating errors in the sales ledger and the purchases ledger.
- A sales ledger control account resembles the account of a credit customer but contains transactions affecting all credit customers.
- A purchases ledger control account resembles the account of a credit supplier but contains transactions affecting all credit suppliers.
- The information to prepare control accounts is obtained from the books of prime entry.
- It is possible to have a balance on each side of a control account.
- If a business is both a customer and a supplier, a contra entry may be made to transfer a balance from the sales ledger account to the purchases ledger account.

Chapter 16 practice questions

1 What is the purpose of preparing a sales ledger control account?

    A to calculate the total credit sales for the period

    B to calculate the total sales for the period

    C to check the arithmetical accuracy of the sales account

    D to check the arithmetical accuracy of the sales ledger accounts [1]

2 What may appear on the debit side of a purchases ledger control account?

    A credit purchases

    B discount allowed

    C payments to credit suppliers

    D returns by credit customers [1]

3 Shilpa's sales ledger control account had an opening credit balance. What does this mean?

    A total amount owing by credit customers

    B goods returned by credit customers

    C interest charged on credit customers' accounts

    D overpayment made by credit customers [1]

4 Hitesh is a trader who maintains a full set of accounting records. He divides his ledger into three sections – nominal (general), sales and purchases.

    a State **one** advantage of dividing the ledger into these sections. [1]

    b State **two** advantages of maintaining a purchases ledger control account. [2]

Hitesh provided the following information for the month of March 20–2.

			$
Mar	1	Debit balances in purchases ledger	105
		Credit balances in purchases ledger	6 786
Mar	31	Totals for the month:	
		Credit purchases	5 735
		Purchases returns	857
		Payments to suppliers	4 853
		Discount received	176
		Interest charged by credit supplier	35

On 31 March 20–2, the total of the debit balances in the individual purchases ledger accounts was $128.

    c Prepare the purchases ledger control account for the month of March 20–2. Balance the account and bring down the balances on 1 April 20–2. [8]

d State the book of prime entry Hitesh would use to provide information about:

   i interest charged by credit supplier

   ii purchases returns

   iii discount received. [3]

[Total: 14]

5 a For each entry A–G state:

   i the book of prime entry from which the information would be obtained [7]

   ii whether each item would appear on the debit side or the credit side of a purchases ledger control account.

     A Contra entry

     B Credit purchases

     C Discount received

     D Dishonoured cheques

     E Interest charges

     F Payments to credit suppliers

     G Returns to credit suppliers [7]

b State why the information required to prepare a purchases ledger control account is not obtained from the purchases ledger. [1]

c Explain why the contra entry to the sales ledger was needed. [2]

[Total: 17]

6 Rita is a trader who maintains a full set of accounting records and prepares control accounts at the end of each month. She provided the following information for the month of March 20–6:

20–6		$
Mar 1	Debit balance in the sales ledger control account	4 290
	Credit balance in the sales ledger control account	180
	Allowance for irrecoverable debts	850
Mar 31	Totals for the month:	
	Credit sales	5 670
	Cash sales	680
	Returns by credit customers	518
	Cheques received from credit customers	3 980
	Dishonoured cheque	325
	Discount allowed	214
	Discount received	236
	Irrecoverable debts	300
	Contra entry	280

On 31 March 20–6, the total of the credit balances in the individual sales ledger accounts was $155.

- a Prepare the sales ledger control account for the month of March 20–6. Balance the account and bring down the balances on 1 April 20–6. [10]

- b State the book of prime entry which would be used as a source of information for each entry (excluding the balances) in the sales ledger control account prepared in **a**. [7]

- c Suggest two items listed that should not appear in a sales ledger control account and explain why they do not appear. [2]

- d Suggest two reasons for the credit balance on the sales ledger control account on 31 March 20–6. [2]

[Total: 21]

CHECK YOUR PROGRESS

How well do you think you have achieved the learning intentions for this chapter? Give yourself a score from 1 (still need a lot of practice) to 5 (feeling very confident) for each learning intention. Provide an example to support your score.

Now I can ...	Score	Example to support score
understand how books of prime entry are used to prepare the purchases ledger control account and the sales ledger control account		
draw up purchases ledger control accounts and sales ledger control accounts		
explain the role of the purchases ledger control account and the sales ledger control account in identifying errors		
explain how control accounts are maintained in a computerised accounting system.		

Chapter 17
Incomplete records

LEARNING INTENTIONS

By the end of this chapter, you will be able to:

- explain the reasons why businesses maintain incomplete records
- calculate profit for the year using statements of affairs
- prepare control accounts to find missing figures
- use mark-ups or gross profit margins to calculate missing figures
- prepare financial statements, including adjustments using incomplete records.

Introduction

The term 'incomplete records' refers to the situation where a business does not maintain accounting records using double entry principles and so is not able to produce a trial balance. A business owner may not think that it is necessary to maintain a full double entry system, or they may lack the skills and knowledge to do so. These are mainly small businesses who may keep a basic cash book. This cash book is the starting point for attempting to construct a full set of accounts and produce a set of financial statements.

ACCOUNTING IN CONTEXT

What financial records are necessary?

Figure 17.1: Goods for sale in a pet shop

People often like the idea of starting a business and becoming self-employed. They may be very knowledgeable about their area of work and feel confident that they will be successful at running their own business. However, they do not always realise what financial records they will have to maintain. Not all business owners will use a full double entry system, and some will keep very few financial records. But almost all business owners will maintain a basic cash book.

Natalia is an animal lover. She decided to open a pet shop and sell food, bedding and toys for a variety of pet animals. Natalia buys goods on credit from wholesalers and pays her credit suppliers by bank transfer at the end of each month. She sells to the general public for cash, but offers credit terms to regular customers who purchase large quantities of goods. Her credit customers pay by cheque at the end of each month.

At the end of each week, Natalia pays the cash and any cheques received into the bank. She records in her cash book all the money that came in and all the money that went out. Natalia is quite happy when more money comes in than goes out, and she regards this as her profit for the week.

Discuss in pairs or in a group:

1. Why is Natalia wrong to regard the change in the bank balance as her profit or loss?

2. What other financial records could Natalia maintain that would provide useful information at the end of each month?

17.1 Complete records and incomplete records

Maintaining a full set of double entry records is important and provides many benefits. These are summarised in Figure 17.2.

Figure 17.2: Advantages of maintaining full accounting records

However, some businesses may not maintain a full set of accounting records. For many small business owners, maintaining a full double entry system would be time-consuming and costly. In addition to this, many small business owners do not have the expertise to maintain double entry records. In these circumstances, it is more likely that they will maintain some records using a single entry system. A business which trades only for cash may consider that recording all their money coming in and going out in a cash book is sufficient for their purposes.

Some of the advantages and disadvantages of not keeping full records are shown in Table 17.1.

Table 17.1: Advantages and disadvantages of not keeping full accounting records

Advantages	Disadvantages
The owner of the business will be able to save time, which can then be used to manage other aspects of the business. The owner may save money by not having to employ a book-keeper to keep their records.	The owner may have to pay additional fees to an accountant when producing the financial statements. The owner may not be aware if the business is making a profit or a loss. The owner may not have enough information available to manage the business successfully. The owner may pay an incorrect amount of tax as the profit may be overstated or understated. The owner may have difficulty raising finance as there will not be evidence to support any loan applications.

17.2 Statement of affairs

If the only records available are those relating to the assets and liabilities of the business, then it is not possible to prepare a statement of profit or loss. These assets and liabilities are listed in a **statement of affairs**, which is similar to a statement of financial position.

If the assets, liabilities and capital of the business are known and no further information is available, then the only way in which the profit can be measured is to compare the change in the capital over the financial period. Capital increases when a profit is made and decreases when a loss is incurred.

Table 17.2 shows the basic formula for calculating profit and how it can be modified if drawings have taken place or if additional capital has been introduced during the period.

Table 17.2: Calculating profit using changes in capital

Formula	Calculation of profit
Basic formula	closing capital − opening capital
If drawings have taken place	closing capital − opening capital + drawings
If additional capital has been introduced	closing capital − opening capital + drawings − capital introduced

An alternative way to calculate profit is to construct a capital account and insert the missing figure of profit.

> **KEY TERM**
>
> **statement of affairs:** a summary of the financial position of a business on a certain date. It is prepared instead of a statement of financial position when double entry records have not been maintained.

> **LINK**
>
> You learnt how to prepare a statement of financial position in Chapter 9.

17 Incomplete records

Dr				Capital account				Cr
			$					$
Year 1				Year 1				
Dec 31	Drawings		xxx	Jan 1	Balance		b/d	xxx
	Balance	c/d	xxx	Dec 31	Bank			xxx
					Profit for the year			?
			───					xxx
			───	Year 2				
				Jan 1	Balance		b/d	xxx

- The dates of 1 January and 31 December have been used for convenience. The first and last days of the financial year of the particular business are used in practice.
- The difference between the opening and closing capital (adjusted for capital introduced and drawings during the year) represents the profit (or loss) for the year.

Calculating profit by comparing the change in the capital is very unsatisfactory. Only an estimate of the profit for the year is possible: it is not possible to show details about gross profit, sales, purchases, expenses and so on. It is not possible to analyse the results and informed decisions about the future cannot be made.

ACTIVITY 17.1

Imagine that you are an accountant and that one of your clients has for many years only maintained a cash book which you have used to calculate their profit for the year. You are aware that this client is opening another branch of their business next year, and you are going to have a meeting with them to discuss their accounting system. You believe that the client needs to be more focussed on the financial aspects of their business if they are to continue to grow.

Prepare some notes that you can take to the meeting to explain why it would be a good idea for your client to start maintaining a full set of accounting records.

WORKED EXAMPLE 17.1

Sara is a sole trader who does not maintain a full set of accounting records. She was able to provide the following information relating to her assets and liabilities:

	1 January 20–6 $	31 December 20–6 $
Bank	3 500	6 430
Inventory	3 790	4 580
Equipment	50 000	50 000
Other payables	520	380
Other receivables	210	–
Trade payables	25 690	32 980
Trade receivables	56 240	65 900

During the year ended 31 December 20–6:
- Sara purchased additional equipment costing $15 000, which she funded from her personal funds. This is in addition to the non-current assets listed.
- Sara's cash drawings during the year amounted to $10 000, and she also took goods costing $1 500 for personal use.

On 31 December 20–6 Sara decided:
- that all equipment owned at that date should be depreciated by 20%
- to create an allowance for irrecoverable debts of 5% of trade receivables.

a Prepare a statement of affairs for Sara at 1 January 20–6.

b Prepare a statement of affairs for Sara at 31 December 20–6.

c Calculate Sara's profit for the year ended 31 December 20–6.

a

Sara Statement of affairs at 1 January 20–6		
	$	$
Non-current assets		
Equipment		50 000
Current assets		
Inventory	3 790	
Trade receivables	56 240	
Other receivables	210	
Bank	3 500	63 740
Total assets		113 740
Capital and liabilities		
Capital		
Balance		87 530
Current liabilities		
Trade payables	25 690	
Other payables	520	26 210
Total capital and liabilities		113 740

17 Incomplete records

> **CONTINUED**

- The figure for capital has been inserted to make the statement of affairs balance.

b

Sara
Statement of affairs at 31 December 20–6

	$ Cost	$ Accumulated depreciation	$ Net book value
Non-current assets			
Equipment	65 000	13 000	52 000
Current assets			
Inventory		4 580	
Trade receivables	65 900		
Less Allowance for irrecoverable debts	3 295	62 605	
Bank		6 430	73 615
Total assets			125 615
Capital and liabilities			
Capital			
Balance			92 255
Current liabilities			
Trade payables		32 980	
Other payables		380	33 360
Total capital and liabilities			125 615

- The figure for capital has been inserted to make the statement of affairs balance.

c

Sara
Calculation of profit for the year ended 31 December 20–6

	$	$
Capital at 31 December 20–6		92 255
Less Capital at 1 January 20–6		87 530
		4 725
Add Drawings: cash	10 000	
goods	1 500	11 500
		16 225
Less Capital introduced		15 000
Profit for the year		1 225

- The capital introduced is the amount spent on additional equipment which Sara funded from her personal funds.

> **CONTINUED**
>
> Alternatively, the profit for the year can be calculated by constructing a capital account:
>
> | Dr | | | | Sara
Capital account | | | Cr |
> |---|---|---|---|---|---|---|---|
> | | | | $ | | | | $ |
> | 20–6 | | | | 20–6 | | | |
> | Dec 31 | Drawings | | 10 000 | Jan 1 | Balance | | 87 530 |
> | | Purchases | | 1 500 | Dec 31 | Equipment | | 15 000 |
> | | Balance | c/d | 92 255 | | Profit for the year | | 1 225 |
> | | | | 103 755 | | | | 103 755 |
> | | | | | 20–7 | | | |
> | | | | | Jan 1 | Balance | b/d | 92 255 |
>
> - The profit is inserted as a 'missing figure' in order to balance the account.

If no instructions are given, the profit calculation can be shown within the closing statement of affairs. In this case, the profit for the year or the loss for the year will be inserted to make the statement of affairs balance.

For Worked example 17.1, Sara's profit for the year ended 20–6 can be shown in the statement of affairs. The assets section and liabilities section will be the same as in Worked example 17.1 and the capital section will be as follows:

	$	$	$
Capital			
Opening balance			87 530
Add Capital introduced			15 000
Profit for the year			1 225
			103 755
Less Drawings (10 000 + 1 500)			11 500
Total capital			92 255

ACTIVITY 17.2

On 1 November 20–8, Aziz's capital account balance was $75 000 and on 31 October 20–9 was $90 000.

During the year ended 31 October 20–9, he introduced additional capital of $10 000 and made a profit of $12 000.

Prepare Aziz's capital account for the year ended 31 October 20–9 and insert the missing figure for drawings.

17 Incomplete records

> **DISCUSSION**
>
> Work with a partner to discuss these questions:
> - Why is it important that the owner has an accurate figure for drawings?
> - What would happen if the owner did not record any goods he took for his own use?
> - What are the consequences for the business if the owner's drawings exceed his profit for the year?

17.3 Preparing financial statements from incomplete records

Even when a business owner has not maintained double entry records, they are sometimes able to provide information in addition to details of the assets and liabilities. If details of money received and paid are available, it is possible to calculate the sales, purchases and expenses. This means that after various calculations, a full set of financial statements can be prepared.

WORKED EXAMPLE 17.2

Chen is a sole trader. He maintains a bank account, but not a full set of double entry records.

He provided the following information for the year ended 30 September 20–5:

	1 October 20–4	30 September 20–5
	$	$
Property at cost	75 000	75 000
Equipment (cost $10 000)	8 000	?
Inventory	8 100	9 800
Trade receivables	26 420	29 200
Trade payables	15 600	18 900
Other payables (general expenses)	500	–
Other receivables (general expenses)	–	360
Bank	22 450	?

Chen records all his receipts and payments in his cash book. They are summarised as follows:

Receipts	$	Payments	$
Receipts from trade receivables	362 700	Payments to trade payables	229 600
Cash sales	12 000	General expenses	21 520
		Drawings	43 800
		Wages	30 000
		Rates	5 900
		Insurance	1 600
		Equipment	6 000

Additional information:

- During the year ended 30 September 20–5, Chen took goods costing $4 000 for his own use.
- On 30 September 20–5, Chen decided to create an allowance for irrecoverable debts of 4% of trade receivables.
- Chen depreciates his equipment at the rate of 10% per annum on the cost of all equipment owned at the year-end.

Prepare the statement of profit or loss of Chen for the year ended 30 September 20–5 and a statement of financial position at 30 September 20–5.

CONTINUED

Step 1 – Calculate the opening capital using a statement of affairs

Chen Statement of affairs at 1 October 20–4			
	$ Cost	$ Accumulated depreciation	$ Net book value
Non-current assets			
Premises	75 000		75 000
Equipment	10 000	2 000	8 000
	85 000	2 000	83 000
Current assets			
Inventory		8 100	
Trade receivables		26 420	
Bank		22 450	56 970
Total assets			139 970
Capital and liabilities			
Capital			
Balance			123 870
Current liabilities			
Trade payables		15 600	
Other payables		500	16 100
Total capital and liabilities			139 970

Step 2 – Calculate the total revenue for the year

Total revenue consists of both credit sales and cash sales. The amount of cash sales can be obtained from the cash book but credit sales have to be calculated. There are two methods for doing this.

Method 1 – Calculation

The total amount of money received from the trade receivables during the year needs to be adjusted to take account of the opening and closing trade receivables to arrive at the total credit sales for the year. The opening balance is deducted as this relates to goods sold the previous financial year, and the closing trade receivables is added as they relate to this financial year.

	$
Receipts from trade receivables	362 700
Less Trade receivables 1 October 20–4	26 420
	336 280
Plus Trade receivables 30 September 20–5	29 200
Credit sales for the year	**365 480**

> **CONTINUED**

Method 2 – Preparation of a sales ledger control account

The same answer can be obtained by preparing a sales ledger control account. The information provided is entered into the account. The balancing figure on the debit side of $365 480 represents the total amount of credit sales. The opening balance is on the debit side as this represents an asset to the business, and the closing trade receivables figure is brought down at the end of the year to represent the current asset at the start of the next year.

Dr				Sales ledger control account				Cr
				$				$
20–4					20–5			
Oct 1	Balance		b/d	26 420	Sept 30	Bank		362 700
20–5						Balance	c/d	29 200
Sept 30	Sales			**365 480**				
				391 900				391 900
20–5								
Oct 1	Balance		b/d	29 200				

To find the total revenue, add together the cash sales and the credit sales:

Total revenue = Cash sales $12 000 + Credit sales $365 480 = $377 480

Step 3 – Calculate the total purchases for the year

Total purchases consists of both credit purchases and cash purchases. The amount of cash purchases can be obtained from the cash book, but credit purchases have to be calculated. There are two methods for doing this.

Method 1 – Calculation

	$
Payments to trade receivables	229 600
Less Trade payables 1 October 20–4	15 600
	214 000
Plus Trade payables 30 September 20–5	18 900
Credit purchases for the year	**232 900**

Method 2 – Preparation of a purchases ledger control account

Dr				Purchases ledger control account				Cr
				$				$
20–5					20–4			
Sept 30	Bank			229 600	Oct 1	Balance	b/d	15 600
	Balance		c/d	18 900	20–5			
					Sept 30	Purchases		**232 900**
				248 500				248 500
					20–5			
					Oct 1	Balance	b/d	18 900

CONTINUED

As there are no cash purchases, the total purchases is equal to the credit purchases calculated.

Step 4 – Calculate the closing bank balance

The bank balance on 1 October 20–4 is given together with details of receipts and payments. A summary of the bank account can be prepared to calculate the closing bank balance. It is not usually necessary to itemise all the transactions.

Dr				Bank account				Cr
				$				$
20–4					20–5			
Oct 1	Balance	b/d	22 450		Sep 30	Total payments		338 420
20–5						Balance	c/d	58 730
Sept 30	Total receipts		374 700					
			397 150					397 150
20–5								
Oct 1	Balance	b/d	58 730					

Step 5 – Prepare the statement of profit or loss

Chen			
Statement of profit or loss for the year ended 30 September 20–5			
	$	$	$
Revenue			377 480
Less Cost of sales			
Opening inventory		8 100	
Purchases	232 900		
Less Goods for own use	4 000	228 900	
		237 000	
Less Closing inventory		9 800	227 200
Gross profit			150 280
Less General expenses		20 660	
Wages		30 000	
Rates		5 900	
Insurance		1 600	
Allowance for irrecoverable debts		1 168	
Depreciation on equipment		1 600	60 928
Profit for the year			89 352

- The figures for revenue and purchases have come from previous calculations.
- The general expenses have been calculated as $21 520 – $500 – $360.
- The allowance for irrecoverable debts has been calculated at 4% of $29 200.
- The depreciation of equipment has been calculated at 10% of ($10 000 + $6 000).

> CAMBRIDGE IGCSE™ AND O LEVEL ACCOUNTING: COURSEBOOK

CONTINUED

Step 6 – Prepare the statement of financial position

Chen Statement of financial position at 30 September 20–5			
	$ Cost	$ Accumulated depreciation	$ Net book value
Non-current assets			
Property	75 000		75 000
Equipment	16 000	3 600	12 400
	91 000	3 600	87 400
Current assets			
Inventory		9 800	
Trade receivables	29 200		
Less Allowance for irrecoverable debts	1 168	28 032	
Other receivables		360	
Bank		58 730	96 922
Total assets			184 322
Capital and liabilities			
Capital			
Opening balance			123 870
Plus Profit for the year			89 352
			213 222
Less Drawings			47 800
			165 422
Current liabilities			
Trade payables			18 900
Total capital and liabilities			184 322

- The depreciation to date on equipment has been calculated as $2 000 + $1 600.
- The figure for bank has come from a previous calculation.
- The drawings have been calculated as $43 800 + $4 000.

LINK

These total accounts are prepared using the same principles as those used for control accounts, which you learnt about in Chapter 16.

ACTIVITY 17.3

A trader's financial year ends on 31 July. They provided the following information:

		$
1 August 20–7	Trade payables	4 300
31 July 20–8	Trade payables	8 000

During the year ended 31 July 20–8

    Payments to credit suppliers   34 000

    Cash purchases   6 000

Calculate the purchases for the year.

REFLECTION

Look through Worked example 17.2 again. As you worked through this example, you will have used skills and understanding you learnt in earlier chapters. The steps in the process for preparing the financial statements are also linked – you cannot complete the later steps until you have completed the earlier steps.

Discuss with a partner:

- Where in Worked example 17.2 did you use skills from earlier chapters?
- Did you notice these connections as you worked through the example?
- What things can you do to help you spot connections between different sections?
- Why do you think it is important to be able to spot connections?

LINK

You learnt how to prepare a full set of financial statements with adjustments in Chapters 11–13.

When a business allows its credit customers a cash discount for an account that is paid within a set time limit, this will affect the calculation of the credit sales. Similarly, any discount received from credit suppliers will affect the calculation of the credit purchases.

TIP

Make sure you include cash discount allowed and cash discount received in the calculation of credit sales and credit purchases. You must also record the discounts in the profit and loss section of the statement of profit or loss.

CAMBRIDGE IGCSE™ AND O LEVEL ACCOUNTING: COURSEBOOK

WORKED EXAMPLE 17.3

Son is a sole trader. He maintains a bank account, but not a full set of double entry records. He provided the following information:

	1 April 20–3	31 March 20–4
	$	$
Trade receivables	26 500	28 790
Trade payables	21 345	22 134

During the year ended 31 March 20–4:

- receipts from credit customers totalled $369 820 (after the deduction of $9 100 cash discount)
- payments to credit suppliers were $265 870 (after the deduction of $8 230 cash discount).

Calculate the credit sales and credit purchases for the year ended 31 March 20–4.

Dr			Sales ledger control account				Cr
			$				$
20–3				20–4			
Apr 1	Balance	b/d	26 500	Mar 31	Bank		369 820
20–4					Discount allowed		9 100
Mar 31	Sales		**381 210**		Balance	c/d	28 790
			407 710				407 710
20–4							
Apr 1	Balance	b/d	28 790				

Dr			Purchases ledger control account				Cr
			$				$
20–4				20–3			
Mar 31	Bank		265 870	Apr 1	Balance	b/d	21 345
	Discount received		8 230	20–4			
	Balance	c/d	22 134	Mar 31	Purchases		**274 889**
			296 234				296 234
				20–4			
				Apr 1	Balance	b/d	22 134

- The amount shown for sales and purchases would appear in the trading section of the statement of profit or loss.
- The amount for discount allowed and discount received would appear in the profit and loss section of the statement of profit or loss.

17.4 Mark-up, gross profit margin and inventory turnover

When dealing with incomplete records, it is sometimes necessary to use percentages to calculate missing information.

Mark-up and gross profit margin

Mark-up and **gross profit margin** (sometimes referred to as margin) are two commonly used ratios which measure the gross profit as a percentage. Their definitions and formulae are shown in Table 17.3.

Table 17.3: Ratios for mark-up and gross profit margin

Ratio	Definition	Formula
Mark-up	Gross profit measured as a percentage of the cost price	$\dfrac{\text{Gross profit}}{\text{Cost of sales}} \times 100$
Gross profit margin	Gross profit measured as a percentage of the selling price	$\dfrac{\text{Gross profit}}{\text{Revenue*}} \times 100$

* Remember the term 'revenue' is often used instead of 'sales'.

> **KEY TERMS**
>
> **mark-up:** the gross profit expressed as a percentage of the cost price.
>
> **gross profit margin:** the gross profit expressed as a percentage of the selling price.

> **WORKED EXAMPLE 17.4**
>
> A trader's turnover for the year was $40 000 and the cost of goods sold was $30 000.
> Calculate the:
> a mark-up
> b gross profit margin
>
> a Mark-up = $\dfrac{\text{Gross profit}}{\text{Cost of sales}} \times 100 = \dfrac{\$10\,000}{\$30\,000} \times 100 = 33.33\%$
>
> b Gross profit margin = $\dfrac{\text{Gross profit}}{\text{Sales}} \times 100 = \dfrac{\$10\,000}{\$40\,000} \times 100 = 25\%$

Applying either gross profit margin or mark-up, it is possible to calculate any one unknown figure in the trading section of a statement of profit or loss.

> ## WORKED EXAMPLE 17.5

The financial year of Taron Trading ends on 30 September. The following information is provided:

	$
Inventory 1 October 20–3	9 000
Inventory 30 September 20–4	11 500
Revenue	84 000

The mark-up is at a standard rate of 25%.

Calculate the purchases for the year ended 30 September 20–4 using the trading section of a statement of profit or loss.

Prepare an outline statement

Insert the figures for revenue, opening inventory and closing inventory, and leave gaps for purchases, cost of sales and gross profit.

<table>
<tr><th colspan="3">Taron Trading
Trading section of statement of profit or loss for the year ended 30 September 20–4</th></tr>
<tr><th></th><th>$</th><th>$</th></tr>
<tr><td>Revenue</td><td></td><td>84 000</td></tr>
<tr><td>Less Cost of sales</td><td></td><td></td></tr>
<tr><td>Opening inventory</td><td>9 000</td><td></td></tr>
<tr><td>   Purchases</td><td>d</td><td></td></tr>
<tr><td></td><td>c</td><td></td></tr>
<tr><td>Less   Closing inventory</td><td>11 500</td><td>b</td></tr>
<tr><td>Gross profit</td><td></td><td>a</td></tr>
</table>

Calculate the gross profit (a) and the cost of sales (b)

The mark-up is 25%, so the gross profit is 25% of the cost of sales.

Revenue = cost of sales + gross profit, so the revenue = 125% of the cost of sales.

- Gross profit = $\frac{25}{125}$ of the revenue, so gross profit = $\frac{25}{125} = \frac{1}{5}$ (or 20%) of $84 000 = $16 800.

- Cost of sales = $\frac{100}{125}$ of the revenue, so cost of sales = $\frac{100}{125} = \frac{4}{5}$ (or 80%) of $84 000 = $67 200.

Alternatively, the cost of sales can be found from the difference between the revenue and the gross profit:

- Cost of sales = $84 000 – $16 800 = $67 200.

Calculate the purchases figure (d)

Work 'backwards' from the cost of sales.
The cost of sales + the closing inventory = $78 700 **(c)**.
This figure less the opening inventory equals the purchases: $78 700 – $9 000 = $69 700.

17 Incomplete records

> **DISCUSSION**
>
> Discuss with a partner:
> 1. How realistic is it for a business to have the same mark-up for all goods purchased?
> 2. Can you think of any difficulties that might occur when using the same mark-up for all goods?

> **ACTIVITY 17.4**
>
>
>
> **Figure 17.3:** Fruit juice for sale at the front of a shop
>
> The financial year of Sunshine Fruit ends on 30 April. The following information was provided:
>
> | | $ |
> |---|---|
> | Inventory 1 May 20–6 | 8 000 |
> | Inventory 30 April 20–7 | 5 000 |
> | Purchases | 135 000 |
>
> All sales were made at a gross profit margin of 25%.
>
> Calculate the revenue for the year ended 30 April 20–7 using the trading section of a statement of profit or loss.

Rate of inventory turnover

It is sometimes necessary to use calculations involving the **rate of inventory turnover** to calculate an unknown figure in the trading section of a statement of profit or loss. The definition and formula for calculating the rate of inventory turnover are shown in Table 17.4.

Table 17.4: Rate of inventory turnover

Ratio	Definition	Formula
Rate of inventory turnover	Number of times a business replaces its inventory in a given period of time.	$\dfrac{\text{Cost of sales}}{\text{Average inventory}}$

> **KEY TERM**
>
> **rate of inventory turnover:** the number of times a business replaces its inventory in a given period of time.

> **LINK**
>
> You will learn about the importance of the rate of inventory turnover in Chapter 22.

WORKED EXAMPLE 17.6

H Palmer is a trader. The financial year ends on 31 July. The following information is provided for the year ended 31 July 20–4.

    Inventory 1 August 20–3 $60 000

    Inventory 31 July 20–4 $40 000

    The gross profit margin is at a standard rate of 20%.

    The rate of inventory turnover is 15 times a year.

Calculate the purchases and revenue for the year ended 31 July 20–4 using the trading section of a statement of profit or loss.

Prepare an outline statement

Insert the figures for opening inventory and closing inventory, and leave gaps for revenue, purchases, cost of sales and gross profit.

H Palmer
Trading section of statement of profit or loss for the year ended 30 September 20–4

		$	$
Revenue			e
Less	Cost of sales		
	Opening inventory	60 000	
	Purchases	c	
		b	
Less	Closing inventory	40 000	a
Gross profit			d

Calculate the average inventory

$$\text{Average inventory} = \frac{\text{Opening inventory} + \text{Closing inventory}}{2}$$

$$= \frac{\$60\,000 + \$40\,000}{2} = \$50\,000$$

Calculate the cost of sales (a)

$$\text{Rate of inventory turnover} = \frac{\text{Cost of sales}}{\text{Average inventory}}$$

$$= \frac{\text{Cost of sales}}{50\,000} = 15$$

Cost of sales = $50 000 × 15 = $750 000

Calculate the purchases figure (c)

Work 'backwards' from the cost of sales:

The cost of sales + the closing inventory = $790 000 **(b)**.

This figure less the opening inventory equals the purchases: $790 000 – $60 000 = $730 000.

17 Incomplete records

> **CONTINUED**
>
> **Calculate the gross profit (d) and revenue (e)**
>
> The gross profit margin is 20%, so the gross profit is 20% of the revenue (sales).
>
> This means the other 80% of the revenue is equal to the cost of sales.
>
> Revenue (100%) = cost of sales (80%) + gross profit (20%)
>
> - Gross profit is $\frac{20}{80} = \frac{1}{4}$ of the cost of sales, so gross profit = $\frac{1}{4}$ (or 25%) of \$750 000 = \$187 500.
> - Revenue = cost of sales + gross profit = \$750 000 + \$187 500 = \$937 500
>
> Alternatively, the revenue is $\frac{100}{80} = \frac{5}{4}$ of the cost of sales, so revenue = $\frac{5}{4}$ (or 125%) of \$750 000 = \$937 500.

ACCOUNTING IN ACTION

Lost and damaged records

Figure 17.4: A furniture store in a shopping mall

Kai is a retailer. He rents a furniture store in an out-of-town shopping mall. Kai offers a wide range of household furnishings and has built up a good reputation for quality products and excellent customer service.

After very heavy rain for several days, the lower floor of the shopping mall was flooded. A lot of the goods in Kai's store were carried away with the flood water and damaged beyond recognition.

A small quantity of goods had been stored on higher shelves away from the floor and these goods could be salvaged.

Kai needs to submit a claim to his insurance company for the damaged goods. Unfortunately, a lot of Kai's paperwork and documents were also destroyed in the flood. However, Kai was able to provide the following information relating to the two months from the start of his financial year to the date of the flood:

- Opening inventory
- Total sales
- Opening and closing trade payables
- Amount paid to trade payables
- Cost of salvaged goods
- Gross profit margin

Discuss in pairs or in a group:

1. Explain, step by step, how Kai could calculate the cost of damaged goods for an insurance claim from the information he has available.
2. Why can Kai only submit a claim for the cost, not the selling price, of the goods that were damaged?

> **CAMBRIDGE IGCSE™ AND O LEVEL ACCOUNTING: COURSEBOOK**

> **SUMMARY**
>
> You should now know:
>
> - A statement of affairs is similar to a statement of financial position and is prepared when a full set of accounting records is not maintained.
>
> - Profit can be measured from the change in the capital over a period of time, taking into consideration drawings and capital introduced.
>
> - The amount received from credit customers does not necessarily equal the credit sales; the amount paid to credit suppliers does not necessarily equal the credit purchases. Adjustments are needed for opening and closing trade receivables and trade payables.
>
> - When records are available of the assets, liabilities and money paid and received, it is possible to prepare a full set of financial statements after calculating revenue and purchases.
>
> - Gross profit can be expressed as gross profit margin (on selling price) and as mark-up (on cost price).
>
> - The rate of inventory turnover is the number of times a business replaces its inventory in a given period of time.

Chapter 17 practice questions

1   On 1 July 20–7, Hanif's capital was $51 800.
    On 30 June 20–8, this had increased to $55 200.
    During the year, he had invested a further $10 000 and had withdrawn cash $1 200 for personal use. How much was the profit or loss for the year?

    A $5 400 loss

    B $5 400 profit

    C $6 600 loss

    D $6 600 profit   [1]

2   Benilda's financial year ends on 31 May. On 1 June 20–2, her trade receivables owed $7 532.

    During the year ended 31 May 20–3, she received $95 620 from trade receivables after allowing cash discount of $1 570. Sales returns during the year totalled $2 640. On 31 May 20–3, the trade receivables owed $8 870.

    How much were the credit sales?

    A $95 888

    B $98 028

    C $99 598

    D $101 168   [1]

3   Isla applies a mark-up of 25% to obtain the selling price of her goods. She provided the following information:

	$
Opening inventory	9 600
Closing inventory	12 400
Revenue	140 000

How much were Isla's purchases for the year?

A $102 200

B $107 800

C $109 200

D $114 800   [1]

4   Leke is a trader. He does not maintain a full set of accounting records, but was able to provide the following information on 1 March 20–7.

	$
Fixtures and fittings at cost	10 000
Motor vehicle at cost	12 000
Inventory	5 800
Trade receivables	5 250
Trade payables	2 700
Long-term loan from Rekha Finance	5 000
Other receivables	460
Bank overdraft	2 660

During the year ended 28 February 20–8, Leke borrowed a further $1 000 from Rekha Finance and took $1 000 from the bank for personal use.

On 28 February 20–8:

- Leke decided that the motor vehicle should be depreciated by 20% on cost and that the fixtures and fittings should be valued at $8 000

- the inventory was valued at $8 100, trade receivables were $6 660, the trade payables were $3 140 and there was $880 in the bank.

a   Prepare a statement of affairs of Leke on 1 March 20–7 showing the total capital at that date.   [6]

b   Prepare a statement of affairs of Leke on 28 February 20–8 showing the total capital at that date.   [7]

c   Prepare a capital account for Leke for the year ended 28 February 20–8 showing the profit or loss for the year.   [4]

[Total: 17]

5 Hafiz is a sole trader who does not maintain a full set of accounting records. He was able to provide the following information.

On 1 January 20–8:

	$
Fixtures (cost $41 000)	34 800
Motor vehicle (cost $20 000)	15 000
Inventory	25 300
Trade receivables	19 500
Balance at bank	7 650
Trade payables	17 550

For the year ended 31 December 20–8:

	$
Receipts – Trade receivables	358 800
Payments – Trade payables	265 820
Motor expenses	12 080
General expenses	15 500
New fixtures	6 000
Drawings	15 000

On 31 December 20–8:

	$
Inventory	23 080
Trade receivables	21 500
Trade payables	15 510

- Fixtures should be depreciated by 10% per annum on the cost of fixtures held at the end of the year.
- The motor vehicle should be depreciated by 20% per annum on cost.

a Prepare the statement of profit or loss for the year ended 31 December 20–8. **[15]**

b Prepare the statement of financial position at 31 December 20–8. Show all calculations. **[11]**

[Total: 26]

6 Malik is a trader. He provided the following information.

	$
Inventory at cost on 1 April 20–5	2 000
For the year ended 31 March 20–6:	
Purchases	45 000
Revenue	55 000

On the evening of 31 March 20–6, a fire destroyed a quantity of goods. The cost of the goods recovered from the fire was $900.

Malik marks up the goods by 25% on cost when calculating the selling price.

a Calculate the cost of goods which were destroyed by using the trading section of a statement of profit or loss. [6]

b Explain the difference between mark-up and gross profit margin. [2]

c Calculate Malik's rate of inventory turnover. Use the total inventory before the fire on 31 March 20–6 when calculating the average inventory. [3]

d State what the answer to the calculation in **c** indicates. [1]

[Total: 12]

CHECK YOUR PROGRESS

How well do you think you have achieved the learning intentions for this chapter? Give yourself a score from 1 (still need a lot of practice) to 5 (feeling very confident) for each learning intention. Provide an example to support your score.

Now I can …	Score	Example to support score
explain the reasons why businesses maintain incomplete records		
calculate profit for the year using statements of affairs		
prepare control accounts to find missing figures		
use mark-ups or gross profit margins to calculate missing figures		
prepare financial statements from incomplete records with adjustments.		

> Chapter 18

Accounts of non-trading organisations (clubs and societies)

LEARNING INTENTIONS

By the end of this chapter, you will be able to:

- understand the difference between receipts and payments accounts and income and expenditure accounts
- prepare receipts and payments accounts and income and expenditure accounts
- prepare financial statements, with adjustments, for clubs and societies
- prepare accounts for activities that generate revenue, such as refreshments and subscriptions
- explain what an accumulated fund is and calculate its value.

18 Accounts of non-trading organisations (clubs and societies)

Introduction

This chapter concentrates on the accounts of **non-trading organisations** such as clubs and societies. The main aim of these organisations is to provide facilities and services for their members; making a profit is not the main objective. Examples of such organisations include youth clubs, sports clubs, music and drama groups, golf clubs and scout groups.

The main source of income of a society is **subscriptions**. These are the amounts members pay, usually annually, to use the facilities provided by the club or society.

A person is appointed to act as treasurer and be responsible for collecting any money due to the society and for paying money owed by the society. In some cases, a full set of double entry records is written up each year, but it is more usual to find that only a record of money received and paid is maintained. At the end of the financial year, the treasurer will usually present financial statements to the members. These financial statements may consist of a receipts and payments account, an income and expenditure account and a statement of financial position. If the club is involved with any buying and selling, such as by running a snack bar, then the treasurer may also prepare a trading account to show the profit or loss on that activity.

> **KEY TERMS**
>
> **non-trading organisation:** an organisation formed to provide facilities and services for members; they are not formed with the aim of making a profit.
>
> **subscriptions:** amounts members of an organisation pay to use the facilities provided by the club or society.

ACCOUNTING IN CONTEXT

Club treasurers

Figure 18.1: A choir might need a club treasurer to manage its finances

It is usual for a club to appoint a treasurer who is responsible for collecting subscriptions and income from other sources, and who is authorised to make payments on behalf of the club. This person may not have any accounting training, but is required to keep appropriate records and to present a summary of the financial position to the members at the end of each financial year.

Ilham runs a choir. They practise together and put on concerts in their local area. The current treasurer is moving away, so a new treasurer needs to be appointed. There are several people who are interested in the role, so Ilham has decided to interview each of them and ask the following questions:

a   Why is the role of treasurer important?

b   What sort of receipts and payments would the treasurer need to keep records of?

Ilham will then be able to choose who she thinks will be better for the role.

Discuss in pairs or in a group:

1   Imagine you want to become the new treasurer. What answers would you give to the two questions?

2   What qualities do you think the new treasurer should possess?

18.1 Preparation of a receipts and payments account

A **receipts and payments account** is regarded as a summary of the cash book for the financial year. All money received is debited and all money paid is credited. The account is balanced, and the balance carried down to become the opening balance for the following financial year. This account does not usually distinguish between cash and bank transactions, so the balance may represent actual cash, money in the bank or a combination of the two.

A debit balance is an asset and represents money owned by the society. A credit balance is a liability and represents a bank overdraft.

A receipts and payments account records all money received and paid (just like a cash book).

It is important to remember that:

- no adjustments are made for other receivables and other payables
- no distinction is made between capital receipts and revenue receipts
- no distinction is made between capital expenditure and revenue expenditure
- non-monetary items such as depreciation are not included.

> **KEY TERM**
>
> **receipts and payments account:** a summary of the cash book which is prepared annually by a non-trading organisation.

> **TIP**
>
> When you prepare a receipts and payments account, remember to include all the money paid and received in that year even if it relates to a different year, such as a subscription for the following year paid in advance.

WORKED EXAMPLE 18.1

The Five Star Athletics Club was formed some years ago to provide various sporting facilities for its members. The club also has a shop where members can purchase sportswear.

On 1 August 20–4, the club had $2 950 in the bank. The treasurer provided the following list of receipts and payments for the year ended 31 July 20–5.

	$
Subscriptions received	7 720
Receipts from shop sales	3 940
Purchases of sportswear for resale	2 930
Wages – Shop assistant	910
Athletics coach	4 800
Rates and insurance	1 620
General expenses	840
Purchase of new sports equipment	3 600
Athletics competition – Entrance fees received	2 200
Expenses	940

All receipts are paid into the bank and all payments are made by bank transfer.

18 Accounts of non-trading organisations (clubs and societies)

CONTINUED

Prepare the receipts and payments account of the Five Star Athletics Club for the year ended 31 July 20–5.

Five Star Athletics Club
Receipts and payments account for the year ended 31 July 20–5

Receipts			$	Payments		$
20–4				20–5		
Aug 1	Balance	b/d	2 950	Jul 31 Purchases		2 930
20–5				Wages –		
Jul 31	Subscriptions		7 720	Shop assistant		910
	Receipts from shop		3 940	Athletics coach		4 800
	Competition entrance fees		2 200	Rates and insurance		1 620
				General expenses		840
				Sports equipment		3 600
				Competition expenses		940
				Balance	c/d	1 170
			16 810			16 810
20–5						
Aug 1	Balance	b/d	1 170			

359

18.2 Preparation of a trading account of a club or society

Although buying and selling is not the main purpose of a club or society, many do carry out a trading activity. Many clubs operate a shop or a cafe where goods are bought and sold. At the end of the financial year, a trading account should be prepared for each separate trading activity to show the profit earned on that activity.

Any expenses which arise as a result of running the trading activity, such as wages of cafe assistants and depreciation of cafe equipment, should be added to the cost of sales in order to calculate the correct profit or loss.

The profit or loss on the trading activity is transferred from the trading account to the income and expenditure account.

Some clubs may not maintain any inventory for the trading activity. For example, members may select goods from a catalogue in the club shop instead of selecting goods from those on display. In cases like this, the calculation of the profit can be shown in the income and expenditure account in the same way as the calculation of profit on any fund-raising activity, so a trading account is not required.

> **LINK**
>
> Income and expenditure accounts are explained in Section 18.3.

WORKED EXAMPLE 18.2

The Five Star Athletics Club was formed some years ago to provide various sporting facilities for its members. The club also has a shop where members can purchase sportswear.

The treasurer provided the following information for the year ended 31 July 20–5:

	$
Receipts from shop sales	3 940
Purchases of goods for resale	2 930
Shop inventory 1 August 20–4	360
Shop inventory 31 July 20–5	520
Wages of shop assistant	910

Prepare the shop trading account of the Five Star Athletics Club for the year ended 31 July 20–5.

Five Star Athletics Club
Shop trading account for the year ended 31 July 20–5

	$	$
Revenue		3 940
Less Cost of sales		
Opening inventory	360	
Purchases	2 930	
	3 290	
Less Closing inventory	520	
	2 770	
Wages of shop assistant	910	3 680
Profit on shop (transferred to income and expenditure account)		260

> **TIP**
>
> When a trading account is prepared for a particular activity, remember to transfer the profit or loss on that activity to the income and expenditure account.

18.3 Preparation of an income and expenditure account

An **income and expenditure account** compares the gains of the club with the expenses of running the club. If the gains are more than the expenses, the difference is referred to as a **surplus** or excess of income over expenditure (this is known as the profit for the year in a business). If the gains are less than the expenses, the difference is referred to as a **deficit** or excess of expenditure over income (this is known as the loss for the year in a business).

An income and expenditure account is prepared using the same principles as those applied in the preparation of a statement of profit or loss of a trading business.

It is important to remember that:

- adjustments must be made for other receivables and other payables
- capital receipts and capital expenditure are not included
- only revenue receipts and revenue expenditure are included
- non-monetary items such as depreciation are included
- assets and liabilities at the beginning and end of the financial year are not included.

Where the club or society holds a fundraising activity, the income and the expenses of that activity should be set off against each other in the income and expenditure account. In this way, the profit or loss on that particular activity can be calculated.

> **KEY TERMS**
>
> **income and expenditure account:** an account prepared annually by a non-trading organisation. It compares the gains and the expenses to calculate the surplus or deficit.
>
> **surplus:** when gains exceed expenses.
>
> **deficit:** when expenses exceed gains.

> **LINKS**
>
> You learnt how to prepare a statement of profit or loss of a business in Chapters 8, 11 and 12.

WORKED EXAMPLE 18.3

The Five Star Athletics Club was formed some years ago to provide various sporting facilities for its members. The club also has a shop where members can purchase sportswear.

The following receipts and payments account was prepared for the year ended 31 July 20–5.

Five Star Athletics Club							
Receipts and payments account for the year ended 31 July 20–5							
Receipts			$	Payments			$
20–4				20–5			
Aug 1	Balance	b/d	2 950	Jul 31	Purchases		2 930
20–5	Subscriptions		7 720		Wages –		
Jul 31	Receipts from shop		3 940		Shop assistant		910
	Competition entrance fees		2 200		Athletics coach		4 800
					Rates and insurance		1 620
					General expenses		840
					Sports equipment		3 600
					Competition expenses		940
					Balance	c/d	1 170
			16 810				16 810
20–5							
Aug 1	Balance	b/d	1 170				

The treasurer provided the following additional information:

1. On 31 July 20–5:
   - insurance prepaid amounted to $56
   - wages of athletics coach outstanding amounted to $200
   - 15 members still owe their annual subscription of $40 each for the current year
   - eight members have paid their annual subscription of $40 each for the following year
   - sports equipment is to be depreciated by $900.

2. The profit on the club's shop for the year ended 31 July 20–5 was $260 (calculated in the shop trading account).

Prepare the income and expenditure account of the Five Star Athletics Club for the year ended 31 July 20–5.

18 Accounts of non-trading organisations (clubs and societies)

CONTINUED

Five Star Athletics Club
Income and expenditure account for the year ended 31 July 20–5

	$	$
Income		
Subscriptions (7720 + 600 – 320)		8 000
Profit on shop		260
Competition – Entrance fees	2 200	
Expenses	940	1 260
		9 520
Expenditure		
Wages – Athletics coach (4 800 + 200)	5 000	
Rates and insurance (1620 – 56)	1 564	
General expenses	840	
Depreciation on equipment	900	8 304
Surplus for the year		1 216

ACTIVITY 18.1

Figure 18.2: Members of a cricket club are likely to be interested in the club's finances

The treasurer of the AB Cricket Club prepared the following receipts and payments account for the year ended 31 May 20–6.

Working with a partner:

1. Consider the account and list the reasons why the members may be concerned.

2. Suggest actions which could be taken to improve the situation in the future.

AB Cricket Club

Receipts and payments account for the year ended 31 May 20–6

Receipts			$	Payments		$
20–5				20–6		
Jun 1	Balance	b/d	2 194	May 31	Competition –	
20–6					Cost of prizes	300
May 31	Subscriptions		3 300		Expenses	333
	Competition –				Groundkeeper's wages	3 000
	Entrance fees		550		General expenses	387
	Balance	c/d	476		Equipment	2 500
			6 520			6 520
				20–6		
				Jun 1	Balance b/d	476

REFLECTION

How confident were you at answering the questions in Activity 18.1?

Were you and your partner able to list all the reasons why the members may be concerned?

What did you need to consider when making suggestions for improvements in the future?

How helpful was it to discuss your ideas with a partner?

ACTIVITY 18.2

Make a copy of this income and expenditure account of the AB Cricket Club.

AB Cricket Club
Income and expenditure account for the year ended 31 May 20–6

	$	$
Income		
Subscriptions (3 300 – ...... – ......)		....
Competition – Entrance fees	....	
Costs (...... + ...)	....	....
		2 917
Expenditure		
Groundkeeper's wages	3 000	
General expenses (387 – ...... + ...)	....	
Depreciation on equipment (10% × (...... + ...))	....	4 577
.... for the year		....

Use the following information and the receipts and payments account shown in Activity 18.1 to complete your copy of the account.

1. The club has 60 members and the annual subscription is $50. On 1 June 20–5, there were subscriptions owing from five members, and on 31 May 20–6, one member had paid the subscription in advance for the following year.

2. On 1 June 20–5, general expenses of $25 were accrued, and on 31 May 20–6, the amount accrued was $15.

3. Equipment held on 1 June 20–5 had cost $9 500 (book value $7 600). Equipment owned at the end of each financial year is depreciated by 10% on cost.

18.4 Differences between a receipts and payments account and an income and expenditure account

Section 18.1 explained how to prepare a receipts and payments account and Section 18.3 explained how to prepare an income and expenditure account. The differences between the two accounts are shown in Table 18.1.

Table 18.1: Differences between a receipts and payments account and an income and expenditure account

Receipts and payments account	Income and expenditure account
Is a summary of a cash book	Is the equivalent of a statement of profit or loss
Shows the opening and closing cash/bank balances	Shows the surplus or deficit for the year
Includes a summary of all money received and all money spent regardless of whether it is capital or revenue	Includes only revenue receipts and revenue expenditures
Includes a summary of all money received and all money spent regardless of the year to which it relates	Includes only income and expenditure which relates to that particular year
Includes only items which can be expressed in monetary terms	Includes non-monetary items

18.5 Preparation of a statement of financial position of a club or society

The principles applied when preparing a statement of financial position of a club or society are similar to those applied in the preparation of a statement of financial position of a business. The statement of financial position of a club or society shows non-current assets, current assets, non-current liabilities and current liabilities in the same way as a statement of financial position of a trading organisation.

If some of the members have not paid their subscriptions due for the year, these subscriptions will appear in the current assets as they are amounts owing to the club. They are often referred to as subscriptions in arrears. It may be that some members have already paid their subscriptions for the following year. These are regarded as a liability to the club and will be included in the current liabilities.

There is no capital in the statement of financial position of a club or society, whereas a business is usually financed by an investment of capital from the owner(s). Members of a club or society do not invest money in the same way as the owner of a business. This means the members are not entitled to make any drawings if a club or society makes a surplus. These surpluses will accumulate within the club to form a capital fund known as the **accumulated fund**. If the club makes a deficit, then the accumulated fund will decrease. This accumulated fund replaces capital in the statement of financial position of a club or society.

> **LINKS**
>
> You learnt how to prepare a statement of financial position of a business in Chapters 9, 11 and 12.

> **KEY TERM**
>
> **accumulated fund:** the surpluses (less any deficits) which have accumulated over the life of the club. It replaces capital in the statement of financial position of a club or society.

18 Accounts of non-trading organisations (clubs and societies)

WORKED EXAMPLE 18.4

The Five Star Athletics Club was formed some years ago to provide various sporting facilities for its members. The club also has a shop where members can purchase sportswear.

On 1 August 20–4, the following balances appeared in the books of the club:

	$
Clubhouse at cost	30 000
Equipment at cost	15 400
Provision for depreciation on equipment	5 160
Balance at bank	2 950
Shop inventory	360
Accumulated fund	43 550

The income and expenditure account for the year ended 31 July 20–5 showed a surplus of $1 216.

During the year ended 31 July 20–5, new equipment costing $3 600 was purchased. The depreciation on equipment for the year amounted to $900.

On 31 July 20–5:

	$
Balance at bank	1 170
Shop inventory	520
Insurance paid in advance	56
Wages of athletics coach outstanding	200
Subscriptions in arrears	600
Subscriptions paid in advance by members	320

> **CONTINUED**
>
> Prepare the statement of financial position of the Five Star Athletics Club at 31 July 20–5.
>
> **Five Star Athletics Club**
> **Statement of financial position at 31 July 20–5**
>
> | Assets | $ Cost | $ Accumulated depreciation | $ Net book value |
> |---|---|---|---|
> | **Non-current assets** | | | |
> | Clubhouse | 30 000 | – | 30 000 |
> | Equipment | 19 000 | 6 060 | 12 940 |
> | | 49 000 | 6 060 | 42 940 |
> | **Current assets** | | | |
> | Shop inventory | | 520 | |
> | Subscriptions in arrears | | 600 | |
> | Other receivables | | 56 | |
> | Bank | | 1 170 | 2 346 |
> | **Total assets** | | | 45 286 |
> | **Accumulated fund and liabilities** | | | |
> | **Accumulated fund** | | | |
> | Opening balance | | | 43 550 |
> | Plus Surplus for the year | | | 1 216 |
> | | | | 44 766 |
> | **Current liabilities** | | | |
> | Other payables | | 200 | |
> | Subscriptions in advance | | 320 | 520 |
> | **Total accumulated fund and liabilities** | | | 45 286 |
>
> - The subscriptions in arrears could have been included under other receivables and the subscriptions in advance could have been included under other payables. In this case, a note to the statement of financial position would show the breakdown of these figures.

18.6 Differences between accounting terms used by a business and those used by a club or society

Accounting in a business context and accounting in the context of a club or society uses different vocabulary. Table 18.2 shows the differences in the accounting terms.

Table 18.2: Differences between the accounting terms used by a business and those used by a club or society

Business	Club or society
Cash book	Receipts and payments account
Statement of profit or loss	Income and expenditure account
Profit for the year	Surplus
Loss for the year	Deficit
Capital/Equity	Accumulated fund

18.7 Subscriptions

The receipts and payments account shows the amount of subscriptions received during the financial year, but the income and expenditure account shows the amount of subscriptions relating to the financial year. This means that the amount received must be adjusted for any subscriptions owed by members and any subscriptions paid in advance by members (see Worked example 18.3). The calculation of the amount relating to the financial year may be shown in the form of a ledger account known as a subscriptions account.

The subscriptions account may be regarded as the account of the members in the books of the club. Subscriptions owing by members are shown as a debit balance on the subscriptions account, and will appear in the statement of financial position as a current asset to the club or society. Subscriptions paid in advance by members are shown as a credit balance on the subscriptions account, and will appear in the statement of financial position as a current liability because the club or society has an obligation to provide a period of membership which has already been paid for. It is possible to have two balances on a subscriptions account as the account is for **all** the members, and some may have paid their subscriptions in advance and some may not have paid their subscriptions.

At the end of the financial year, the account is closed by a transfer to the income and expenditure account of the amount relating to that financial year. The club will also maintain a register of members. This records the details of each individual member of the club, including if their subscription has been paid.

WORKED EXAMPLE 18.5

The Five Star Athletics Club was formed some years ago to provide various sporting facilities for its members.

On 1 August 20–4, there were no subscriptions owing by members and no members had paid their subscriptions in advance.

During the year ended 31 July 20–5, the club received subscriptions totalling $7 720 from members. This included subscriptions of $40 each from eight members for the following financial year.

On 31 July 20–5, subscriptions of $40 each for the current financial year were still outstanding from 15 members.

During the year ended 31 July 20–6, the club received subscriptions from members totalling $6 920. On 31 July 20–6, there were subscriptions outstanding of $360.

Prepare the subscriptions account in the books of the Five Star Athletics Club for **each** of the **two** years ended 31 July 20–5 and 31 July 20–6.

Five Star Athletics Club

Dr				Subscriptions account				Cr
				$				$
20–5					20–5			
July 31	Balance	c/d	320		July 31	Bank/cash		7 720
	Income & expenditure		8 000			Balance	c/d	600
			8 320					8 320
20–5					20–5			
Aug 1	Balance	b/d	600		Aug 1	Balance	b/d	320
20–6					20–6			
July 31	Income & expenditure		7 000		July 31	Bank/cash		6 920
						Balance	c/d	360
			7 600					7 600
20–6								
Aug 1	Balance	b/d	360					

- At the end of each financial year, the difference on the account is transferred to the income and expenditure account. This represents the subscriptions which relate to that particular financial year.

A club may have a policy that subscriptions which remain unpaid after a certain period of time are written off. The entries are similar to those made when a business writes off an irrecoverable debt. The subscriptions account is credited with the amount written off before the subscriptions for the year are transferred to the income and expenditure account. These irrecoverable debts will be included in the expenses in the income and expenditure account.

TIP

When you prepare a subscriptions account, remember that subscriptions owing are a debit balance and subscriptions paid in advance are a credit balance.

18 Accounts of non-trading organisations (clubs and societies)

ACTIVITY 18.3

Figure 18.3: Members of a football club usually pay a subscription to use the club's facilities

The financial year of the Woodfield Football Club ends on 31 March.
On 1 April 20–5, the club had 420 members. The annual subscription is $30.

The following account appeared in the ledger.

Working in pairs, discuss the account and answer the following questions:

1 What does the balance of $90 on 1 April 20–4 represent?

2 State what the entry on the credit side of the account of $12 870 represents.

3 Why was it necessary to make the entry on 31 March 20–5 transferring $30 to the income and expenditure account?

4 What does the transfer of $12 600 to the income and expenditure account on 31 March 20–5 represent?

5 What does the balance of $210 on 1 April 20–5 represent?

\multicolumn{7}{c}{**Woodfield Football Club**}
\multicolumn{7}{c}{**Subscriptions account**}
Date	Details		$	Date	Details	$
20–4				20–5		
Apr 1	Balance	b/d	90	Mar 31	Bank	12 870
20–5					Income & expenditure	30
Mar 31	Balance	c/d	210			
	Income & expenditure		12 600			
			12 900			12 900
				20–5		
				Apr 1	Balance b/d	210

371

> **DISCUSSION**
>
> Imagine you are the treasurer of a drama club. You have noticed that the amount of subscriptions unpaid at the end of each financial year has increased considerably.
>
> **Discuss in a small group:**
>
> 1 Why might this be happening?
>
> 2 In what ways may this be affecting the club?
>
> 3 What can be done to encourage members to pay their subscriptions on time?
>
> Select a member of the group to present a summary of your discussion to the rest of the class.

18.8 Calculation of sales and purchases

As the accounts of a club or society are often incomplete, it may be necessary to calculate credit purchases (and sometimes credit sales if goods are sold on credit) before the preparation of the trading account. The method used to calculate credit sales and credit purchases for a business which does not have a full set of accounting records can also be applied to a club or society.

> **LINK**
>
> You learnt how to calculate purchases and sales for businesses which do not have complete accounting records in Chapter 17.

> **WORKED EXAMPLE 18.6**
>
> The Five Star Athletics Club has a shop where members can purchase sportswear. All the sales are made for cash and all purchases are made on credit terms.
>
> The treasurer provided the following information:
>
> | | $ |
> |---|---|
> | Trade payables 1 August 20–6 | 310 |
> | Trade payables 31 July 20–7 | 296 |
> | Amount paid to credit suppliers during the year ended 31 July 20–7 | 3 088 |
>
> Prepare a total payables account to calculate the purchases for the year ended 31 July 20–7.
>
> **Five Star Athletics Club**
>
> | Dr | | | Total payables account | | | Cr |
> |---|---|---|---|---|---|---|
> | | | $ | | | | $ |
> | 20–7 | | | 20–6 | | | |
> | July 31 | Bank | 3088 | Aug 1 | Balance | b/d | 310 |
> | | Balance c/d | 296 | 20–7 | | | |
> | | | | July 31 | Purchases | | 3074 * |
> | | | 3384 | | | | 3384 |
> | | | | 20–7 | | | |
> | | | | Aug 1 | Balance | b/d | 296 |
>
> * This represents the purchases for the year and will appear in the shop trading account.

18.9 Calculation of accumulated fund

It is sometimes necessary to calculate the accumulated fund of a club or society. This can be calculated by applying the same formula used to calculate the capital of a business.

In a business	Assets	=	Capital	+	Liabilities
In a club or society	Assets	=	Accumulated fund	+	Liabilities

WORKED EXAMPLE 18.7

On 1 August 20–7, the assets and liabilities of the Five Star Athletics Club were as follows:

	$
Clubhouse at cost	30 000
Equipment at cost	23 000
Provision for depreciation on equipment	7 060
Balance at bank	1 846
Shop inventory	420
Trade payables for shop supplies	296

Calculate the accumulated fund on 1 August 20–7.

Calculation of accumulated fund on 1 August 20–7			
		$	$
Assets	Clubhouse at cost		30 000
	Equipment at cost	23 000	
	Less Accumulated depreciation	7 060	15 940
	Balance at bank		1 846
	Shop inventory		420
			48 206
Liabilities	Trade payables		296
Accumulated fund			47 910

ACTIVITY 18.4

The treasurer of a youth club provided the following information at the end of the financial year on 30 September 20–8.

	$
Equipment at book value	19 750
Petty cash	94
Trade payables for shop supplies	579
Shop inventory	695
Bank overdraft	1 990
Rent of meeting room prepaid	120

The income and expenditure account for the year ended 30 September 20–8 showed a deficit of $1 600.

Calculate the accumulated fund on 1 October 20–7.

ACCOUNTING IN ACTION

Greenways Football Club

Figure 18.4: A football club might need to borrow money for a particular purpose if they do not have enough from subscriptions

Greenways Football Club rents the football pitches and clubhouse at an annual rent of $8 000 payable in full on the first day of their financial year, which is 1 January.

The average bank balance is $12 000. There are 200 members and the annual subscription is $100.

On 31 August 20–3, the owner of the football pitches and clubhouse offered to sell them to the club for $100 000. A decision has to be made before 31 October 20–3 and the property will have to be paid for on 31 December 20–3.

Five members have suggested the following ways to raise the necessary funds:

A Organise fundraising activities

B Increase the annual subscription

C Use the accumulated fund, which is currently $25 000

D Take out a ten-year 6% bank loan of $50 000

E Take out a five-year 5% loan of $60 000, which has been offered by a member of the club.

Working in groups:

1 Prepare a comment on each of these suggestions.

2 Advise the club which, if any, of these five suggestions should be acted upon. Give a reason for your recommendation.

Discuss your group's recommendations with the rest of the class.

18 Accounts of non-trading organisations (clubs and societies)

SUMMARY

You should now know:

- A club or society is often referred to as a non-trading organisation.
- At the end of the financial year, a club will usually prepare a receipts and payments account, which is a summary of the cash book.
- If a club carries out a trading activity, it may be necessary to prepare a trading account for that activity at the end of the financial year.
- At the end of the financial year, a club will prepare an income and expenditure account, which is similar to a statement of profit or loss.
- The statement of financial position of a club is very similar to that of a business except that the capital is replaced by the accumulated fund.
- The main source of income for a club is the subscriptions received from its members for the use of the facilities provided by the club.

Chapter 18 practice questions

1 A club provided the following information:

	$
Subscriptions paid in advance at the start of year	250
Subscriptions received during the year	4 900
Subscriptions owing at the end of the year	300

How much was included for subscriptions in the income and expenditure account?

A $4 850

B $4 950

C $5 200

D $5 450   [1]

2 A sports club was formed on 1 January 20–4. During the year ended 31 December 20–4, the club purchased sports equipment by cheque.

In which of the financial statements would this be included?

	Receipts and payments account	Income and expenditure account	Statement of financial position
A	✓	✓	✓
B	✓	✓	
C	✓		✓
D		✓	✓

[1]

3 On 1 January 20–4, the accumulated fund of a club amounted to $15 750. During the year ended 31 December 20–3, the only item of income was subscriptions of $4 960. The expenses for the year ended 31 December 20–3 included running costs of $5 100 and depreciation of $360. How much was the accumulated fund on 1 January 20–3?

   A $15 250   B $15 610   C $15 890   D $16 250   [1]

4 The treasurer of the ABC Club provided the following information for the year ended 30 April 20–8:

	$
Balance at bank 1 May 20–7	844
Subscriptions received:	
for the year ended 30 April 20–7	1 800
for the year ended 30 April 20–8	15 000
for the year ending 30 April 20–9	1 200
Proceeds of sale of old sports equipment	856
Cost of new sports equipment	?
Rent paid for 13 months to 31 May 20–8	5 460
Insurance	640
Repayment of loan	5 500
Loan interest	250
General expenses	2 045
Bank balance 1 May 20–8	495 credit

Prepare a receipts and payments account for the year ended 30 April 20–8 showing the amount paid for new sports equipment during the year. [7]

5 The Arrows Archery Club was formed on 1 June 20–1. The following information was provided for the year ended 31 May 20–2.

		$
Receipts	Subscriptions	7 440
	Tickets for archery competition	950
	Loan from SportingHelp	2 000
Payments	Rent	4 950
	Insurance (15 months to 31 August 20–2)	750
	Expenses of archery competition	630
	Archery equipment	1 260

Additional information:

   1 The club has 90 members. The annual subscription is $80. On 31 May 20–2, two members had not paid their subscriptions and five members had paid their subscriptions in advance for the following year.

2   On 31 May 20–2, general expenses accrued amounted to $124 and rent accrued amounted to $450.

3   A five-year loan from SportingHelp was received on 1 December 20–1. Interest is payable at 5% per annum.

4   Equipment is to be depreciated at the rate of 10% per annum based on the cost of equipment owned at the end of the financial year.

a   Prepare the income and expenditure account for the year ended 31 May 20–2. [8]

b   Prepare a statement of financial position at 31 May 20–2. [9]

[Total: 17]

6   In addition to providing sports facilities for members, the KY Running Club also has a shop selling sports clothing to members and guests. All purchases are made on credit terms and all sales are made for cash.

The treasurer provided the following information:

	1 July 20–4 $	30 June 20–5 $
Shop inventory	1 420	1 960
Subscriptions owing by members	150	–
Subscriptions prepaid by members	–	300
Rent payable accrued	–	500
Amounts owing to credit suppliers	1 100	930
Sports equipment at cost	19 100	?
Provision for depreciation on sports equipment	7 640	?

During the year ended 30 June 20–5:

Receipts	Subscriptions	16 200
	Receipts from shop sales	15 350
	Tournament entrance fees	1 710
Payments	New sports equipment	1 500
	Credit suppliers to shop	9 300
	Rent	4 000
	Tournament prizes	1 620
	Wages – Shop assistant	4 920
	Sports coach	6 180
	General expenses	4 940

The sports equipment is being depreciated at the rate of 20% per annum using the straight line method. A full year's depreciation is charged in the year of purchase.

a   Prepare the shop trading account for the year ended 30 June 20–5. [7]

b   Prepare the income and expenditure account for the year ended 30 June 20–5. [8]

[Total: 15]

CHECK YOUR PROGRESS

How well do you think you have achieved the learning intentions for this chapter? Give yourself a score from 1 (still need a lot of practice) to 5 (feeling very confident) for each learning intention. Provide an example to support your score.

Now I can ...	Score	Example to support score
understand the difference between receipts and payments accounts and income and expenditure accounts		
prepare receipts and payments accounts and income and expenditure accounts		
prepare financial statements, with adjustments, for clubs and societies		
prepare accounts for activities that generate revenue, such as refreshments and subscriptions		
explain what an accumulated fund is and calculate its value.		

Chapter 19
Partnerships

LEARNING INTENTIONS

By the end of this chapter, you will be able to:

- explain the advantages and disadvantages of forming a partnership and why a partnership agreement is important
- understand and prepare appropriation accounts
- prepare and make adjustments to financial statements
- record interest on loans, capital and drawings
- record partners' salaries and the division of the balance of profit or loss
- understand and prepare partners' capital and current accounts.

Introduction

The earlier chapters (except Chapter 18) related to businesses which were owned by only one person (a sole trader). Another very common form of business is a **partnership**. A partnership is a business in which two or more people work together as owners with the aim of making profits.

Professional people such as accountants and solicitors often operate as partnerships. A large number of family businesses also run as partnerships. Sometimes a new business is formed as a partnership, or a partnership is formed when a sole trader wishes to expand their business, or a partnership is formed when two or more sole traders agree to combine their businesses.

A partnership business will maintain double entry records in the same way as a sole trader. Just like a sole trader, a partnership business can be a manufacturing business, a trading business, a service business or a combination of these. Whichever type of business it is, a partnership business must prepare financial statements at the end of each financial year.

If the partnership is a manufacturing business, then a manufacturing account and a statement of profit or loss will be prepared at the end of each financial year. If the partnership is a trading or a service business, a statement of profit or loss will be prepared. However, a partnership will prepare an extra account after the statement of profit or loss. This is known as an appropriation account. This account will show how the profit for the year is divided among all the partners in accordance with their partnership agreement.

> **KEY TERM**
>
> **partnership:** a business in which two or more people work together as owners with the aim of making a profit.

> **LINKS**
>
> You learnt about financial statements of sole traders in Chapters 8–9.
>
> You will learn about manufacturing accounts in Chapter 20.

ACCOUNTING IN CONTEXT

Forming a partnership

Figure 19.1: Business owners discussing the advantages and disadvantages of forming a partnership

Sole traders who have been successfully running a business for some time may look for new ways to expand their business further. They might consider forming a partnership with another sole trader who has a business in a related area.

Aisha has been manufacturing children's clothes for some years as a sole trader. Her cousin, Fatini, has been in business as a retailer of children's clothes for a similar length of time. At a family party, they discussed the possibility of forming a partnership and merging their businesses.

Aisha gave the proposal serious thought during the next few days and decided it would be a good idea to merge the businesses. She contacted Fatini to discuss the possible partnership in more detail.

Discuss in a pairs or in a group:

- What are the advantages to Aisha and Fatini of forming a partnership?
- What might be some of the disadvantages of forming a partnership?

19.1 The advantages and disadvantages of partnership businesses

Before agreeing to enter into a partnership business, a person must consider the advantages and disadvantages of such an arrangement. These are summarised in Table 19.1.

Table 19.1: Advantages and disadvantages of a partnership

Advantages	Disadvantages
Additional finance is available.	Profits have to be shared among the partners.
Additional knowledge, experience and skills are available.	Decisions have to be recognised by all partners.
The responsibilities are shared.	Decisions may take longer to put into effect.
The risks are shared.	One partner's actions on behalf of the business are binding on all the partners.
Discussions can take place before decisions are taken.	Disagreements can occur.
	All partners are responsible for the debts of the business.

> **LINK**
>
> You learnt about the advantages and disadvantages of sole trader businesses in Chapter 1.

> **DISCUSSION**
>
> Imagine that you are a sole trader and that you own a retail store selling bicycles and cycling equipment. You think it is possible to increase the size of your business and you are considering asking an old school friend to join you in the business as a partner.
>
> Working in pairs, list the things you would consider before going into business with someone. The list should contain both financial and non-financial considerations.
>
> Justify the items on your list to the rest of the class.

19.2 Partnership agreement

Although it is not legally necessary to draw up a **partnership agreement** when forming a partnership, it is a good idea to do so. Drawing up an agreement can avoid misunderstandings and arguments later on. The clauses of a partnership agreement cover many aspects of the business, including those shown in Table 19.2.

> **KEY TERM**
>
> **partnership agreement:** a document setting out the rules for operating the business, including profit-sharing arrangements.

Table 19.2: Financial clauses which may be included in a partnership agreement

Terms of the partnership agreement	Reason
Amount of capital invested by each partner	Partners do not need to invest equal amounts.
How profits and losses are to be shared	Profits and losses may be shared equally, or in proportion to capital invested or in some other ratio.
If interest on partners' capital is to be paid, and at what rate	This interest is a reward for investing in the business rather than elsewhere. If all partners invest the same amount, it may not be necessary to pay interest. Where partners invest different amounts, interest can be a form of compensation to the person who has invested the most capital.
If partners' salaries are to be paid, and what amount	If all partners share the work and responsibilities equally, it may not be necessary to pay salaries. A salary can be a form of compensation where one partner has a greater share of the work and responsibilities.
If an upper limit is to be placed on partners' drawings, and what amount	The business will benefit if partners keep drawings as low as possible.
If interest on partners' drawings is to be charged, and at what rate	This is a method of discouraging partners from making drawings from the business (especially early in the financial year). Interest on the amount withdrawn is calculated from the date of withdrawal until the end of the financial year.
If interest on partners' loans is to be paid, and at what rate	If extra finance is required, a partner may make a loan to the business. To compensate for the loss of interest they could otherwise earn, interest on the loan may be paid.

> **ACTIVITY 19.1**
>
> Make a list of non-financial factors you think would be included in a partnership agreement. The list should contain a minimum of four items.
>
> Compare your list with a partner's list and discuss any differences.

19.3 Loans from partners

A partnership may borrow money from one of the partners if extra finance is required (particularly if it is needed for a fixed period of time). Loans from partners are **not** part of the capital of the business and are treated in the same way as any other loan. Unlike investing additional capital, money lent to a partnership business by a partner will be repaid at an agreed time. Interest on the loan is a business expense and is not affected by the amount of profit or loss. Interest on a loan from a partner is entered in the statement of profit or loss in the same way as interest on any other loans.

When a loan is received from a partner

- Debit the bank account.
- Credit the loan from X (partner) account.

When a loan is repaid to a partner

- Debit the loan from X (partner) account.
- Credit the bank account.

When interest is paid on a partner's loan

- Debit the interest on loan account.
- Credit the bank account.

When interest is due (but not paid) on a partner's loan

- Debit the interest on loan account.
- Credit the Partner X current account. (Current accounts are explained in Section 19.5.)

At the end of the financial year

- Debit the statement of profit or loss.
- Credit the interest on loan account.

> **TIP**
>
> When you are completing financial statements, remember that interest on a loan from a partner is an expense in the statement of profit or loss; it is not an appropriation of profit.

> **ACTIVITY 19.2**

Maria and James formed a partnership a few years ago providing equal amounts of capital to open a taxi business. The business now owns several cars and a minibus, and employs ten drivers. Maria and James would like to expand their business, which would include replacing two of the cars with newer models and purchasing an electric car.

There is not enough money in the business to finance this and an extra $20 000 will be required. Maria cannot invest further capital. James has available funds but is not sure whether to invest further capital or make a loan to the business.

Working in small groups, consider whether James should invest further capital or make a loan to the business.

Write down the advantages and disadvantages for James of each action.

19.4 Preparation of an appropriation account of a partnership

The **appropriation account** for the financial year is prepared after the statement of profit or loss and shows how the profit for the year is shared between the partners.

The profit for the year is transferred to this account from the statement of profit or loss. Any interest on drawings charged to the partners increases the amount available to share and this must be added to the profit. The appropriations (profit shares) detailed in the partnership agreement for interest on capital and partners' salaries are deducted. The remaining figure is known as the **residual profit** and is shared between the partners in the agreed profit-sharing ratio.

> **KEY TERMS**
>
> **appropriation account:** one of the year-end financial statements. It shows the division of the profit or loss between the partners.
>
> **residual profit:** the profit remaining after adjusting for interest on drawings, interest on capital and partners' salaries.

WORKED EXAMPLE 19.1

Ahmed and Basma are in partnership. Their financial year ends on 31 May. They provided the following information:

		$
Capital on 1 June 20–8	Ahmed	70 000
	Basma	30 000
Drawings for the year ended 31 May 20–9	Ahmed	16 000
	Basma	12 000
Profit for the year ended 31 May 20–9		26 000

The partnership agreement includes the following terms:
- Interest on capital is allowed at 6% per annum.
- Interest on drawings is charged at 3%.
- Basma is entitled to a partnership salary of $11 000 per annum.
- Residual profits are shared in proportion to capital invested.

Prepare the appropriation account for the year ended 31 May 20–9.

Ahmed and Basma
Appropriation account for the year ended 31 May 20–9

		$	$	$
Profit for the year				26 000
Add Interest on drawings	Ahmed		480	
	Basma		360	840
				26 840
Less Interest on capital	Ahmed	4 200		
	Basma	1 800	6 000	
Partner's salary	Basma		11 000	17 000
Residual profit				9 840
Profit shares*	Ahmed		6 888	
	Basma		2 952	9 840

* The profit shares are calculated:

Ahmed $\dfrac{70\,000}{100\,000} \times \dfrac{9\,840}{1}$ Basma $\dfrac{30\,000}{100\,000} \times \dfrac{9\,840}{1}$

ACTIVITY 19.3

Figure 19.2: Partnership agreements are important as they can help avoid misunderstandings

When Jamala and Sade formed a partnership some years ago, they each contributed $50 000 as capital and agreed to share profits and losses equally. Their financial year ends on 31 March. On 1 July 20–1, Jamala introduced additional capital of $20 000. On 1 January 20–2, Sade made a loan to the business of $10 000. The partners agreed that Sade would receive loan interest of 4% per annum.

Their partnership agreement provides for interest on capital at 5% per annum, interest on drawings at 4% and an annual salary of $5 000 for Sade. On 1 October 20–1, Sade's annual salary was increased to $6 000.

During the year ended 31 March 20–2, Jamala's drawings amounted to $7 000 and Sade's amounted to $11 000.

The profit before interest for the year ended 31 March 20–2 was $18 100.

Calculate:

a   the profit for the year ended 31 March 20–2 after loan interest

b   the residual profit for the year ended 31 March 20–2.

> **TIP**
>
> You should pay attention to the date when capital is introduced. If it was partway through a financial year, the interest is calculated from the date the funds were received by the partnership.

REFLECTION

How confident were you with completing Activity 19.3? Did you refer back to Worked example 19.1?

How can you make the best use of the worked examples to help you in your learning?

19.5 Partners' ledger accounts

Capital accounts

Similar to a sole trader, each partner has their own capital account in the nominal ledger. These usually record permanent increases or decreases in the capital invested by the individual partner. Capital accounts prepared in this way are referred to as fixed capital accounts.

A capital account has a credit balance as the business owes this to the partner.

Current accounts

Each partner usually has a current account. Anything which the partner becomes entitled to, such as interest on capital, interest on loan, partner's salary and profit share, is credited to this account. Anything which the partner is charged with, such as drawings and interest on drawings, is debited to this account.

A credit balance on a current account represents the amount owed to the partner, and a debit balance represents the amount owed by the partner to the business. If a partner's drawings are more than their total share of profit, the current account will have a debit balance as the partner owes this to the business. If a partner's drawings are less than their total share of profit, the current account will have a credit balance as the business owes this to the partner.

If the partners decide not to maintain current accounts, then interest on capital, partners' salaries, profit share, drawings and interest on drawings are recorded in the capital account.

Drawings accounts

Each partner usually has a drawings account. The total of this account is transferred to the partner's current account at the end of the financial year.

WORKED EXAMPLE 19.2

Ahmed and Basma are in partnership. Their financial year ends on 31 May. They provided the following information:

	Ahmed	Basma
On 1 June 20–8:	$	$
Capital account	70 000	30 000
Current account	2 390 Cr	650 Dr
For the year ended 31 May 20–9:		
Drawings	16 000	12 000
Interest on drawings	480	360
Interest on capital	4 200	1 800
Partner's salary		11 000
Profit share	6 888	2 952

> ### CONTINUED
>
> Prepare the capital account and the current account of Ahmed for the year ended 31 May 20–9.
>
> | Ahmed and Basma | | | | | |
> |---|---|---|---|---|---|
> | **Dr** | | **Ahmed – Capital account** | | | **Cr** |
> | | $ | | | | $ |
> | | | 20–8 | | | |
> | | | Jun 1 | Balance | b/d | 70 000 |
>
> | Dr | | | Ahmed – Current account | | | Cr |
> |---|---|---|---|---|---|---|
> | | | $ | | | | $ |
> | 20–9 | | | 20–8 | | | |
> | May 31 | Drawings | 16 000 | Jun 1 | Balance | b/d | 2 390 |
> | | Interest on drawings | 480 | 20–9 | | | |
> | | | | May 31 | Interest on capital | | 4 200 |
> | | | | | Profit share | | 6 888 |
> | | | | | Balance | c/d | 3 002 |
> | | | 16 480 | | | | 16 480 |
> | 20–9 | | | | | | |
> | Jun 1 | Balance | b/d | 3 002 | | | |
>
> - Ahmed is entitled to interest on capital and share of profits, and he is charged with drawings and interest on drawings during the year, so they are entered into Ahmed's current account.

It is important to maintain both a capital account and a current account for each partner. The capital account shows the amount invested in the partnership and makes it easy to calculate the interest on capital. The current account shows the partner's total profit share and whether the drawings exceed the total profit share.

It saves time to show partners' capital accounts and current accounts side by side using a column for each partner.

WORKED EXAMPLE 19.3

Using the information in **Worked example 19.2**, prepare the capital and current accounts of Ahmed and Basma for the year ended 31 May 20–9.

	Ahmed and Basma						
Dr			**Capital accounts**				**Cr**
	Ahmed	Basma				Ahmed	Basma
	$	$				$	$
			20–8				
			Jun 1	Balance	b/d	70 000	30 000

CONTINUED

Dr					Current accounts					Cr
				Ahmed	Basma				Ahmed	Basma
				$	$				$	$
20–8						20–8				
Jun 1	Balance	b/d			650	Jun 1	Balance	b/d	2 390	
20–9						20–9				
May 31	Drawings			16 000	12 000	May 31	Interest on capital		4 200	1 800
	Interest on drawings			480	360		Salary			11 000
	Balance	c/d			2 742		Profit share		6 888	2 952
							Balance	c/d	3 002	
				16 480	15 752				16 480	15 752
20–9						20–9				
Jun 1	Balance	b/d		3 002		Jun 1	Balance	b/d		2 742

ACTIVITY 19.4

Naji and Taha are in partnership. Their partnership agreement provides for interest on capital at 6% per annum, interest on drawings at 3%, an annual salary of $15 000 for Naji, with the residual profit shared according to capital invested. The profit for the year ended 31 March 20–5 was $60 000.

1 Copy the following current accounts of Naji and Taha and insert the missing figures.

				Naji and Taha						
Dr				Current accounts						Cr
				Taha	Naji				Taha	Naji
				$	$				$	$
20–4						20–4				
Apr 1	Balance	b/d			14 000	Apr 1	Balance	b/d	1 000	
20–5						20–5				
Mar 31	Drawings			………	………	Mar 31	Interest on capital		18 000	12 000
	Interest on drawings			300	600		Salary			………
	Balance	c/d		………			Profit share		………	6 360
							Balance	c/d		………
				………	………				………	………
20–5						20–5				
Apr 1	Balance	b/d			………	Apr 1	Balance	b/d		………

2 Discuss with a partner how you calculated Taha's profit share. How else could you have worked it out?

19.6 Preparation of a statement of financial position of a partnership business

A statement of financial position of a partnership is very similar to the statement of financial position of a sole trader. The only difference is in the capital section where, for a partnership, the capital account and current account of each partner must be shown separately. The partners may decide to include only the closing balance on each current account instead of listing all the details.

WORKED EXAMPLE 19.4

Ahmed and Basma are in partnership. Their financial year ends on 31 May. Their capital accounts and current accounts are shown in **Worked example 19.3**.

Prepare a relevant extract from the statement of financial position of Ahmed and Basma at 31 May 20–9.

Ahmed and Basma			
Extract from statement of financial position at 31 May 20–9			
	Ahmed $	Basma $	Total $
Capital accounts	70 000	30 000	100 000
Current accounts	(3 002)*	2 742	(260)
	66 998	32 742	99 740

* The debit balance on Ahmed's current account is shown in brackets as it is a minus figure, which reduces the amount owed by the business to Ahmed.

Sometimes the partners may decide to include all the details of each current account in the statement of financial position.

> ### WORKED EXAMPLE 19.5
>
> Ahmed and Basma are in partnership. Their financial year ends on 31 May. Their capital accounts and current accounts are shown in **Worked example 19.3**.
>
> Prepare a relevant extract from the statement of financial position of Ahmed and Basma on 31 May 20–9 showing full details of their current accounts.
>
> **Ahmed and Basma**
> **Extract from statement of financial position at 31 May 20–9**
>
> | | Ahmed $ | Basma $ | Total $ |
> |---|---|---|---|
> | **Capital accounts** | 70 000 | 30 000 | 100 000 |
> | **Current accounts** | | | |
> | Opening balance | 2 390 | (650) | |
> | Interest on capital | 4 200 | 1 800 | |
> | Partner's salary | | 11 000 | |
> | Profit share | 6 888 | 2 952 | |
> | | 13 478 | 15 102 | |
> | Less Drawings | 16 000 | 12 000 | |
> | Interest on drawings | 480 | 360 | |
> | | 16 480 | 12 360 | |
> | | (3 002) | 2 742 | (260) |
> | | | | 99 740 |

ACCOUNTING IN ACTION

Figure 19.3: Some businesses will need to invest in specialist equipment

Charles has a business making jewellery.

Charles wants to purchase additional specialised equipment costing at least $35 000 but is unable to fund this from the business and can only provide $10 000 from his personal money. He estimates that the profit will increase by 15% if this equipment is purchased. Charles's profit for the year was $6 000 after deducting the salary of the office manager.

The office manager, Susie, has worked for Charles for many years. She is paid an annual salary of $20 000. Susie has savings of $25 000 and has offered to invest this amount in the business provided that she is made a partner and is entitled to a partnership salary of $10 000 and half of the residual profit. Susie would continue to manage the office.

Calculate the profit share Charles would receive if he admitted Susie as a partner.

List the advantages and disadvantages to Susie of entering into a partnership with Charles.

SUMMARY

You should now know:

- A partnership is a business in which two or more people work together as owners with the aim of making profits.
- There are both advantages and disadvantages of being a member of a partnership business.
- It is advisable to draw up a partnership agreement when the partnership is formed.
- A partner may make a loan to the business. This is treated in a similar way to all other loans.
- An appropriation account is prepared after the statement of profit or loss to share out the profit between the partners.
- Each partner usually has a capital account and a current account.
- In the statement of financial position of a partnership, the balances on each partner's capital account and current account must be shown separately.

Chapter 19 practice questions

1. What is a disadvantage of being a partner?

    A additional capital is available

    B additional skills are available

    C profits are shared

    D risks are shared [1]

2. Which item would **not** appear in the appropriation account of a partnership?

    A drawings

    B interest on capital

    C interest on drawings

    D partner's salary [1]

3. Chen and Hua are partners. Chen's capital is $90 000 and Hua's is $45 000. The partnership agreement provides for interest on capital at 4% per annum and an annual salary for Hua of $9 000. Profits and losses are shared in proportion to capital invested.

    The profit for the year ended 31 December 20–5 was $17 400. How much was credited to Hua's current account on 31 December 20–5?

    A $5 800

    B $11 800

    C $13 600

    D $16 600 [1]

4. Jabar and Tanvir are in partnership. Their financial year ends on 31 July.

    Their partnership agreement provides for:

    - interest on capital at 5% per annum
    - an annual salary of $5 000 for Tanvir
    - interest on drawings at 2%
    - residual profits and losses to be shared in the ratio of 3:2.

    The following information is available:

	Jabar $	Tanvir $
Capital account at 1 August 20–4	75 000	45 000
Current account at 1 August 20–4	3 000 (Cr)	150 (Dr)
Drawings during the year	5 000	4 000

    The profit for the year ended 31 July 20–5 was $13 250.

    a Prepare the appropriation account for the year ended 31 July 20–5. [7]

    b Prepare Tanvir's current account for the year ended 31 July 20–5. Balance the account and bring down the balance on 1 August 20–5. [5]

c State **two** reasons why a partnership maintains both a capital account and a current account for each partner. [2]

[Total: 14]

5 Adeel and Fahad are in partnership. Their financial year ends on 30 April. They provided the following information after the preparation of the statement of profit or loss for the year ended 30 April 20–7.

		Dr $	Cr $
Profit for the year			59 000
Capital account 1 May 20–6	Adeel		160 000
	Fahad		140 000
Current account 1 May 20–6	Adeel		9 000
	Fahad	100	
Drawings	Adeel	14 100	
	Fahad	6 500	
Property at cost		260 000	
Machinery at cost		150 000	
Provision for depreciation on machinery			83 200
Fixtures and equipment at cost		80 000	
Provision for depreciation on fixtures and equipment			36 000
Loan (repayable May 20–9)			37 000
Trade receivables		16 000	
Other receivables		2 180	
Trade payables			28 500
Other payables			400
Bank balance		5 120	
Inventory		19 100	

The partners are entitled to interest on capital at 5% per annum and share profits and losses equally.

Fahad invested an additional $20 000 capital on 1 February 20–7. No entries were made in the books of the partnership. On the same date, it was decided that Adeel would be entitled to a partnership salary of $10 000 per annum.

a Prepare the appropriation account for the year ended 30 April 20–7. [7]

b Prepare the statement of financial position at 30 April 20–7 (showing the current accounts in full). [15]

[Total: 22]

6   Leyna and Rana are in partnership. Their financial year ends on 31 December. On 31 December 20–4, their capitals were: Leyna $80 000 and Rana $90 000. The incomplete current accounts for the year ended 31 December 20–5 were as follows:

		Leyna $	Rana $				Leyna $	Rana $
20–5				20–5				
Jan 1	Capital	10 000		Jan 1	Balance	b/d	11 000	3 000
Dec 31	Drawings	6 000	8 000	Dec 31	Interest on capital		4 500	4 500
	Interest on drawings	240	320		Interest on loan			800
	Share of loss	200	200					

a   State the meaning of the entry on 1 January 'Capital $10 000'. [1]

b   Calculate the profit or loss for the year before appropriations. [3]

c   Calculate the percentage rate of interest on capital the partners received. [1]

d   Calculate the percentage rate of interest charged on partners' drawings. [1]

e   Calculate the ratio in which the partners shared the loss. [1]

f   State the balance on each partner's current account on 1 January 20–6, indicating whether each balance is debit or credit. [2]

g   State how a debit balance on a partner's current account may arise. [1]

h   Suggest one reason why Rana made a loan to the business instead of investing additional capital. [2]

[Total: 12]

CHECK YOUR PROGRESS

How well do you think you have achieved the learning intentions for this chapter? Give yourself a score from 1 (still need a lot of practice) to 5 (feeling very confident) for each learning intention. Provide an example to support your score.

Now I can …	Score	Example to support score
explain the advantages and disadvantages of forming a partnership and why a partnership agreement is important		
understand and prepare appropriation accounts		
prepare and make adjustments to financial statements		
record interest on loans, capital and drawings		
record partners' salaries and the division of the balance of profit or loss		
understand and prepare partners' capital and current accounts.		

Chapter 20
Manufacturing accounts

LEARNING INTENTIONS

By the end of this chapter, you will be able to:

- understand the difference between direct costs and indirect costs
- explain direct materials, direct labour and prime cost
- understand and identify factory overheads
- understand and make adjustments for work in progress
- calculate factory cost of production
- prepare manufacturing accounts, statements of profit or loss and statements of financial position, including adjustments.

20 Manufacturing accounts

Introduction

The previous chapters (except Chapter 18) relate to businesses which are involved in trading (such as wholesale or retail businesses that buy goods and sell them without changing the goods in any way) or service businesses. There are also manufacturing businesses which buy raw materials and convert these into finished products, which they then sell.

A manufacturing business will maintain double entry records similar to those of retail and wholesale businesses. At the end of the financial year, in addition to a statement of profit or loss and a statement of financial position, a manufacturing business will prepare a **manufacturing account**. The purpose of this account is to calculate how much it has cost the business to manufacture the goods produced in the financial year.

> **KEY TERM**
>
> **manufacturing account:** an annual financial statement that is used to calculate the cost of goods produced.

> **LINKS**
>
> You learnt about statements of profit or loss and statements of financial position in Chapters 8–9.

ACCOUNTING IN CONTEXT

The cost of production

Figure 20.1: A manufacturing business produces final goods from raw materials

Many businesses buy goods and sell these same goods without changing them in any way. A manufacturing business obtains raw materials and converts them into finished products, which it then sells. For example, a car maker will purchase steel and use it to make parts of cars, and a clothing factory will purchase fabric and make it into items of clothing.

Kuda manufactures high-quality honey. He purchases raw honey from a local beekeeper. The honey is then processed and put into jars, which Kuda sells to local shops and also online. Kuda has been concerned recently that a local supermarket has been selling jars of honey more cheaply than he is able to sell his honey.

At the end of each financial year, Kuda's accountant prepares a manufacturing account in addition to a statement of profit or loss and a statement of financial position. The manufacturing account shows the total cost of producing the honey. From his own records, Kuda knows how many jars of honey he produces each year.

Discuss in pairs or in a group:

1. How can Kuda use the information in the manufacturing account to calculate the cost of producing one jar of honey? How might this information be useful?

2. a Other than the cost of the raw materials, what other things need to be considered when working out the cost of production?

   b Why do you think a supermarket is able to sell jars of honey more cheaply than Kuda does?

20.1 The elements of cost

The cost of manufacture is made up of four main elements. These are divided into **direct costs** and **indirect costs**, as shown in Figure 20.2.

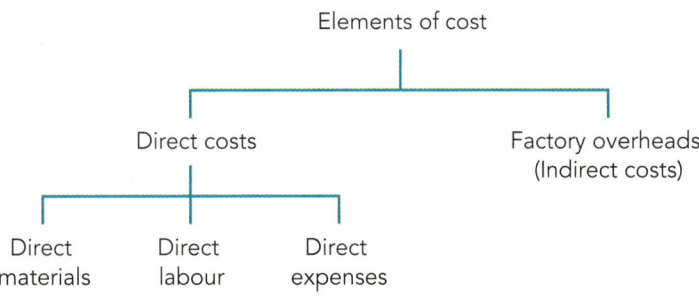

Figure 20.2: Cost of manufacture

> **KEY TERMS**
>
> **direct costs:** costs which can be linked to the making of the product.
>
> **indirect costs:** costs which are not directly linked to the making of the product.

Direct material

The first thing a manufacturer needs is raw material to make the finished goods. This raw material takes many forms depending on the type of business – a baker will need flour, a furniture maker will need wood, a car maker will need steel and so on. The cost of material used in production is often referred to as the cost of material used or the cost of material consumed.

Direct labour

The next essential cost for a manufacturer is the cost of the wages of the people who are employed in the factory making the goods. Depending on the type of business, these may be bakers, carpenters, machine operators and so on. This cost is sometimes referred to as direct wages.

The term direct labour includes only those people who are actually involved in the production of the finished goods. It does not include the wages of supervisors, maintenance staff, factory cleaners and so on. These people have important roles to play within the factory, but are regarded as indirect labour.

Direct expenses

These are any expenses which a manufacturer can link directly with the product being manufactured. It may be that for every item produced, a manufacturer has to pay a fee (known as a royalty) to the person who originally invented the product. A manufacturer may have to hire a special piece of equipment to complete the manufacturing process. These expenses are regarded as direct expenses.

Factory overheads

These are sometimes referred to as indirect factory expenses. They include all the costs involved in operating the factory but which cannot be directly linked with the product being manufactured. Expenses such as factory rent and rates, factory heat and light, factory machinery repairs, depreciation of factory machinery and indirect factory wages are all regarded as factory overheads.

ACTIVITY 20.1

Figure 20.3: There are many different types of cost associated with manufacturing clothes

A clothing factory provided the following information about some of its costs.

Copy and complete the table by inserting a tick (✓) to indicate whether each cost is direct material, direct labour or factory overhead.

Cost	Direct material	Direct labour	Factory overhead
Electricity used in factory			
Sewing machine operators' wages			
Purchase of suit fabric			
Factory supervisor's wages			
Purchase of spare parts for machine			
Cost of fitting spare parts to machine			
Purchase of buttons and threads			

20.2 Preparation of a manufacturing account

The cost of manufacturing the goods produced is calculated in the manufacturing account.

Step 1

The first item in a manufacturing account is direct material. The cost of the raw material used during the year is calculated in a similar way to that in which a retailer or a wholesaler calculates the cost of goods sold. The cost of raw material actually used during the year is calculated as:

Direct material = Opening inventory of raw materials + Purchases of raw materials − Purchases returns + Carriage inwards on purchases of raw materials − Closing inventory of raw materials

Step 2

The cost of the direct labour is then added to the direct material. Any direct expenses are then also added.

The total of these three elements of cost is known as the **prime cost**.

Prime cost = Direct material + Direct labour + Direct expenses

Step 3

The factory overheads are added to the prime cost to get the total **cost of production**.

Cost of production = Prime cost + Factory overheads

> **KEY TERMS**
>
> **prime cost:** the total of the direct materials, direct labour and direct expenses. It is the cost of the essentials necessary for production.
>
> **cost of production:** prime cost plus factory overheads, adjusted for any work in progress at the start and at the end of the year. It is the total cost of manufacturing the completed goods.

> **TIP**
>
> Remember that the manufacturing account includes only costs relating to the making of the goods, so you must not include revenue in this account.

20 Manufacturing accounts

WORKED EXAMPLE 20.1

The following information was provided by Awang Manufacturing Company on 30 April 20–6:

	$
Raw materials – Inventory 1 May 20–5	15 200
Inventory 30 April 20–6	16 450
Purchases	203 100
Carriage on purchases	4 050
Factory wages – Direct	179 600
Indirect	95 200
Royalties	2 000
Factory insurance	2 010
Factory rent and rates	3 430
Factory general expenses	6 110
Depreciation on factory machinery	10 500

Prepare the manufacturing account of Awang Manufacturing Company for the year ended 30 April 20–6.

Awang Manufacturing Company
Manufacturing account for the year ended 30 April 20–6

	$	$
Cost of material consumed		
Opening inventory of raw material	15 200	
Purchases of raw material	203 100	
Carriage on purchases	4 050	
	222 350	
Less Closing inventory of raw material	16 450	205 900
Direct wages		179 600
Direct expenses – Royalties		2 000
Prime cost		387 500
Factory overheads		
Indirect wages	95 200	
Insurance	2 010	
Rent and rates	3 430	
General expenses	6 110	
Depreciation on machinery	10 500	117 250
Cost of production		504 750

ACTIVITY 20.2

Figure 20.4: An employee checking the quality of furniture produced in a factory

Max imports timber, which he then makes into wooden furniture that is sold to large retail stores.

At the end of his first year, he made the following list of his 12 costs.

- General factory expenses
- Purchase of timber
- Wages – Machine operators
    - Factory cleaners
    - Factory supervisor
- Carriage on timber
- Insurance of factory building
- Machinery – Repairs
    - Hire of special cutting machine
- Depreciation – Machinery
    - Hand tools
- Customs duty on timber

Draw up a table with the headings shown and complete it by listing the costs under the correct headings. The first one has been competed as an example.

Prime cost			Factory overheads
Cost of material consumed	Direct labour	Direct expenses	
			General factory expenses

> **REFLECTION**
>
> How confident are you that you:
>
> - understand the differences between direct costs and indirect costs
> - can prepare a manufacturing account without looking back to Worked example 20.1?
>
> Some strategies that might help you include:
>
> - Writing down definitions
> - Explaining your thoughts to a partner
> - Practising with other examples
> - Writing a checklist of steps to follow
>
> What other learning strategies can you think of? Which do you find most helpful and why?

20.3 Work in progress

Goods which are partly completed at the end of the financial year are known as **work in progress**. The work in progress is excluded from the cost of production as these goods cannot be sold until they are completed. However, they do have some value as it has cost something to get them to their present condition – some material has been used and some direct wages have been incurred and so on – so it is necessary to place a value on the work in progress.

The partly made goods at the end of the financial year are known as closing work in progress. These goods will become the opening work in progress at the start of the following financial year.

In a manufacturing account, it is necessary to adjust the cost of production so that it represents only the cost of goods actually completed in the year. This adjustment is done in the same way as for any other type of inventory – the opening inventory is added and the closing inventory is deducted.

> **KEY TERM**
>
> **work in progress:** goods which are partly completed at the end of the financial year.

> **WORKED EXAMPLE 20.2**
>
> The following information was provided by Awang Manufacturing Company on 30 April 20–6.
>
> | | $ |
> |---|---|
> | Prime cost | 387 500 |
> | Factory overheads | 117 250 |
> | Work in progress – Inventory 1 May 20–5 | 9 150 |
> | Inventory 30 April 20–6 | 8 900 |

CONTINUED

Prepare the manufacturing account of Awang Manufacturing Company for the year ended 30 April 20–6.

Awang Manufacturing Company
Manufacturing account for the year ended 30 April 20–6

	$	$
Prime cost*		387 500
Factory overheads*		117 250
		504 750
Add Opening work in progress		9 150
		513 900
Less Closing work in progress		8 900
Cost of production		505 000

* Full details would be shown as in **Worked example 20.1**.

20.4 Calculation of unit cost

Where a manufacturer makes only one type of identical product, the cost of making one item (or unit) can be found by dividing the production cost of goods completed by the number of items manufactured.

WORKED EXAMPLE 20.3

Awang Manufacturing Company makes one type of identical product. The cost of production during the year ended 30 April 20–6 was $505 000, and a total of 125 000 articles were completed.

Calculate the unit cost.

$$\text{Unit cost} = \frac{\text{Cost of production}}{\text{Number of units produced}} = \frac{\$505\,000}{125\,000} = \$4.04$$

ACTIVITY 20.3

Look back to Worked example 20.1.

The costs were:

	$
Direct material	205 900
Direct wages	179 600
Royalties	2 000
Factory overheads	117 250

The owner of Awang Manufacturing Company is looking ahead to the following financial year.

He expects to produce 125 000 units but estimates:

- cost of direct material will decrease by 2% as he intends to purchase cheaper materials
- direct wages will increase by 4%
- royalties will remain the same
- factory overheads will increase by 2%

a Calculate the estimated cost of production (ignoring work in progress). Show your workings.

b Calculate the estimated unit cost.

20.5 Preparation of a trading section of a statement of profit or loss of a manufacturing business

The gross profit of a manufacturing business is calculated in the trading section of the statement of profit or loss. This is very similar to the trading section of a statement of profit or loss prepared by a wholesale or retail business. The main difference is that because the business actually makes the goods it sells, purchases is replaced by the production cost of goods completed.

Sometimes a manufacturing business may purchase some finished goods which it does not manufacture itself. This may occur when:

- production does not meet demand
- it is cheaper to buy the goods rather than make them
- those particular items cannot be made by the business.

Purchases of finished goods are added to the production cost of goods completed in the statement of profit or loss. In the trading section of the statement of profit or loss, the proceeds from the sale of finished goods are compared with the cost of those finished goods. This means that the inventories included are the inventories of finished goods held by the manufacturer at the start and end of the financial year.

DISCUSSION

Figure 20.5: Sometimes it may be cheaper to buy finished goods rather than manufacture them

Akshata owns a leather goods manufacturing business. During the last three months, she has experienced an increase in orders and has been struggling to meet demand.

Akshata is undecided whether to increase output by purchasing more machinery and employing more workers, or whether to purchase finished goods from another manufacturer.

Working with a partner:

1. Discuss what Akshata should consider before making a decision.
2. Summarise your discussion by making a list of points which could help Akshata make a decision.

> **CAMBRIDGE IGCSE™ AND O LEVEL ACCOUNTING: COURSEBOOK**

WORKED EXAMPLE 20.4

The following information was provided by Awang Manufacturing Company on 30 April 20–6:

	$
Cost of production*	505 000
Revenue	696 300
Finished goods – Inventory 1 May 20–5	32 150
Inventory 30 April 20–6	28 130
Purchases	18 380

* Calculated in the manufacturing account.

Prepare the trading section of the statement of profit or loss of Awang Manufacturing Company for the year ended 30 April 20–6.

Awang Manufacturing Company
Trading section of statement of profit or loss for the year ended 30 April 20–6

	$	$
Revenue		696 300
Less Cost of sales		
Opening inventory of finished goods	32 150	
Cost of production	505 000	
Purchases of finished goods	18 380	
	555 530	
Less Closing inventory of finished goods	28 130	527 400
Gross profit		168 900

20.6 Preparation of a profit and loss section of a statement of profit or loss of a manufacturing business

The profit for the year of a manufacturing business is calculated in the profit and loss section of the statement of profit or loss. This is very similar to the profit and loss section of a statement prepared by a wholesale or retail business. Expenses relating to the manufacturing process have already been entered in the manufacturing account, so only administration expenses, selling and distribution expenses and financial expenses will appear in the profit and loss section of the statement of profit or loss.

Where an expense relates to the whole of the business, it may be necessary to share this out between the factory and the offices. Expenses such as insurance of buildings, rent and rates, and heat and light often have to be shared out in this way. For example, the insurance of the buildings may be shared ¾ to the factory and ¼ to the offices. This means that if the total cost of insurance was $2 680, then an amount of $2 010 would be included in the manufacturing account and $670 in the profit and loss section of the statement of profit or loss.

WORKED EXAMPLE 20.5

The following information was provided by Awang Manufacturing Company on 30 April 20–6.

	$
Gross profit*	168 900
Office wages	76 200
Office insurance	670
Office rent and rates	1 715
General office expenses	3 155
Depreciation on office equipment	3 500

* Calculated in the trading section of the statement of profit or loss.

Prepare the profit and loss section of the statement of profit or loss of Awang Manufacturing Company for the year ended 30 April 20–6.

Awang Manufacturing Company
Profit and loss section of statement of profit or loss for the year ended 30 April 20–6

		$	$
Gross profit			168 900
Less	Office wages	76 200	
	Office insurance	670	
	Office rent and rates	1 715	
	Office general expenses	3 155	
	Depreciation on office equipment	3 500	85 240
Profit for the year			83 660

20.7 Preparation of a statement of financial position of a manufacturing business

The statement of financial position of a manufacturing business is similar to that prepared by a wholesale or retail business. There is only one main difference, which is that a manufacturer may have three different inventories – raw material, work in progress and finished goods.

It is usual to show each of these inventories separately in the current assets section of the statement of financial position.

> **CAMBRIDGE IGCSE™ AND O LEVEL ACCOUNTING: COURSEBOOK**

WORKED EXAMPLE 20.6

On 30 April 20–6, Awang Manufacturing Company had inventories valued as follows:

	$
Raw material	16 450
Work in progress	8 900
Finished goods	28 130

Prepare a relevant extract from the statement of financial position of Awang Manufacturing Company at 30 April 20–6.

Awang Manufacturing Company Extract from statement of financial position at 30 April 20–6		
	$	$
Current assets		
Inventories – Raw materials	16 450	
Work in progress	8 900	
Finished goods	28 130	53 480

20.8 Year-end adjustments

This chapter has concentrated on the difference between the financial statements of a manufacturing business and those of a trading business. In order to emphasise these differences, the only year-end adjustment included was deprecation on factory machinery.

A manufacturer may have to make year-end adjustments for items such as accrued and prepaid expenses and incomes, and allowance for irrecoverable debts. These are recorded in exactly the same way as year-end adjustments in a wholesale or retail business.

> **LINKS**
>
> You learnt about year-end adjustments in Chapters 11–13.

20 Manufacturing accounts

ACCOUNTING IN ACTION

Decreasing the cost of production

Figure 20.6: A tableware business might try to keep their production costs low in order to increase their profits

Marlena is the owner of a business which manufactures tableware such as plates, cups, saucers and soup bowls. She supplies products to wholesalers and large retail businesses. In the factory, Marlena employs 15 factory operatives and a factory supervisor. There are also three warehouse staff and four office workers.

The manufacturing account for the last financial year showed the following costs (ignoring work in progress):

	$
Cost of material used	270 000
Direct wages	330 000
Factory overheads	126 000 (includes depreciation on factory machinery at 20% per annum)

Marlena would like to decrease the cost of production. She is considering spending $30 000 on additional factory machinery. This new machinery would mean that the cost of the direct labour could be reduced by one third. Repairs and maintenance of factory machinery would be decreased by $8 000 but the factory overheads would be increased by the annual depreciation on the new machinery.

Discuss in pairs or in a group:

1. Would you advise Marlena to go ahead with the purchase of the new machinery? Explain why or why not.

2. Prepare a list of the advantages and disadvantages which you could present to Marlena. You should consider both financial and non-financial factors.

SUMMARY

You should now know:

- A manufacturing account is used to calculate the cost of making goods produced in the financial year. It consists of direct materials + direct labour + direct expenses + factory overheads.

- Direct materials + direct labour + direct expenses = prime cost.

- The cost of production may have to be amended for the goods partly made at the end of the financial year, known as work in progress.

- In the trading section of the statement of profit or loss of a manufacturer, the cost of production is included together with any purchases of finished goods.

- In the statement of financial position of a manufacturer, it may be necessary to show three different inventories.

Chapter 20 practice questions

1. How is cost of production calculated?

    A prime cost + factory overheads + increase in work in progress

    B prime cost + factory overheads − increase in work in progress

    C prime cost − factory overheads + increase in work in progress

    D prime cost − factory overheads − increase in work in progress [1]

2. What may be included in prime cost?

    1 salary of factory manager
    2 salary of supervisor of production workers
    3 wages of machine maintenance workers
    4 wages of production workers

    A 1, 2 and 3

    B 2, 3 and 4

    C 3 and 4

    D 4 only [1]

3. Sophia provided the following information:

	$
Prime cost	145 000
Factory overheads	23 500
Opening work in progress	12 600
Closing work in progress	13 400

    How much was the cost of production?

    A $120 700

    B $122 300

    C $167 700

    D $169 300 [1]

4 The financial year of Seniya ends on 30 September. She provided the following information:

	$
At 1 October 20–7:	
Inventory – Raw materials	43 100
Finished goods	60 700
Work in progress	21 240
For the year ended 30 September 20–8:	
Purchases of raw materials	503 300
Purchases of finished goods	5 650
Revenue	915 400
Factory direct wages	69 600
Factory indirect salaries	32 450
Office and sales salaries	40 110
Factory general expenses	50 750
At 30 September 20–8:	
Inventory – Raw materials	44 800
Finished goods	58 350
Work in progress	18 920

a Select the relevant figures and prepare Seniya's manufacturing account for the year ended 30 September 20–8. [9]

b Select **two** of the items in this list which should not appear in a manufacturing account and explain why they are not included. [4]

[Total: 13]

5 a Explain the difference between:

  i direct costs and indirect costs [2]

  ii prime cost and cost of production. [2]

b State the meaning of the term 'work in progress'. [1]

c Explain why a manufacturer may purchase finished goods as well as raw materials. [2]

Bruno is a manufacturer. He provided the following information for the year ended 31 May 20–9:

	$
1 June 20–8 Inventory of raw materials	5 160
Inventory of work in progress	6 250
31 May 20–9 Inventory of raw materials	5 410
Inventory of work in progress	5 270

For the year ended 31 May 20–9:

	$
Purchases of raw materials	62 400
Direct factory wages	70 330
Indirect factory wages	32 250
Carriage on raw materials	4 120
Factory direct expenses	3 100
Factory indirect expenses	51 370

d i Calculate the prime cost. [5]

  ii Calculate the cost of production. [4]

[Total: 16]

6 Wendy started a manufacturing business on 1 April 20–5. She provided the following information:

	$
On 1 April 20–5:	
Cost of factory machinery	32 000
Cost of factory hand tools	1 100
Cost of office fixtures and fittings	9 900
For the year ended 31 March 20–6:	
Purchases of raw materials	34 700
Purchases of finished goods	11 900
Carriage on raw materials	2 150
Revenue	124 600
Wages and salaries – Factory operatives	30 300
Office staff	16 400
Factory supervisor	12 000
General expenses	6 500
Rent and rates	6 300
At 31 March 20–6:	
Inventory – Raw materials	3 120
Work in progress	3 030
Finished goods	8 250
Value of factory hand tools	850

Additional information:

1. The general expenses are to be apportioned ⅘ to the factory and ⅕ to the offices.

2. The rent and rates are to be apportioned ⅔ to the factory and ⅓ to the offices.

3. The factory machinery is to be depreciated at 20% per annum on cost, and the office fixtures and fittings by 10% per annum on cost. No additional non-current assets were purchased during the year.

a Prepare the manufacturing account for the year ended 31 March 20–6. [11]

b Prepare the statement of profit or loss for the year ended 31 March 20–6. [9]

[Total: 20]

CHECK YOUR PROGRESS

How well do you think you have achieved the learning intentions for this chapter? Give yourself a score from 1 (still need a lot of practice) to 5 (feeling very confident) for each learning intention. Provide an example to support your score.

Now I can …	Score	Example to support score
understand the difference between direct costs and indirect costs		
explain direct materials, direct labour and prime cost		
understand and identify factory overheads		
understand and make adjustments for work in progress		
calculate factory cost of production		
prepare manufacturing accounts, statements of profit or loss and statements of financial position, including adjustments.		

Chapter 21
Limited companies

LEARNING INTENTIONS

By the end of this chapter, you will be able to:

- explain the advantages and disadvantages of operating as a limited company
- understand the meaning of the terms limited liability and equity
- understand that the capital of a limited company can consist of ordinary share capital, general reserve and retained earnings
- understand and distinguish between issued, called-up and paid-up share capital, and between ordinary share capital and loan capital (debentures)
- understand that limited companies may be trading, service or manufacturing businesses (or a combination of some of these)
- prepare and make adjustments to financial statements for limited companies.

21 Limited companies

Introduction

A **limited company** is a legal entity which has a separate identity from its shareholders, whose liability for the company's debts is limited.

The capital of a limited company is divided into parts, which are known as shares. The people who own those shares are known as shareholders and they are the owners of the company. If the company earns a profit, part of that profit will be divided between the shareholders, and this is known as a share dividend.

An important difference between a sole trader or a partnership business and a limited company is that the owners of the company (the shareholders) are not responsible for the debts of the company. If a limited company fails and cannot pay its debts, then effectively these debts 'die' with the company. If this happens, the shareholders will have to pay anything they owe to the company but that is where their liability ends. Similarly, if a business or individual takes legal action against a limited company, this action is against the company and not the owners of that company as the company is a separate legal entity.

The business entity concept applies to limited companies in the same way as it applies to sole traders and partnerships. The limited company is completely separate from the owners of that company and the accounting records relate only to the business and not the owners (shareholders).

Sometimes a new business is formed as a limited company and sometimes a limited company is formed when a sole trader or partnership wishes to expand their business. Just like a sole trader or a partnership, a limited company can be a manufacturing business, a trading business, a service business or a combination of these.

> **KEY TERM**
>
> **limited company:** a legal entity which has a separate identity from its shareholders, whose liability for the company's debts is limited.

> **LINK**
>
> You learnt about the business entity concept in Chapter 10.

ACCOUNTING IN CONTEXT

Buying and selling shares

Figure 21.1: Selling agricultural machinery to a farmer

All businesses need capital. The capital of a sole trader is provided from the business owner's personal funds. Similarly, the capital of a partnership is provided by some or all of the partners. The capital of a limited company is provided by the shareholders. In all cases, some initial capital is required to set up the business and then further capital may be added when required.

A few years ago, Greg and Andreas established a limited company, G&A Agriculture Limited. The company buys agricultural machinery such as tractors, trailers, ploughs and milking machines from manufacturers, and sells them to farmers who are within 100 km of their premises.

Greg and Andreas have been very successful and now want to expand their business by opening a new branch in another part of the country. They have obtained a bank loan for half of the amount required, but they do not have enough personal funds to invest in the company.

> **CONTINUED**
>
> Marcia has worked for G&A Agriculture Limited for several years and has expressed an interest in becoming a shareholder in the company.
>
> **Discuss in pairs or in a group:**
>
> 1 Why do you think Marcia might be interested in buying shares in G&A Agriculture Limited?
>
> 2 What are the advantages and disadvantages to Marcia of buying shares in G&A Agriculture Limited compared to investing the money in a bank savings account?

21.1 The nature of a limited company

The capital of a company is divided into units known as shares, which can be of any monetary amount. The members (shareholders) of the company are only liable for the debts of the company up to the amount they agree to pay for their shares. Since a company can have a large number of members whose liability is limited, a large amount of capital can be raised. The shares of a company have a face value (par value) such as $5, $1, $0.50, etc. Profits are distributed among the members in the form of dividends, which are often stated in terms of a percentage of the face value of the shares.

> **WORKED EXAMPLE 21.1**
>
> GX Limited has a total capital of 300 000 shares of $2 each. It was decided to pay the shareholders a dividend of 13%.
>
> a What is the total amount payable?
>
> b What is the amount payable per share?
>
> a Total amount payable is $78 000 (13% of $600 000)
>
> b Amount payable per share is $0.26 (13% of $2)

There are two types of limited company – a public limited company, which may offer its shares to the public, and a private limited company, which is usually a smaller company and is not allowed to offer its shares to the public. Operating as a limited company has both advantages and disadvantages. These are summarised in Table 21.1.

Table 21.1: Advantages and disadvantages of a limited company

Advantages	Disadvantages
The company can attract more investors and higher capital because the principle of **limited liability** means that shareholders are not responsible for the debts of the business.	Limited companies can be complicated and expensive to establish as there are many legal requirements.
Shares can be transferred easily in a public limited company, which may be attractive to shareholders.	Annual accounting statements have to be filed, which can be expensive and time-consuming.
Companies may find it easier to borrow money from financial institutions as they may be regarded as a lower risk than sole traders and partnerships.	It is not always easy for shareholders in a private limited company to transfer shares.
Because a company is a separate legal entity, it continues to exist even though individual shareholders sell or transfer their shares.	In larger companies, shareholders are often not able to take an active part in the management of the company, which is run by a board of directors.
In some countries, limited companies may be more tax-efficient than sole traders and partnerships.	

> **KEY TERM**
>
> **limited liability:** the owners of a business are not personally liable for the debts of the business beyond what they agree to contribute as capital.

21.2 Share capital

Limited companies raise money by issuing shares to shareholders. In addition to issuing shares when the company is first set up, shares can be issued at any point in the life of the company when additional funds are required. The money received from the shareholders is debited to the company's bank account and credited to the share capital account. The company usually requires shareholders to pay the total amount due for the shares immediately. If the company does not require all the money immediately, then shareholders may pay for the shares in instalments. Once the money has been received by the company, it becomes part of the permanent capital of the company and a shareholder cannot request repayment.

Issued share capital

Issued share capital is the amount of share capital which is issued to the shareholders (members) when the company is formed. If more capital is required later, further shares can be issued.

Called-up capital

A company may not immediately require all the money due on the shares it issues. **Called-up capital** is the amount of the issued share capital that the company has

> **KEY TERMS**
>
> **issued share capital:** the amount of share capital issued to the shareholders.
>
> **called-up capital:** the amount of the issued share capital for which the company has requested payment from shareholders.

actually requested from its shareholders. In this situation, shareholders may be allowed to pay in 'instalments', at times and amounts fixed by the company. This amount may be less than the issued share capital, as a company may only 'call up' the amount it actually requires at a specific date.

Paid-up capital

Paid-up capital is that part of the called-up capital which the company has actually received from its shareholders.

> **KEY TERM**
>
> **paid-up capital:** the part of the called-up share capital which shareholders have actually paid to the company.

WORKED EXAMPLE 21.2

MMF Limited was formed on 1 January 20–8. A total of 400 000 $1 shares were issued on that date and shareholders were asked to pay 60% of the sum due immediately, and the other 40% in January 20–9.

By 1 May 20–8, holders of 380 000 shares had paid the amount due.

State:

a The issued capital of MMF Limited on 1 May 20–8.

b The called-up capital of MMF Limited on 1 May 20–8.

c The paid-up capital of MMF Limited on 1 May 20–8.

a The issued capital is $400 000 consisting of 400 000 shares of $1 each.

b The called-up capital is $240 000 consisting of $0.60 called up on 400 000 shares.

c The paid-up capital is $228 000 consisting of $0.60 paid up on 380 000 shares.

ACTIVITY 21.1

UDX Limited was formed on 1 July 20–4 when a total of 200 000 shares of $0.50 each were issued. Shareholders were asked to pay 60% of the sum immediately on 1 July 20–4, 20% of the sum on 1 January 20–5 and 20% of the sum on 30 June 20–5.

All the amounts due were paid in full on 1 July 20–4 and 1 January 20–5. Holders of 40 000 shares did not pay the last instalment until August 20–5.

Calculate:

a the issued capital on 1 July 20–4

b the called-up capital on 1 July 20–4

c the called-up capital on 1 January 20–5

d the paid-up capital on 30 June 20–5.

21.3 Types of shares

The share capital of a limited company may be divided into different types of shares. The most common ones are **ordinary shares** and preference shares. (Preference shares carry a fixed rate of dividend and are ranked before ordinary shares. However, preference shares are outside the scope of this coursebook.)

The below list summarises the main features of ordinary shares.

Ordinary shares

- They are also known as equity shares.
- The holders are usually entitled to vote at shareholders' meetings on the basis of one vote per share.
- The dividend is only payable after profit has been allocated for preference share dividend.
- The amount of dividend is recommended by the directors and may vary from year to year. If trading results are poor, the ordinary shareholders may receive no dividend at all, but they may receive high dividends if trading results are good.
- If the company is wound up (closed down), the outside liabilities and the preference shares are repaid before any monies are returned to the ordinary shareholders.

> **KEY TERM**
>
> **ordinary shares:** shares which receive a variable rate of dividend and have voting rights.

ACTIVITY 21.2

Figure 21.2: Ordinary shareholders can attend shareholders' meetings

The financial year of KQB Limited ends on 31 March. The company has capital consisting of 300 000 ordinary shares of $1 each.

On 1 September 20–2, the company paid an interim dividend on the ordinary shares totalling $7 000.

On 30 March 20–3, the company paid a final dividend on the ordinary shares totalling $14 000.

Calculate:

a   the total percentage dividend paid to ordinary shareholders

b   the total amount per share paid to ordinary shareholders.

21.4 Debentures

In addition to the funds provided by the owners (shareholders), a company may also obtain funds from **debentures**. The main features of debentures are summarised as follows:

- Debentures are long-term loans.
- They carry a fixed rate of interest, which is payable whether or not the company makes a profit.
- The loan agreement will specify the rate of interest, how often it is to be paid and when the debentures have to be repaid.
- The loan interest appears as a finance cost in the statement of profit or loss.
- If the company is wound up, the debenture holders will be repaid before any capital is repaid to shareholders.
- The holders are not members of the company and so are not entitled to vote at shareholders' meetings.

> **KEY TERM**
>
> **debenture:** a long-term loan which has a fixed rate of interest, payable irrespective of the profit of the company.

> **DISCUSSION**
>
> YXX Limited has an ordinary share capital of 650 000 shares of $1 each, and a long-term loan of $50 000 repayable in three years' time. The directors want to raise long-term funds in order to expand the business and are considering either issuing $100 000 in 6% debentures or issuing 100 000 ordinary shares of $1 each.
>
> Discuss with a partner how the directors' decision may affect Suella who holds 40 000 ordinary shares.

21.5 Financial statements of a limited company

Just like a sole trader or a partnership business, a limited company can be a manufacturing business, a trading business, a service business or a combination of these. Whichever type of business it is, a limited company must prepare financial statements at the end of each financial year.

If the limited company is a manufacturing business, then a manufacturing account and a statement of profit or loss will be prepared at the end of each financial year. If the limited company is a trading or a service business, then a statement of profit or loss will be prepared.

The manufacturing account of a limited company is prepared in exactly the same way as the manufacturing account for a sole trader or a partnership. The statement of profit or loss for a limited company is prepared in the same way as for any other type of business. The only difference is that debenture interest may be included in the finance costs.

A limited company will prepare an annual statement of financial position in the same way as other forms of business. But, before the statement of financial position is prepared, a limited company must first prepare a statement of changes in equity to show how the profit is allocated.

> **LINKS**
>
> Statements of profit or loss were covered in Chapter 8 and manufacturing accounts were covered in Chapter 20.
>
> You learnt about profit and loss appropriation accounts of partnerships in Chapter 19.

21.6 Statement of changes in equity

A partnership business needs to prepare an appropriation account to show how the profit and loss is divided between partners. In a similar way, a limited company must prepare a statement showing how the profit for the year is used. This statement is known as a **statement of changes in equity**.

The term **equity** refers to the total funds provided by the shareholders of a company. The ordinary shareholders provide the share capital, but they are also entitled to the profit earned by the business. Some of the profit for the year will have been paid out to the shareholders in the form of dividends. The profit not distributed is known as the **retained earnings**. Profit is also often retained in the form of a general reserve.

Ordinary share capital, retained earnings and general reserve form the equity of a limited company. The statement of changes in equity summarises the changes during the year to the ordinary share capital, retained earnings and general reserve.

Ordinary share capital

- This is the total amount of ordinary share capital which the company had at the start and end of the financial year. It will only change if shares have been issued during the year.

Retained earnings

- The balance at the start of the financial year represents the profit not distributed in the previous years.
- The profit for the year calculated in the statement of profit or loss will increase the retained earnings. Any ordinary share dividend which has actually been paid during the financial year is recorded in the statement of changes in equity for that particular year as it reduces the retained earnings.

> **KEY TERMS**
>
> **statement of changes in equity:** a statement showing the changes in a company's ordinary share capital, retained earnings and general reserves over the financial year.
>
> **equity:** the total funds provided by the shareholders of a company.
>
> **retained earnings:** the profit which has not been distributed to shareholders.

- Sometimes the directors will recommend an interim dividend (halfway dividend) to be paid during the year on ordinary shares. This will appear in the statement of changes in equity for that particular year as it reduces the retained earnings.

- At the end of each financial year, the directors of a company propose that ordinary share dividends are paid and that these will be paid early in the following year. These proposed dividends are not included in the statement of changes in equity for the current year. Proposed dividends are only what the directors recommend and have to be approved by the shareholders.

- Even if a limited company wished to distribute the whole profit, it would not be possible if there was not enough cash available.

- At the end of the financial year, a transfer may be made from the retained earnings to the general reserves, which reduces the retained earnings.

General reserve

- In addition to leaving a balance of retained earnings, many companies will transfer an amount from the profit for the year to a general reserve. This is another way of ploughing back profits into the company to help it grow.

- The balance at the start of the year represents the total amount transferred to the general reserve in previous years.

- The amount of the general reserve will be increased if a transfer is made from the retained earnings.

> **TIP**
>
> In a statement of changes in equity, you should add each column vertically and then add the first three column totals to make sure you get the same total for the final column.

WORKED EXAMPLE 21.3

AB Plants Limited was formed several years ago. By 30 June 20–6, 800 000 ordinary shares of $0.50 each had been issued and were fully paid.

The following information is provided:

1. On 1 July 20–5:

   the ordinary share capital consisted of 800 000 shares of $0.50 each
   the general reserve amounted to $49 000
   the retained earnings brought forward amounted to $37 000.

2. The profit for the year ended 30 June 20–6 was $66 000.

3. The proposed final ordinary share dividend of $30 000 for the year ended 30 June 20–5 was paid on 30 September 20–5.

4. An interim dividend of $32 000 was paid on 31 March 20–6.

5. On 30 June 20–6, the directors recommended a transfer of $7 000 to the general reserve and the payment of an ordinary share dividend of 6%.

CONTINUED

Prepare a statement of changes in equity of AB Plants Limited for the year ended 30 June 20–6.

AB Plants Limited Statement of changes in equity for the year ended 30 June 20–6				
	Ordinary share capital $	General reserve $	Retained earnings $	Total $
Balance at 1 July 20–5	400 000	49 000	37 000	486 000
Profit for the year			66 000	66 000
Divided paid (final)			(30 000)	(30 000)
Dividend paid (interim)			(32 000)	(32 000)
Transfer to general reserve		7 000	(7 000)	
Balance at 30 June 20–6	400 000	56 000	34 000	490 000

- After entering the opening balances, each item is entered in the appropriate column and also in the total column.
- The final dividend paid relates to the previous year but is entered in the statement as the dividend was paid during the current year.
- The interim dividend is entered on the statement as it was paid in the current year.
- The dividend proposed at the end of the current year does not appear as it has not yet been paid.
- A figure in brackets indicates that it is reducing the amount in that column.
- The totals should be added vertically and then cross-checked horizontally.

ACTIVITY 21.3

The financial year of KTL Limited ends on 31 December. The following information is provided:

On 1 January 20–9, the company had 6% debentures totalling $50 000 and 520 000 ordinary shares of $0.50 each.

Profit for the year ended 31 December 20–9 before debenture interest was $32 000.

A final ordinary share dividend of $8 000 for the year ended 31 December 20–8 was paid in February 20–9.

An interim ordinary share dividend of $0.01 per share for the year ended 31 December 20–9 was paid in August 20–9.

A final ordinary share dividend of $0.10 per share for the year ended 31 December 20–9 was proposed.

On 31 December 20–9, a transfer of $5 000 was made to general reserve.

Copy out the following statement of changes in equity. Complete by inserting the missing words and figures.

KTL Limited Statement of changes in equity for the year ended 31 December 20–9				
	Ordinary share capital $	General reserve $	Retained earnings $	Total $
Balance at 1 January 20–9	260 000	34 000	11 000	305 000
....	....	....	....	....
....	....	....	....	....
....	....	....	....	....
....	....	....	....	....
Balance at 31 December 20–9	....	....	....	....

REFLECTION

Working in a small group, compare your answers to Activity 21.3.

Discuss any differences and try to agree on an answer before checking whether it is correct.

Three common errors may have been:

- showing the profit for the year as $32 000
- including the interim dividend paid as $2 600
- including the proposed dividend.

Explain why each of these is wrong.

How does comparing answers and talking about any mistakes help your understanding?

21.7 Statement of financial position of a limited company

In the statement of financial position of a limited company, the assets section and the current liabilities section are presented in exactly the same way as for a sole trader or a partnership.

The non-current liabilities section may include debentures and any other non-current liabilities. The capital section has to be modified so that it shows details of the shares and reserves of the company. Section 21.6 explained that the ordinary share capital, general reserve and retained earnings form the equity of a limited company, so instead of using the heading 'capital' the heading 'equity' is used. The general reserve and the retained earnings are added to the share capital as they represent profits which have been retained in the company, and therefore belong to the ordinary shareholders.

> **LINK**
>
> You learnt about statements of financial position of sole traders in Chapter 9.

WORKED EXAMPLE 21.4

Using the information and the statement of changes in equity provided in **Worked example 21.3**, prepare an extract from the statement of financial position of AB Plants Limited at 30 June showing the equity section.

AB Plants Limited	
Extract from statement of financial position at 30 June 20–6	
	$
Equity	
Ordinary share capital	400 000
General reserve	56 000
Retained earnings	34 000
	490 000

> **TIP**
>
> Use the totals of the columns in the statement of changes in equity to enter the items in the equity section of the statement of financial position.

CAMBRIDGE IGCSE™ AND O LEVEL ACCOUNTING: COURSEBOOK

ACCOUNTING IN ACTION

Raising additional funds

Figure 21.3: A coach tour for a group of tourists

Daniel, Erin and Caitlin formed a partnership many years ago and established a business running bus and coach tours. They purchased minibuses for small groups and a coach for larger groups of tourists making longer journeys.

On 1 May 20–4, they decided to convert their partnership into a limited company, which they named DEC Tours Limited. The three partners became the sole shareholders and the directors of the new business. They are now considering how to raise additional funds in order to replace two of the minibuses with modern electric vehicles.

The statements prepared by the accountant of DEC Tours Limited at the end of the financial year on 30 April 20–5 included the following statement of changes in equity instead of an appropriation account. Daniel, Erin and Caitlin have never seen this sort of statement before and are finding it difficult to understand.

DEC Tours Limited				
Statement of changes in equity for the year ended 30 April 20–5				
	Ordinary share capital $	General reserve $	Retained earnings $	Total $
Balance at 1 May 20–4	350 000			350 000
Profit for the year			38 000	38 000
Dividend paid (interim)			(10 500)	(10 500)
Transfer to general reserve		7 500	(7 500)	
Balance at 30 April 20–5	350 000	7 500	20 000	377 500

Discuss in pairs or in a group:

1 The directors have the following questions:

　a　What is equity?

　b　Why is there an opening balance in the ordinary share capital column but not in the other columns?

　c　What is general reserve and why was a transfer made to it?

　d　Why is the 5% dividend that we are going to get next week not included?

　What answers would you give to the directors' questions?

2 What options could the directors consider in order to raise additional finance to purchase the electric minibuses?

> **SUMMARY**
>
> You should now know:
>
> - A limited company is a legal entity which has a separate identity from its shareholders, whose liability is limited.
> - Issued share capital is the amount of share capital issued to shareholders.
> - Called-up capital is the amount of issued share capital for which payment has been requested, and the paid-up capital is the amount of called-up share capital that has actually been paid.
> - Debentures are a form of long-term loan.
> - A statement of changes in equity summarises the changes during the year to ordinary share capital, retained earnings and general reserve.

Chapter 21 practice questions

1. Which statement about debentures is correct?

    A Debentures carry a fixed rate of dividend.

    B Debentures carry a fixed rate of interest.

    C Debentures are part of the equity of a limited company.

    D Debenture holders are allowed to vote at shareholders' meetings. [1]

2. XZ Limited was formed on 1 August 20–1. Which items may appear in the statement of changes in equity for the year ended 31 July 20–2? [1]

	Debenture interest paid	Ordinary share dividend for current year paid	Ordinary share dividend for current year proposed	Transfer to general reserve
A	✓	✓	✓	
B	✓			✓
C		✓	✓	✓
D		✓		✓

3. Which items are included in the equity section of the statement of financial position of a limited company?

1	bank loan	2	debentures
3	general reserve	4	ordinary shares

    A 1 and 2

    B 1 and 3

    C 2 and 4

    D 3 and 4 [1]

4 DG Limited provided the following information:

On 1 January 20–9:

	$
Ordinary shares of $1 each	100 000
Retained earnings	16 700

During the financial year ended 31 December 20–9, an interim dividend of $12 500 was paid on the ordinary shares.

The profit for the year ended 31 December 20–9 was $31 000.

On 31 December 20–9, the directors recommended the payment of a final ordinary share dividend of 5% and a transfer to general reserve of $5 000.

Calculate the retained earnings at 31 December 20–9. [4]

5 TX Limited have issued 500 000 ordinary shares of $0.50 each. All the shares are fully paid.

The following information relating to the year ended 30 June 20–8 is available:

			$
20–7			
Jul 1		Retained earnings	10 100
		General reserve	13 250
Dec 31		Interim dividend of 5% paid on ordinary shares	
20–8			
Jun 30		Profit for the year	51 000

On 30 June 20–8, the directors:

- recommended a transfer of $8 000 to the general reserve
- proposed a final dividend of 10% on the ordinary shares.

a Prepare the statement of changes in equity of TX Limited for the year ended 30 June 20–8. [5]

b Prepare a relevant extract from the statement of financial position of TX Limited at 30 June 20–8 showing the equity section. [3]

c Explain which dividends (if any) would appear in the statement of financial position of TX Limited at 30 June 20–8. Give reasons for your answer. [3]

[Total: 11]

6 DC Limited provided the following information:

	$
On 1 May 20–4:	
Ordinary share capital	350 000
General reserve	19 000
Retained earnings	41 500
On 1 August 20–4, the final ordinary share dividend for the year ended 30 April 20–4 was paid	14 000
On 1 November 20–4, an interim ordinary share dividend for the year ended 30 April 20–5 was paid	10 500
Profit for the year ended 30 April 20–5	68 000

On 30 April 20–5, the directors decided to transfer $15 000 to general reserve and proposed a final ordinary share dividend of 4%.

Additional information at 30 April 20–5:

	$
Property at cost	400 000
Equipment at cost	130 000
Motor vehicles at cost	70 000
Provision for depreciation on equipment	80 100
Provision for depreciation on motor vehicles	34 000
Trade payables	36 100
Trade receivables	31 000
Other payables	770
Other receivables	520
Allowance for irrecoverable debts	930
5% debentures	40 000
Bank overdraft	12 370
Inventory	26 750

a Prepare the statement of changes in equity for the year ended 30 April 20–5. [6]

b Prepare the statement of financial position at 30 April 20–5. [10]

[Total: 16]

CHECK YOUR PROGRESS

How well do you think you have achieved the learning intentions for this chapter? Give yourself a score from 1 (still need a lot of practice) to 5 (feeling very confident) for each learning intention. Provide an example to support your score.

Now I can ...	Score	Example to support score
explain the advantages and disadvantages of operating as a limited company		
understand the meaning of the terms limited liability and equity		
understand that the capital of a limited company can consist of ordinary share capital, general reserve and retained earnings		
understand and distinguish between issued, called-up and paid-up share capital, and between ordinary share capital and loan capital (debentures)		
understand that limited companies may be trading, service or manufacturing businesses (or a combination of some of these)		
prepare and make adjustments to financial statements for limited companies.		

Chapter 22
Analysis and interpretation

LEARNING INTENTIONS

By the end of this chapter, you will be able to:

- calculate and interpret profitability, liquidity and efficiency ratios
- identify the different users of accounting information and their requirements
- use ratios to perform an inter-business comparison
- understand the limitations of accounting statements.

Introduction

It is necessary to analyse and interpret the financial statements of a business in order to assess its performance and progress. Analysis consists of a detailed examination of the information in a set of financial statements of a business. The results of this analysis are then interpreted in order to assess the performance of the business. Interpretation can include comparing to the results of other similar businesses and also comparing within the business (with the results for previous years and with targets and budgets). This chapter explains ways in which this analysis and interpretation can be carried out.

ACCOUNTING IN CONTEXT

Comparing financial statements

Figure 22.1: Working as a painter and decorator

At the end of each financial year, the accountant for a business will provide the owners with a set of financial statements. The business owners can use the statement of profit or loss to see the profit made on the sale of goods (the gross profit) and the total profit or loss for the year. They can use the statement of financial position to see a summary of the assets, liabilities and capital at the end of the year.

Liam is a painter and decorator. He does not understand very much about financial matters, but he is able to maintain adequate day-to-day records for his accountant to prepare annual financial statements. Liam is very pleased to learn that he has made a profit and that his accountant considers the business to be in a satisfactory financial position. The accountant suggested that Liam would find it useful to compare the financial statements with those for the previous year.

Liam also compared his financial statements with those of his brother, Will, who owns a jewellery store. Liam was disappointed to find that Will had earned a much larger profit and that Will's assets had a much higher value.

Discuss in pairs or in a group:

1. Why do you think the accountant suggested that Liam should compare the financial statements with those of the previous financial year?

2. Why should Liam not be disappointed when he compares his financial statements with Will's financial statements?

22.1 Using financial statements

To enable comparisons between businesses or within businesses to be carried out in a meaningful way, the results of the analysis are usually expressed as accounting ratios. This is a general term which includes calculations in the form of ratios, percentages and time periods. Ratios are usually divided into three main groups: profitability ratios, liquidity ratios and efficiency ratios, as shown in Figure 22.2.

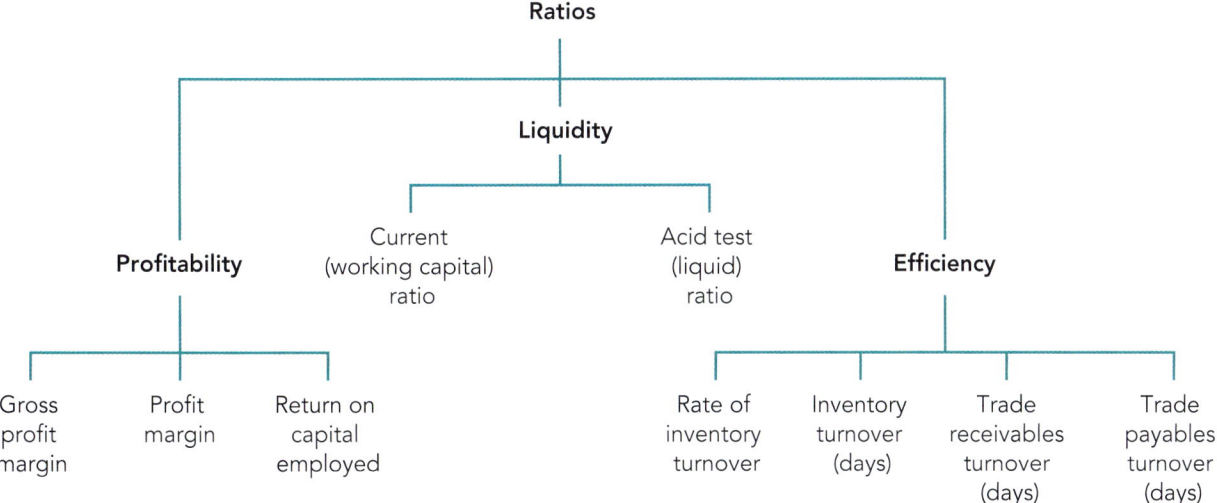

Figure 22.2: Accounting ratios

The information needed to calculate the ratios is found in a business's financial statements.

Aarav is a trader who has been in business for several years. His financial year ends on 30 June.

The following financial statements will be used in the Worked examples in this chapter.

Aarav
Statement of profit or loss for the year ended 30 June 20–6

		$	$
Revenue –	Cash sales	20 000	
	Credit sales	100 000	120 000
Less	Cost of sales		
	Opening inventory	25 500	
	Purchases (all on credit)	85 000	
		110 500	
	Less Closing inventory	20 500	90 000
Gross profit			30 000
Less Administration and selling expenses			10 000
Profit from operations			20 000
Less Finance costs			2 000
Profit for the year			18 000

Aarav
Statement of financial position at 30 June 20–6

	$	$
Non-current assets (at book value)		159 500
Current assets		
Inventory	20 500	
Trade receivables	5 500	
Bank	4 000	30 000
Total assets		189 500
Capital and liabilities		
Capital		
Opening balance	160 000	
Plus Profit for the year	18 000	
	178 000	
Less Drawings	13 000	165 000
Non-current liabilities		
Loan – Fax Finance		9 500
Current liabilities		
Trade payables		15 000
Total capital and liabilities		189 500

22.2 Profitability ratios

Profitability ratios are used to relate the profit figures to other figures within the same set of financial statements. Table 22.1 describes the three main ratios that are used to measure profitability.

Table 22.1: Profitability ratios

Ratio	What the ratio measures	Formula
Gross profit margin	The amount of profit on the goods sold	$\dfrac{\text{Gross profit}}{\text{Revenue}} \times 100$
Profit margin	How much profit has been made after all expenses have been deducted	$\dfrac{\text{Profit for the year}}{\text{Revenue}} \times 100$
Return on capital employed (ROCE)	The return that investors in the business have achieved on their investment	$\dfrac{\text{Profit for the year before interest}}{\text{Capital employed}} \times 100$

The profit for the year before interest is sometimes referred to as profit from operations.

The capital employed can be calculated in two ways:

- owner's capital + non-current liabilities
- non-current assets + working capital, where working capital is the difference between current assets and current liabilities.

KEY TERM

profitability ratio: a way to measure the performance of the business by comparing the profit to other figures in the same set of financial statements.

LINKS

You learnt how to calculate gross profit, profit for the year before interest and profit for the year in Chapter 8. You learnt how to calculate working capital and capital employed in Chapter 9.

> **WORKED EXAMPLE 22.1**
>
> Using the financial statements shown in Section 22.1, calculate the:
> a gross profit margin
> b profit margin
> c return on capital employed.
>
> a Gross profit margin = $\dfrac{\text{Gross profit}}{\text{Revenue}} \times 100 = \dfrac{\$30\,000}{\$120\,000} \times 100 = 25\%$
>
> b Profit margin = $\dfrac{\text{Profit for the year}}{\text{Revenue}} \times 100 = \dfrac{\$18\,000}{\$120\,000} \times 100 = 15\%$
>
> c Return on capital employed = $\dfrac{\text{Profit for the year before interest}}{\text{Capital employed}} \times 100$
>
> $= \dfrac{\$20\,000}{\$159\,500 + \$15\,000} \times 100 = \dfrac{\$20\,000}{\$174\,500} \times 100 = 11.46\%$

Interpretation of ratios

Gross profit margin

A gross profit margin of 25% indicates that for every $100 of revenue, $25 of gross profit was earned before any expenses. Different types of industries and trades tend to have different gross profit percentages. The same business may have a similar gross profit margin from year to year. Generally speaking, the higher the gross profit margin the more profitable the business. However, if the gross profit margin is reduced slightly by reducing the selling price, the business may sell more goods. This would mean that a higher monetary gross profit would be earned even though the gross profit margin is lower.

The gross profit margin can be improved by measures such as:

- increasing selling prices
- obtaining cheaper supplies
- changing the proportions of different types of goods sold (by selling more of the goods which have a higher gross profit margin and less of the goods which have a lower gross profit margin).

However, these measures may have some negative effects. For example, increasing the selling price may result in customers going elsewhere, and obtaining cheaper supplies may result in a lower quality of goods.

If the gross margin changes significantly from one year to another, the cause should be investigated. A fall in the gross margin may be caused by:

- increasing the rate of trade discount
- selling goods at cheaper prices
- not passing on increased costs to customers.

Profit margin

A profit margin of 15% indicates that for every $100 of revenue, $15 of profit was earned after all expenses are accounted for. The higher the return, the more profitable is the business. This ratio acts as an indicator of how well a business is able to control its expenses. If the profit margin of a business increases, it indicates that the operating expenses are being controlled. This ratio will be influenced by the different types of expense: some expenses increase in proportion to sales (e.g. commission paid on sales) but other expenses remain the same whatever the sales are (e.g. insurance of buildings). Any change in the gross margin will also affect the profit margin.

The profit margin can be improved by measures such as:

- increasing the gross margin
- controlling expenses
- increasing other income.

A fall in the profit margin may be caused by:

- a decrease in the gross profit
- an increase in expenses
- a decrease in other income
- a change in the type of expense.

The difference between the gross profit margin and the profit margin represents the percentage of the expenses to the revenue. This indicates the ability of the business to control its expenses. If the difference between a business's gross profit margin and profit margin increases, it indicates that more of the business's revenue is being used to cover its expenses, so the business may not be controlling its expenses well. But if the difference between gross profit margin and profit margin stays the same or decreases, it indicates the business has better control of its expenses.

Return on capital employed

A return on capital employed of 11.46% means that for every $100 invested in the business, the owner earns $11.46 profit. The higher the return, the more efficiently the capital is being employed within the business. If the capital employed increases with no increase in the profit for the year, then the ratio will decrease. If the profit for the year increases with no increase in the capital employed, then the ratio will increase.

ACTIVITY 22.1

At the end of his financial year, Santana reported that his profit for the year was $50 000 with revenue of $125 000. He operates on a gross profit margin of 75%.

His capital employed at the end of the year was $200 000.

Calculate:

1 gross profit margin

2 profit margin

3 return on capital employed.

22.3 Liquidity ratios

Liquidity ratios measure the ease and speed with which assets can be turned into cash.

Table 22.2 gives details of the two main ratios that are used to measure liquidity.

Table 22.2: Liquidity ratios

Ratio	What the ratio measures	Formula
Current (working capital) ratio	The ability of a business to meet its current liabilities when they fall due	Current assets : Current liabilities
Acid test (liquid) ratio	The ability of a business to meet its current liabilities without selling its inventory	Current assets – Inventory : Current liabilities

> **KEY TERM**
>
> **liquidity ratio:** a way to measure the ability of the business to turn assets into cash to pay its short-term debts.

WORKED EXAMPLE 22.2

Using the financial statements shown in Section 22.1, calculate:

a   the current (working capital) ratio

b   the acid test (liquid) ratio.

a   Current assets : Current liabilities = $30 000 : $15 000

    = 2 : 1

b   Current assets – Inventory : Current liabilities = $30 000 – $20 500 : $15 000

    = 0.63 : 1

Interpretation of ratios

Current ratio

A current ratio of 2 : 1 means that for every $1 of liabilities, there are $2 of current assets. This is considered to be satisfactory as the business is able to meet its short-term debts.

Ratios between 1.5 : 1 and 2 : 1 are generally regarded as satisfactory, but it is important to consider the size and type of business. Some businesses necessarily need a large amount of non-current assets whereas other businesses have a higher proportion of current assets; some businesses always purchase goods on credit whereas others always pay cash; some businesses obtain long-term loans whereas others make use of short-term loans or a bank overdraft. If the current ratio is over 2 : 1, it may indicate poor management of the current assets.

The working capital of a business must be adequate to finance the day-to-day trading activities. A business which is short of working capital may encounter the following problems:

- cannot meet immediate liabilities when they are due
- have difficulties in obtaining further supplies on credit

- cannot take advantage of cash discounts
- cannot take advantage of business opportunities when they arise.

Ways to improve the working capital include:

- the owners introducing further capital
- obtaining long-term loans (non-current liabilities)
- selling surplus non-current assets
- delaying purchasing non-current assets
- increasing profit
- reducing drawings by the owners (or reducing dividends).

The cash position can also be improved by measures such as delaying payments to credit suppliers, increasing the proportion of cash sales and reducing the period of credit allowed to credit customers. These measures may also have some negative effects such as being refused further supplies on credit, and customers moving to other suppliers where longer credit is allowed.

Acid test (liquid) ratio

An acid test (liquid) ratio of 0.63 : 1 is considered unsatisfactory as this indicates that in the short term, the business will be unable to pay its immediate debts without selling its inventory. If a business is not able to pay its credit suppliers or expenses such as wages, this may result in further problems.

Inventory is the least liquid of the current assets. Where sales are made on credit, inventory is two steps away from being money: the goods have to be sold and then the money has to be collected from the credit customers.

An acid test (liquid) ratio of 1 : 1 is considered satisfactory as immediate liabilities can be met out of the liquid assets without having to sell inventory. If the acid test (liquid) ratio is over 1:1, it may indicate poor management of liquid assets, such as having too high a balance on a bank current account, which could be invested elsewhere to provide a return.

ACTIVITY 22.2

At the end of the financial year, two different businesses reported the following results:

	Business X	Business Y
	$	$
Profit for the year	58 000	58 000
Closing inventory	35 000	50 000
Current assets	100 000	60 000
Current liabilities	35 000	25 000

1 Calculate for each business:

   a current (working capital) ratio

   b acid test (liquid) ratio.

Give your answers correct to two decimal places.

2 Suggest reasons why even though both businesses have the same profit for the year, their liquidity positions are significantly different.

22.4 Efficiency ratios

Efficiency ratios measure how effectively a business manages its resources to generate revenue and ultimately profit. They are sometimes classified as liquidity ratios.

Table 22.3 gives details of the four main ratios that are used to measure efficiency.

Table 22.3: Efficiency ratios

Ratio	What the ratio measures	Formula
Rate of inventory turnover	The number of times inventory is sold and replaced in the period	$\dfrac{\text{Cost of sales}}{\text{Average inventory}}$
Inventory turnover (days)	The number of days inventory is held before being sold	$\dfrac{\text{Average inventory}}{\text{Cost of sales}} \times 365 \text{ days}$
Trade receivables turnover (days)	How long it takes on average for the credit customers to pay their debts	$\dfrac{\text{Trade receivables}}{\text{Credit sales}} \times 365 \text{ days}$
Trade payables turnover (days)	How long it takes on average for the business to pay its credit suppliers	$\dfrac{\text{Trade payables}}{\text{Credit purchases}} \times 365 \text{ days}$

- Answers to inventory turnover, trade receivables turnover and trade payables turnover are always rounded up to the next whole day.

WORKED EXAMPLE 22.3

Using the financial statements shown in Section 22.1, calculate:

a rate of inventory turnover

b inventory turnover

c trade receivables turnover

d trade payables turnover.

KEY TERM

efficiency ratio: a way to measure how well a business is using their resources to generate revenue or how well a business is managing their resources.

LINK

You learnt about the rate of inventory turnover in Chapter 17.

TIP

When calculating ratios, you should show your workings as it makes it easier to check your answers.

> **CONTINUED**
>
> a Rate of inventory turnover = $\dfrac{\text{Cost of sales}}{\text{Average inventory}} = \dfrac{\$90\,000}{\$23\,000} = 3.9$ times
>
> b Inventory turnover = $\dfrac{\text{Average inventory}}{\text{Cost of sales}} \times 365 \text{ days} = \dfrac{\$23\,000}{\$90\,000} \times 365 \text{ days} = 94 \text{ days}$
>
> c Trade receivables turnover = $\dfrac{\text{Trade receivables}}{\text{Credit sales}} \times 365 \text{ days} = \dfrac{\$5\,500}{\$100\,000} \times 365 \text{ days}$
> $= 21 \text{ days}$
>
> d Trade payables turnover = $\dfrac{\text{Trade payables}}{\text{Credit purchases}} \times 365 \text{ days} = \dfrac{\$15\,000}{\$85\,000} \times 365 \text{ days}$
> $= 65 \text{ days}$

> **TIP**
>
> Remember to include the correct description after the value, such as %, 'times' and 'days'.

Interpretation of ratios

Rate of inventory turnover and inventory turnover

These two ratios are effectively indicating the same thing – how often the inventory is replaced. Aarav replaces his inventory 3.9 times a year, or every 94 days, which may be considered satisfactory depending on the nature of the business.

Businesses selling luxury goods such as expensive jewellery or private jet planes will have a low rate of inventory turnover, whereas businesses selling low value everyday items such as fresh bread or newspapers will have a high rate of inventory turnover.

A business may have a similar rate of inventory turnover from year to year. If the rate increases, it may indicate improved efficiency; if the rate decreases, it may indicate that the business has too much inventory or that the sales are slowing down. The quicker the rate of inventory turnover, the less time funds are tied up in inventory. This can be beneficial for the business because inventory is regarded as the least liquid of the current assets.

The rate of inventory turnover can affect the profit of the business. If business activity slows down, both the gross profit and the profit for the year will decrease.

A lower rate of inventory turnover can be caused by factors such as:

- lower sales (resulting in higher inventory levels)
- purchasing too much inventory
- too high selling prices
- falling demand
- business activity slowing down
- business inefficiency.

> **LINKS**
>
> You learnt about the effects of an incorrect inventory valuation in Chapter 10 and about the rate of inventory turnover in Chapter 17.

Trade receivables turnover

This ratio indicates that Aarav's credit customers take on average 21 days to pay their invoices.

The answer to this calculation – the length of time credit customers actually take to pay their accounts – should be compared with the terms of credit allowed to them. The quicker the customers pay their accounts, the better it is because the money can then be used for other purposes within the business. The longer a business has to wait for a debt to be paid, the greater the risk that the debt becomes irrecoverable.

The same business may have a similar trade receivables turnover from year to year. If the period decreases, it may indicate that the credit control policy is being applied more effectively. If the period increases, it may indicate that the credit control policy is inefficient, or that longer credit terms are being allowed in order to maintain the quantity of credit sales.

The rate of the trade receivables turnover can be improved by measures such as:

- improving credit control policy (sending regular statements of account, 'chasing' overdue accounts and so on)
- offering cash discount for early settlement
- charging interest on overdue accounts
- refusing further supplies until any outstanding debt is paid.

> **LINK**
>
> You learnt about irrecoverable debts in Chapter 13.

Trade payables turnover

This ratio indicates that Aarav takes on average 65 days to pay his credit suppliers.

The answer to this calculation should be compared with the terms of credit allowed by the suppliers.

The same business may have a similar trade payables turnover from year to year. If the period decreases, the business is paying the suppliers more quickly; if the period increases, it may indicate that the business is short of immediate funds and is finding it difficult to meet debts when they fall due. This ratio can also be influenced by the trade receivables turnover: if the credit customers do not settle their accounts promptly, the business may not be able to pay the credit suppliers promptly. Taking longer to pay the suppliers means that the business can use the funds for other purposes, but there can be negative effects such as:

- the supplier refusing credit in the future
- the supplier refusing further supplies
- the loss of any cash discount for early settlement
- damage to the relationship with the supplier.

> **ACTIVITY 22.3**
>
> At the end of the financial year, two different businesses reported the following results.
>
> | | Business E | Business F |
> |---|---|---|
> | Rate of inventory turnover | 4 times | 355 times |
> | Inventory turnover | 92 days | 1 day |
> | Trade receivables turnover | 45 days | 14 days |
> | Trade payables turnover | 30 days | 30 days |
>
> Answer these questions, giving reasons for your decisions:
>
> 1 Which business uses its resources more efficiently?
> 2 One of the businesses is a clothing retailer and the other is a fresh food store. Which business is which? Give a reason to explain your answer.
> 3 Which business would you prefer to supply goods to on credit?
>
> Share your answers with a partner and discuss any differences.

> **DISCUSSION**
>
> Discuss these questions with a partner:
> 1 What is the difference between profitability, liquidity and efficiency?
> 2 Which do you think is most important to a business owner? You should justify your choice.
>
> Be prepared to share your ideas with the rest of the class.

22.5 Interpretation of business trends using ratios

Ratios can be used to measure a business's performance over a one-year period. However, it may be more meaningful for the business to use the ratios to analyse and compare the business's performance over a longer period. This will enable business owners to spot any trends and take appropriate action to improve the performance of the business.

WORKED EXAMPLE 22.4

Ayaz is a trader who has been in business for several years. He provided the following ratios for his business for the last three years:

Ratio	20–7	20–6	20–5
Gross profit margin	25%	25%	25%
Profit margin	12%	15%	18%
Return on capital employed	8%	10%	12%
Current (working capital) ratio	1.8 : 1	2 : 1	2.5 : 1
Acid test (liquid) ratio	0.8 : 1	1 : 1	1.5 : 1
Rate of inventory turnover	15 times	20 times	25 times
Trade receivables turnover	40 days	35 days	30 days
Trade payables turnover	30 days	30 days	30 days

Using the ratios in the table, compare the performance of the business over the three years in terms of profitability, liquidity and efficiency.

Profitability

The stable gross profit margin shows that over the three years, Ayaz has maintained his selling price relative to the cost of buying the goods. The profit margin has decreased from 18% to 12% over the three years, which indicates that even though the gross profit margin was maintained, his expenses have been increasing. This decrease in profit margin affected the return on capital employed, which decreased from 12% to 8%. Ayaz is now achieving less profit for the capital he has invested. He should review all his expenses and find ways of controlling the expenses in order to improve his profit margin and return on capital employed.

Liquidity

The liquidity position has also become worse over the three years. The current ratio has fallen below the satisfactory value of 2 : 1 and the acid test (liquid) ratio has fallen below the satisfactory value of 1:1. This may affect the ability of the business to meet its short-term debts when they fall due.

The current (working capital) ratio has reduced from 2.5 : 1 to 1.8 : 1, which indicates that the business is still able to meet its debts, but the overall trend indicates that action needs to be taken. The acid test (liquid) ratio is now 0.8 : 1, which indicates that Ayaz would need to sell some inventory to meet all his short-term debts. Ayaz should consider ways in which he can improve his liquidity position.

22 Analysis and interpretation

> **CONTINUED**
>
> **Efficiency**
>
> The rate of inventory turnover has also decreased from 25 times a year to 15 times a year, which indicates that it is taking longer for Ayaz to sell his inventory and make a profit. This may have contributed to the decrease in liquidity. Poor inventory management could lead to increased costs of storage and an increased risk of inventory become obsolete, which will reduce profits.
>
> The trade receivables turnover shows that credit customers are taking longer to pay their debts. Invoices are usually due for payment within 30 days. This was met in 20–5 but increased to 40 days in 20–7. This increases the risk of irrecoverable debts and also affects the ability to pay credit suppliers as cash is not coming in on time.
>
> The trade payables turnover has remained steady at 30 days over the three years. This will improve Ayaz's relationship with his credit suppliers. He may also be able to benefit from cash discount for prompt payment. But paying the suppliers on time when the credit customers are taking longer to pay will negatively affect the liquidity of the business.

> **TIP**
>
> When you are commenting on how a ratio has changed, you should explain whether it has improved or worsened. Mentioning only whether it has increased or decreased does not indicate whether it has got better or worse.

> **ACTIVITY 22.4**
>
> Choose one of the ratios that you have learnt about so far in this chapter.
>
> Design a poster to explain:
>
> - how to calculate the ratio and what information it gives about the state of the business
> - why a business owner would be interested in knowing the value of the ratio
> - what a business can do to improve the value of the ratio.

> **REFLECTION**
>
> Look back at what you have learnt so far in this chapter about the different accounting ratios and what these tell us about the health of a business.
>
> What areas are you most confident with?
>
> Are there areas where you are less confident? If so, what can you do to improve your understanding?

22.6 Inter-business comparison

Comparing the ratios calculated for the current financial year with those of previous years can measure the progress and performance of a business and indicate the trends in profitability, liquidity and so on.

Another useful comparison is to compare the ratios of one business with the ratios of a similar business.

WORKED EXAMPLE 22.5

Aarav is a trader who has been in business for several years. Mahika started a similar business in another town two years ago. The financial year for both businesses ends on 31 December and the following information was available on 31 December 20–7:

Ratio	Aarav	Mahika
Gross profit margin	25%	30%
Profit margin	15%	10%
Return on capital employed	11.46%	10.1%
Current (working capital) ratio	2 : 1	1.5 : 1
Acid test (liquid) ratio	0.63 : 1	0.9 : 1
Rate of inventory turnover	3.9 times	10.3 times
Trade receivables turnover	21 days	40 days
Trade payables turnover	65 days	37 days

Use the ratios in the table to compare the performance of the two businesses.

Profitability

Mahika has achieved a higher gross profit margin than Aarav. This may be because Mahika sells goods at a higher price or purchases goods at a lower price. However, even though Aarav has a lower gross profit margin, he has achieved a higher profit margin, which may indicate that he has better control of his expenses.

Aarav achieved the higher return on capital employed. This may indicate that Mahika is not employing the capital in the most effective way.

Liquidity

Aarav's current ratio of 2 : 1 is quite satisfactory. Mahika's current ratio of 1.5 : 1 may be regarded as too low. She needs to improve her working capital position so she can meet her current liabilities when they fall due, and take advantage of cash discounts or business opportunities when they arise.

CONTINUED

Aarav's acid test (liquid) ratio is not satisfactory as the current assets excluding inventory are less than the current liabilities, so he will not be able to meet his short-term debts without having to sell his inventory. Mahika's acid test (liquid) ratio is quite reasonable as her liquid assets and her current liabilities are almost equal. However, she will have to monitor her current assets, particularly trade receivables, to ensure that she can meet her short-term debts.

Efficiency

Mahika has achieved a quicker rate of inventory turnover than Aarav. This may indicate that Mahika is more efficient. Aarav could consider reducing his inventory levels and trying to increase his rate of sales.

Aarav's credit customers are paying their accounts in an average of 21 days, but Mahika's credit customers are taking an average of 40 days. Mahika's credit control policy may be inefficient or it may be that she is not offering cash discounts. To be more meaningful, these figures should be compared to the credit allowed by each business. The longer it takes to receive payment from a credit customer, the greater the chances of debts becoming irrecoverable, which will reduce the profit for the year.

Aarav's credit suppliers are being paid in an average of 65 days, whereas Mahika takes an average of 37 days to pay her credit suppliers. This may mean that Aarav is not able to take advantage of cash discounts. The relationships with his credit suppliers may become worse and credit supplies may be refused.

DISCUSSION

Imagine that three of your friends are sole traders, each operating a retail business. Each of them would like another investor and you have $50 000 to invest in one of their businesses.

You have obtained the following information about the three businesses in order to help you make your decision:

	Business A	Business B	Business C
Gross profit margin	30%	40%	50%
Profit margin	10%	20%	15%
Return on capital employed	12%	10%	8%

Discuss with a partner which business may be the best investment based on the ratios provided.

Are there any other factors you should consider before making a final decision?

TIP

When comparing the ratios of two businesses, in addition to comparing the actual figures, you should try to suggest why the businesses have different values and the consequences of low or high ratios.

22.7 Problems of inter-business comparison

A business owner can often obtain valuable information by comparing their accounting ratios with those of another business, but they must be aware of the limitations of such a comparison. Every business is different and has different requirements and accounting policies. A comparison is only meaningful if it is between two or more businesses that are the same type, the same size, and operating in the same trade.

The problems of comparison include the following:

- The businesses may apply different accounting policies, such as using different methods of depreciation.

- The businesses may apply different operating policies such as renting premises or purchasing premises, obtaining long-term finance from capital only or using capital and long-term loans. These sorts of policy will affect both the profit for the year and the statement of financial position.

- Non-financial matters such as the skill of the workforce, the goodwill of the business and the location of the business do not appear in the accounting records as they cannot be expressed in monetary terms, but are very important in the success of the business.

- It is not always possible to obtain all the information about another business which is needed to make a true comparison. For example, the inventory shown in the financial statements may not represent the average amount held during the year, and the financial statements do not show the age of the non-current assets and when they need replacing.

- The information relating to other businesses may be for one financial year only, so it is not possible to calculate business trends. That particular year may also not be a 'typical' year.

- The financial years may end on different dates, which can make comparison difficult. For example, the year end for one business may be at a time when inventories are particularly low, whereas the year end for another business may be when inventories are particularly high.

- The accounts are based on historic cost and do not show the effects of inflation.

DISCUSSION

A student has made the following statement:

> 'As there are so many limitations when comparing accounting ratios of different businesses, I don't think there is any value in the information the analysis provides.'

Discuss with a partner whether you agree with this student.
Justify your conclusion.

22.8 Users of accounting statements

It is not only the owner who is interested in analysing and interpreting the financial statements of an organisation. Various other people are also interested in different aspects of the accounts.

Table 22.4 shows the main users of financial information and the reasons why they may be interested in the information.

Table 22.4: Users of financial information

Interested party	Why they are interested
Owners	The owners of a business, such as a sole trader or partners, will be interested in all aspects of the business, including profitability, liquidity and efficiency in order to assess the business's performance and progress. Any potential partners are interested in the profitability of the business. The shareholders and potential shareholders of a limited company are interested in the profitability of the company.
Managers	In many small businesses, the owners manage the business, but in some cases, an employee may be the manager. Like the owners, managers are interested in all aspects of the business. They may use ratios to assess past performance, plan for the future and take action to improve things where necessary.
Banks	If a business requests a bank loan or an overdraft facility, the bank manager will require the financial statements of the business. The bank manager will need to know whether there is adequate security to cover the amount of the loan or overdraft, whether interest can be paid when due and whether the amount borrowed can be repaid when due.
Other lenders	Anyone who has made a loan to a business (and any potential lenders) will be interested in the security available, the repayment of the loan when due and the payment of interest when due.
Credit suppliers	Anyone who has supplied a business with goods on credit terms (and any potential credit supplier) is interested in the liquidity position and the trade payables turnover. These factors may be considered when determining the credit limit and the length of credit allowed.
Local authorities/ Local community	The local authority may wish to check if they can provide any grants to the business. The local community may be interested in the effect the business has on their community, such as positive employment opportunities.
Customers	Customers of the business are interested in knowing whether the business is likely to continue supplying goods.
Employees and trade unions	Employees and trade unions want to know that the company is able to continue operating, and so maintain jobs and continue to pay adequate wages (and, in some cases, contribute to pension schemes).
Potential buyers of the business	Potential buyers of the business are interested in the profitability of the business and the market value of the assets of the business.
Government	Government departments may want information for purposes such as compiling business statistics and checking that the correct amount of tax is being paid.
Club members	The members of a club or society want to know that the club is being well-managed financially so the club can continue to exist and provide facilities to members.

22.9 Limitations of accounting statements

Accounting statements and the ratios calculated from them provide valuable information about a business. They do, however, have limitations and are not able to provide a complete picture of the performance and position of a business. Their limitations include the following:

Time factor

The accounting statements are a record of what has happened in the past, not a guide to the future. There is also a gap between the end of the financial year and when the accounting statements are prepared. In that time significant events such as changes in inventory levels and purchasing of non-current assets may have taken place.

Historic cost

The only way to record financial transactions is to use the actual cost price. However, comparing transactions taking place at different times can be difficult because of the effect of inflation. For example, in times of inflation, it would cost more to buy a machine in 20–8 identical to one purchased in 20–1.

Accounting policies

All businesses should apply the accounting principles of prudence and consistency, which should help with making comparisons. However, there are several acceptable accounting policies which may be applied, such as different methods of calculating depreciation. Where businesses have used different accounting policies, it is difficult to make a meaningful comparison of their results. Similarly, where a business changes its policy, a comparison with the results of previous years is difficult.

Different definitions

Where a business has borrowed money, such as in the form of loans or debentures, the statement of profit or loss may show the profit from operations and then deduct the finance costs to give the profit for the year. Businesses may use a different definition of 'profit' when calculating profitability ratios.

A comparison of profit and profitability ratios is only meaningful if 'like is compared with like' and the same definitions are applied.

Money measurement

Accounts only record information which can be expressed in monetary terms. This means that there are many important factors which influence the performance of a business that will not appear in the accounting statements.

The factors which are within the control of the business include the quality of management, the skill and reliability of the workforce, the goodwill of the business, the age and condition of the non-current assets and the ability to adapt in response to changing market conditions.

Other factors are outside the control of the business. These include government policies, competition, the impact of new technology and future long-term prospects for the particular trade or industry.

> **LINKS**
>
> You learnt about the concepts of prudence, consistency, historic cost and money measurement in Chapter 10.

22 Analysis and interpretation

ACCOUNTING IN ACTION

Improving profitability ratios

Figure 22.3: A hot air balloon in flight

Serena buys and sells hot-air balloons. She buys the balloons from the manufacturer and sells them to businesses which organise hot-air balloon trips for the general public. She also sells to private individuals who are keen balloonists.

Serena understands that accounting ratios can be used to assess the performance of her business. She decided to ask her accountant to compare the accounting ratios calculated at the end of the previous financial year with the accounting ratios calculated using this year's financial statements. Looking at the profitability ratios provided by the accountant, Serena noticed the following:

Last year   gross profit margin 35% and profit margin 9%

This year   gross profit margin 30% and profit margin 8%

The revenue for the two years was exactly the same.

Discuss in pairs or in a group:

1   How are these ratios calculated and what do they measure?

2   a   How would you explain to Serena what may have caused the differences in these ratios?

    b   What measures could Serena take to improve these ratios?

SUMMARY

You should now know:

- There are three ratios which measure profitability: gross profit margin, profit margin and return on capital employed.
- There are two ratios which measure liquidity: current (working capital) ratio and acid test (liquid) ratio.
- There are four ratios which measure efficiency: rate of inventory turnover, inventory turnover, trade receivables turnover and trade payables turnover.
- Ratios can be used to compare the current year with previous years and with other similar businesses. Problems can arise when making inter-business comparisons.
- Certain aspects of the accounting statements of a business are of interest to users such as owners, managers, banks and lenders, credit suppliers, potential buyers, customers, employees and trade unions, local authorities and local communities, and government departments.
- Accounting statements and the ratios calculated from them provide valuable information, but they have limitations and are not able to provide a complete picture of the performance and position of a business.

Chapter 22 practice questions

1. A trader provided the following information about his current (working capital) ratio:

Year 1	Year 2	Year 3
1.45 : 1	1.75 : 1	2.00 : 1

   What would explain the change in this ratio?

   A decrease in cash at bank

   B decrease in inventory

   C decrease in trade payables

   D decrease in trade receivables [1]

2. Tomass provided the following information at the end of the first year of trading:

Cash sales	$9 600
Credit sales	$150 000
Trade receivables	$14 800

   At the end of the year, Tomass decided to write off $1 400 as irrecoverable debts.

   What was the trade receivables turnover?

   A 31 days

   B 33 days

   C 34 days

   D 37 days [1]

3. Why may Joshi, a credit supplier, be interested in the financial statements of Parminder, a new customer?

   A to calculate Parminder's current assets

   B to calculate Parminder's trade payables turnover

   C to set the rate of cash discount to be allowed to Parminder

   D to set the rate of trade discount to be allowed to Parminder [1]

4. Raham is a trader. His financial year ends on 31 March. He provided the following information on 1 April 20–5:

	$
Inventory	9 240
Trade payables	4 150
Trade receivables	10 680
Bank overdraft	5 320
Loan from Theo repayable 31 March 20–6	5 000
Loan from Sara repayable 31 March 20–8	10 000

a Calculate the amount of working capital. [3]

b Suggest two problems Raham may encounter if his working capital is inadequate. [2]

Raham is considering adopting one of four possible courses of action aimed at increasing his working capital.

c Explain the effect on the working capital of each of the following proposals:

Proposal 1 Introduce an additional $15 000 capital.

Proposal 2 Convert the loan from Sara into a bank loan repayable on the same date.

Proposal 3 Sell 25% of the inventory to a cash customer at cost price.

Proposal 4 Pay the trade payables immediately and earn a 5% cash discount. [8]

d Suggest **two** other things Raham could consider to increase his working capital. [2]

[Total: 15]

5 Victoria runs a wholesale furniture business. All goods are sold on credit terms. She provided the following information at the end of her second year of trading:

	$
On 1 January 20–1:	
Inventory	10 200
Capital employed	150 000
For the year ended 31 December 20–1:	
Revenue	120 000
Cost of sales	95 000
Loan interest	3 000
Profit for the year	12 900
At 31 December 20–1:	
Inventory	8 200
Trade receivables	9 120

Victoria decided to compare her results with those of JT Limited, a food wholesaler.

a   Copy and complete the following table to show the ratios for Victoria's business for the year ended 31 December 20–1. The answers should be correct to two decimal places. [8]

	Victoria	JT Limited
Gross profit margin		17.50%
Profit margin		9.25%
Return on capital employed		6.76%
Rate of inventory turnover		16.44 times

b   Suggest **two** reasons for the difference in the gross profit margin. [2]

c   State which business has better control of its expenses.
    Give a reason for your answer. [2]

d   Suggest **two** reasons for the difference in the rate of inventory turnover. [2]

e   Suggest **four** factors which Victoria should consider when comparing her results with those of JT Limited. [4]

[Total: 18]

6   Roberto is a trader. He provided the following information on 31 August 20–4:

	$
Inventory	6 140
Cash at bank	5 650
Trade payables	4 970
Trade receivables	3 960
Loan repayable 31 July 20–5	5 000

a   State the formula for the calculation of the acid test (liquid) ratio. [1]

b   Calculate the acid test (liquid) ratio. [1]

c   Comment on your answer to **b**. [2]

d   State why the acid test (liquid) ratio is a more reliable indicator of liquidity than the current (working capital) ratio. [2]

e Copy and complete the table by stating the effect of each of the following on Roberto's current (working capital) ratio and acid test (liquid) ratio. The first one has been completed as an example. [6]

	Current (working capital) ratio	Acid test (liquid) ratio
Sold old inventory at cost price to credit customer	no effect	increase
Purchased a new machine paying by cheque		
Purchased inventory on credit		
Arranged for loan repayment date to be extended for two years		

f Name **four** interested parties, apart from Roberto, who may wish to look at the financial statements of Roberto. Give a reason in each case. [8]

[Total: 20]

CHECK YOUR PROGRESS

How well do you think you have achieved the learning intentions for this chapter? Give yourself a score from 1 (still need a lot of practice) to 5 (feeling very confident) for each learning intention. Provide an example to support your score.

Now I can …	Score	Example to support score
calculate and interpret profitability, liquidity and efficiency ratios		
identify the different users of accounting information and their requirements		
use ratios to perform an inter-business comparison		
understand the limitations of accounting statements.		

> Chapter 23
Technology and sustainability

LEARNING INTENTIONS

By the end of this chapter, you will be able to:

- understand how digital applications can be used for all or part of the accounting records
- understand the importance of storing accounting data safely and sustainably and the risks associated with not storing accounting data safely and securely
- describe different types of storage systems: manual, data storage devices and cloud services
- explain the advantages and disadvantages of the different types of storage systems.

23 Technology and sustainability

Introduction

It is increasingly important for businesses to operate in a sustainable way. The negative impact of human activities on the environment can be clearly seen, and businesses have a responsibility to ensure they do their best to preserve and replace resources for the future rather than waste them.

Good use of technology can be an important part of incorporating environmentally friendly practices into financial management. It can reduce the number of paper documents that need to be produced, stored and transported from one business to another. This chapter looks at how technology can be used and considers some of the advantages and disadvantages for businesses.

ACCOUNTING IN CONTEXT

Figure 23.1: A sustainable garden nursery

Sustainability in business refers to the actions and strategy a business puts in place to decrease the negative environmental and social impacts which result from business practices. This can include using technology to make the financial management system more environmentally friendly.

Swavi runs a garden nursery, and she would like to apply these principles to run her nursery in a sustainable manner. Swavi is concerned about the environment. She thinks it is very important to try to preserve and protect the environment by not consuming more resources than necessary and to look for sustainable ways of living.

Swavi uses environmentally friendly materials for growing and selling her plants. She also uses a system for watering her plants that prevents too much water being wasted. However, Swavi currently keeps her accounts using a manual system and she is worried about the amount of paper that she is using and the effect this could be having on the environment.

Discuss in pairs or in a group:

1. Why is it a good idea for Swavi to focus on sustainability within her business?

2. What should Swavi consider before changing from a manual system to a digital system for maintaining her accounting records?

23.1 Digital applications

The traditional, manual method of keeping accounts involves recording transactions by hand in journals and ledgers. Computerised accounting uses specialised software known as **digital applications** to record transactions and process the information.

By using digital applications in a computerised system and preparing statements electronically, a business can greatly reduce the number of physical records that need to be kept and the amount of paper that needs to be used.

Businesses can make further improvements in sustainability by investing in energy-efficient computers and servers, and by making use of software programs which

> **KEY TERM**
>
> **digital applications:** any software or program which runs on an electronic device such as a computer, tablet or mobile phone.

457

reduce energy consumption. These programs track and analyse a business's energy use and make recommendations on how to increase energy efficiency and cut energy costs. Businesses can also implement policies to reduce waste and promote recycling. These policies should include how to deal with electronic waste and outdated technology.

Digital applications can be used to record and manage the day-to-day financial transactions of a business. A complete accounting system keeps track of a business's assets, liabilities, revenues and expenses. It posts the information into the relevant ledgers and then across into the financial statements. Business owners, book-keepers and accountants can access the records in the accounting system and view the financial statements in order to monitor the financial performance of the business. All transactions are recorded in the computerised accounting system and so no paper records are needed.

> **DISCUSSION**
>
> In a small group, discuss what difference you think it could make and what influence it would have on other businesses if a large, well-known company implemented sustainable financial management methods.

23.2 The safety and security of accounting data

Most business owners are concerned about keeping their data safe. This means preventing data from being stolen and preventing it from being corrupted or lost on a digital application.

If sensitive data such as bank account numbers, transaction records or personal identification information is stolen, it may result in significant financial losses. Clients and customers could lose confidence in the business and the business's reputation may be damaged. If the stolen information becomes available to any competitors, it may give them an advantage. There could also be legal consequences.

If the data is corrupted or lost on a digital application, the time taken to input all the information is wasted and there will be extra costs involved in replacing or recovering the information.

To try prevent these problems, businesses using digital applications should make sure that they follow good **data security** practices to protect their accounting software and systems.

Figure 23.2 describes measures that should be put in place to protect the security of the data.

> **KEY TERM**
>
> **data security:** a safeguarding process of securing digital information from corruption, theft or unauthorised access.

23 Technology and sustainability

Cyber training
Staff should receive regular training about new viruses and cyber problems so that they learn to recognise suspicious-looking activity or email scams. Phishing is a common form of scam which involves using deceptive emails, messages or websites to attempt to steal personal information or break into online accounts.

Data encryption
A code is placed on the data so that only parties who have the key to the code can unscramble and access the data. Data should be encrypted when it is exchanged between businesses and also when it is being stored to ensure that unauthorised individuals cannot access sensitive financial information.

Policy for computer use
Employers should have a policy in place to regulate how employees use the computer system. For example, this could involve restricting access to certain websites to reduce the chance of introducing viruses and to prevent hackers from being able to easily access the system. Employees should also be aware of the consequences of not following this policy.

Restricted access
Restrict employee access to certain parts of the application so workers can only access the data they need to work with to complete their job. This limits the number of people who can access and potentially steal data.

Data security measures

Backing up work
Saving work often is essential to ensure records are not lost and time is not wasted with the input of the transactions. If files are also saved somewhere else (backed up), it means that the data can be retrieved if the computer system is damaged by a computer virus.

Strong passwords
Always choose passwords which cannot be easily discovered, and change passwords regularly. Multi-factor authentication can also prevent attackers from accessing the system.

Automatic logging out
Systems should be put in place so that if there has been no activity for 2–3 minutes, the user is automatically logged out. This reduces the risk of someone being able to access the data if an employee leaves their computer unattended.

Antivirus package
Computer viruses can cause different problems. Some corrupt or steal data, and others cause the system to shut down. A spyware virus can steal confidential data. Some viruses can steal money and divert payments to different accounts. It is very important for all computers using digital applications to have up-to-date antivirus packages.

Figure 23.2: Security measures to protect data

DISCUSSION

In a small group, discuss whether you think it is safer to use an accounting system where your information is saved on an online platform, or to use a manual system where records are locked away in a safe at the office. Why do you think your preferred system is safer?

> **ACTIVITY 23.1**
>
> Work with a partner to research a real-world example of a data breach and answer the following questions:
>
> - What happened?
> - How did it affect the financial aspects of the business?
> - How did it affect the non-financial aspects of the business?
> - How does this example demonstrate the importance of storing accounting data securely?
> - What could the business do to avoid a similar data breach in the future?
>
> Share your findings with the rest of the class.

> **REFLECTION**
>
> After your research for Activity 23.1, how has your understanding grown in relation to the importance of securing accounting data and the consequences of not securing the data?

23.3 Different types of storage systems

Accounting firms and businesses can use different methods to store their accounting data. If accounts are maintained manually, then the records will be kept on paper, but if accounts are maintained digitally, then there are several storage methods to choose from.

Each method of storage has unique features and benefits. In addition to considering which method best meets their particular needs, businesses may think about which systems are the most sustainable and will minimise the impact on the environment.

Manual storage

Manual storage systems are used when accounts are maintained using traditional methods and records are kept by hand, using pen and paper to record transactions and maintain accounting records.

Manual accounting involves entering the information from business documents into the physical books of prime entry and then posting the information to the relevant ledgers. These records are then used to prepare the trial balance and financial statements.

All of this information is recorded on paper, so a secure space is needed to store all the records.

> **KEY TERM**
>
> **manual storage:** a system where accounting records are stored physically in books and on paper.

23 Technology and sustainability

Figure 23.3: Manual storage means that records are kept on paper and in books

Table 23.1: Advantages and disadvantages of a manual storage system

Advantages	Disadvantages
It is a simple and convenient system, and no special technology or training is needed.	A single copy only of the records is kept in a manual storage system, and the records cannot be backed up easily.
The records can be accessed without electricity, so financial work can continue if there is a power cut or a problem with internet access.	The books and ledgers require more physical space than is needed for storing digital records.
There will not be any problems from computer errors or file corruption and there is no risk of cyberattacks.	Physical records are at risk of damage or loss from fire, flood or theft.
	It may be harder to keep track of all the data using this system, and it is more complicated to analyse and interpret the financial data, so decision-making is more difficult.
	Maintaining records manually uses a lot of paper, which has an impact on the environment as both trees and water are needed to produce paper.

Data storage devices

A **data storage device** is a piece of technology used to store information. Examples include external hard drives, DVDs and USB flash drives. An electronic document management system (EDMS) is another digital system where a business's digital content is stored in a centralised place.

> **KEY TERM**
>
> **data storage devices:** digital devices such as external hard drives or USB flash drives, which can be used to store accounting records.

CAMBRIDGE IGCSE™ AND O LEVEL ACCOUNTING: COURSEBOOK

Figure 23.4: USB flash drives and DVDs are examples of data storage devices

Table 23.2: Advantages and disadvantages of a data storage device

Advantages	Disadvantages
There are no physical ledgers and journals, so space is saved.	There may be high costs associated with purchasing and maintaining computers and software, as well as in training staff to use the system.
It is easy to make backup copies of data.	
It is more environmentally friendly because less paper is used.	Computers might crash due to power cuts or program failures and data may be lost.
Data stored on CDs, DVDs, USB flash drives or computer hard drives can be accessed without an internet connection and can be protected by a password.	Devices are vulnerable to technical problems. For example, external hard drives and USB flash drives can become corrupt.
Financial data that is stored digitally is easier to analyse and interpret, which helps with making well-informed decisions.	Some data storage devices are small and so may be more easily stolen than larger physical books.
	Computers use electricity when managing and processing data and to run the necessary cooling systems. This results in increased carbon emissions.

Cloud services

A server is a computer that provides information to other computers on a network. **Cloud services** are a method of storing digital data on computers through a server in an off-site location. The servers are maintained by a third-party service provider who is responsible for hosting, managing and securing data on their servers.

The cloud service provider ensures that data is always accessible via a public or private internet network. This means that businesses are able to store and access their accounting records, reports or financial statements from anywhere there is an internet connection.

Cloud accounting uses accounting software hosted on a safe, remote server. A business can sign up for a subscription and it will then receive a licence to make use of the accounting software. Users input the information into the software program where it is processed and safely stored. Multiple users can access the information at the same time from their own devices.

A cloud-based system can be used by businesses of any size, and it provides a business with the same benefits as a non-cloud-based digital accounting system.

> **KEY TERM**
>
> **cloud services:** a system which involves using third-party services to store data online.

23 Technology and sustainability

Figure 23.5: A cloud-based system means that information can be accessed from anywhere with an internet connection

Table 23.3: Advantages and disadvantages of cloud services

Advantages	Disadvantages
Financial information can be accessed from anywhere and on any device, as long as there is an internet connection.	The system is available online only, so a poor internet connection may cause problems.
Cloud-based accounting systems often run directly in a browser or through a mobile app. This allows for more flexibility and cost-effectiveness.	The licence to use the system is an ongoing cost to the business. There may also be a cost associated with training staff to use the system.
Technical support is available from the third-party provider should it be required.	Cyberattacks, privacy breaches, security threats and viruses are a threat to the system, so strong security practices are required.
The servers used in cloud systems may be more energy-efficient than local servers. This means cloud accounting reduces a business's electricity consumption, and therefore reduces its carbon emissions.	
Cloud accounting means that accounting records can be viewed online by everyone who needs to access them, so records do not have to be printed and less paper is used. This is better for the environment, is more cost-effective and saves office space.	

> **TIP**
>
> It is helpful to remember that manual accounting systems have a lower initial cost but higher labour costs; digital and cloud-based accounting systems have a higher initial cost but lower labour costs.

ACTIVITY 23.2

Anika has been running her business for several years and has always maintained the business's accounts using the traditional method and recording transactions by hand. Recently, Anika decided to change to a digital system so that she does not have to store so much paperwork. Anika is unsure exactly what the difference is between a data storage device and cloud-based storage.

Write a short description of each of the two systems and explain the similarities and differences.

Compare your description with that of a partner and compare your answers. If your partner has included things that you have missed, add them to your description.

DISCUSSION

In a small group, discuss whether a growing business should use a manual or a computerised system of accounting. Provide reasons for your answer.

ACCOUNTING IN ACTION

Figure 23.6: The owner of a grocery store

Basil owns a grocery store. He is responsible for ensuring the safety and security of the accounting data for his business. The business has been growing rapidly and the manual accounting system is becoming difficult to manage. Basil is concerned that errors will be made.

Basil thinks that he should consider moving to a computerised accounting system, but he has concerns about data security. He can remember reading about incidents where businesses had their data stolen and sensitive financial information was made public.

Basil is determined to try to avoid these problems.

Discuss in pairs or in a group:

1. What research do you suggest Basil should carry out before making a decision?

2. What advice would you give to Basil about things he could do to improve the security of a computerised accounting system?

SUMMARY

You should now know:

- Sustainable accounting practices aim to minimise any negative impact on the environment.

- Digital applications allow accounts to be maintained electronically. This may increase efficiency, reduce the likelihood of accounting errors and make it easier to analyse financial information.

- Businesses that store information digitally should follow data security practices such as encrypting data, restricting access to information, using antivirus programs, using strong passwords, backing up data and ensuring staff are trained to recognise cybersecurity threats.

- Manual accounting means accounts are maintained by hand and so all records are stored in books and paper files. This is a simple system with few costs, but it can be slower and there is a greater risk of accounting errors.

- Digital storage devices include external hard drives, USB flash drives and DVDs. These require little storage space, reduce the amount of paper that is needed and make it possible to back up data easily. However, it may be expensive to buy and maintain the computers and software, and to train staff to use them.

- Cloud storage involves using third-party services to store data on a remote server. The data can be accessed from anywhere with an internet connection, but strong security practices should be followed to reduce the risk of cyberattacks.

Chapter 23 practice questions

1   Which action will **not** help to keep data secure within a computerised accounting system?

   A   frequently backing up all work entered into the accounting system

   B   making sure that antivirus protection is put in place

   C   making use of updates from the accounting software provider

   D   using a single password to allow access to the entire accounting system   [1]

2   What is a benefit of using cloud-based accounting systems?

   A   access to data from anywhere with internet access

   B   annual licensing costs

   C   increased manual data entry

   D   limited access to data   [1]

3   What is an advantage of using sustainable accounting software?

   A   higher costs

   B   increased complexity

   C   limited functionality

   D   reduced environmental impact [1]

4   Identify why it is important for companies to integrate sustainability into their financial management practices. [3]

5   List two advantages and two disadvantages of a manual accounting storage system and a data storage device. [8]

6   Jane runs a small business and currently uses a manual accounting system. She is finding that the amount of space required for all the files and paperwork is reducing the amount of shop space that is available. She is also concerned about the environmental sustainability of all the paper used in a manual system. Jane is considering switching to a cloud-based accounting system to save physical space and reduce the amount of paper used.

   a   State how a cloud-based accounting system could benefit Jane's business. [2]

   b   Identify the challenges Jane might face when switching to a cloud-based accounting system. [2]

   [Total: 4]

CHECK YOUR PROGRESS

How well do you think you have achieved the learning intentions for this chapter? Give yourself a score from 1 (still need a lot of practice) to 5 (feeling very confident) for each learning intention. Provide an example to support your score.

Now I can ...	Score	Example to support score
understand how digital applications can be used for all or part of the accounting records		
understand the importance of storing accounting data safely and sustainably, and the risks associated with not storing accounting data safely and securely		
describe different types of storage systems: manual, data storage devices and cloud services		
explain the advantages and disadvantages of the different types of storage systems.		

Section 4 practice questions

1. Which would result in a cheque being dishonoured?

   1. The amount written in words is different to the amount written in figures.
   2. The cheque is out of date.
   3. The signature is incorrect or missing.
   4. There are insufficient funds in the bank for the cheque to be paid.

   A   1 only
   B   1, 2 and 3 only
   C   1, 2, 3 and 4
   D   4 only [1]

2. Goods returned to Zelda, $200, were credited to Zelda's account as $2 000.

   What entries are required to correct this error?

	Account to be debited	$	Account to be credited	$
A	suspense	1 800	Zelda	1 800
B	suspense	2 200	Zelda	2 200
C	Zelda	1 800	suspense	1 800
D	Zelda	2 200	suspense	2 200

   [1]

3. A sports club provided the following information at the end of its first financial year:

	$
Subscriptions received during the current year	5 550
Subscriptions owing for the current year	650
Subscriptions received in advance for the following year	1 200

   How much should be shown in the income and expenditure account for subscriptions?

   A $4 350
   B $5 000
   C $5 550
   D $6 100 [1]

4 Which should be included in a manufacturing account?

   1   carriage inwards on raw materials

   2   carriage outwards on finished goods

   3   returns inwards of finished goods

   4   returns outwards of raw materials

   A 1 only

   B 1 and 4 only

   C 3 and 4 only

   D 1, 2, 3 and 4   [1]

5 Which is the main advantage of cloud-based storage compared to other data-storage systems?

   A It allows multiple users to share processing power.

   B It enables the business to reduce the size of computers.

   C It makes the business look more professional.

   D It means the business owns more hardware.   [1]

6 On 30 November 20–7, Tomas downloaded the following bank statement for his business account.

ZZY Bank Limited

PO Box 2345

Penang

Customer: Tomas Trading (Business Account)   **Date:** 30 November 20–7

Account: 321987

Date		Details	Debit $	Credit $	Balance $
November	1	Balance			5 432 Cr
	2	Cheque 1234	1 780		3 652 Cr
	5	Card payment	1 910		1 742 Cr
	9	Deposit		3 200	4 942 Cr
	20	Bank transfer – Elgar		3 100	8 042 Cr
	21	SO Rent	600		7 442 Cr
	26	Cheque 1235	932		6 510 Cr
	28	DD Electricity Company	255		6 255 Cr
	29	Dishonoured cheque – Rio	235		6 020 Cr
	30	Bank charges	78		5 942 Cr

The following is Tomas's cash book (bank columns only) for November 20–7.

Tomas Trading								
Dr			Cash book (bank columns only)					Cr
				$				$
20–7					20–7			
Nov	1	Balance	b/d	3 652	Nov	2	Purchases	1 910
	9	Cash		3 200		20	Purchases	932
	29	Cash		2 800		29	S Moon	1 423
						30	Wages	2 500
						30	Balance c/d	2 778
				9 652				9 652
Dec	1	Balance	b/d	2 778				

Tomas compared the two documents and found there were differences. He also found that the balance on 1 December should have been $2887 as the credit side had been added incorrectly.

a Make any additional entries which are required in the bank columns of Tomas's cash book and bring down an updated balance on 1 December 20–7. [7]

b Prepare a bank reconciliation statement at 30 November 20–7. [5]

c Explain why the entries on a bank statement are on the opposite side to where they appear in the cash book. [2]

[Total: 14]

7 On 1 January 20–5, Daria started a business by transferring $275 000 from his private bank account to a business bank account. In addition, he took out a bank loan of $25 000. On the same day, he purchased business property $80 000, equipment $20 000 and inventory $10 000. These were all paid using online transfers from the business bank account.

a Prepare the opening journal entry on 1 January 20–5. A narrative is required. [4]

On 1 July 20–5, Daria transferred his personal motor vehicle to the business at a valuation of $9 500.

b Prepare the journal entry to record this transaction. A narrative is required. [3]

On 1 November 20–5, Daria purchased an additional motor vehicle, $20 000, on credit from BK Autos.

c Prepare the journal entry to record this transaction. A narrative is required. [3]

On 31 December 20–5, Daria:

- wrote off a debt of $500 owing by Ruhee as irrecoverable
- created an allowance for irrecoverable debts of $750
- depreciated **all** motor vehicles by 20% on cost.

  d Prepare journal entries to record these transactions.
     Narratives are required. [9]

  [Total: 19]

8 At the end of her financial year on 31 December 20–6, Elise drew up a trial balance, which did not balance. She proceeded to prepare draft financial statements including the statement of financial position shown below.

Elise			
Draft statement of financial position at 31 December 20–6			
	$	$	$
Assets			
Non-current assets at net book value			165 750
Current assets			
Inventory		25 000	
Trade receivables	32 050		
Less Allowance for irrecoverable debts	1 250	30 800	
Bank		3 900	
Cash		250	59 950
Total assets			225 700
Capital and liabilities			
Capital			
Opening balance			165 000
Plus Draft profit for the year			48 000
			213 000
Less Drawings			27 800
			185 200
Non-current liabilities			
Bank loan			25 000
Current liabilities			
Trade payables			17 050
			227 250
Suspense			1 550
Total capital and liabilities			225 700

The following errors were later discovered:

- No adjustment had been made for insurance paid in advance on 31 December 20–6, $500.
- A payment of $500 from Zaira, a credit customer, had been correctly entered in the bank account but entered in Zaira's account as $50.
- Sales on credit, $4 500, had not been entered in the accounting records.
- The total of the purchases account had been understated by $800.
- No adjustment had been made for an increase in the allowance for irrecoverable debts of $250.
- Inventory withdrawn by Elise for her personal use, $1 200, had been correctly entered in the purchases account but no other entries had been made.
- Cash drawings, $1 100, had been recorded in the wages account.

a Write up the suspense account starting with the difference on trial balance of $1 550 on the debit side. [4]

b Calculate the correct profit for the year. [6]

c Prepare a corrected statement of financial position at 31 December 20–6. [13]

[Total: 23]

9 Simone, a trader, maintains a full set of accounting records and prepares monthly control accounts.

  a Explain how Simone can use control accounts to verify the balances in her sales ledger and purchases ledger. [2]

On 30 June 20–6, Simone provided the following information:

	Debit	Credit
Sales ledger balances on 1 June 20–6:	$5 678	$90
Sales ledger balances on 30 June 20–6:	?	$75

Totals for the month of June 20–6:

	$
Cash sales	1 321
Contra entries	375
Credit sales	12 432
Discount allowed	85
Discount received	102
Interest charged by credit suppliers	35
Interest charged to credit customers	52
Irrecoverable debts	245
Allowance for irrecoverable debts	350
Receipts from credit customers	11 908
Sales returns	327
Purchases returns	198

b Suggest one reason why a sales ledger control account may have a credit balance. [1]

c Select the relevant figures and prepare the sales ledger control account for June 20–6.
Balance the account and bring down the balances on 1 July 20–6. [10]

d Explain why a contra entry may be required. [2]

[Total: 15]

10 Odette, a trader, sells all goods on credit at a mark-up of 25%.

She does not maintain a full set of double entry records but was able to provide the following information at the end of her financial year on 31 May 20–2.

	$
Trade receivables on 1 June 20–1	5 432
For the year ended 31 May 20–2:	
Receipts from trade receivables	24 231
Discount allowed	560
Irrecoverable debts	300
Trade receivables on 31 May 20–2	6 521

a Calculate for the year ended 31 May 20–2:

　i credit sales [3]

　ii gross profit [2]

　iii cost of sales. [2]

b State **one** advantage and **one** disadvantage to Odette of using a computerised accounting package to maintain her sales ledger. [2]

[Total: 9]

11 The Rialto Art Society was formed to provide members with an opportunity to create and display art in their art studio. The club charges an annual subscription and members are able to purchase their art supplies from the club shop at a reduced rate.

The club provided the following information for the year ended 30 April 20–6.

	1 May 20–5 $	30 April 20–6 $
Subscriptions in advance	850	1 000
Subscriptions in arrears	720	650
Inventory – Art supplies	2 100	3 450
Trade payables – Art supplies	3 456	4 321
Other payables – General expenses	300	350
Art studio – Cost	250 000	250 000
Equipment – Cost	39 500	45 000
Equipment – Accumulated depreciation	9 500	?
Balance at bank	31 560	?

The club bank account shows the following receipts and payments for the year.

Receipts	$
Subscriptions	8 900
Club shop sales	25 358
Competition entrance fees	4 500
Payments	
Trade payables	9 245
Club shop wages	5 000
Insurance	1 325
General expenses	8 650
Competition prizes	215
Competition expenses	1 200
Equipment	5 500

The club policy is to depreciate equipment at 20% per annum using the reducing balance method. A full year's depreciation is charged in the year of acquisition and none in the year of disposal.

a   For the year ended 30 April 20–6, prepare the:

   i   receipts and payments account   [5]

   ii   subscriptions account   [6]

   iii trading account for the club shop   [5]

   iv   income and expenditure account.   [8]

b   Prepare the statement of financial position at 30 April 20–6.   [10]

c   State two ways in which the use of accounting software could assist
    the treasurer of the Rialto Art Society.   [2]

[Total: 36]

12 Green Spaces Gardening Club was established on 1 August 20–4. The club owns a selection of gardening tools which members are allowed to borrow free of charge. The club also arranges for visitors to speak about various aspects of gardening at their monthly meetings.

On 1 August 20–6, the club had 50 members. The annual subscription is $90, which is payable on 1 August each year.

On 1 August 20–6, the club received a three-year loan of $2 000 from a member. The loan was used to purchase additional gardening tools. Interest on the loan of 4% per annum is payable in arrears in two instalments on 31 January and 31 July each year.

The treasurer provided the following information for the year ended 31 July 20–7:

		$
On 1 August 20–6		
Balance at bank		850

Receipts and payments during the year ended 31 July 20–7

			$
Subscriptions	for the year ended 31 July 20–6		990
	for the year ended 31 July 20–7		3 870
	for the year ending 31 July 20–8		450
Loan			2 000
Interest on loan			20
Hire of meeting room (14 months to 30 September 20–7)			1 050
Gardening tools			3 940
General expenses			1 070

a Prepare the receipts and payments account for the Green Spaces Gardening Club for the year ended 31 July 20–7. Balance the account and bring down the balance on 1 August 20–7. [7]

b Identify three items in the receipts and payments account which will **not** appear in the income and expenditure account. Give reasons for your answers. [6]

c Identify two items in the receipts and payments account which will appear in the income and expenditure account, but which will show a different amount. Give reasons for your answers. [4]

d Identify one item of expenditure which may appear in the income and expenditure account of the Green Spaces Gardening Club for the year ended 31 July 20–7, which does **not** appear in the receipts and payments account. [1]

e State why members of the Green Spaces Gardening Club cannot expect to receive a share of the surplus for the year. [1]

[Total: 19]

13 Alex has been in business as a sole trader for several years. He has been considering forming a partnership business with a friend, but is undecided.

a Suggest three advantages of continuing in business as a sole trader. [3]

Alex finally made a decision, and on 1 January 20–6, he formed a partnership with his friend Kahili. They each introduced $80 000 as capital. Kahili also made a loan to the business of $20 000.

Their partnership agreement included the following terms:

Interest on capital to be allowed at 4% per annum

Interest to be charged on drawings at 3%

Alex to be entitled to an annual salary of $8 000

Interest on partners' loans to be allowed at 3% per annum

Profits and losses to be shared equally.

On 1 July 20–6, Alex introduced an additional $10 000 as capital.

It was agreed that from 1 July 20–6, Alex's salary would increase to $10 000 per annum.

During the year ended 31 December 20–6, Alex's drawings were $11 000 and Kahili's were $7 000.

The profit before loan interest for the year ended 31 December 20–6 was $28 000.

b Prepare the appropriation account for the year ended 31 December 20–6. **[8]**

c State two possible reasons why Kahili decided to make a loan to the business rather than invest additional capital. **[2]**

[Total: 13]

14 Lottie, Fatima and Daniel are in partnership. Their financial year ends on 31 May. Profits and losses are shared in the ratio 5 : 3 : 2.

The following information is available.

At 1 June 20–8:

	Lottie	Fatima	Daniel
	$	$	$
Capital account	80 000	60 000	40 000
Current account	35 120 Cr	1 120 Dr	980 Dr
5% Loan account			20 000

During the year ended 31 May 20–9:

Drawings	4 000	7 000	2 000

The profit before loan interest for the year ended 31 May 2009 was $12 800.

The following information was prepared for inclusion in the appropriation account for the year ended 31 May 20–9:

			$	$
Profit for the year				?
Interest on drawings	Lottie		120	
	Fatima		210	
	Daniel		60	390
Interest on capital	Lottie		3 200	
	Fatima		2 400	
	Daniel		1 600	7 200
Partner's salary	Fatima			6 000

a State the significance of a debit balance on a partner's current account. **[1]**

b i Calculate the rate of interest which the partners were charged on their drawings. **[1]**

  ii Calculate the rate of interest which the partners received on their capital. **[1]**

  iii Suggest one reason why Fatima was entitled to a partnership salary. **[1]**

c i Calculate the residual profit or loss for the year ended 31 May 20–9. **[4]**

  ii Calculate Daniel's share of the residual profit or loss for the year ended 31 May 20–9. **[1]**

d Prepare Daniel's current account for the year ended 31 May 20–9. Balance the account and bring down the balance on 1 June 20–9. **[6]**

[Total: 15]

15 Hodan runs a manufacturing business. She produces embroidery machines, which she sells to local businesses who embroider T-shirts, sports clothing and school wear.

Hodan provided the following information for the financial year ended 31 August 20–3:

	$
At 1 September 20–2:	
Inventory – Raw materials	19 430
Work in progress	21 290
Finished goods	25 940
Factory machinery at cost	60 000
Provision for depreciation on factory machinery	21 600
For the year ended 31 August 20–3:	
Purchases of raw materials	96 200
Purchases of finished goods	26 150
Carriage inwards on raw materials	12 750
Revenue	385 000
Direct factory wages	68 560
Indirect factory wages	24 284
General expenses	14 400
Factory rates and insurance	7 870
Factory repairs and maintenance	2 866
Factory light, hear and power	6 790

Section 4 practice questions

At 31 August 20–3:

Inventory – Raw materials	18 780
Work in progress	22 220
Finished goods	26 150

Additional information:

- Direct factory wages accrued at 31 August 20–3 amounted to $3 950.
- Factory rates and insurance prepaid at 31 August 20–3 amounted to $1 240.
- The general expenses are to be apportioned ¾ to the factory and ¼ to the offices.
- Factory machinery is being depreciated at 20% per annum using the reducing balance method.

a Prepare the manufacturing account for the year ended 31 August 20–3. [12]

b Prepare the trading section of the statement of profit or loss for the year ended 31 August 20–3. [5]

c Give two possible reasons why Hodan purchased finished goods. [2]

Hodan is concerned about the cost of heat, light and power for the factory and is considering installing solar panels on the factory roof.

d Identify factors which Hodan should consider when making a decision about solar panels. [4]

[Total: 23]

16 The financial year of ZYV Limited ends on 31 October.

On 1 November 20–6:	$
Ordinary share capital $1 shares	100 000
General reserve	9 000
Retained earnings	13 000
5% debentures	40 000

Payments during the year ended 31 October 20–7:	
Final ordinary share dividend for the year ended 31 October 20–6	5 500
Interim ordinary share dividend for the year ended 31 October 20–7	3 500
Profit for the year ended 31 October before debenture interest	21 000

On 31 October 20–6, the directors recommended:	
Payment of a final dividend on ordinary share	6 000
The transfer to general reserve	3 600

a Prepare a statement of changes in equity for the year ended 31 October 20–7. [6]

b State the meaning of the word equity. [1]

c Calculate the interim ordinary share dividend as a percentage of the ordinary share capital for the financial year ended 31 October 20–7. [1]

d Suggest one reason why the directors recommended a transfer to general reserve. [1]

e State three ways in which debentures differ from ordinary shares. [3]

f State why debenture interest does not appear in the statement of changes in equity. [1]

g Prepare an extract from the statement of financial position at 31 October 20–7 to show the equity section. [2]

[Total: 15]

17 XY Limited was formed on 1 May 20–5. On that date, 180 000 ordinary shares of $1 each were issued. The company also issued 600 4% debentures of $100 each. No further shares or debentures were issued until 1 November 20–7 when 20 000 additional ordinary shares were issued.

The profit for the year ended 30 April 20–8 after debenture interest was $23 200.

The partly completed statement of changes in equity for the year ended 30 April 20–8 has been provided.

XY Limited				
Partly completed statement of changes in equity for the year ended 30 April 20–8				
	Ordinary share capital $	General reserve $	Retained earnings $	Total $
Balance at 1 May 20–7	180 000	12 000	3 000	
Share issue				20 000
Profit for the year			23 200	
Dividend paid (interim)			(4 000)	
Transfer to general reserve		2 000		
Balance at 30 April 20–8				

a Copy out the statement of changes in equity and insert the missing figures. [3]

XY provided the following information at 30 April 20–8.

1 The allowance for irrecoverable debts equalled 5% of the trade receivables at 30 April 20–8.

2 Twelve months' interest on debentures was accrued on 30 April 20–8.

3 Other balances on the books on 30 April 20–8 were:

	$
Property at cost	205 000
Machinery and equipment at cost	80 000
Motor vehicles at cost	26 000
Trade receivables	22 200
Other receivables	950
Trade payables	16 720
Bank	6 200 debit
Provision for depreciation on machinery and equipment	38 800
Provision for depreciation on motor vehicles	12 120
Inventory	25 000

b Prepare the statement of financial position at 30 April 20–8. [10]

The directors of XY Limited are concerned about the low bank balance and have decided to issue 200 debentures in order to raise $20 000.

c Explain how this decision may affect:

  i XY Limited [2]

  ii the ordinary shareholders. [2]

[Total: 17]

18 Marion is a sole trader. She extracted the following information from her statement of financial position on 31 May 20–4:

	$
Bank balance	1 450 debit
Inventory	5 435
Other payables	350
Other receivables	130
Petty cash	1 250
Trade payables	7 679
Trade receivables	6 932

a Calculate the working capital at 31 May 20–4. [3]

b I State the formula for the calculation of the current ratio. Calculate the current ratio of Marion, correct to two decimal places. [2]

  ii State the formula for the calculation of the acid test (liquid) ratio. Calculate the acid test (liquid) ratio of Marion, correct to two decimal places. [2]

Marion provided the following additional information for the previous two years:

Ratio	31 May 20–2	31 May 20–3
Current (working capital)	2.93 : 1	2.22 : 1
Acid test (liquid)	1.64 : 1	1.43 : 1

c Discuss the change in liquidity over the three years. [4]

d State two ways in which Marion can improve her liquidity position. [2]

[Total: 13]

19 SJ Traders buys and sells goods on credit only. They provided the following information at the end of their financial year on 30 June 20–3:

SJ Traders
Statement of profit or loss for the year ended 30 June 20–3

	$	$
Revenue		300 000
Less Cost of sales		
Opening inventory	35 000	
Purchases	175 000	
	210 000	
Less Closing inventory	30 000	180 000
Gross profit		120 000
Less Expenses		45 000
Profit for the year		75 000

SJ Traders
Statement of financial position at 30 June 20–3

	$	$
Assets		
Non-current assets at net book value		113 960
Current assets		
Inventory	30 000	
Trade receivables	50 000	
Bank	6 040	86 040
Total assets		200 000
Capital and liabilities		
Capital		
Opening balance		143 000
Profit for the year		75 000
		218 000
Less Drawings		43 000
		175 000
Current liabilities		
Trade payables		25 000
Total capital and liabilities		200 000

a   Calculate the following ratios, correct to two decimal places. In each case, state the formula used.

   i   gross profit margin [2]
   ii   profit margin [2]
   iii return on capital employed [2]
   iv   trade receivables turnover (rounded up to the next whole day) [2]
   v   trade payables turnover (rounded up to the next whole day). [2]

SJ Traders obtained the following data for another business in the same trade.

Ratio	
Gross profit margin	35.33%
Profit margin	25.42%
Return on capital employed	38.18%
Trade receivables turnover	30 days
Trade payables turnover	30 days

b   Compare each of SJ Traders' ratios with those of the other business and state which business has the better ratio. Give a reason for each answer. [10]

c   State, giving reasons, whether SJ Traders will be satisfied with the results of their ratio analysis for the year ended 30 June 20–3. [5]

[Total: 25]

Glossary

accounting — the process of using book-keeping records to prepare financial statements and to assist in decision-making.

accrued expense — an expense relating to a particular accounting period which is unpaid at the end of that period.

accrued income — income relating to a particular accounting period which has not been received at the end of that period.

accumulated depreciation — the total of all the depreciation which has been charged on a non-current asset.

accumulated fund — the surpluses (less any deficits) which have accumulated over the life of the club. It replaces capital in the statement of financial position of a club or society.

allowance for irrecoverable debts — an estimate of the amount a business will lose in a financial year due to irrecoverable debts.

analysis columns — columns in a petty cash book used to divide the payments into different categories.

appropriation account — one of the year-end financial statements. It shows the division of the profit or loss between the partners.

assets — anything owned by or owing to the business.

balance — the difference between the debit side and the credit side on a ledger account.

bank overdraft — when a business has taken more out of its bank account than has been paid in.

bank reconciliation statement — a document prepared by a business to explain why the updated bank balance in the cash book does not agree with the balance on the bank statement.

bank statement — a copy of a customer's account in the books of the bank which is sent to the customer at regular intervals.

bank transfer — a transaction where funds are moved directly from one bank account into another.

book of prime entry — a book where transactions are recorded before being entered in the ledger.

book-keeping — the process of recording details of all the financial transactions of a business.

business entity concept — this means that the business is treated as being completely separate from the owner of the business.

called-up capital — the amount of the issued share capital for which the company has requested payment from shareholders.

capital employed — the total long-term finance which is being used by a business.

capital expenditure — money spent on purchasing, improving or extending non-current assets.

capital — the total resources provided by the owner. It represents what the business owes the owner.

capital receipt — money received by a business that is not from normal trading activities.

carriage — the cost of transporting goods.

carriage inwards — the cost of bringing the goods to the business.

carriage outwards — the cost of delivering the goods to the customer.

cash book — the book where the cash account and the bank account are maintained side-by-side.

cash discount — an allowance given to a credit customer when an account is settled within a time limit set by the supplier.

cheque	a written order to a bank to pay a stated sum of money to the person or business named on the order.	**digital applications**	any software or program which runs on an electronic device such as a computer, tablet or mobile phone.
cloud services	a system which involves using third-party services to store data online.	**direct costs**	costs which can be linked to the making of the product.
consistency concept	this means that accounting methods must be used consistently from one accounting period to the next.	**dishonoured cheque**	a cheque which the bank will not accept when it is presented for payment.
contra entry	an entry that appears on both sides of the cash book.	**double entry book-keeping**	the process of making a debit entry and a credit entry for each transaction.
cost	the purchase price of the goods plus any additional costs to bring the goods to their present position and condition.	**drawings**	any value taken from the business by its owner.
cost of production	prime cost plus factory overheads, adjusted for any work in progress at the start and at the end of the year. It is the total cost of manufacturing the completed goods.	**duality concept**	this means that every transaction is recorded twice – once on the debit side and once on the credit side.
		efficiency ratio	a way to measure how well a business is using their resources to generate revenue or how well a business is managing their resources.
credit note	a document issued by a credit supplier to notify of a reduction in a previous invoice.	**equity**	the total funds provided by the shareholders of a company.
current assets	short-term assets whose amounts are constantly changing.	**going concern concept**	this means that the accounting records are maintained on the basis that the business will continue to operate for an indefinite period of time.
current liabilities	amounts owed which are due for repayment within the next 12 months.		
data security	a safeguarding process of securing digital information from corruption, theft or unauthorised access.	**goodwill**	the amount by which the value of a business as a whole exceeds the value of the separate assets and liabilities.
data storage devices	digital devices such as external hard drives or USB flash drives, which can be used to store accounting records.	**gross profit**	the difference between the selling price and the cost price of the goods.
		gross profit margin	the gross profit expressed as a percentage of the selling price.
debenture	a long-term loan which has a fixed rate of interest, payable irrespective of the profit of the company.	**historic cost concept**	this means that all assets and expenses are initially recorded at their actual cost.
debit note	a document issued by a credit customer to request a reduction in the invoice received.	**imprest system**	the amount spent each period is restored so the amount of petty cash at the start of each period is the same.
deficit	when expenses exceed gains.		
depreciation	an estimate of the loss in value of a non-current asset over its expected working life.		

Glossary

income and expenditure account	an account prepared annually by a non-trading organisation. It compares the gains and the expenses to calculate the surplus or deficit.
indirect costs	costs which are not directly linked to the making of the product.
inventory	the goods a business has available at any point in time.
invoice	a document issued by a credit supplier showing details, quantities and prices of goods supplied.
irrecoverable debt	an amount owing to a business which will not be paid by the credit customer.
irrecoverable debt recovered	when a credit customer pays some or all of the debt after it was written off as irrecoverable.
issued share capital	the amount of share capital issued to the shareholders.
journal	a book of prime entry used to record transactions which cannot be recorded in any other book of prime entry.
liabilities	anything owed by the business.
limited company	a legal entity which has a separate identity from its shareholders, whose liability for the company's debts is limited.
limited liability	the owners of a business are not personally liable for the debts of the business beyond what they agree to contribute as capital.
liquidity ratio	a way to measure the ability of the business to turn assets into cash to pay its short-term debts.
manual storage	a system where accounting records are stored physically in books and on paper.
manufacturing account	an annual financial statement that is used to calculate the cost of goods produced.
mark-up	the gross profit expressed as a percentage of the cost price.
matching/accruals concept	this means that the revenue of the accounting period is matched against the costs of the same period.
materiality concept	this means that individual items which will not significantly affect either the profit or the assets of a business do not need to be recorded separately.
money measurement concept	this means that only information which can be expressed in terms of money can be recorded in the accounting records.
net book value	the cost price of a non-current asset minus the accumulated depreciation to date.
net realisable value	the estimated receipts from selling the goods less any costs of completing or selling those goods.
nominal (general) ledger	the ledger where accounts for assets, liabilities, expenses, income, sales, purchases and returns are maintained.
non-current assets	assets which are obtained for use and not for resale, which help the business earn revenue.
non-current liabilities	amounts owed which are not due for repayment within the next 12 months.
non-trading organisation	an organisation formed to provide facilities and services for members; they are not formed with the aim of making a profit.
ordinary shares	shares which receive a variable rate of dividend and have voting rights.
paid-up capital	the part of the called-up share capital which shareholders have actually paid to the company.
partnership	a business in which two or more people work together as owners with the aim of making a profit.
partnership agreement	a document setting out the rules for operating the business, including profit-sharing arrangements.
paying-in slip	a document showing the amounts of coins, notes and cheques being paid into a bank account.
petty cash book	a book used to record low-value cash payments.
prepaid expense	an expense paid during a particular accounting period which relates to a future accounting period.

prepaid income	income received during a particular accounting period which relates to a future accounting period.	**receipt**	a written acknowledgement of money received and acts as proof of payment.
prime cost	the total of the direct materials, direct labour and direct expenses. It is the cost of the essentials necessary for production.	**receipts and payments account**	a summary of the cash book which is prepared annually by a non-trading organisation.
profit for the year	the final profit after any other income has been added to the gross profit and the running expenses have been deducted.	**reducing balance method of depreciation**	the method where the depreciation charged each year decreases as it is calculated on the net book value rather than the cost.
profit from operations	the profit after deducting all expenses from the gross profit with the exception of finance charges such as interest paid.	**residual profit**	the profit remaining after adjusting for interest on drawings, interest on capital and partners' salaries.
		residual value	the value of a non-current asset at the end of its useful life.
profitability ratio	a way to measure the performance of the business by comparing the profit to other figures in the same set of financial statements.	**retained earnings**	the profit which has not been distributed to shareholders.
		revaluation method of depreciation	the method where the opening and closing values of a non-current asset are compared (after adjusting for any additions during the year) to determine the depreciation for the year.
prudence concept	this means that profits and assets should not be overstated, and losses and liabilities should not be understated.		
purchase order	a document issued by a buyer to a credit supplier showing the goods or services they wish to purchase.	**revenue expenditure**	money spent on running a business on a day-to-day basis.
		revenue receipt	money received by a business from normal trading activities.
purchases journal	a record of the names of credit suppliers, the value of the goods purchased and the date of the purchase.	**sales journal**	a record of the names of credit customers, the value of the goods sold and the date of the sale.
purchases ledger	the ledger where the accounts of credit suppliers are maintained.	**sales ledger**	the ledger where the accounts of credit customers are maintained.
purchases ledger control account	an account summarising the balances of all the accounts of the trade payables.	**sales ledger control account**	an account summarising the balances of all the accounts of the trade receivables.
purchases returns journal	a record of the names of credit suppliers to whom goods have been returned, the value of the goods returned and the date of the return.	**sales returns journal**	a record of the names of credit customers who have returned goods, the value of the goods returned and the date of the return.
		service business	a business which provides a service.
rate of inventory turnover	the number of times a business replaces its inventory in a given period of time.	**sole trader**	a person who owns and operates a business individually.
realisation concept	this means that revenue is only regarded as being earned when the legal title to goods passes from the seller to the buyer.	**statement of account**	a document issued by a credit supplier to summarise the transactions for the month.

Glossary

statement of affairs — a summary of the financial position of a business on a certain date. It is prepared instead of a statement of financial position when double entry records have not been maintained.

statement of changes in equity — a statement showing the changes in a company's ordinary share capital, retained earnings and general reserve over the financial year.

statement of financial position — a statement of the assets, liabilities and capital of a business on a certain date.

statement of profit or loss — a statement prepared for a trading period to show the gross profit and profit for the year.

straight line method of depreciation — the method where the same amount of depreciation is charged each year.

subscriptions — amounts members of an organisation pay to use the facilities provided by the club or society.

surplus — when gains exceed expenses.

suspense account — a temporary account opened in order to make the totals of a trial balance agree.

trade discount — a reduction in the selling price of goods.

trade payable — a credit supplier of goods to whom the business owes money.

trade receivable — a credit customer who owes money to the business.

trading business — a business which buys and sells goods.

trial balance — a list of the balances on the accounts in the ledger at a certain date.

work in progress — goods which are partly completed at the end of the financial year.

working capital — the difference between the current assets and the current liabilities.

Appendix: commonly used accounting ratios

You should make sure that you are familiar with the following ratios for this course:

Profitability ratios

Gross profit margin (%) $\dfrac{\text{Gross profit}}{\text{Revenue}} \times 100$

Mark-up (%) $\dfrac{\text{Gross profit}}{\text{Cost of sales}} \times 100$

Profit margin (%) $\dfrac{\text{Profit for the year}}{\text{Revenue}} \times 100$.

Return on capital employed (ROCE) (%) $\dfrac{\text{Profit for the year before interest}}{\text{Capital employed}} \times 100$

Capital employed = issued shares + reserves + non-current liabilities

Liquidity ratios

Current (working capital) ratio $\dfrac{\text{Current assets}}{\text{Current liabilities}}$

Answer presented as a ratio

Acid test (liquid) ratio $\dfrac{\text{Current assets} - \text{inventory}}{\text{Current liabilities}}$

Answer presented as a ratio

Efficiency ratios

Rate of inventory turnover (times) $\dfrac{\text{Cost of sales}}{\text{Average inventory}}$

Inventory turnover (days) $\dfrac{\text{Average inventory}}{\text{Cost of sales}} \times 365 \text{ days}$

Trade receivables turnover (days) $\dfrac{\text{Trade receivables}}{\text{Credit sales}} \times 365 \text{ days}$

Trade payables turnover (days) $\dfrac{\text{Trade payables}}{\text{Credit purchases}} \times 365 \text{ days}$

> Acknowledgements

The authors and publishers acknowledge the following sources of copyright material and are grateful for the permissions granted. While every effort has been made, it has not always been possible to identify the sources of all the material used, or to trace all copyright holders. If any omissions are brought to our notice, we will be happy to include the appropriate acknowledgements on reprinting.

Thanks to the following for permission to reproduce images:

Cover Eugene Mymrin/Getty Images; *Inside* **Chapter 1** Douglas Sacha/GI; Morsa Images/GI; Peter Dazeley/GI; Westend61/GI; M_a_y_a/GI; Alex Liew/GI; **Chapter 2** Donglpix/Shutterstock; Connect Images/GI; MoMo Productions/GI; Westend61/GI; AsiaVision/GI; Luis Alvarez/GI; ljubaphoto/GI; Maskot/GI; Zephyr18/GI; **Chapter 3** Oxygen/GI; JackF/GI; SrdjanPav/GI; Sean Gladwell/GI; Krittiraj Adchasai/GI; Jay Yuno/GI; **Chapter 4** Donglpix/Shutterstock; Bet_Noire/GI; Charnchai/GI; Miniseries/GI; Tetra Images/GI; Alvarez/GI; **Chapter 5** Oxygen/GI; Gahsoon/GI; FilippoBacci/GI; Pascal Deloche/GI; LittleCityLifestylePhotography/GI; LaylaBird/GI; **Chapter 6** John Lund/GI; Tang Ming Tung/GI; ArLawKa AungTun/GI; Hispanolistic/GI; Westend61/GI; MTStock Studio/GI; DMP/GI; **Chapter 7** Jose A. Bernat Bacete/GI; Hispanolistic/GI; Cineberg/GI; TravelCouples/GI; Svetikd/GI; Hispanolistic/GI; **Chapter 8** Robbie Goodall/GI; Westend61/GI; Deepak Sethi/GI; Iryna Inshyna/GI; Maria Toutoudaki/GI; HEX/GI; Domoyega/GI; Maskot/GI; Luis Alvarez/GI; **Chapter 9** Baac3nes/GI; Caia Image/GI; Halfpoint Images/GI; tdub303/GI; Baona/GI; Ariel Skelley/GI; **Chapter 10** Baac3nes/GI; Maskot/GI; Andrii Iemelyanenko/GI; Halfpoint/GI; Ralf Hahn/GI; shapecharge/GI; hphimagelibrary/GI; **Chapter 11** Baac3nes/GI; Nick David/GI; Liubomyr Vorona/GI; DuxX/GI; AmnajKhetsamtip/GI; Drazen/GI; UntitledImages/GI; Mint Images/GI; **Chapter 12** merrymoonmary/GI; Thana Prasongsin/GI; Viti/GI; MoMo Productions/GI; Maskot/GI; Sturti/GI; JackF/GI; Gahsoon/GI; **Chapter 13** kampee patisena/GI; Extreme-Photographer/GI; 10'000 Hours/GI; Shapecharge/GI; Katleho Seisa/GI; Prasit photo/GI; Gorodenkoff/GI; KLH49/GI; **Chapter 14** Coneyl Jay/GI; JGI/Jamie Grill/GI; Courtneyk/GI; Shapecharge/GI; Wasan Tita/GI; **Chapter 15** Dulyanut Swdp/GI; xPACIFICA/GI; MartinPrescott/GI; SolStock/GI; Serts/GI; Jamie Grill/GI; **Chapter 16** Baac3nes/GI; boonchai wedmakawand/GI; PixelsEffect/GI; Kilito Chan/GI; Anderson Coelho/GI; **Chapter 17** Baac3nes/GI; JackF/GI; AsiaVision/GI; Insta_photos/GI; Nick Brundle Photography/GI; Kosamtu/GI; **Chapter 18** oxygen/GI; Maskot/GI; Vitranc/GI; SolStock/GI; Mayur Kakade/GI; Matimix/GI; Ratnakorn Piyasirisorost/GI; JohnnyGreig/GI; **Chapter 19** Constantine Johnny/GI; Xavierarnau/GI; Izusek/GI; 10'000 Hours/GI; Jose Luis Pelaez Inc/GI; Nitat Termmee/GI; Katleho Seisa/GI; Cavan Images/GI; **Chapter 20** John Lund/GI; Noah Saob/GI; Vithun Khamsong/GI; Boonchai wedmakawand/GI; Andresr/GI; AnSyvanych/GI; Comezora/GI; Wirestock/GI; **Chapter 21** Yaroslav Kushta/GI; Smederevac/GI; Matej Kastelic/GI; Lorado/GI; Xavierarnau/GI; **Chapter 22** Glow Images/GI; South_agency/GI; Monkeybusinessimages/GI; Juanmonino/GI; MoMo Productions/GI; Wallis Yu/GI; **Chapter 23** MirageC/GI; Tara Moore/GI; Piyaphun/GI; Rankomm/GI; SBdigit/GI; Andresr/GI

Key: GI = Getty Images

Thanks to Sharon Elan-Puttick for her contribution to this publication.

Index

accounting, definition 4
accounting concepts 175–7
accounting equation 7–8
accounting in action
   accrued and prepaid income 212
   assets and liabilities 12
   bank reconciliation 281–2
   books of prime entry 124
   business documents 106
   correcting errors 307
   cost of production 409
   data security 464
   deciding who to sell to 69
   different methods of recording 83
   different types of expenditure 186
   error location 51
   Greenways Football Club 374
   improving profitability ratios 451
   irrecoverable debts 254
   limited companies 425
   lost and damaged records 351
   partnerships 392
   statements of financial position 168
   trading options 38
accounting in context
   accounting rules 174
   bank statements 271
   books of prime entry 287
   business documents 96
   club treasurers 357
   comparing financial statements 432
   control accounts 314, 326–7
   cost of production 397
   different types of transactions 113–14
   encouraging prompt payment 56
   falling profits 237
   financial statements 137
   irrecoverable debts 242
   limited companies 415
   non-current assets 218
   partnerships 380
   paying in advance or paying later 191
   record keeping 3
   small transactions 75
   statements of financial position 159
   statements of profit or loss 153
   sustainability 457
   traditional or digital accounts 17
   trial balances 43
   what financial records are necessary? 332
accounting ratios 433
   efficiency ratios 440–2
   inter-business comparisons 446–8
   interpretation of business trends 443–5
   limitations 450
   liquidity ratios 438–9
   profitability ratios 435–7
accounting rules 174
accounting software 123
   bank reconciliation 280–1
   role of control accounts 325–6
accounting statements see financial statements
accruals concept 176, 219, 248
accrued expenses 192–4
accrued income 203–5, 212
accumulated depreciation 231
accumulated funds 366, 368
   calculation of 373
acid test (liquid) ratio 438, 439
allowance for irrecoverable debts
   adjustment of 251–3
   creation of 249–50
analysis 432
   see also accounting ratios
analysis columns 78, 80–1
appropriation accounts 384–5
asset disposal accounts 234–6
assets 5, 12, 160–2
   accounting equation 7–8
   depreciation *see depreciation*
   recording in ledger accounts 20–1
   see also non-current assets

back-ups 458–9
balancing ledger accounts 24–5
bank account, discrepancies with bank statements 272–3
bank loans 63
bank overdrafts 62–3
   bank reconciliation 278–9
bank reconciliation 274–8, 281–2
   advantages 281
   in a computerised accounting system 280–1
   when there is a bank overdraft 278–9
bank reconciliation statements 275, 278

Index

bank statements 271–2
    discrepancies with the bank account 272–3
bank transfers (credit transfers) 19
book-keeping 4
    double entry 17
        see also ledger accounts
books of prime entry 113, 124, 287
    purchases journals 119, 121–2
    purchases returns journals 119–22
    sales journals 114, 115, 117
    sales returns journals 114–17
    using accounting software 123
    see also cash books; journals; petty cash books
business documents 95–6
    cheques 66–9, 103, 273
    credit notes 101
    debit notes 100
    digital records 106
    invoices 97–9
    purchase orders 96
    receipts 104–5
    statements of account 102–3
business entity concept 175
business trends 443–5

called-up capital 417–18
capital 5, 162–3
    accounting equation 7–8
capital accounts, partnerships 387–8
capital employed 167
capital expenditure 181, 182
capital receipts 182
carriage 31
carriage inwards 31–3
carriage outwards 31–3
cash, comparison with profit 142–3
cash accounts 21
cash books 57, 58, 61, 64
    bank overdrafts 62
    contra entries 58
    discrepancies with bank statements 272–3
    dishonoured cheques 67–9
    items not recorded until bank statement is received 273
    three-column 64–5
    see also petty cash books
cash discounts 64–5, 97, 345
cheques 103
    dishonoured 66–9
    unpresented 273
cloud storage 462–3
clubs and societies *see non-trading organisations*

combined expense accounts 201–3
combined trading and service businesses, statements of profit or loss 150–2
commission, errors of 49
compensating errors 49
complete reversal, errors of 49
computerised accounting systems *see accounting software*
confidentiality 184
consistency concept 175
consultancies 150
contra entries (inter-ledger transfers, set-offs) 58, 61, 323–5
control accounts (total accounts) 314, 326–7
    advantages of 315
    contra entries 323–5
    credit and debit balances 321–2
    purchases ledger control accounts 318–20
    role in computerised accounting systems 325–6
    sales ledger control accounts 315–18
cost, definition 177
cost of production 397, 400–1, 409
    elements of 398–9
    unit cost calculation 404
cost of sales 140
credit, goods purchased on 26
credit, goods sold on 27–8
credit balances 321–2
credit cards 19
credit control 247
credit notes 101
current accounts, partnerships 387–9
current assets 161–2
current liabilities 163
current (working capital) ratio 438–9
cyber training 458–9

data encryption 458–9
data security 458–9, 464
    storage systems 460–3
data storage devices 461–2
debentures 420
debit balances 322
debit cards 19
debit notes 100
debts *see irrecoverable debts*
deficits 361
depreciation 218, 237
    accumulated 231
    causes 219
    effect on financial statements 219
    methods of calculation 220–5
    recording in financial statements 231–3

recording in the ledger 225–31
reducing balance method 222–3
revaluation method 224–5
straight line method 221–2
digital applications 457–8
data security 458–9
digital records 106
direct costs 398
direct debit 19
discounts
cash 64–5
trade 97, 98, 99
dishonoured cheques 66–9
double entry book-keeping 17
see also ledger accounts
drawings, recording in ledger accounts 34
drawings accounts, partnerships 387
duality concept 175

efficiency ratios 440–2
environmental impact *see sustainability*
equity 421
equity shares *see ordinary shares*
error correction
effect on profit 304–5
effect on the statement of financial position 306
errors 307
of commission 49
compensating 49
of complete reversal 49
finding the location of 48, 51
of omission 49
of original entry 49
of principle 49
which affect a trial balance 301–3
which are not shown by a trial balance 49, 299–301
ethical principles 184
expense accounts
combined 201–3
opening balances 198–200
expenses
accrued 192–4
direct 398
prepaid 195–7
recording in ledger accounts 22–4

factory overheads 399
financial statements 4, 137
analysis 432–3
see also accounting ratios
effect of depreciation 219
limitations 450

preparation from incomplete records 339–44
recording depreciation 231–3
users of 449
see also statements of financial position; statements of profit or loss
fixed capital accounts 387
floats *see imprest system*
full accounting records, advantages of 333

general reserve 422
going concern concept 175
going out of business 254
goods 6
goodwill 161
gross profit 139–40
gross profit margin 347–8, 351, 435, 436

historic cost concept 175

imprest system 77
income
accrued 203–5, 212
prepaid 206–8, 212
recording in ledger accounts 22–4
income accounts, opening balances 208–10
income and expenditure accounts 361–3
difference from receipts and payments accounts 365–6
income statements *see statements of profit or loss*
incomplete records 332, 351
advantages and disadvantages 334
calculation of credit sales and credit purchases 346
mark-up and gross profit margin 347–8, 351
non-trading organisations 372
preparation of financial statements 339–44
profit calculation 334–8
rate of inventory turnover 349–50
statements of affairs 334, 337
indirect factory expenses (factory overheads) 399
intangible non-current assets 161
integrity 184
inter-business comparisons 446–7
problems of 448
inter-ledger transfers *see contra entries*
inventories 6
inventory turnover 440–1
inventory valuation 177–8
effects of incorrect valuation 179–80
invoices 97–9
irrecoverable debts 242, 254
recording in the journal 292–3
reducing the possibility of 247

subscriptions 370
    writing off 243
irrecoverable debts, allowance for 248
    adjustment of 251–3
    creation of 249–50
irrecoverable debts recovered 244–7
    recording in the journal 294–5
issued share capital 417

journals 287
    layout 288
    opening entries 288–90
    recording non-regular transactions 292–6
    recording purchase and sale of non-current assets 291

labour, costs of 398
ledger accounts
    balancing 24–5
    interpretation 37
    layout 18–19
    partnerships 387–9
    recording assets and liabilities 20–1
    recording carriage inwards and carriage outwards 31–3
    recording depreciation 225–31
    recording drawings 34
    recording expenses and income 22–4
    recording sales, purchases and returns 26–30
    recording year-end transfers 297–8
    three-column running balance format 35–6
    transferring totals to statements of profit or loss 145–7
    see also nominal ledgers; purchases ledgers; sales ledgers
ledgers 17
    division into specialist areas 56–7, 59–61
liabilities 5, 12, 162, 163
    accounting equation 7–8
    recording in ledger accounts 20–1
limited companies 415–16
    advantages and disadvantages 417
    debentures 420
    financial statements 421
    share capital 417–18
    statements of changes in equity 421–3, 426
    statements of financial position 425
    types of shares 419
liquidity ratios 438–9
loans from partners 383

manual storage systems 460–1
manufacturing accounts 397
    elements of cost 398–9

limited companies 421
    preparation of 400–1
    statements of financial position 407–8
    statements of profit or loss 405–7
    work in progress 403–4
    year-end adjustments 408
mark-up 347–8
matching concept 176, 219, 248
materiality concept 176
materials, costs of 398, 400–1
money measurement concept 176

net book value (written down value) 222
net realisable value 177
nominal ledgers 57, 60
non-current assets 160–1
    depreciation *see depreciation*
    disposal of 234–6
    purchase and sale of 291
non-current liabilities 163
non-regular transactions 292
non-trading organisations 357, 374
    calculation of accumulated fund 373
    calculation of sales and purchases 372
    differences in accounting terms 369
    income and expenditure accounts 361–3, 366
    receipts and payments accounts 358–9, 366
    statements of financial position 366–8
    subscriptions 369–70
    trading accounts 359–61

objectivity 184
omission, errors of 49
opening balances
    on expense accounts 198–200
    on income accounts 208–10
opening journal entries 288–90
ordinary share capital 421
ordinary shares (equity shares) 419
original entry, errors of 49
overdrafts *see bank overdrafts*

paid-up capital 418
partnership agreements 382
partnerships 380, 392
    advantages and disadvantages 381
    appropriation accounts 384–5
    ledger accounts 387–9
    loans from partners 383
    statements of financial position 390–1
passwords 458–9
paying-in slips 104

payment, early, encouragement of 56, 64
payment methods 19
cheques 66–9, 103, 273
petty cash books 75
   imprest system 77
   layout and recording entries 78–81
   maintenance 76
   methods of recording 83
preference shares 419
prepaid expenses 195–7
prepaid income 206–8, 212
prime cost 400
principle, errors of 49
private limited companies 416
professional behaviour 184
professional competence 184
profit
   calculation from changes in capital 334–8
   comparison with cash 142–3
   effect of correcting errors 304–5
   gross 347–8, 351
   residual 384
profit for the year 142
profit from operations 142
profit margin 435, 436–7
profit sharing, partnerships 384–5
profitability ratios 435–7, 451
prudence concept 176, 219, 243, 248
public limited companies 416
purchase orders 96
purchases 6
   recording in ledger accounts 26–7
purchases journals 119, 121–2
purchases ledger control accounts (total trade payables accounts) 314–15, 318–20
   see also control accounts
purchases ledgers 57, 59
purchases returns journals 119–22

rate of inventory turnover 349–50, 440–1
realisation concept 176
receipts 104–5
receipts and payments accounts 358–9
   difference from income and expenditure accounts 365–6
record keeping 3, 17
   see also ledger accounts
reducing balance method of depreciation 222–3
   recording in the ledger 225–8
residual profit 384
retained earnings 421
return on capital employed (ROCE) 435, 437

returns, recording in ledger accounts 29
returns inwards books *see sales returns journals*
revaluation method of depreciation 224–5
   recording in the ledger 230–1
revenue expenditure 181–2
revenue receipts 182

sales 6
   recording in ledger accounts 27–8
sales journals 114, 115, 117
sales ledger control accounts (total trade receivables accounts) 314–18
   see also control accounts
sales ledgers 57, 59
sales returns journals 114–17
service businesses
   definition 148
   statements of profit or loss 148–52
set-offs *see contra entries*
share capital 417–18
shareholders 415, 416
shares 415, 416
   types of 419
small transactions *see petty cash books*
solo traders 6
standing orders 19
statements of account 102–3
statements of affairs 334, 337
statements of changes in equity 421–3, 426
statements of financial position 4, 9–11, 137, 159, 166, 168
   assets 160–2
   capital and liabilities 162–3
   effect of correcting errors 306
   inclusion of depreciation 219
   limited companies 421, 425
   manufacturing businesses 407–8
   non-trading organisations 366–8
   partnerships 390–1
   preparation from incomplete records 340–4
   recording depreciation 231–3
   using a trial balance 163–5
   working capital and capital employed 167
statements of profit or loss 137, 138, 153
   of combined trading and service businesses 150–2
   combining the two sections 144
   inclusion of depreciation 219
   limited companies 421
   manufacturing businesses 405–7
   preparation from incomplete records 340–3
   profit and loss section 142–3, 406–7
   recording depreciation 231–3
   of service businesses 148–9

Index

trading section 139–41, 405–6
transferring ledger account totals 145–7
using a trial balance 138–9
storage systems 460
   cloud services 462–3
   data storage devices 461–2
   manual storage 460–1
straight line method of depreciation 221–2
   recording in the ledger 225–8
subscriptions 357, 366, 368, 369–70
subsidiary books *see books of prime entry*
surpluses 361
suspense accounts 301–3
sustainability 457
   digital applications 457–8

'T' account format 35
   see also ledger accounts
tangible non-current assets 160
three-column cash books 64–5
three-column running balance accounts 35–6
total accounts *see control accounts*
trade discount 97, 98, 99
trade payables 6, 26
trade payables turnover 440, 442
trade receivables 6, 27–8
trade receivables turnover 440, 442

trading accounts 359–61
trading businesses 6
   definition 148
trading options 38
treasurers 357
trial balances 43
   error location 48, 51
   errors which affect them 301–3
   errors which do not affect them 49, 299–301
   failure to balance 48
   preparation of 44–7
   preparation of statements of financial position 163–5
   preparation of statements of profit or loss 138–9
   purpose of 44

unit cost 404

work in progress 403–4
working capital 167
working capital, current ratio 438–9
writing off irrecoverable debts 243
written down value *see net book value*

year-end adjustments 191
   manufacturing businesses 408
year-end transfers
   ledger postings 297–8
   recording in the journal 295–6